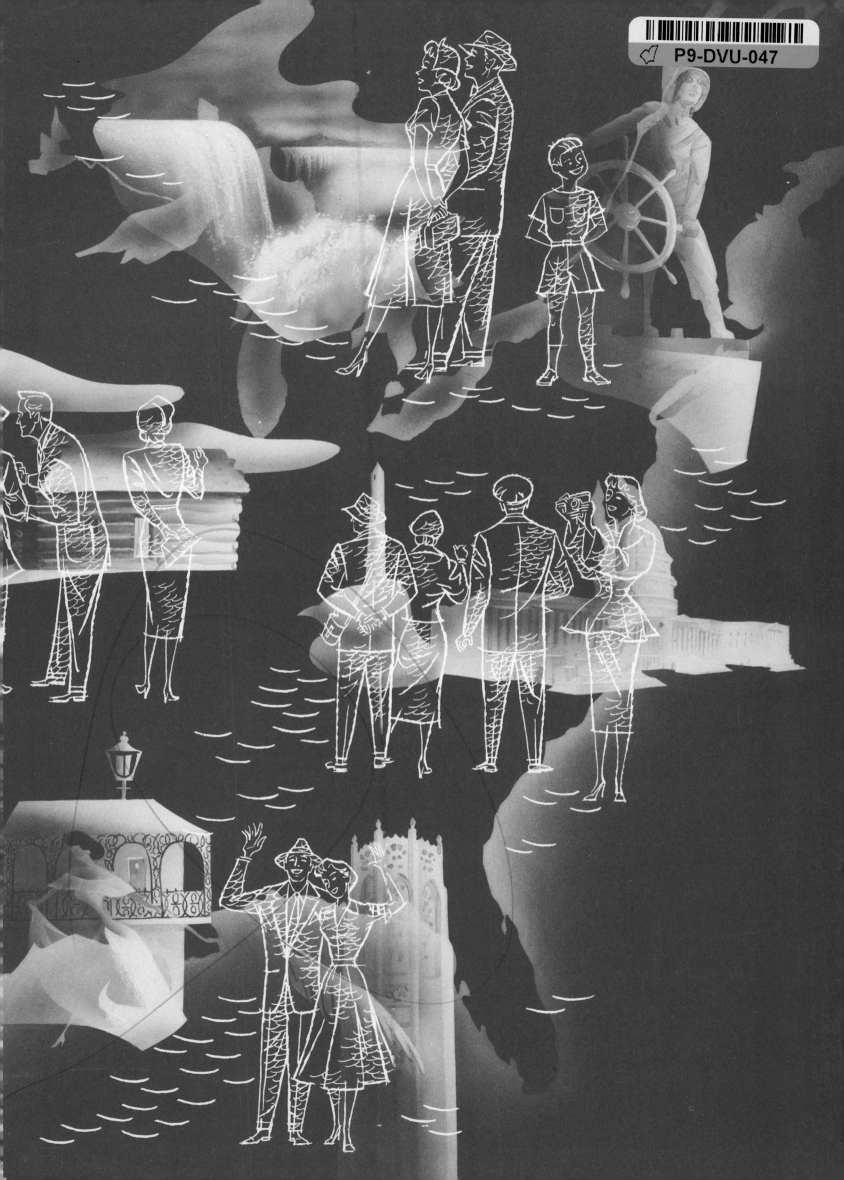

Hammond's

Pictorial Travel Atlas of Scenic America

By

E. L. JORDAN, PH.D.

Rutgers University

WITH THE ASSISTANCE OF A GROUP OF PRIVATE AND OFFICIAL
AGENCIES WHICH SPECIALIZE IN TRAVEL INFORMATION

220 Color Photographs

By

Outstanding Landscape Photographers

C. S. Hammond and Company

MAPLEWOOD, N. J.   NEW YORK, N. Y.

Foreword

THE BEAUTY of scenic America is like that of a diamond: Not until the jewel is ground and cut does its brilliance appear. As to our continent, the task of shaping and cleaning, polishing and brightening its surface is performed by a host of people: highway engineers, auto mechanics, builders of motor courts, navigators of airplanes, officials of national parks, rangers of wilderness areas and innumerable others, among them the author of this book.

For a long time it had been known that our continent contained every type of scenic beauty encountered anywhere on earth: sky-high mountains and living deserts, white beaches and huge inland lakes, northern forests and southern palm groves, shiny glaciers and tropical islands. But as long as only isolated Americans saw single parts of the American scene and took their knowledge for granted, our scenic splendor did not penetrate into our national consciousness, nor did it become part of our national heritage Those who had the means for getting acquainted with the various sections of America preferred to sail to Europe.

But during the last two or three decades this situation changed through a combination of factors. Good highways and superb turnpikes, modern motels and free maps, information on travel and mass-produced cars, a broadly extended airway system, improved railroads and paid vacations, blended with the innate wanderlust of a people who had always been explorers and "movers," helped to make available, accessible and enjoyable the grandeur and beauty of the continent as a whole.

As the new travel opportunities multiplied, the people responded enthusiastically, and today the country's vacation travelers are counted by the tens of millions. The amount spent annually in American motor travel alone touches the ten billion dollar mark. Never have Americans been as travel-minded and interested in seeing their country as now.

Considering this situation, the author and the executives of the publishing house of C. S. Hammond & Co. held many a conference to discuss the question: Should there not be a modern travel atlas that would embrace the new concept? Such a work would, in one large volume, present scenic America to its readers as a fascinating field of travel open and available to practically every American family. Out of these deliberations the present volume emerged: *Hammond's Pictorial Travel Atlas of Scenic America.*

In determining the special features of the Atlas, the following plan was decided upon: In several hundred color pictures, most of them created by the country's leading landscape photographers; in 120 color maps, all of them designed in one of America's oldest and most distinguished cartographic work shops, and in a series of lively travelogs, the volume sets out to present the approximately *100 Most See-Worthy Travel Spots in America, the Sightseeing Gazetteer of the United States and Canada* and a series of general maps and notes on highway, railroad and air travel, plus various tables with additional travel information.

The purpose of the Atlas is, in the first instance, a practical one. With its maps, its numerous hints and suggestions and its Sightseeing Gazetteer of the United States and Canada, the Atlas will answer almost any practical travel question that may arise, particularly if used in conjunction with the free road maps which can be obtained at any gas station, and the free routing of trips offered by the tourist service departments of all major oil companies and by the automobile clubs to their members.

The second, equally important purpose of the Atlas is the dramatizing of America as a travel land. With its combination of color photographs, color maps and word pictures, the Atlas attempts to show the dramatic grandeur, beauty and infinite variety of America. By stressing the background, the appeal, the mood, the atmosphere, it will enable the traveler to explore for himself the permanent and inspirational values of travel in America and to discover, in his own mind, the deep roots of our country and our nation—roots not anchored in New Jersey or Oklahoma or California but stretching out in all directions and reaching far and wide from coast to coast.

Acknowledgments

THIS BOOK is a cooperative venture. Much of the information presented here was gathered by means of correspondence and questionnaires, with the active and friendly cooperation of a host of federal, state, county and municipal agencies, like the National Park Service, the Forest Service, the state agencies concerned with tourism (usually the Departments of Commerce or special Development Commissions), chambers of commerce, regional associations and others. All helped in assembling the material and in presenting a well-balanced picture of the travel and sightseeing opportunities in Scenic America. The author is particularly indebted to the following officials:

Herbert Evison, Chief of Information, National Park Service, U.S. Dept. of the Interior; Elmer P. Thompson, Director of Information, Air Transport Association of America; Albert A. Beatty, Assistant Vice President, Association of American Railroads; P. J. Campbell, Chairman, National Bus Traffic Association; Michael Frome, American Automobile Association; Miss Virginia Schwartz, Supervisor, Mexican State Tourist Bureau; Miss Miriam Raab, State News Bureau, Dept. of Conservation and Development, State of North Carolina; John N. Johnson, Editor, Division of Publicity, Commonwealth of Kentucky; J. Herbert Walker, Director, Vacation and Recreation Bureau, Dept. of Commerce, Commonwealth of Pennsylvania; Philip Florman, Senior State Publicity Editor, Dept. of Commerce, State of New York; Carl G. Hodges, Superintendent, Division of Department Reports, Dept. of Finance, State of Illinois; Robert J. Furlong, Executive Secretary, State of Michigan Tourist Council; Prentiss Mooney, Assistant Director, Missouri Division of Resources and Development; E. C. Johns, Executive Secretary, Washington State Advertising Commission; Eric Bergman, Assistant Director, Travel Information Division, Oregon State Highway Department; J. E. Carpenter, Director, Travel and Recreation Department, California State Chamber of Commerce; Fred T. Bennett, Engineer, Texas Highway Department; Lenox E. Bigelow, General Representative, Dept. of Commerce, Commonwealth of Massachusetts; Dan E. C. Campbell, Director, Travel Bureau, Province of Alberta, Canada.

The pictorial material has come from many sources, and the author is proud to count among his collaborators outstanding landscape photographers like R. S. Hibshman, Fred G. Korth, Ted Lagerberg, Harvey Meston and Paul W. Nesbit. Mr. Nesbit, photographer, naturalist and writer of Colorado Springs, was particularly helpful in "tracking down" hard-to-find pictures, and never tired of establishing contacts for the author. Also Mr. Winston Pote of Lancaster, N. H., proved a most understanding and cooperative expert.

Many fine pictures were contributed by government agencies, railroad companies (especially the Union Pacific) and airlines. As all of these agencies and corporations employ the services of recognized professionals, their material is of outstanding quality and highly welcome. Finally a number of friends, all color-photo hobbyists of long standing, furnished kodachromes from their files, particularly of regions for which professional photographic material was not easily available. This group of collaborators consisted of an interesting variety of people, including a ranger in Yosemite Park, the comptroller of the country's largest insurance company, a pharmacist in a small canyon-bottom town in Colorado, a biology professor in Ohio, a doctor in Indiana, a college student in Virginia—all united in their enthusiasm for color photography.

Final thanks are due to the many people who helped the author along on his travels and saw to it that he noticed and appreciated the right sights and views, and had the best possible travel impressions from Quebec to Miami, from British Columbia to California.

As in the case of *Hammond's Nature Atlas of America,* my wife, Mrs. Ethel A. Jordan, acted as typist, secretary, assistant, critic and inspiration in general.

E. L. J.

Contents

Travel by Ship. All passages are bought through the offices of the steamship company or a travel agent. Escorted all-expense tours and prearranged individual tours including hotels and sightseeing are obtained through a travel agent.

Travel by Plane. Straight passages or organized all-expense tours are purchased from the airline or a travel agent; for prearranged individual tours including hotels and sightseeing, see a travel agent. The "fly-now, pay-later" arrangement makes air travel on the installment plan possible. Families may save through the "family fare plan"; under this system, a family group traveling on a Monday, Tuesday or Wednesday, on any standard flight, can buy a full-price ticket for one parent and half-price tickets for the other parent and any children under 21 years of age.

Travel by Railroad. Straight tickets are normally purchased at railroad stations but can also be secured through travel agents. The latter are particularly glad to arrange long round trips, i.e. from the East to Yellowstone Park, or from a western location to New York. They also sell all-expense, escorted tours and organize prearranged individual tours including hotels and sightseeing.

Travel by Bus. Tickets are sold at the offices of Greyhound (or other bus companies operating on a national scale) or through travel agents who hold appointments by the bus company. Greyhound offers complete vacation tours, including transportation, hotels, sightseeing. Individual prearranged, all-expense tours by bus will be organized by travel agents holding a bus company appointment.

Travel by Car. The method that has evolved as the most satisfactory for a majority of modern automobile travelers is a combination of sightseeing, including new impressions and new experiences, with relaxation at one or a few particularly congenial places. After selecting the desired vacation region in general, some prefer to establish a headquarters there, as a base for exploring the surrounding territory; others travel with a definite idea of what they want to see but without too rigid a schedule. If on their travels they come upon a lake or resort having a special personal appeal, they'll stay there for an extra day, or two or three, before moving on. This alternating of new sights and new impressions with a carefree rest at some beauty spot has proved an ideal vacation method for many. I remember one afternoon when my family and I drove along the Columbia River Highway, headed for Portland, and in spite of the grand vistas, the heat and the dust from new construction projects proved quite annoying. So a conference over a map and an inter-

view with a gas station manager caused us to turn to the left into the Cascade Mountains. The road was very poor, but after 12 miles it ended at a small blue mountain lake in which the snowy peak of Mt. Hood was mirrored; a camp was available in a forest of huge Douglas Firs; we stayed for five days. Such unscheduled side excursions often turn out to be the most memorable experiences.

The Stimulus of Variety. If you can include a boat excursion with your motor trip, that will be a pleasant change. Opportunities are innumerable; almost every large lake, river or coastal body of water offers them. It may be a small fishing boat on a New Jersey inlet that seems interesting to you, or a floating craft in the Ozarks, or a sea-going steamer across Puget Sound to Victoria, or an excursion boat on the Mississippi, at St. Louis or New Orleans. If you are a sportsman you will stop where the trout fishing is good, or where you can go out to sea with the commercial fleet at daybreak and return in the afternoon with a couple of salmon. If you are a horseback rider, you will find innumerable opportunities for an afternoon ride over mountain trails or for pack trips of several days.

Sometimes local attractions are discovered unexpectedly, and should be enjoyed as a bonus. I remember coming upon a natural granite swimming pool near the lodge where we stayed in the Great Smoky Mountains, with crystal-clear mountain water flowing through it, a forest of virgin hemlocks bordering its edges and a flock of great, brilliantly blue butterflies hovering above it. There is no better swimming anywhere. With equal pleasure I like to think of the small canyon-bottom town of Ouray, Colorado, where we discovered an enterprise called "Scenic Jeep Tours." In a sturdy, especially adapted jeep we were taken over old mining roads to the very roof of America, a perfectly unique experience. Be on the lookout for opportunities of that kind!

Planning. A vacation trip is like every other project: The better planned, prepared and organized it is, the more successful and enjoyable it will be. Half a year before vacation time is not too early a date to start thinking about it; in preparation, the following steps are suggested:

(1) Look through this volume, compare and check the various possibilities; determine which travel area or areas interest you most at the time.

(2) Write to the Tourist Service Department of any major gas company and ask for a map or maps with the exact outline of your trip, specifying either the shortest or the most scenic route. This service is free.

(3) If you plan to visit one or more national parks, write to the "Superintendent of ——National Park in

—," requesting a folder. While such a step is not necessary, it is often helpful to know in advance the latest
regulations, fees, etc.

(4) If there are some questions which this volume
does not answer, it is suggested that you write to the
tourist bureaus of the state or states in which you plan
to spend your vacation. The exact names and addresses
can be found in the Sightseeing Gazetteer, page 209,
at the head of each state section.

(5) It is strongly recommended that you get a copy of
one of the recognized guides to good eating places. The
best-known book is Duncan Hines' *Adventures in Good
Eating;* it can be bought through any book store, and
many restaurants sell it. If you have difficulty finding a
copy, write to *Adventures in Good Eating,* Box 907,
Bowling Green, Kentucky. The *Gourmet Guide* is also
popular, and a number of regional guides list and rate
restaurants.

(6) Just use your own judgment concerning all other
preparations (clothes, equipment, etc.).

Motels. Many motor car travelers have adopted the
system of starting out early and stopping between four
and five in the afternoon; in that fashion it is possible to
select a motel which appeals to you. Should you make an
advance reservation? For regular vacation travel that will
not be necessary, if you conclude your day's journey in
the afternoon; it is also advisable to see the motor court
personally before deciding to put up there for the night.
There is another difficulty involved in the matter of reservations: Many courts will not hold them beyond five
o'clock, and many will not accept them at all unless they
are prepaid. This situation has been brought about by
the tourists themselves, who too often made reservations
by telephone and then never appeared. If it is necessary
to cover a great deal of territory and to drive until nine
or ten at night, it is best to work with an organization
like Quality Courts, whose members will accept paid advance reservations for any other member-motel. In the
solving of special problems, membership in the American Automobile Association (AAA) will be helpful.

Camping. This form of vacation travel increases in
popularity from year to year, especially in the West,
where camping facilities in national and state parks are
numerous. Camping is, of course, a very individual venture, depending on the size, the living standard and the
general preferences of the family concerned. The sporting goods stores are able to fill every need in equipment,
and supplies are usually available not far from the camping site. Write to the following address for a map indicating the available camp sites: Superintendent of
Documents, Washington 25, D.C.—Map of Recreational
Areas of the United States, Catalog No. I 29.8: R 24/948.

Enclose 25 cents. Or get the *Handbook of Auto Camp-
ing and Motorist's Guide to Public Campgrounds,* by
George and Iris Wells, published by Harper & Brothers,
New York, N. Y. The price is $3.00.

Restaurants, Food. As was mentioned before, it is
worth while to take along a copy of Duncan Hines or a
similar guide to good eating. Be sure to have the latest
edition. Guidance of this kind is especially valuable if
you find yourself in a strange town, with several restaurants on each side of the street, all looking more or less
alike. With your guide book you will pick the right one.
The books, by the way, do not list only expensive restaurants but also many medium-priced eating places of good
quality. Considering the enormous number of restaurants in the United States, it is unavoidable that some
good ones are not listed in the various guides, and that
some of those listed do not come up to expectations. But
on the whole, the books are reliable.

In most large cities there are famous restaurants, particularly in New Orleans, San Francisco, New York,
which in themselves are sightseeing attractions. Otherwise, you will find the food good but a little monotonous
throughout the country. The same seven or eight dishes
from ham and steak to chicken and turkey will appear
again and again on every menu. The restaurateurs assert that traveling Americans want just those standard
dishes and ignore local specialties if and when they are
listed. That may be so; there is, however, a more imaginative minority of travelers who like to enjoy whatever traditional foods each region has to offer. If you
belong to that group, you are advised to study the notes
in Duncan Hines, and to watch signs along the road and
perhaps talk about local cooking with the manager of
the gas station or the general store. A table of some
famous regional dishes from the various parts of America can be found on page 9.

Sightseeing Buses. All larger cities have grave traffic
problems, and a stranger who is not familiar with the
town's layout and system of one-way streets will have a
difficult time finding his way to the various sightseeing
attractions. On the other hand, the sightseeing bus lines
are well operated, and although some tours are stretched
a bit and include some very minor sights, sightseeing
buses are, on the whole, the best and simplest means of
getting acquainted with our large cities. The announcers
in these buses are either objective and interesting, or of
the gushing kind, calling their passengers "you lovely
people," telling stale jokes and even singing songs. You
will have to bear patiently with the latter type of "lec-
turer."

Chair Lifts. Wherever there are mountains, from New

England to the Rockies and the Sierras, new chair lifts are carrying tourists in summertime and skiers during the winter to peaks and hilltops, with views gradually broadening as the chair ascends. Each ride is a little adventure.

Museums. The organizers and operators of museums have learned a great deal, during these last years, about the art of presenting their collections in a dramatic and stimulating way; many museums, especially those in the National Parks, are lively and excellent supplements to your own actual experiences. For example, in Mesa Verde National Park you visit the ancient cliff dwellings, and the park museum explains the nature, origin and final fate of the cliff dwellers who lived there. Similarly happy relationships between a sightseeing attraction and its museum will be found in many other travel spots. As to historical, art and natural history museums, you will visit them only if you are genuinely interested.

Cameras. Almost everybody in America is taking pictures, and especially the number of 35 mm-color-slide enthusiasts is increasing by leaps and bounds. Photography on a vacation trip is a wonderful pastime that will definitely enhance your travel enjoyment. By placing into focus and framing, in the viewer of your camera, the sights that impress you most, and by jockeying for the best position, the best light and the best background, you become much more conscious of the interesting and scenic features of your surroundings than if you merely look and proceed without stopping. Often your photo hobby will induce you to climb to some elevated vantage point which otherwise you would be too lazy to tackle, and a surprisingly fine panorama will reward you. Showing colored travel slides at home, after the journey is over, has almost become a national pastime. However, when doing so, use your discretion. If you show only a restricted number of your very best slides, that will be infinitely more enjoyable to your audience than showing all the 250 pictures you took while away, including the ones that are technically poor or near-duplications or show a topic that seemed interesting at that time, in the viewer of the camera, but did not turn out that way on the slide.

Binoculars. Anyone interested in wildlife should take along a pair of good binoculars; the 7 × 35 type is popular and satisfactory for all regular purposes. Particularly in the Western mountains where you can observe mule deer and elk, moose and bear, bighorn antelopes and Rocky Mountain goats; along the Pacific Coast where sea lions play on the rocks and innumerable varieties of sea birds fill the air; on the Florida coast and in the Everglades or in the Southern mountains where song-birds abound, a handy pair of binoculars will greatly increase the pleasure of your journey.

Souvenirs. One old lady from Germany who was visiting her relatives in the U.S.A. found some lovely, typically American toys at a souvenir stand in the White Mountains; little birch canoes, with Indian dolls at the paddle. She bought several to take home to various young grandnieces and nephews. When she packed them, the small seat in one of the canoes came loose and fell out. On the underside it was stamped: "Made in Germany." Such disillusioning experiences are quite frequent, and on the whole the only travel souvenirs worth while buying are those arts and crafts native to the region, like redwood platters in northern California, vases or bowls made of native alabaster in Colorado, products of native woodcraft in the mountains of North Carolina, Tennessee and other southern states and similar souvenirs that have a "genuine ring."

Native Advice on Sightseeing. Don't trust it. Sometimes it will be accurate and useful if given by persons who have seen more of the world than just their own home region, but just as often the local scenic beauty will not be appreciated at all by the residents and will not even be mentioned by them, while they will direct you to some nearby monument, museum or aquarium of which they are proud but which may prove very insignificant. It is far better to get your information from this atlas or other guide books, and to use your own judgment.

Weather. Some of your travel experiences will be disappointing, and in most such cases the weather will be the villain. In a fog or a drizzling rain all scenic beauty is reduced to the vanishing point. In visiting the various regions of America it is of importance to do so at the right seasons, and if the tremendous climatic variety of our continent sometimes poses problems, they can always be solved with a little common sense. For instance, most people who have to cross the desert during the summer, now travel at night. You may rest in an air-conditioned motel in Reno till midnight, and then set out eastward through a pleasantly cool and possibly cold night, to arrive at Salt Lake City in the morning. The sunrise over the desert is a splendid spectacle.

The Right Frame of Mind. Your personal attitude is the key to a successful vacation. If you take things the easy way, let the other members of the family have their turns at the wheel, are willing to put up with certain inconveniences and imperfections and are inclined to see the humorous side of the little mishaps which are bound to occur, you will have mastered the art of travel. Bon voyage and happy landing.

A Selective List of America's Regional Foods

Some of the dishes listed in this table are strictly regional; she-crab soup, for example, can probably be obtained only in and around Charleston, S. C., and pollo relleno only in the Southwest. Other dishes have spread to many parts of the U.S. and Canada, but still are especially delicious in their original regions.

NEW ENGLAND

Maine lobster; New England clam chowder; fish chowder; codfish cakes; Narragansett clams steamed on hot rocks; Vermont turkey; New England boiled dinner (corned beef, lean pork, quartered green cabbage, carrots, turnips, beets, potatoes, horse-radish sauce, mustard pickles); succotash; baked beans and brown bread; Parker House rolls; hot cakes with maple syrup; pumpkin pie with Vermont cheese; Boston cream pie; squash pie; cranberry pie; huckleberry pie; New Hampshire deep-dish blueberry pie; apple and huckleberry cobbler; maple sugar; country cider.

METROPOLITAN NEW YORK

Good, international cuisine, but hardly any local specialties. Birthplace of Manhattan clam chowder and the Manhattan cocktail.

PHILADELPHIA AND THE PENNSYLVANIA-DUTCH COUNTRY

Philadelphia pepperpot; Philadelphia snapper soup; Philadelphia peach ice cream; scrapple; Lebanon sausage; head-cheese; snits and knepp (dried apples, smoked ham, dump-lings); 7 sweets and 7 sours (including apple butter, jam, spiced peaches, rhubarb, honey, chowchow, coleslaw, cucumber pickles, watermelon pickles, quince preserve); Reading pretzels; schmierkäse; shoo-fly pie.

SOUTH

Pan-roasted oysters; fried soft-shell crabs; crab flakes, Mary-land; shrimp pie; green corn and shrimp pudding; she-crab soup (Charleston, S.C.); diamond-back-terrapin stew; Virginia ham; Smithfield ham; Arkansas ham; hog jowl; Maryland fried chicken; squab pie; beaten biscuits; hot breads; hush puppies; hominy and butter; grits and gravy; red beans and rice; pecan pie; ambrosia.

MIDWEST

Great Lakes whitefish; Great Lakes perch; Minnesota pike; Michigan smelts; Indiana chicken pot pie; Wisconsin roast goose; Chicago porterhouse or T-bone steak with home-fried potatoes and hot buttered corn; Kansas City sirloin steak; pork loin roast; jellied pigs feet; Kassler Rippchen (smoked rib chops) with sauerkraut, prepared with apples and caraway seeds; blood sausage; tongue sausage; Dakota buffalo steak.

NEW ORLEANS

Bayou oysters; oysters Rockefeller; crayfish; bouillabaisse; shrimp Creole; pompano; gumbo (with shellfish and rice); jambalaya (rice plus crabmeat, shrimps, oysters, ham, sausages, pork, turkey, chicken); chicken Creole; pommes soufflées; crêpes suzettes; cherries jubilee; café diable.

SOUTHWEST

Chile con carne; pollo relleno (baked chicken with sharply seasoned ground beef); tamales; tacos; frijoles; tortillas; en-chiladas; pinto beans and barbecue sauce.

SOUTHERN CALIFORNIA

Barbecued spare ribs; Japanese sukiyaki; fresh-vegetable salads; fresh-fruit salads; various salad dressings, mostly with sweet overtones, like cream flavored and colored with berry juice; boysenberry pie.

SAN FRANCISCO AND THE NORTHWEST

Columbia salmon; smoked salmon; jerked salmon; abalone steak; crabmeat flakes, Lorenzo; broiled crab legs with butter; Dungeness crab; cioppino (the Italian version of bouillabaisse); Oriental foods; various Oriental teas.

CANADA

The east coast of Canada enjoys the same seafood specialties that are popular in Maine; in fact, the world's largest lobster packing plant is in St. Andrews-by-the-Sea, in the Province of New Brunswick. On the Pacific coast the luscious seafoods of San Francisco and Seattle are also available in Vancouver and Victoria. Quebec has a wonderful French cuisine, and the British-Canadian sections are fond of roast beef with Yorkshire pudding, and other English dishes.

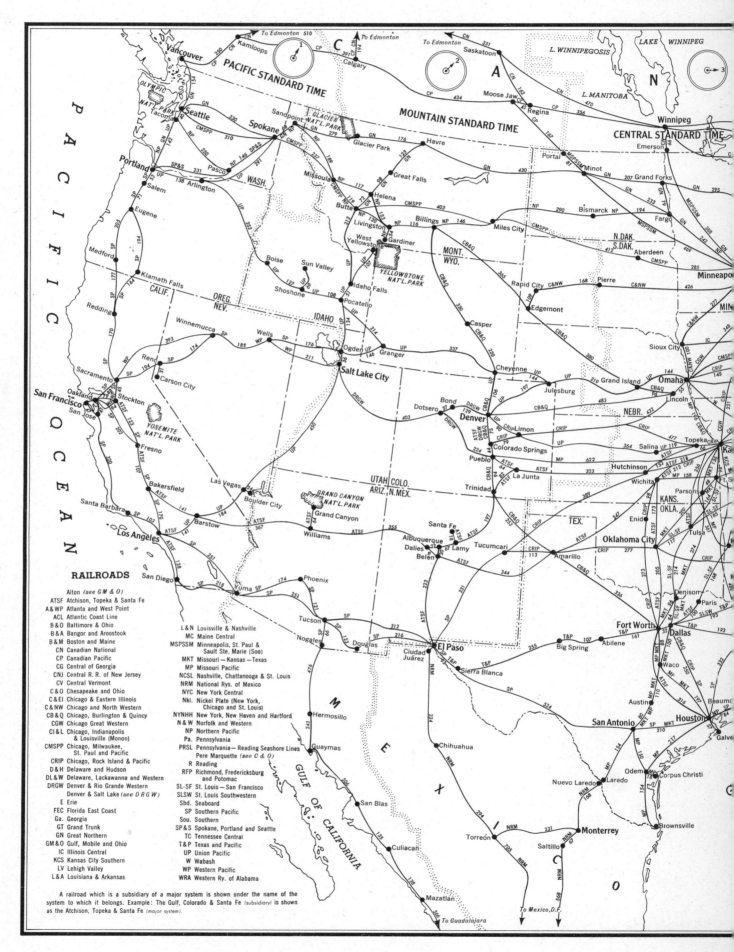

RAILROADS

Alton (see GM & O)
ATSF Atchison, Topeka & Santa Fe
A&WP Atlanta and West Point
ACL Atlantic Coast Line
B&O Baltimore & Ohio
B&A Bangor and Aroostook
B&M Boston and Maine
CN Canadian National
CP Canadian Pacific
CG Central of Georgia
CNJ Central R.R. of New Jersey
CV Central Vermont
C&O Chesapeake and Ohio
C&EI Chicago & Eastern Illinois
C&NW Chicago and North Western
CB&Q Chicago, Burlington & Quincy
CGW Chicago Great Western
CI&L Chicago, Indianapolis
 & Louisville (Monon)
CMSPP Chicago, Milwaukee,
 St. Paul and Pacific
CRIP Chicago, Rock Island & Pacific
D&H Delaware and Hudson
DL&W Delaware, Lackawanna and Western
DRGW Denver & Rio Grande Western
 Denver & Salt Lake (see D R G W)
E Erie
FEC Florida East Coast
Ga. Georgia
GT Grand Trunk
GN Great Northern
GM&O Gulf, Mobile and Ohio
IC Illinois Central
KCS Kansas City Southern
LV Lehigh Valley
L&A Louisiana & Arkansas

L&N Louisville & Nashville
MC Maine Central
MSPSSM Minneapolis, St. Paul &
 Sault Ste. Marie (Soo)
MKT Missouri — Kansas — Texas
MP Missouri Pacific
NCSL Nashville, Chattanooga & St. Louis
NRM National Rys. of Mexico
NYC New York Central
Nkl. Nickel Plate (New York,
 Chicago and St. Louis)
NYNHH New York, New Haven and Hartford
N&W Norfolk and Western
NP Northern Pacific
Pa. Pennsylvania
PRSL Pennsylvania — Reading Seashore Lines
 Pere Marquette (see C & O)
R Reading
RFP Richmond, Fredericksburg
 and Potomac
SL-SF St. Louis — San Francisco
SLSW St. Louis Southwestern
Sbd. Seaboard
SP Southern Pacific
Sou. Southern
SP&S Spokane, Portland and Seattle
TC Tennessee Central
T&P Texas and Pacific
UP Union Pacific
W Wabash
WP Western Pacific
WRA Western Ry. of Alabama

A railroad which is a subsidiary of a major system is shown under the name of the system to which it belongs. Example: The Gulf, Colorado & Santa Fe (subsidiary) is shown as the Atchison, Topeka & Santa Fe (major system).

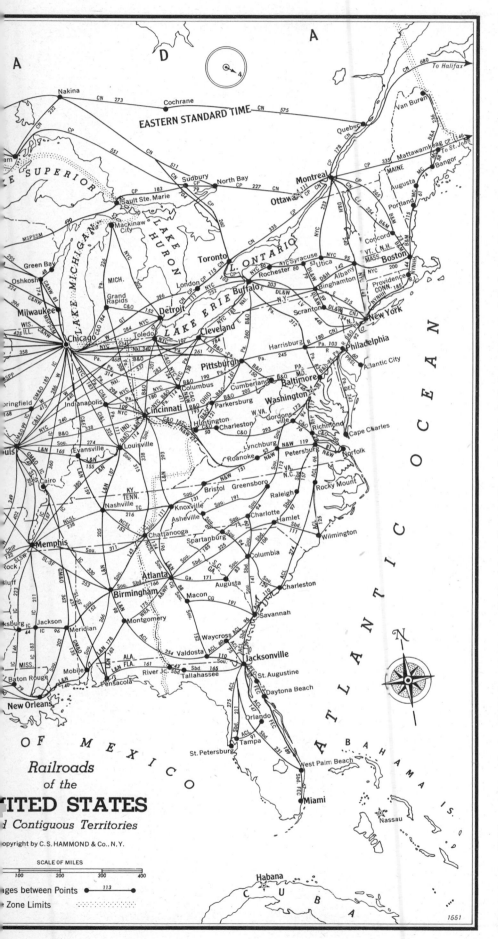

Railroads
of the
UNITED STATES
and Contiguous Territories

Copyright by C.S. HAMMOND & Co., N.Y.

SCALE OF MILES

100   200   300   400

Mileages between Points   113

Zone Limits

VACATION TRAVEL BY RAILROAD

A considerable share of vacation travel in America is in the hands of the railroads, which stress the safety and comfort they can offer their passengers, regardless of weather conditions. Streamlined Diesel and electric trains, roomettes, modern dining facilities and the new "vista domes" for scenic routes are attractions indeed. Some vista domes are even equipped with sets of floodlights which throw strong diffused beams on the scenery on both sides of the track so that the sightseeing can continue at night. Some railroads have family-fare plans, some operate credit plans and many feature all-expense package tours. The two Canadian railroad systems —Canadian Pacific and Canadian National —are even more strongly geared to tourist and vacation travel: In Canada's principal vacation areas they own hotels, lodges and chalets, among them such famous hostelries as Banff Springs Hotel, the Chateau Lake Louise, the Jasper Park Lodge and the Empress Hotel in Victoria. They also own fleets of steamers which make rail-and-steamboat tours possible in the beautiful Puget Sound region, to southern Alaska and elsewhere. Canadian railroads also cross some of the wildest and most magnificent parts of our continent, regions which cannot be reached either by car or by plane.

In New England, the New Haven Railroad features more than thirty all-expense Pilgrim Tours, some of them extending into Eastern Canada. In the Middle-Atlantic states the New York Central System provides an Eastern Circle Trip which includes Chicago, Detroit, Niagara Falls, New York, Washington, D.C., Philadelphia and Colonial Virginia. Between New York and Florida the streamlined Silver Star, Silver Meteor, Champion and Orange Blossom Special are famous trains. In the Rocky Mountains the Denver & Rio Grande Western operates vista-dome trains through the most scenic sections of the Rockies, including the spectacular Royal Gorge. The Southwest is served mostly by the Santa Fe Lines, which together with several national travel agencies, offer two-to-three-week trips to such famous sightseeing points as the Grand Canyon, Santa Fe and Carlsbad Caverns. In western all-expense tours the Union Pacific Railroad, in conjunction with the Chicago and North Western, is outstanding, offering a wide range of all-expense tours to Yellowstone, the Rockies, the great western national parks, and the California coast. The Southern Pacific features package tours to the Southwest, California and Oregon. The Great Northern features an all-expense circle trip to Glacier National Park, the Pacific Northwest, California and the Southwest.

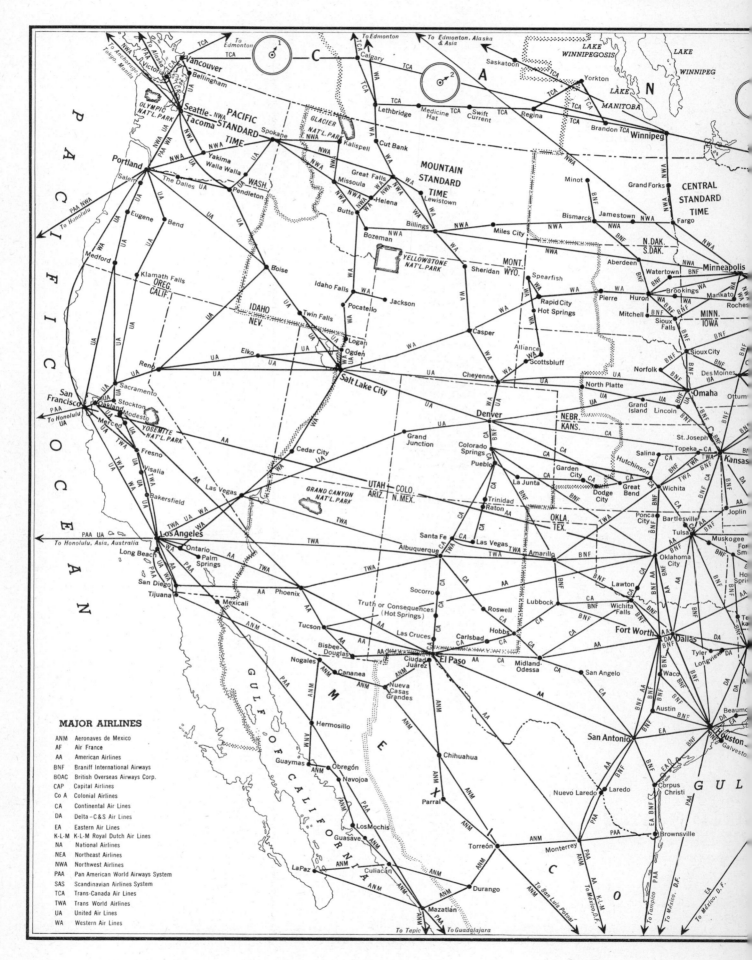

MAJOR AIRLINES

ANM	Aeronaves de Mexico
AF	Air France
AA	American Airlines
BNF	Braniff International Airways
BOAC	British Overseas Airways Corp.
CAP	Capital Airlines
Co A	Colonial Airlines
CA	Continental Air Lines
DA	Delta–C&S Air Lines
EA	Eastern Air Lines
K-L-M	K-L-M Royal Dutch Air Lines
NA	National Airlines
NEA	Northeast Airlines
NWA	Northwest Airlines
PAA	Pan American World Airways System
SAS	Scandinavian Airlines System
TCA	Trans-Canada Air Lines
TWA	Trans World Airlines
UA	United Air Lines
WA	Western Air Lines

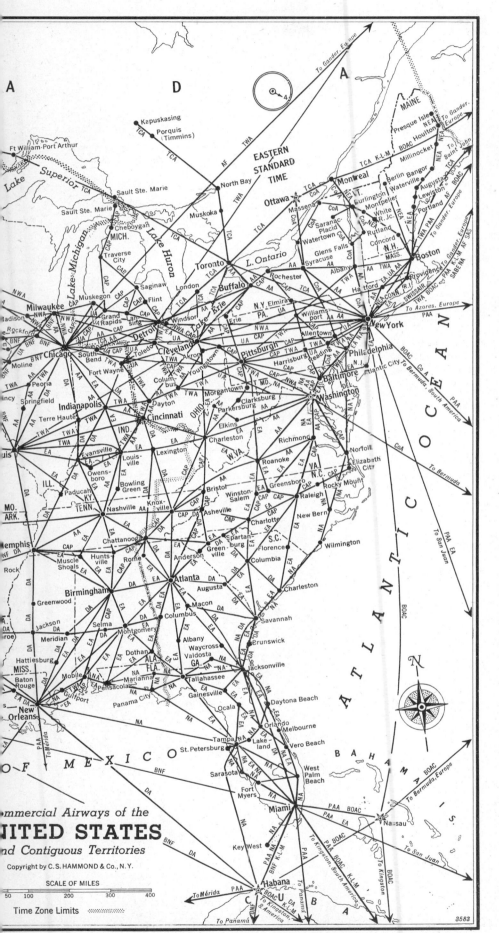

Commercial Airways of the
UNITED STATES
and Contiguous Territories

Copyright by C. S. HAMMOND & Co., N.Y.

SCALE OF MILES
50 100   200   300   400

Time Zone Limits

VACATION TRAVEL BY AIR

Every major vacation and sightseeing spot in the United States and Canada can be reached by air, and such fairly general arrangements as the Fly-Now, Pay-Later Plan or the Family-Fare Plan (husband pays full-fare ticket; wife and children under 22 pay half-price tickets, Monday to Wednesday) make air travel financially attractive. U-Drive-It cars are available at most airports; a combined airplane-and-car vacation can be most enjoyable and highly practical if the traveler's time is limited. But most popular are the all-expense package tours offered by many airlines. Southern Florida trips, with Miami Beach as headquarters, are featured during the summer season by National Airlines and Eastern Air Lines, from Chicago by Eastern and Delta Air Lines and from Pittsburgh by Capital Airplanes. 7- and 15-day package tours to California are offered by United Airlines. Their Golden West Air Cruise of 15 days includes Yellowstone National Park, Salt Lake City, San Francisco, Yosemite National Park, Los Angeles with Beverly Hills, Hollywood and San Diego. United Airlines features also a popular Rocky Mountain tour to Denver, with motor coach trips to Rocky Mountain National Park, Idaho Springs and Colorado Springs with Pikes Peak. Trans-World Air Lines offers package tours to the Grand Canyon and the Southwest in general. Northwest Air Lines covers the Pacific Northwest; from its vacation headquarters in Seattle it conducts all-expense 2-day motor tours of Mt. Rainier National Park and 5-day all-expense tours of Olympic National Park. Capital Airlines features package tours of 5 or 7 days to the Great Smoky Mountains, also to New Orleans and Virginia Beach. American Airlines offers many all-expense tours to the California coast, Yosemite National Park, Grand Canyon National Park, Niagara Falls and New York City; some of these tours combine airplane travel with U-Drive-It car travel.

A typical package vacation to Southern California includes all the famous sights from Santa Barbara to San Diego: Hollywood's "Sunset Strip" and the movie stars' homes in Beverly Hills, Universal Pictures and Walt Disney Studios, San Fernando Valley and Hollywood Bowl, San Juan Capistrano Mission and Tiajuana in Old Mexico, an evening at Ciro's and tickets to famous radio and TV shows. You'll ride through citrus groves and past ocean oil wells, over the spectacular Sulphur Mountain Drive and via the magnificent Los Angeles Freeway. The trip lasts one week and a weekend and costs about $85, including hotels, plus your air fare to and from Los Angeles.

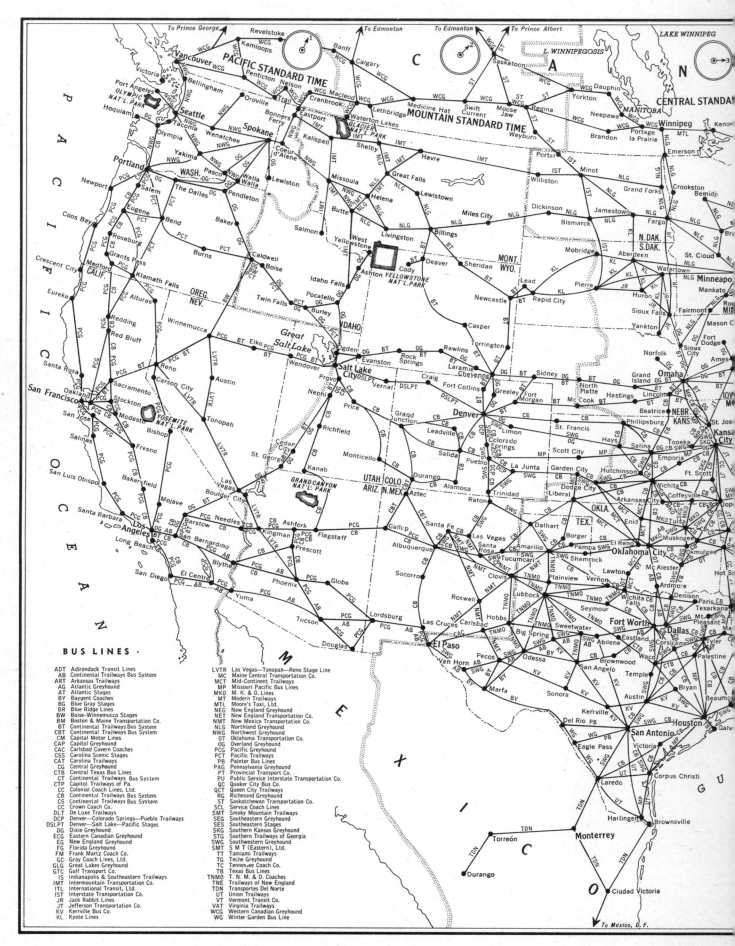

BUS LINES

ADT	Adirondack Transit Lines	LVTR	Las Vegas—Tonopah—Reno Stage Line
AB	Continental Trailways Bus System	MC	Maine Central Transportation Co.
ART	Arkansas Trailways	MCT	Mid-Continent Trailways
AG	Atlantic Greyhound	MP	Missouri Pacific Bus Lines
AT	Atlantic Stages	MKO	M. K. & O. Lines
BY	Baygent Coaches	MT	Modern Trailways
BG	Blue Gray Stages	MTL	Moore's Taxi, Ltd.
BR	Blue Ridge Lines	NEG	New England Greyhound
BW	Boise-Winnemucca Stages	NET	New England Transportation Co.
BM	Boston & Maine Transportation Co.	NMT	New Mexico Transportation Co.
BT	Continental Trailways Bus System	NLG	Northland Greyhound
CBT	Continental Trailways Bus System	NWG	Northwest Greyhound
CM	Capital Motor Lines	OT	Oklahoma Transportation Co.
CAP	Capitol Greyhound	OG	Overland Greyhound
CAC	Carlsbad Cavern Coaches	PCG	Pacific Greyhound
CSS	Carolina Scenic Stages	PCT	Pacific Trailways
CAT	Carolina Trailways	PB	Painter Bus Lines
CG	Central Greyhound	PAG	Pennsylvania Greyhound
CTB	Central Texas Bus Lines	PT	Provincial Transport Co.
CT	Continental Trailways Bus System	PU	Public Service Interstate Transportation Co.
CTP	Capitol Trailways of Pa.	QC	Quaker City Bus Co.
CC	Colonial Coach Lines, Ltd.	QCT	Queen City Trailways
CB	Continental Trailways Bus System	RG	Richmond Greyhound
CS	Continental Trailways Bus System	ST	Saskatchewan Transportation Co.
CC	Crown Coach Co.	SCL	Service Coach Lines
DLT	De Luxe Trailways	SMT	Smoky Mountain Trailways
DCP	Denver—Colorado Springs—Pueblo Trailways	SEG	Southeastern Greyhound
DSLPT	Denver—Salt Lake—Pacific Stages	SES	Southeastern Stages
DG	Dixie Greyhound	SKG	Southern Kansas Greyhound
ECG	Eastern Canadian Greyhound	STG	Southern Trailways of Georgia
EG	New England Greyhound	SWG	Southwestern Greyhound
FG	Florida Greyhound	SMT	S M T (Eastern), Ltd.
FM	Frank Martz Coach Co.	TT	Tamiami Trailways
GC	Gray Coach Lines, Ltd.	TG	Teche Greyhound
GLG	Great Lakes Greyhound	TC	Tennessee Coach Co.
GTC	Gulf Transport Co.	TB	Texas Bus Lines
IS	Indianapolis & Southeastern Trailways	TNMO	T. N. M. & O. Coaches
IMT	Intermountain Transportation Co.	TNE	Trailways of New England
ITL	Intermountain Transit, Ltd.	TDN	Transportes Del Norte
IST	Interstate Transportation Co.	UT	Union Trailways
JR	Jack Rabbit Lines	VT	Vermont Transit Co.
JT	Jefferson Transportation Co.	VAT	Virginia Trailways
KV	Kerrville Bus Co.	WCG	Western Canadian Greyhound
KL	Kyote Lines	WG	Winter Garden Bus Line

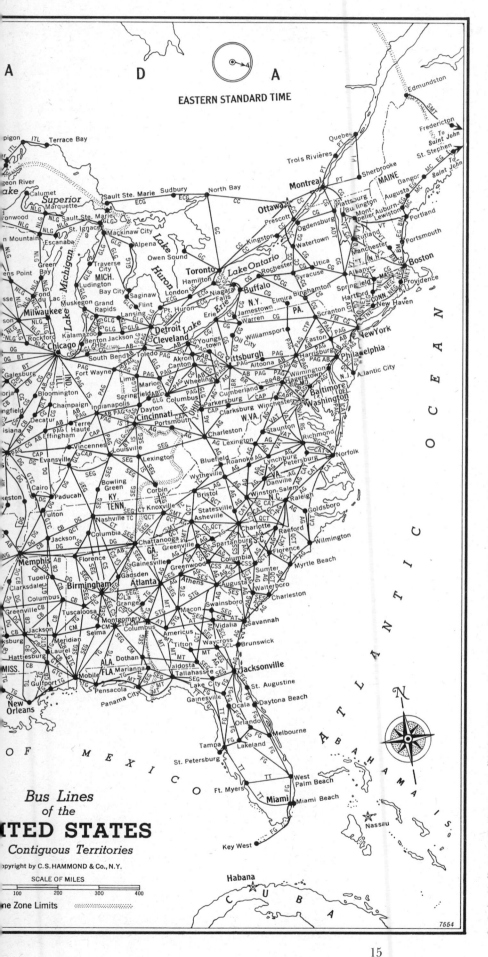

Bus Lines
of the
ITED STATES
Contiguous Territories
opyright by C.S. HAMMOND & Co., N.Y.
SCALE OF MILES
100   200   300   400
ne Zone Limits

EASTERN STANDARD TIME

VACATION TRAVEL BY BUS

Autobusses play an important part in American vacation travel. Even tourists who ride in their own cars or use railroads and planes will find the sightseeing bus trips conducted by the Gray Line and other companies the easiest and most comfortable way of getting acquainted with our larger cities and their surroundings. Bus travel for a complete vacation has the advantage of low cost; in addition to inexpensive fares, most bus package tours provide only overnight accommodations in hotels but not meals, these being obtained by each passenger individually—another source of economy. The largest nation-wide operator, the Greyhound Lines, offers all-expense tours to every scenic area in the United States, Canada and Mexico. There are 87 Greyhound Travel Bureaus, ready to make the necessary arrangements; also a number of travel agencies are authorized to sell Greyhound tickets and package tours. Among the line's most popular tours are the following: Colonial Virginia and Shenandoah Valley, 6 days; New England Circle, 6 days; Cape Cod, 5 days; White Mountains, 6 days; International, including Niagara Falls and Eeastern Canada, 10 days; Montreal-Quebec, 6 days; Thousand Islands, N.Y., 6 days; Washington D.C., 3 days; Philadelphia-Atlantic City, 4 days; Williamsburg, Va., 4 days; Great Smoky Mountains, 8 days; Florida Circle, 13 days; Yellowstone National Park, 15 days; Rocky Mountain National Park, Denver and Colorado Springs, 15 days; Canadian Rockies, 21 days; California, 21 days; California-Yellowstone Park, 31 days; "To and Through the Golden West," 31 days, including the Pacific Northwest, California and the Southwest. Some Greyhound all-expense trips are off the beaten path, for instance the 15-day Gulf Coast Tour which winds its way from St. Augustine and Marineland in Florida along the charming Gulf coast resorts of Mississippi to New Orleans; or the 16-day tour through the Ozarks and Kentucky Caves; or the 14-day Paul Bunyan-Minnesota Tour which explores the "Land of 10,000 Lakes" or the restful 6-day Muskoka Lakes Tour which combines bus and steamer travel, starting from Buffalo and proceeding to Toronto and the Lakes.

The American Bus Lines of Lincoln, Nebraska, feature an 18-day California tour from New York, a 9-day Rocky Mountain tour from San Diego and a 9-day trip to the Historic East from Joplin, Missouri. The National Trailways System of Chicago, Ill., specializes in independent all-expense tours from any and to any point in the U.S. Among its popular arrangements are an 8-day dude-ranching trip and a 16-day Chicago-New Orleans-Florida tour.

20–21	Red Cliffs, Gaspé; Percé, Gaspé	E. B. Norris
21	Chateau Frontenac	Chateau Frontenac
22	Maine Birches	Maine Development Commission
23	Small Plane; Airplane view, Northwoods	H. Randall Pease
25–29	Portland Light; Mt. Chocorua; Covered Bridge; Mt. Washington; Peacham, Vt.	Winston Pote
30–31	Boston Fish Pier; Boston Swan Boat; Indian Statue	Massachusetts Dept. of Commerce
33	Old Mill Point	Kelsey, Cape Cod Chamber of Commerce
35	Lower Manhattan	Winston Pote
36–41	Bear Mountain Bridge; Hudson River Day Line; Storm King Highway; Fishing Stream; Whiteface Mt.; Ausable Chasm; Seneca Lake; American Falls, Niagara; Niagara Falls, Goat Island	NYSPIX—Commerce
43	Atlantic City	Atlantic City Convention Bureau
44–47	Independence Square; Betsy Ross Room; Valley Forge; Susquehanna Valley; Penna-Dutch Soap-making; Lower Buck Hill Falls	Pennsylvania Dept. of Commerce
49	Washington, D. C.	Winston Pote
50–51	Shenandoah, Jewel Hollow; Falls Trail; Grand Cavern	Royalpix, Front Royal, Va.
52	Old Church, Jamestown	Walter H. Miller
53	Capitol, Williamsburg; Governor's Palace	Press Bureau, Colonial Williamsburg
56–57	Kitty Hawk; Wreckage, Cape Hatteras	North Carolina News Bureau
57	Play "Lost Colony"	Dare County Tourist Bureau
59	Blue Ridge Parkway	North Carolina News Bureau
60–63	Great Smokies, Mt. Lodge; Granite Pool; Fontana Dam; Old Houses, Charleston, S. C.; Middleton Gardens; Country Church	E. L. Jordan
64–68	Shrimp Boats, Savannah; Iron Lace House; Drayton Arms; Okefenokee Swamp; American Egret; Fort Frederica	Meston's Travels
68	Florida Beach	Florida News Bureau
69	St. Augustine, Oldest House; A Porpoise Acrobat	Jack Brandon
70	Sarasota Jungle Gardens	Sarasota Jungle Gardens
71	John and Mable Ringling Museum of Art	John and Mable Ringling Mus. of Art
71	Sponge Fisher	Ted Lagerberg
72	Orange Blossoms and Fruit	Florida News Bureau
73	Florida Cypress Gardens	Fla. Cypress Gardens Assn.
73–74	Bok Tower; Palm Beach	Florida News Bureau
75	Miami Beach Hotel	City of Miami Beach, Fla.
75	Key West Bridge	C. E. Bennett, Jr.
76	Nature Walk, Everglades	National Park Service
77	Everglades Bear; Brahma Cattle	Ted Lagerberg
78–79	Bellingrath Gardens; Mardi Gras, Mobile; Azalea Country	Official Alabama State Photograph by Curtis Frizzell
80	Biloxi Lighthouse	Mississippi Agricultural and Industrial Board
82–83	Court of Two Sisters French Quarter, Grillwork; Mardi Gras, New Orleans	Meston's Travels
84–85	State Capitol, Baton Rouge; Bayou Country; Shrimp Boats, Morgan City	State of Louisiana Dept. of Commerce and Industry
86–87	Dunleith Mansion, Natchez; Auburn Mansion; Vicksburg Military Park	Mississippi Agricultural and Industrial Board
90–91	Isle Royale; Rock of Ages Lighthouse	Karl Gilbert
91	Northern Lake	Carl Dommerstern
92–93	Mackinac Island; Soo Locks; Northern Lakeshore	Michigan Tourist Council
94–95	State Capitol, Madison; Wisconsin Dells; Wisconsin Lake	State of Wisconsin Conservation Dept.
97	Chicago's Gold Coast	Fred G. Korth
98–99	Wright Brothers Shop, Greenfield Village; Detroit Zoo; Cranbrook	Michigan Tourist Council
100	Lincoln Home, Springfield, Ill.	Illinois Division of Dept. Reports
101	Mark Twain House, Hannibal, Mo.; Becky Thatcher House, Hannibal, Mo.	Becky Thatcher Book Shop, Hannibal, Mo.
102	Mississippi Boat, New Style	Missouri Division of Resources and Development
103	Mississippi Boat, Old Style	Becky Thatcher Book Shop, Hannibal, Mo.
103–107	St. Louis, Old Cathedral; Mammoth Cave, Ky., Underground River; Green River Ferry; Mammoth Cave; Needles Drive, Badlands; Mt. Rushmore Memorial	Meston's Travels
107	Elk in Black Hills	E. L. Jordan
111	Ozark Stream	Missouri Division of Resources and Development
112	Will Rogers Memorial	Oklahoma Planning and Resources Board
113	Oklahoma State Capitol with oil well	Edwin C. Alberts
113	Buffaloes	Paul W. Nesbit
114–115	Indian Lodge, Davis Mts.; Roadside Park, Sierra Blanca Mts.; Balmorhea State Park	Meston's Travels
117	San Jacinto Battlefield, Houston	Texas Highway Dept.
118–119	Crocket Hotel, Alamo Gateway, Alamo Walkway, all San Antonio	Meston's Travels
121	Big Bend Nat. Pk., Texas	National Park Service
122	Carlsbad Caverns, Giant Dome	Raymond C. Douglas
123	White Sands of N. Mexico	National Park Service
123	Carlsbad Caverns, Setting Hen Grotto	Raymond C. Douglas
125–127	Santa Fe Fiesta; Taos Pueblo; Indian Dancers at Gallup; San Felipe Church, Albuquerque	New Mexico State Tourist Bureau
130–131	Bow Lake; Trail Riding, Canadian Rockies; Snowmobile, Columbia Icefield	E. L. Jordan
132	Ramparts Range, Jasper Nat. Pk.	Canadian National Railway System
135	Swiftcurrent Falls, Glacier Nat. Pk.	Great Northern Railway Color Photo by John Kabel
136–139	View from Artist Point, Hot Pool, Old Faithful, all Yellowstone N. P.; Grand Tetons near Jenny Lake	Union Pacific Railroad Colorphoto
141	Sun Valley from Penny Mountain	Steve Hannegan Associates
142–143	Columbia River; Grand Coulee Dam; Man-made Desert Lake	Columbia Basin Project, U.S. Dept. of the Interior
144–145	Prospect Point, Lion's Gate Bridge, Vancouver, B. C.	Otto C. Schallerer
145	Ocean Falls, B. C.	E. L. Jordan
147	The Olympic Mts., Washington	Washington State Advertising Commission
148–149	Seattle Skyline; Floating Bridge, Wash. Lake	R. S. Hibshman
149–150	Sightseeing Coaches in Victoria, B. C.; Mountain Lake in Mt. Rainier, N. P.	E. L. Jordan
151	Mt. Rainier from Ricksecker Point	Meston's Travels
152–153	Multnomah Falls, Oregon; Crown Point View, Columbia River Highway; Portland with Mt. Hood	Oregon State Highway Commission
155	Mt. Hood and Lost Lake	Union Pacific Railroad Colorphoto
156–157	Newport Harbor, Oregon; Otter Crest State Park, Oregon; Yaquina Head Lighthouse	E. L. Jordan
160–163	Long's Peak from Bear Lake; Big Thompson Canyon; Indian Paint Brush; Denver, City and County Bldg.; Red Rocks Amphitheater	Paul W. Nesbit
163	Autumn in the Rockies	Frank L. Massard
164–165	Royal Gorge, Colo.; Colorado Springs with Pike's Peak	Paul W. Nesbit
165	Garden of the Gods	E. L. Jordan
166–167	Cliff Palace, Mesa Verde N. P.; "Apartment" in Canyon Wall, M. V. N. P.	Donald Watson
167	Sun Temple, Mesa Verde N. P.	Paul W. Nesbit
168	Mormon Temple, Salt Lake City	E. L. Jordan
169	Sea Gull Mon., Salt Lake City	Paul W. Nesbit
170	Indians at Monument Valley	Meston's Travels
171	Double Arch	E. P. Wood
171	Winter picture, Yebechai Group	Meston's Travels
173–175	Bryce Canyon; Grand Canyon N.P.; Bright Angel Point	Union Pacific Railroad Colorphoto
176	Walnut Canyon Ruins	E. K. Field
177	Navaho Indian Country; Sheep on Desert Pasture	L. W. Moore
178–179	Hotel Biltmore, Phoenix, Ariz.; Saguaro Cactus; Mission San Xavier del Bac	Paul W. Nesbit
181	Tucson, Desert	American Airlines Photo
182–183	Colorado River; Hoover Dam; Lake Mead	U. S. Dept. of the Interior, Bureau of Reclamation Region III
184	Rhyolite, Nev.	Wayne W. Bryant
185	Virginia City, Crystal Bar	Louise Bowman
185	Reno at Night	Meston's Travels
186	Shasta Dam	U. S. Forest Service
187	Mt. Lassen	Emil Muench
188	Lake Tahoe, Emerald Bay	Wayne W. Bryant
189	Lake Tahoe from Donner Pass Bridge	Raymond C. Douglas
189	Reno Ski Bowl	Reno Chamber of Commerce
190–191	El Capitan, Yosemite N.P.; Yosemite Falls	Wayne W. Bryant
191	Half Dome, Yosemite N.P.	Meston's Travels
192	King's Highway, Kings Canyon N. P.	Louise Bowman
193	Base of General Sherman Tree	Paul West
193	Mt. Whitney	Wayne W. Bryant
194–195	Scotty's Castle, Death Valley; Bad Water, Death Valley	Paul W. Nesbit
195	20-Mule Team, Death Valley	National Park Service
196–197	Palm Springs Biltmore; Chuck-Wagon Breakfast, San Jacinto Mountains	Palm Springs Chamber of Commerce
197	Joshua Tree	Paul W. Nesbit
198	Redwood Highway, Chandelier Tree	Meston's Travels
199	Timber Truck	R. S. Hibshman
199	Light and Shadow, Redwood Highway	E. L. Jordan
200	San Francisco, Fisherman's Wharf	E. L. Jordan
201	San Francisco, Cable Car; San Francisco, Cliff House	Atkins Travel Slides
202–203	Monterey Peninsula, Witsch Tree; Monterey Peninsula, Midway Point	Emil Muench
203	Window in Robert Louis Stevenson House	E. L. Jordan
205	Los Angeles, Douglas McArthur Park	Union Pacific Railroad Colorphoto
206–207	Torrey Pines, San Diego; San Diego from Pt. Loma; Mission San Diego de Alcala	San Diego City and County Visitors Bureau

KEY TO SECTIONAL MAPS

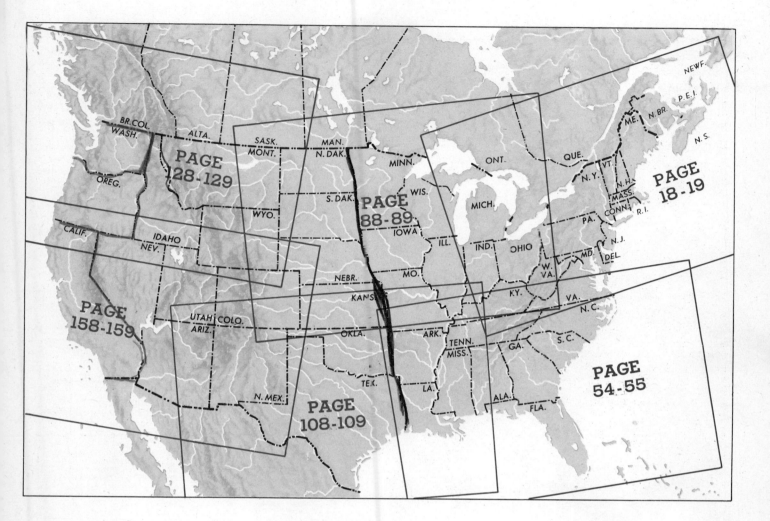

LEGEND

National Parks and Monuments	▪ ▮
National Parkways	
Completed sections	═════
Projected or under construction	═══════
National Recreational Areas	▲ ▮
Indian Reservations and Reserves	◉ ▮
National Wildlife Refuges	○ ▯
National Forests and Forest Reserves	⋈ ▱
State and Provincial Parks	△ ▱
State and Provincial Forests	⋈ ▱
Highways to National Park Service Areas	─────
Highways to State and Provincial Recreational Areas	─────
U.S. Highway Numbers	⬡
State and Provincial Highway Numbers	②
Trails	··········
National Boundaries	─·─·─
State and Provincial Boundaries	─··─··
Cities and Towns	●
National Capitals	⊛
State and Provincial Capitals	✳
Deserts	░
Mountain Peaks	+

LIST OF ABBREVIATIONS

C.H.=Court House
CHAN.=Channel
CO.=County
CR.=Creek
EXPER. STA.=Experimental Station
FED.=Federation
I., IS.=Island, Islands
IND. RES., I.R.=Indian Reservation or Reserve
MEM'L FOR.=Memorial Forest
MT., MTN., MTS.=Mount, Mountain, Mountains
NAT'L MEM'L=National Memorial
NAT'L MON.=National Monument
N.F.=National Forest
N.W.=Northwest
N.W.R.=National Wildlife Refuge
PKWY.=Parkway
PROV.=Provincial
P.S.=Plant Sanctuary
R.A.=Recreational Area
R.D.A.=Recreational Demonstration Area
S.F., S.F.P.=State Forest, State Forest Park
S.P.=State Park

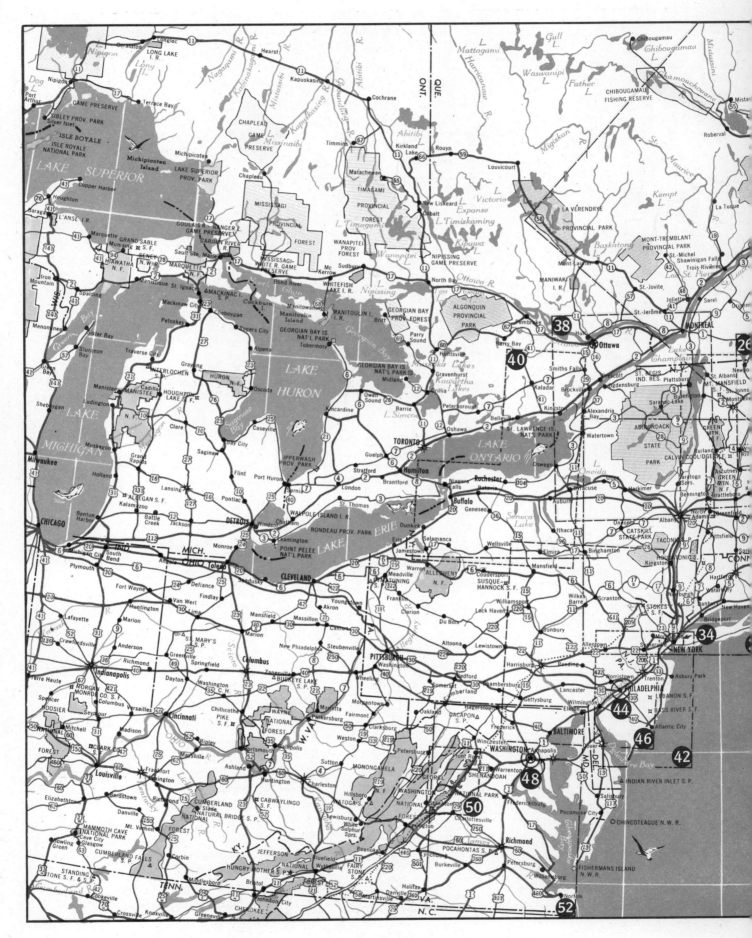

What to See in the Northeast Section

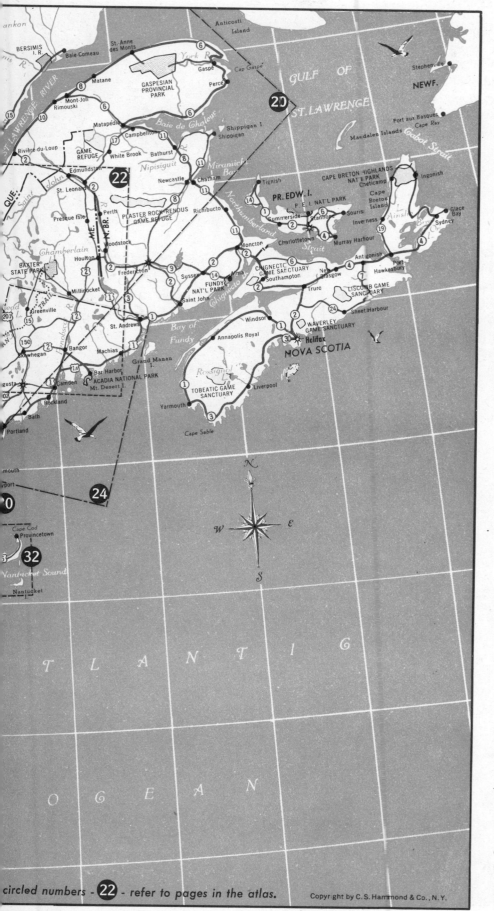

circled numbers - ②② - refer to pages in the atlas.

15-DAY TRIP THROUGH EASTERN CANADA, from Montreal to St. Andrews. See pictures and maps on pages 20 and 21, also the Sightseeing Gazetteer.—Suggested stops: Montreal—Quebec—Murray Bay—Gaspé Peninsula, in or near Cap Chat—Percé—Chatham, New Brunswick—by ferry to Charlottetown, Prince Edward Island—by ferry to Nova Scotia, the Pictou-New Glasgow area—Cape Breton Highlands National Park, at Ingonish or Neils Harbour—Halifax or Lunenburg—by ferry to St. John, New Brunswick—St. Andrews. 11 overnight stops in 15 days allow for 2-day stopovers in Quebec, Percé, Cape Breton Highlands National Park or elsewhere.

14-DAY TRIP THROUGH NEW ENGLAND. See pictures and maps on pages 22 to 31, also Sightseeing Gazetteer. — Suggested stops: New York City—the Great Barrington area in the Berkshires of Massachusetts—Bennington, Vermont, and the Green Mountains—the Meredith-Laconia area on Lake Winnipesaukee, N.H.—the Woodstock to Gorham area in the White Mountains of N.H.—Bar Harbor, Maine—Portland, Me.—Boston, Mass.—New York City.—7 overnight stops in 14 days allow for 2- and 3-day stopovers at the Green Mountains, the White Mountains, Bar Harbor, or elsewhere.

10-DAY TRIP TO CAPE COD AND NANTUCKET. See pictures and maps on pages 32 and 33, also the Sightseeing Gazetteer.—Suggested stops: Plymouth, Mass.—Dennis on Cape Cod—Provincetown—Chatham—Hyannis—Woods Hole—take ferry to Martha's Vineyard—take ferry to Nantucket—take ferry back to Woods Hole and proceed to Buzzards Bay—Plymouth. Two days are recommended for Nantucket.

10-DAY TRIP THROUGH NEW YORK STATE. See pictures and maps on pages 34 to 41, also the Sightseeing Gazetteer.—Suggested stops: New York City—Catskill Mountains in or near Cairo—Watkins Glen—Niagara Falls—Thousand Islands, between Clayton and Alexandria Bay—Lake Placid—Lake George—New York City.—6 overnight stops for 10 days allow for 2-day stopovers at the Catskills, Niagara Falls, Thousand Islands, the Adirondacks, or elsewhere.

10-DAY TRIP THROUGH PENNSYLVANIA. See pictures and maps on pages 44 to 47, also the Sightseeing Gazetteer.—Suggested stops: Philadelphia—the Stroudsburg area in the Pocono Mountains—Eagles Mere—Wellsboro—Erie—Pittsburgh—Gettysburg—via Lancaster and the Pennsylvania-Dutch country to Valley Forge and Philadelphia. 7 overnight stops for 10 days allow for 2-day stopovers in the Poconos, Pittsburgh, Gettysburg, or elsewhere.—Alternate route: Philadelphia—via Harrisburg along the picturesque Susquehanna to Millersburg area—Eagles Mere, etc.

19

GRAND WELCOME. There may be more central maritime approaches to America, but nowhere will the New World receive you in a grander manner. The ocean gradually narrows down to an inland sea, to blue waters surrounded by cliffs and hills, with immense black pine forests on the slopes, and small, straight white church steeples in the tiny village ports. By the river's bank two great and civilized cities arise where the little-explored northern wilderness begins. This gateway is of huge proportions, and the traveler who wants to get acquainted with the St. Lawrence may easily spend his whole vacation on or near its shores. A leisurely ride around the Gaspé Peninsula alone will take a week, and many full days may be spent at Murray Bay and the Laurentians, in Quebec and Montreal.

LA GASPÉ: REPLICA OF AN OLD FRENCH COUNTRYSIDE.

If you like roads that run by the sea, and views that encompass bays and shores, the Gaspé Peninsula will offer you many a reward. One of its most famous sights is the Percé Rock; facing the ocean toward the east, it stands in the blue waters like an oversized battleship; the scenery around the village of Percé belongs to America's most spectacular sights. Besides, there are the ingredients of a colorful peasant civilization that is preserving many an old custom from the French homeland: The bulky outdoor ovens in which delicious bread is baked; the large, good-natured dogs that pull carts

The red cliffs of the Gaspé set off the dark forests and the blue water.

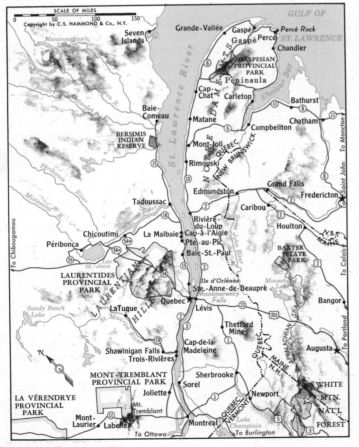

See sectional map, page 18

heaped with vegetables; the piles of wood stacked high behind the houses for winter use; the frail horse-buggies converging upon the village church on a Sunday morning; the crucifixes by the road; and the small country hotels where good meals can be eaten.

SWANK AND WILDERNESS IN THE LAURENTIAN HILLS.

Jumbled and without any regular pattern of orderly ranges, the Laurentians cover an enormous territory on the northwestern shore of the St. Lawrence. Cruises up the Saguenay River reveal a grandiose, lonely landscape of cliffs and forests, but farther south where a particularly picturesque group of Laurentian hills touch the broad, lake-like St. Lawrence, the famous summer resort of Murray Bay is flourishing. This "Northwoods Newport" is in a class with Bar Harbor, Palm Beach, and Carmel-by-the-Sea; its estate owners—for instance the Cabots, Ryans, Tafts of Ohio, and Hamilton Fish's—form an exclusive social group, but also mere tourists find the resort wonderful; its natural beauty has a French accent: Neither the government nor the mails know a place called Murray Bay. That name is merely a tradition. Officially the resort consists of three French-Canadian towns with the romantic designations of La Malbaie, Cap-à-l'Aigle and Pointe-au-Pic. The showplace of the region is the Manoir Richelieu, a luxury hotel owned by the Canada Steamship Lines. Built into a cliff, it offers its guests a stunning view of the 15-mile wide river, all sports, and a fabulous collection of Canadiana; 45 miles to the north it operates a camp from which 32 lakes may be fished. The inland Laurentians are still a lonely wilderness, but during recent years many private and public fishing, hunting and skiing lodges have been built, often in a gaily colored French-Canadian style. That does not mean that the hills are becoming crowded; it rather points up a typically Canadian resort specialty—the fine, comfortable hotel-lodge in an untamed, wild forest country where fishing is superb. Skiing facilities are developed especially north of the two great cities. The "Maple Leaf Trail" is a unique 80-mile path for cross-country skiing, beginning at the logging town of Labelle and running southward through Mt. Tremblant, the ski resort, and a host of picturesque little French-Canadian towns.

THE ROCKS AND RAMPARTS OF QUEBEC. Cities built on hills by the water are always spectacular, but Quebec has one advantage over such hill-town-sisters as San Francisco or Rio de Janeiro: It is all of one piece, monolithic, easily encompassed by the human eye. There is the old town with its little criss-cross streets along the river, and towering on the rock above stands Château Frontenac. When Willa Cather, the poet, saw this picture gleaming at night with a million lights, it seemed to her like "an altar with many candles," like the vision of "a holy city in an old legend." To enjoy the majestic sweep of "the rock," and to view the picturesque Montmorency

The fortress-like Rock of Percé is the most spectacular sight of the Gaspé.

Falls which are 100 feet higher than the drop of the Niagara, an excursion-boat ride on the St. Lawrence is recommended; getting acquainted with the old town and the ramparts—Quebec is the only walled city in America—is a venture best performed on foot. From above, the panorama is glorious from the Château Frontenac, the famous hotel that looks like a huge French castle, and from the terrace surrounding it. For exploring the upper town with its parliament building, monuments and gardens, an old-fashioned horse-drawn *calèche* is usually hired, the driver explaining the sights or just chatting about his family. The city is altogether charming.

MONTREAL, A TWO-NATION COMMUNITY. This largest city of Canada is fascinating because of its contrasts. From Mount Royal, the green hill in the center of Montreal Island, you look into the vast, rich plains to the south and feel, quite correctly, that you are in the center of a great inland empire. Then suddenly the big white hull of the "Empress of Canada" or a huge tanker or a freighter from Liverpool or Rotterdam, looms at the bend of the river, and you realize that this is also a great world port, 1,000 miles away from the ocean. Montreal is an ancient seat of religion and culture; it has probably more churches than any other American community, and McGill is one of the continent's leading universities. Yet it lies at the edge of the wilderness that stretches uninterrupted to the North Pole.

Chateau Frontenac, the hotel-castle that is the landmark of Quebec.

SILENT LAKES AND INDIAN TRAILS. Since Thoreau wandered through the deep woods and canoed over the lonely lakes of Northern Maine, almost a hundred years ago, there have been some changes, but not in the way anticipated by Thoreau. He was afraid that settlements and towns would encroach upon the wilderness while in fact the woods and streams are lonelier today than ever. They shelter more deer and bears, beavers and otters, foxes and wildcats than lived there in Thoreau's time, and the fishing about which he complained occasionally, is infinitely better now because the lakes and brooks are stocked. Of course, the white pines and balsam firs, the red spruce and hemlocks, the rock maples and aspen poplars are in their third or fourth growth now, but Thoreau did not see the virgin giants either; they had gone by 1857. On the whole he would still feel entirely at home at Moosehead Lake, the starting point of his wilderness trip, a water body which cuts for 35 miles through almost trackless forests. About midway on its westerly side, Mount Kineo rises abruptly above its surface like a wounded giant cow moose lying by the shore, a striking comparison from Indian lore. Greenville at the southern end is a pleasant resort and outfitters' town, and in the north the portage to the West Branch of the Penobscot and the canoe trip to Chamberlain Lake are still a great experience in solitude and freedom.

White birches blend with cool, blue lakes into a northern picture.

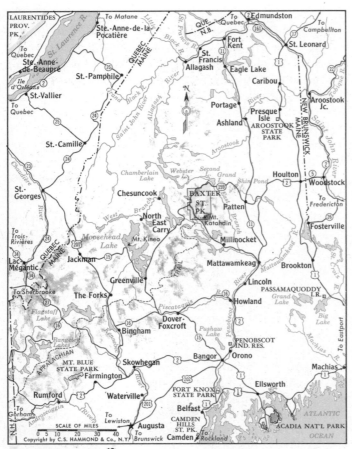

See sectional map, page 18

Chamberlain Farm where Thoreau borrowed some sugar, is still there, ancient and weatherbeaten but deserted, and also the decaying remnants of a lumber steamer in a shallow cove testify to the victory of nature over civilization. Allen Nugent's sporting camp, a more recent settlement, fits well into the Northwoods scene. The rest of the trip, over Webster Lake and through the turbulent Webster Brook, through Second Lake and Grand Lake and down the East Branch of the Penobscot to Millinocket, is quite the same today as it was a century ago, or as it ever was. There are innumerable similar wilderness jaunts; best known among them is the Allagash River trip which according to the guides in Greenville is "the finest on the continent." It runs through solid deep forest, encompasses the eight remote and untouched Allagash lakes, includes some exciting samples of white water travel, and is interrupted by few portages.

THE BIRD'S EYE VIEW. One twentieth-century touch of the Northwoods is the presence of small planes that have become an accepted means of transportation. Such points as Greenville or Augustine's Shin Pond House northwest of Patten have become water airports. From there hunters and especially fishermen like to be flown to remote lakes which are not accessible by road and offer wonderful hunting and fishing. Also amateur nature photographers find such flights most rewarding.

Thoreau's Beloved Wilderness

On clear days the deep-green, endless expanse of forests and hills, the hundreds of shiny lakes, and the unknown blue mountain ranges far away on the horizons, blend into an unforgettable panorama which Thoreau would have loved. Flying is also a lazy man's way of observing wildlife. Turning around a mountain slope, at a moderate altitude, there will be six or seven bears grazing in the blueberry bushes and scattering in all directions. Two moose will stand in a little lake, their heads completely immersed in the water in their search for bottom plants, paying no attention to the big bird. Upon landing, an old red fox may watch you from a bushy peninsula, and a worried loon mother will take her two baby loons under her wings and dive with them out of sight. A look through your binoculars will confirm that the huge nest on a dead tree on a tiny island is occupied: A bald eagle family lives there Ashore a bed of bright scarlet cardinal flowers may welcome you. However, one warning is in order here: During the early summer the mosquitoes and flies are often most annoying.

THE MOUNT KATAHDIN STORY The highest peak of Maine is Mount Katahdin situated approximately in the center of the half-circle described by Thoreau It lies in Baxter State Park, one of America's great fish and game preserves. With a height of 5,258 feet and a geographical location far east of New York, it is the

From an airplane the Northwoods appear like a huge green-and-blue nature map.

first spot in the United States to be touched by the rays of the rising sun. No one has described the peak better than Thoreau: It is "a vast aggregation of loose rocks, as if at some time it had rained rocks, and they lay as they fell on the mountain, nowhere firmly at rest, but leaning on each other, all rocking stones.—" There are a number of camps for vacationers at the foot of the mountain, and the ascent is neither easy nor difficult. About Katahdin, the mountain-god, the Abnaki Indians have an ancient tale: Once a beautiful girl who loved the mountain, vanished while berry-picking. She came back three years later with a lovely, strong boy who had eyebrows of stone. The camp buzzed with gossip, but nobody asked the indiscreet question. Later a famine descended upon the land, and the Abnaki would have perished if the boy had not shown supernatural powers and provided food: With his finger he pointed to a moose or a wild goose in flight, and the game's dead body fell to the ground. Gossip and insinuations became stronger, and finally the curious women made the tactless inquiry. "You fools," replied the angry and weary mother. "My boy is the son of Katahdin, sent to you to save you. But now your folly has destroyed his work." She took her child and wandered off toward the top of the great mountain. The Abnakis, however, were doomed. White man came and robbed and killed them. It's a Lohengrin tale of the Northwoods.

Small planes are favorites with hunters and fishermen in search of hidden lakes.

THE TENFOLD COASTLINE. If you fly from the southernmost to the northernmost point of the Maine shore, your speedometer will indicate that you have traveled less than 250 miles. If you sail along the coastline, you will ride for 2,500 miles. There is a geological explanation for this "folded" coast: A mountainous country has gradually sunk into the sea, the valleys have become inlets and bays, and the outlying mountain peaks have turned into islands. This grandiose seascape begins with restraint at the southern end around the well-known resorts of Kennebunkport and Old Orchard Beach but gathers momentum at Portland. The white spray of the breakers that dashes over the granite cliffs of Portland Head Light has a wild, rugged touch. A steamboat ride around Portland's Casco Bay has more amiable overtones. The rocky islands on which the boat calls, are pleasant resorts. Between Brunswick where famous Bowdoin College lies in a stately grove of cathedral pines, to Rockland, the great lobster harbor, the coast sends far out into the sea a number of thin, long, rocky fingers, creating a thousand vacation spots of blue coves lined with granite and shaded by pines, with seals sunning themselves on the cliffs and birds singing in the trees. Boothbay Harbor has a varied resort life with summer theater and art exhibits, excursions to the old sailing ships of Wiscasset or to Fort Edgecomb, built about 1808, with a wonderful view of bays and woods; sails to Squirrel Island or Monhegan Island are popular. Camden (home of the "Windjammer Cruises") Belfast, Blue Hill and the large islands, all easily reached by bridges or by ferry, offer innumerable opportunities for individual exploration.

THE STEEPEST CAPES, THE DEEPEST HARBORS. The life of the shore comes to a grand crescendo in Mount Desert Island; this is the highest point of the Atlantic coast north of Rio de Janeiro, and the meeting place of the Temperate Zone and the Northern Zone. Its most picturesque part has been converted into Acadia National Park, created by purchases and donations of land, a monument to civic responsibility and generosity. A fine automobile road leads to the summit of Mount Cadillac, so named in honor of the first owner of the island, the Sieur de la Mothe Cadillac. From its peak (1,532 feet high) you will see one of America's great land-and-ocean vistas; Frenchman Bay, deep enough for the biggest ocean vessels, lies below you; the Porcupine Islands look like ducks swimming out into the blue Atlantic. On the other side Katahdin, the great peak of the Northwoods, and the outline of New Hampshire's White Mountains will be visible on a clear day. The trails of the park will lead you to many a point where you stand on top of a cliff rising abruptly out of the sea, or to crystal-clear mountain lakes where wildflowers thrive between lichen-clad rocks. At migration time the land and sea birds of the north form mammoth congregations here.

J. P. MORGAN AND THE PIRATES. At the eastern shore of the island, Bar Harbor is Maine's most famous vacation spot. Once the proud northern summer outpost of eastern society, it is now one of "the last resorts" where dozens of huge Edwardian mansions are still kept up. Bar Harbor had its heyday when J. P. Morgan's yacht *Corsair* lay in the harbor, and the resort's "Pot and Kettle" Club represented 85 per cent of America's wealth. One of the public cruises through Mount Desert waters is strongly recommended. There is a northern frontier atmosphere over the cold, choppy waves, the lonely wooded islands, the seals and the porpoises, the ospreys and the occasional bald eagle surveying the scene from a high dead branch. One sight delights the imagination: Every so often two granite promontories jut out into the ocean, thunderously sprayed with white foam, and between them, secretly tucked away between high granite walls there lies a short, white, sandy beach, a silent cove that is the perfect setting for a swords-and-treasure pirate story.

FROM THE SOUTH SEAS TO VACATIONLAND. The Maine Coast has more to offer than just natural beauty; about its piers and ports, its villages and towns there is that very real atmosphere that only history can create. It is a history far more fascinating than that of battles and diplomatic disputes: It is the true story of a world-wide shipping empire that is no more. America's

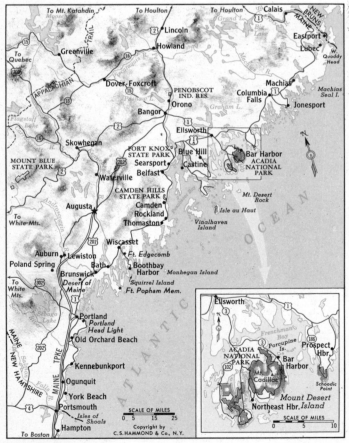

See sectional map, page 18

Our Most Rugged Stretch of Atlantic Shore

Famous Portland Head Light with its breakers and granite cliffs is a symbol of Maine's rugged, "folded" coast. This much-indented shore line covers almost 2,500 miles, equalling about the same number of miles that separate New York from South America.

first vessels were built here, on quiet coves, with native timber. White pine boards were a prime export article, and could be sold at great profit even in jungle-covered Sumatra and Java. So Maine-made square riggers with Maine captains and Maine crews took their Maine lumber to the seven seas, and came home from China and Hawaii, the East Indies and the South Seas with spices and silks and oriental wares. Sometimes one lucky trip made a man rich. In the 1820's Bangor was the world's leading lumber port, with a waterfront life that rivaled that of San Francisco's Barbary Coast in gold rush days. Then suddenly the great venture collapsed, due to the steamboats, the depletion of the forests, and the lack of

a populous hinterland. But there were still lobstering and fishing and farming, a good way of life, until in the 20th century a new cash crop was thrust upon the coast: Tourism. Natural scenic beauty, ideal fishing and sailing, wonderful lobster dinners and a race of fine, sincere, hearty Americans living along the coves and the docks, combined to attract vacationers and travelers by the thousands. When the state introduced automobile license plates that proclaimed Maine as "Vacationland" nobody protested but the undertakers. They did not think that such propaganda would be dignified on a hearse carrying a corpse to the cemetery; for them special plates were made, with the simple legend "Maine."

"THE SECOND - GREATEST SHOW ON EARTH!" These were Mr. Barnum's words when he admired the view from the summit of Mt. Washington. Other celebrities were more subtle but not less lavish in their praise of New Hampshire's White Mountains. Thoreau and Agassiz, Daniel Webster and Washington Irving, Dana and Emerson traveled there and told the world; Hawthorne was inspired to write "The Great Stone Face" and Longfellow to compose his ode on "Chocorua's Curse"; Whittier penned his White Mountain ballads, and others collected the Indian legends and the ancient stories about the ranges. At a time when America's other mountains "just stood," the peaks of New Hampshire were glorified loudly throughout the land. The reasons for this early recognition were threefold: The White Mountains were indeed beautiful; they were easily accessible, and since on clear days they could even be seen from ships at sea, had been known since the days of exploration; and they towered in the heart of New England which in the 19th century was the most articulate section of our country.

COGS AND NOTCHES. The charm of the White Mountains lies in a perfect integration of civilization—white little churches, well-kept valley farms, neat villages gay with flowers—and nature in the grand manner—endless wooded hills, towering granite peaks, rushing mountain streams, sky-blue lakes. Today most visitors on a

Early settlers called this land bewitched. An Indian curse lay on Mt. Chocorua.

New Hampshire holiday cross and recross the White Mountains on highways 3, 302, and 16, the roads forming a huge N on the map. After a ride through the foothills, the first group of famous sights is ready for inspection north of North Woodstock around Franconia Notch (notch being the Yankee word for pass). There is the Flume, a deep canyon with vertical granite walls through which a cold mountain stream makes a spraying and gurgling 700-foot dash. The Lost River Reservation will take you into magnificent mountain scenery and through a series of caverns with such extravagant names as Cave of Lost Souls and the Judgment Hall of Pluto. Behind Profile Lake, 1,500 feet above the water, the rocky outline of the Old Man of the Mountain's stern face is clear and distinct, a landmark of New England and the inspiration of a classic. To get an impression of the surrounding mountainous countryside, a ride on the aerial tramway to the top of Cannon Mountain is recommended. This is a more conservative conveyance than most of the other White Mountain chairlifts which serve sightseers in summertime and skiers during the winter. Proceeding in a northeasterly direction, Crawford Notch was the scene of New England's most famous landslide. The Willey cabin stood there; when in 1826 during a terrible storm the mountain behind gave way and roared down toward the farm house, the nine residents rushed out to seek shelter in the notch. All were caught in the

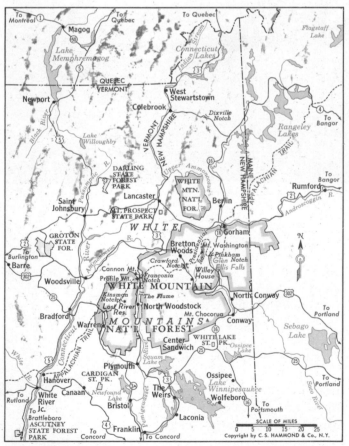
See sectional map, page 18

maelstrom and literally ground to death while a boulder divided the slide just above the cabin and left it untouched. All would have lived had they stayed inside. The tragic irony of the incident has been immortalized in a Hawthorne story. At Bretton Woods the sumptucus Mount Washington Hotel is decoratively surrounded by the Presidential Range, and near there the cogwheel railroad to the summit of Mt. Washington may be boarded. Of the world's railways this is the oddest (its toy-like pusher locomotive has a tilted boiler to remain horizontal on a slope), the safest (never an accident on a regular run), the shortest (3½ miles), and possibly the most expensive (if figured in cents per mile). It is also one of the oldest, opened in 1869, and one of the most ingenious; it was the first one to use the cogwheel principle which later was copied dozens of times in the Alps. On a clear day New England's tallest mountain (6,288 feet) offers a view of 130 miles in any direction. It's a stormy peak, and the worst wind ever recorded anywhere on earth was recorded here: In April, 1934, it once blew at the rate of 231 miles an hour. Back at the base you proceed through Crawford Notch around the range to Glen Ellis Falls and Pinkham Notch where an eight-mile toll road leads automobiles to the top of Mt. Washington, with innumerable hairpin turns that offer broad mountain vistas. Of course, thousands of people climb to the summit over various trails. There are hundreds of

Mt. Washington with a head of October snow rivals the great mountains of the West.

miles of trails throughout the White Mountains, supplemented by a chain of huts where simple food and lodging may be obtained along the trail. From Pinkham Notch on, the ride north leads into New Hampshire's forest primeval; at Dixville Notch the wilderness is pointed up by The Balsams, a large modern luxury hotel. The area from North Conway to Berlin is a skier's paradise.

THE WREATH OF LAKES. It seems quite proper that these amiable mountains should be surrounded by groups of lovely lakes in whose clear waters wooded hills are mirrored. The scattering of small lakes and the beautiful Connecticut River in the west; the Connecticut Lakes in the north; Sebago and the Rangeley Lakes of Maine, the myriad of New Hampshire lakes of which Winnipesaukee is the largest, and the Ossipees in the east; and Lakes Squam and Newfound in the south combine to make a perfect stage for the "Great White Hills." Winnipesaukee, an Indian name meaning "the Smile of the Great Spirit," has become a thriving tourist center. It has natural beauty, with great expanses of blue water, a shoreline of 183 miles, 274 tree-shaded islands, and the dark-blue outline of the White Mountains as a backdrop. It has shore areas crowded with tourist cabins, and others with spacious, exclusive beach clubs, modest summer camps and sumptuous island estates, and at The Weirs there are water carnivals and bathing beauty contests, outboard races and parachute jumps.

Covered bridges are practical in winter sleet and summer sun.

BEAUTIFUL, LOVELY, HARMONIOUS, EX-QUISITE, GRACEFUL." These adjectives, descriptive of Vermont's Green Mountain landscape, do not come from the Chamber of Commerce but are from Dorothy Canfield Fisher, herself a Vermonter who, supposedly, is given to understatement. Perhaps it is for that reason that she calls the reader's attention to the fact that she does not say "sublime, magnificent, gorgeous, or spectacular." Such words, she feels, should be reserved for the Rockies. Be that as it may, all visitors will agree with her, particularly those who do not just hurry through the Green Mountain country but stay for a while. The finest place to enjoy the essence of Vermont is the ridge of a hill pasture where you can sit down under a tall elm, with a "four-town view" beneath. The horizon is a rhythmic chain of mountains, crossing and re-crossing. The fields and meadows are green and yellow rectangles set off by light hedgerows or heavy, golden-grey stone fences. In the valleys the gables of white farm houses or white church steeples rise above green trees. This is not the wild, untamed beauty of the West, but a perfect harmony between soil and man, landscape and village, although the Vermonters had only two centuries to achieve it; it is reminiscent of the European countryside. One excellent way of getting acquainted with the Green Mountains is a hike over the Long Trail which for 260 miles winds its way over the ridges from Blackin-

ton, Massachusetts, to Canada. Shelters are numerous.

CATAMOUNT AND SMUGGLERS' NOTCH. No great cities intrude here. Driving to the capital, for instance, a golden dome suddenly emerges above the hills and trees, and you are at the state capital at Montpelier. In the south, Bennington is an interesting town, especially Old Bennington, just to the west of the modern business district. It is a veritable outdoor museum with such attractions as the world's tallest battle monument, standing 306 feet above the ridge of the hill. The First Congregational Church on the Old Burying Ground is one of New England's most beautiful buildings, and the Catamount Monument—the bronze figure of a large wildcat—recalls tumultous frontier days. Here was the site of the Catamount Tavern whose sign was a stuffed catamount on a tall pole, the cat's wicked bare teeth facing the New York border. Here the Green Mountain Boys, excited by rum and hard cider, bragged that they could take Fort Ticonderoga from the British, which they did. To the north, Manchester is the foremost summer resort of the Green Mountains, a lovely spot for those who appreciate a quiet, cultured setting. Incidentally, a trip over Mt. Equinox Skyline Drive, just west of Manchester, affords an excellent view of the surrounding countryside. Burlington, partly a creation of those fascinating Vermont brothers Ethan and Ira Allen, lies on the three terraces of a mountain that faces Lake Champlain. On the highest level the campus of the University of Vermont offers a splendid panorama of the town and the broad expanse of the blue lake; beyond its waters the Adirondacks stand against the sky, in light and dark blue sheets, like a Chinese water color. Watching the sunset from here, William Dean Howells compared it to sunset over the Bay of Naples, but he gave the crown to Burlington. East of Burlington, Stowe has become the Green Mountains' ski center; it lies at the southern end of the Smugglers' Notch Road, once a notorious thoroughfare for the duty-free importation of goods from Canada, and in the shadow of Mount Mansfield, with 4,393 feet the tallest peak of the chain. Ideal hill contours and plenty of snow combine with chair lifts, ski jumps and pleasant inns to make Stowe one of the most popular winter sports resorts in the East.

GRANITE, MARBLE, MAPLE SUGAR. Among the material contributions of these mountains to the country at large, granite and marble must be mentioned; both occur here in seemingly inexhaustible quantities. Barre is the granite center, and Proctor near Rutland the great marble producer; quarrying operations are fascinating to watch, and it is well worth-while to visit one of the granite or marble "sheds" as the mills are called, to watch the sawing, carving and polishing of the stone. The Vermont stone cutters are interesting people: The granite workers are largely Scotsmen who erected a fine Robert Burns statue in Barre, and among the marble

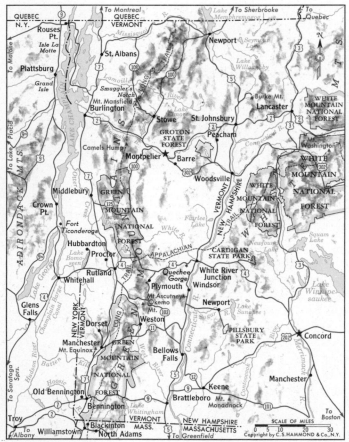

See sectional map, page 18

Peacham, Vermont, shows the harmonious integration of landscape and village that is reminiscent of the European countryside. It is this harmony between man and the soil that makes the Vermont countryside a delight to behold.

cutters there are many Italian-Americans whose ancestors worked in Carrara, Italy; they are the descendants of quarrymen who shaped marble columns for the Forum of Augustus Imperator in Rome. Even better known than Green Mountain stone is Vermont maple sugar, although these days the production rather runs into maple syrup. The "harvest" begins in mid-March; a 40-year-old maple will yield 10 gallons of sap annually.

CHARACTER RATHER THAN CASH. One of the best features of a Green Mountain vacation is the chance of getting acquainted with Vermonters. In their communities the latter never had any "gentry," and never kept slaves; so they remained a very homogeneous group of American folks in the best and most democratic sense

of the word. Self-reliant and independent, they will react very negatively to an address like "Hey, Mac!," but will prove friendly and helpful to all courteous comers. Innumerable stories reflect their good humor. An Iowa farmer once watched a Vermont ploughman and remarked that at home in Iowa they would never bother to work a rocky soil like that. "May be so," replied the Green Mountain man. "Sometimes I wonder myself how we make a living here and even save enough money to buy mortgages on Iowa farms." Classical is the remark of the Vermont farmer who, after a rectification of the state line, was told that he now lived in New Hampshire. "Good," he said. "I don't think I could have stood another one of those Vermont winters."

29

ACOMPLEX PERSONALITY. Ralph Waldo Emerson called Boston "the town which was appointed to lead the civilization of North America." Oliver Wendell Holmes felt that more than any other city "Boston has opened and kept open the turnpikes that lead straight to free thought and free speech and free deeds." Lincoln Steffens thought differently. "Boston," he wrote, "has carried the practice of hypocrisy to the nth degree of refinement and failure." Such conflicting views about America's "Mother of Freedom" are quite the rule, and the city's pattern is so complex that no mere visitor can hope to analyze the Boston spirit. The descendants of the Puritans are a small minority by now, but the Lowells and Reveres, Adamses and Cabots are still very much alive, and strong in finance and politics. U.S. Senator Leverett Saltonstall, for instance, belongs to the 12th generation of the American branch of his family, and to the 10th that graduated from Harvard. There may be innumerable caricatures of stuffy and overly proper Bostonians, but it is due to their wealth, public spirit, and cultural interest that Boston has one of the world's top symphony orchestras, that its museums contain unique art treasures, that Harvard is not only our country's oldest but also its richest university, and that Massachusetts Institute of Technology is America's leading engineering school.

THE FREEDOM TRAIL. As a sightseeing town Bos-

Fish Pier. Boston is still a great fishing port.

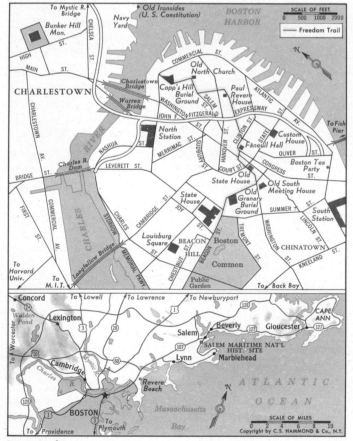

See sectional map, page 18

ton is historic rather than scenic although the approach from the sea presents the city quite handsomely, especially when the sun is setting behind the towering skyline. Since most of Boston's historic shrines are concentrated in the compact downtown district, it is recommended to see them on a walking tour which is marked by easily followed pointers. The "Freedom Trail" begins at the State House with its golden dome and its Hall of Flags; in the Hall of Representatives hangs the symbol of this coast: the Sacred Cod. Your next stop will be Boston Common, the old cow pasture and training ground where stocks, pillory and gallows used to stand. The Old Granary Burial Ground is a hall-of-fame cemetery; you will see there the graves of Samuel Adams and John Hancock, Paul Revere and Peter Faneuil, the parents of Benjamin Franklin and Mother Goose who was a lady with the name of Mary Goose. Old South Meeting House with its 180-foot steeple was the scene of the most violent revolutionary oratory, and the Boston Tea Party was planned there. The Old State House, dating from 1713, is an interesting historical and marine museum; nearby is the scene of the Boston Massacre. Faneuil Hall is a free meeting hall open to any group of citizens; so many loud and angry protests against the British were voiced there, before the Revolution, that it is called the "Cradle of Liberty." The weathervane of its steeple is a Boston curiosity: It represents a big grasshopper. The Paul Revere

House, built in the 1660's or 70's, is the oldest in Boston; with its overhanging second story and its diamond-shaped panes, it is reminiscent of medieval England. The Old North Church was the lookout from which the British approach was signaled with the help of lanterns: "One if by land, and two if by sea, and I on the opposite shore will be." Ironically, the bells that hung above the warning lanterns, are inscribed: "We are the first ring of bells cast for the British Empire in North America." Copp's Hill Burial Ground concludes the Freedom Trail tour.

SWAN BOATS AND OLD IRONSIDES. Other typical Boston sights are the Public Garden with its labeled trees and bright flower beds, adjacent to the Common, on "made land" that was once a marsh along the Charles and is still called "the Back Bay." A feature of the park is a ride on a swan boat. A ship of a different nature may be seen at the Navy Yard, across the Charlestown Bridge: Old Ironsides, the U.S. Frigate Constitution may be inspected there; it is conserved in all its glory. Lovers of architecture will enjoy Beacon Hill on Chestnut Street north of the Common, where the Boston "Brahmins" live or used to live, and Louisburg Square.

PHILOSOPHERS AND CAPTAINS COURAGE-OUS. Across the Charles River in Cambridge the Harvard campus is well worth visiting; the Agassiz Museum's collection of glass-blown flowers, authentic in every detail, is

Chief Massasoit's statue stands near Plymouth Rock (see page 32).

The Swan Boats of the Public Garden are a cherished Boston institution.

famous. In Lexington, the pleasant suburb of minute-men tradition, the Revolutionary War began, and in nearby Concord the shot heard around the world was fired. Another of the town's claims to fame can be read on the gravestones of its Sleepy Hollow Cemetery: Emerson and Thoreau are buried there, Alcott and Hawthorne. In its own way, Concord was once an American Florence or Weimar when "Transcendentalism" and "Nature," "Tanglewood Tales" and "Walden" (the drowsy pond is not far from town) were topics of the day. North of Boston the city of Salem has the embarrassing memories of the witch trials and the glorious ones of clipper ship days. Its old sea captains' houses are, architecturally, among the country's finest buildings; also the House of Seven Gables of Hawthorne's classic is located there. The rock-fringed harbor of Marblehead is the yachting capital of the Northeast; its winding streets are lined with elms and hollyhocks. Race Week in early August is a great water sports event. On Cape Ann, a resort area that combines ruggedness (huge boulders, promontories, coves) with gentleness (flowers, villas, woods), the city of Gloucester has been America's greatest fishing port for 300 years. Its early sailors to the Grand Banks have found a magnificent chronicler in Rudyard Kipling whose "Captains Courageous" has become a classic. More than 10,000 Gloucester men never returned from the sea; a famous statue commemorates their heroism.

THE GREAT ADVENTURE. Plymouth Rock is almost certainly a myth, not history. But that does not matter in the least. All Americans who see the famous stepping stone with the "1620" carved into it, feel that they are standing at one of the deep-reaching foundations on which America is built. This spot has been the scene of agony and humility, and for that we remember it proudly. Only 17 men went ashore here, the others stayed aboard ship where snow covered the decks and scurvy and ship fever raged. Between Christmas and March nearly half the company died. The pilgrims had a few friends, though, and to one of them, the Indian chief Massasoit, a fine bronze statue has been erected on top of Cole's Hill, near the Rock. But the true significance of this hill is expressed by its sculptured sarcophagus: To this spot the new-comers carried the corpses of their people at night, buried them secretly, and planted corn on the graves. For terror was in their hearts, and they did not want the Indians to know that so many were dying.—The cradle of the first white child born here, and other interesting objects may be inspected at Pilgrim Hall.

THE YANKEE SPIRIT AND THE BOHEMIAN TOUCH. Cape Cod has the shape of a man's arm bent upward to show off its muscles. The "arm" is 65 miles long, 20 miles broad at the "shoulder," and 2 miles wide at the "wrist." It is a seaside resort area that could hardly

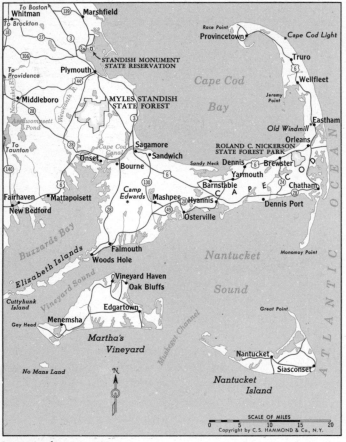

See sectional map, page 18

be improved upon: There are gleaming white dunes, lovely marshlands, dark evergreen forests, numerous inlets for sailing, and 200 freshwater lakes. Some stretches, particularly at the "elbow," are bleak with high, lonely bluffs; others, especially on the south shore, are well groomed with sea vistas framed in roses and tall trees, with yacht clubs and golf courses. This sunny and breezy peninsula increases its regular population fivefold each summer, and since the visitors are the main source of income, a certain commercialism is unavoidable. To the amusement of the Cape Codders most travelers expect the natives to be salty and quaint, and while the latter are not different from any other small-town Americans, they are glad to oblige and act the expected part. Real estate operators look like sea captains, and oldsters who sell carved knick-knacks at road stands, whittle on a piece of wood. All this professional Yankeedom, however, is carried on in a good-natured, unobjectionable way; such venerable old Cape towns as Sandwich (birthplace of the famous Sandwich glass, now a collector's item) and Barnstable, Woods Hole (a world center for oceanographic research) and Falmouth, Hyannis and Chatham still have a great deal of the genuine Yankee spirit. In contrast, Provincetown at the tip of the peninsula has a different though not less intriguing atmosphere. Its regular population, the fishermen and storekeepers, are not to any extent of British-American stock but rather Portuguese from the Azores whose ancestors worked on Yankee whaling ships and settled here. The summer population is also different: It has been of an artistic bend ever since the first art school was opened there in 1899. More than a dozen such institutions are in existence now, and inevitably the real artists have been joined by pseudo-artists, amateurs and hangers-on in search of *Bohème* rather than art. The well-known playhouse exerts also a considerable influence on the summer colony, and the total result is that of an animated Greenwich Village.

FAMOUS VISITORS' ROSTER: FROM LEIF ERICSON TO EUGENE O'NEILL. You cannot see history, of course, but somehow it is in the air; the fact that history has often touched Cape Cod, is one of the peninsula's main attractions. Long Viking ships with tall carved dragons in the bow landed at these shores half a millennium before the latter were officially discovered. The man who charted the Cape's harbors was no other than Champlain, in 1606. The name Cape Cod emerged from Captain John Smith's expedition in 1614. The Pilgrim Fathers, as everybody knows, landed in Provincetown before they settled across the bay. One of the first tourists on the Cape was Thoreau, and his report on what he saw is a classic. After that, the visiting celebrities were legion, from Daniel Webster to Grover Cleveland. In 1916 a future Nobel Prize winner, Eugene O'Neill, was living in an abandoned Coast Guard station near Provincetown, and one of his

Old Mill Point. Dozens of windmills once operated on the Cape, pumping sea water into shallow vats, for the manufacture of salt. Although now in disuse, some still stand as picturesque landmarks. Some windmills are still operated to grind fresh corn meal.

first plays, "Bound East for Cardiff," was staged in a fish house on a wharf. Since the drama takes place on a ship, and since the audience could hear the harbor water splash around the poles beneath their improvised theater, the realism was unsurpassed.

THE SHAPELY SEA WITCH. Of course, the Cape has also a wonderful folklore of its own. Many of its yarns run into the supernatural and the humorous. One of the most colorful, semi-legendary figures was Ichabod Paddock, the first great whaling captain. Once, when chasing whales near Nantucket, he noticed that a big bull whale seemed immune; no harpoon took hold. So the captain decided to investigate and swam through

the huge throat of the beast into its stomach. To his surprise he discovered that a shapely young sea witch with red hair and green eyes lived there. She invited him to stay for the night, and he did. From then on he made his excursions into the bull whale two or three times a week, until Mrs. Paddock decided to stop her husband's amorous aberrations. She persuaded another skipper to harpoon the whale with a sterling silver harpoon against which the witch was powerless. So the bull was caught and cut open. What they found inside were these ominous objects: a strand of red sea weed, like a head of woman's hair; two oval green beach plums; and jellyfish the color of human flesh.

THE FIRST GLANCE. Libraries could be filled with the books, guides and articles that have been written about the world's largest community, that "ragged purple dream, the wonderful, cruel, enchanting, bewildering, fatal, great city,"—as O. Henry expressed it. In the limited space available here we want to present only a few suggestions to the visitor who is interested in the atmosphere and the mood of the city rather than in a great many details. Your first impression of New York will be disheartening if you approach it by rail from the north, through endless blocks of factories and tenements. It will be doubtful if, en route to New York, you cross the Jersey Meadows by train or car, and from the burning garbage and the delapidated piggeries a formidable stench arises to your nostrils. It will be a pleasant surprise if you ride on one of the parkways, and out of a bright forest landscape you drive into a majestic river scene, the Hudson and the Palisades to your right, the big town to your left. And it will be a vision of unearthly beauty if you approach New York from the sea, and watch its skyline and the Statue of Liberty emerge from the morning mist.

THE SECOND GLANCE. For a general survey of the city two excursions are recommended: A trip to the top of the Empire State Building and a steamer tour around the Island of Manhattan. From the 102nd story of the world's tallest tower you will have a stunning view of

Manhattan, and although, of course, New York City is very much larger than just the island, it is Manhattan's huge ship of rock below you that is the visitor's New York. This gigantic vessel, loaded with magnificent buildings and millions of human beings from every corner of the earth, points toward the ocean, as if setting out on its journey into the future.—The circle tour around Manhattan by steamer will offer you an unobstructed view of many a famous "castle in the sky," will give you a feel of the harbor when you hear "the hoarse notes of the great ships in the river," and will give you a close-up view of New York's splendid bridges, particularly George Washington Bridge and the famous Brooklyn Bridge.

STREETS THAT ARE IDEAS. The best sights are free in New York, as everywhere else. Just to walk along the streets whose names are known around the world is fun. Every avenue has a reputation of its own, and it is a pleasant pastime to check on it. Is Broadway, the stretch around Times Square, gaudy and vulgar? You look at the over-loud neon signs, the "spectaculars," the shooting galleries and the cheap souvenir stores, and you agree. And then you glance into one of Broadway's side streets of the theater district, and you read the famous names on marquee after marquee, and wind your way through the well dressed, festive crowds, and cross the street between slowly moving taxis where a policeman on horseback surveys the scene like a general, and you will register your impressions as "civilized and sophisticated." Is Fifth Avenue "like a smart woman, clad in the newest and most elegant raiment, perfumed and furred and bejeweled . . . modern and self-assured to her gleaming fingertips," as Silas Spitzer describes it? Fifth Avenue names like Tiffany, Lord & Taylor, Georg Jensen, Sloane, Bergdorf Goodman, the Plaza and a host of others have indeed real glamour. Central Park is a resort in itself, and its southern end a paradise for camera enthusiasts. You can photograph its line of gleaming hotel skyscrapers framed by the branches of elms and maples, or mirrored in a lake, or jutting out beyond rugged stone cliffs that seem to be transplanted from the Rockies.—Then there are the foreign sections; unfortunately, as time goes by and new American-born generations grow up, those neighborhoods lose more and more of their native flavor. Chinatown around Mott Street offers good Chinese food and imports, but it is in rather a slum area. The German section in Yorkville, at the eastern end of 86th Street, still has German cafés with Viennese waltzes, but there, as in the Italian and Spanish quarters, the food display is almost the only specialty left.

BUILDINGS THAT ARE SYMBOLS. Every visitor to New York is bound for Rockefeller Center, and rightly so. There is nothing in the world like this proud monument to America. Take the architectural angle: For three centuries we copied Europe slavishly. Here now is

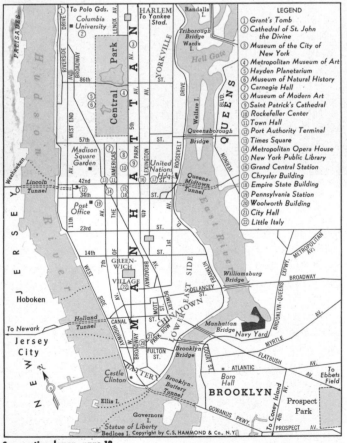

LEGEND
1. Grant's Tomb
2. Cathedral of St. John the Divine
3. Museum of the City of New York
4. Metropolitan Museum of Art
5. Hayden Planetarium
6. Museum of Natural History
7. Carnegie Hall
8. Museum of Modern Art
9. Saint Patrick's Cathedral
10. Rockefeller Center
11. Town Hall
12. Port Authority Terminal
13. Times Square
14. Metropolitan Opera House
15. New York Public Library
16. Grand Central Station
17. Chrysler Building
18. Empire State Building
19. Pennsylvania Station
20. Woolworth Building
21. City Hall
22. Little Italy

See sectional map, page 18

"One hears the hoarse notes of the great ships in the river, and one remembers suddenly the princely girdle of proud, potent tides that bind the city . . . . a magnificent jewel in its fit setting of sea, earth and stars."—Thomas Wolfe

something new, monumental, truly American. Take its antecedents: The building complex stands on land owned by a great university (Columbia), and it was erected by the descendants of a famous millionaire benefactor. Take its size: There are more than a million doorkeys, lush roof gardens, a theater seating 6200 people, ten miles of underground corridors, the world's most precise precision ballet, the Rockettes, a skating rink, and fascinating stores, displays, and restaurants. Both the tours of the Center proper and of the National Broadcasting Company are very worthwhile. Another must is a tour of the United Nations Buildings on the East River. If you are in town during a session of the U.N.,

try by all means to attend a meeting. To put on your ear phones and listen to the speaker in English, Spanish, French, Russian or Chinese, depending on the button you press, is a thrill in itself.—As to New York as the city of music, the drama, the opera, the nightclubs, and of excellent eating places, the latest number of *Cue* or the *New Yorker* will furnish the desired information. Of the town's more than 50 museums the Metropolitan Museum of Art and the American Museum of National History are the best-known; but whatever your special interest, whether it is numismatics or Indian totem poles, you will find a top-ranking museum collection of your hobby in New York.

THE AMERICAN RHINE. The likeness between the Hudson and the great European artery has often been noted: The broad current, the mountain-lined banks, the surprising perspectives at each bend, the sloping vineyards, and the old legends and folk tales are of a similar nature. Around the turn of the century some wealthy shore proprietors carried the Old-World touch even farther and erected on the river's banks medieval castles of spurious antiquity; some built "ruins" on their estates, as fitting ornaments for the hills by the water. In reality both the turrets and the ruins were a reflection of our new and unaccustomed wealth, at a time when "we catered to the condescending snobs of Europe."

In fact, the Hudson is as beautifully and interestingly American a river as can be found anywhere on the continent. On its rather short course it ties together two typically American elements: the wilderness and the metropolis, the untouched, primeval nature and the vanguard of civilization. It accomplishes this by rising on the highest peak of the Adirondacks, lonely Mt. Marcy, at Lake Tear-of-the-Clouds; by flowing for a hundred and fifty miles between high mountains, through wild country of rocks and trees where only hunters and lumberjacks touch its shores; and by gradually maturing into a great river that forms the world's busiest, skyscraper-studded port. Downstream

At Bear Mountain Bridge the Hudson resembles the Rhine.

where the piers, the transatlantic freighters and the smokestacks begin to crowd out nature, the river presents as a last gesture of independence a steep, yellowish, towering wall of rock: the rampart-like Palisades.

EXPLORING THE HUDSON VALLEY. It is easy enough to do so. The New York Central is a "water-level route," and on both banks of the river highways lead north to Saratoga and Lake George, the Adirondacks and Montreal. On the eastern bank there is Tarrytown with Washington Irving's "Sunnyside," an idyl which the poet himself described as "full of angles and corners as an old cocked hat"; North Tarrytown with the Phillipse Castle, a gambrel-roofed stone mansion that has been standing there since 1683; Ossining with Sing Sing; Beacon (opposite Newburgh) with the Mount Beacon Inclined Railroad; Poughkeepsie where girls study at Vassar College and boys from various universities formerly competed, every June, for the Intercollegiate Rowing Championship in an exciting race, as throngs of spectators watched and cheered on the west shore; the Hyde Park estate of the Roosevelts with the Franklin D. Roosevelt Library, the nation's storehouse of Rooseveltiana; Staatsburg with the Mills Memorial Museum; Rhinebeck which has a lovely distinction: It is America's violet capital, growing ninety per cent of all the violets marketed in this country; in spring-

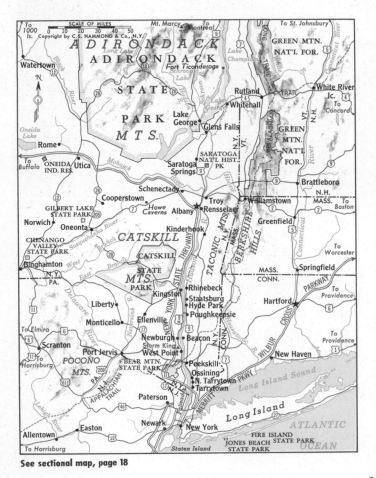

See sectional map, page 18

A Patrician River Turns to the Common Man

time a veritable cloud of fragrance sometimes hovers over town and river; Kinderhook with President Van Buren's home Lindenwald; finally there is Rensselaer with Fort Crailo.

On the western bank beyond the Palisades, Bear Mountain State Park is a popular excursion goal. Farther north the Storm King Highway and West Point offer some of the most magnificent views of the river, and beyond Kingston the Catskill Mountains beckon; there in the dark of the night the Headless Horseman of Sleepy Hollow may gallop by your car. At that spot where picturesque ridges and wooded hills meet the swift waters, the only school of painting arose which America has produced so far: the Hudson River School whose members saw, behind the picturesque romanticism of the river, the hand of God. Beyond Albany your road will leave the Hudson for a while as you cross Saratoga Springs, but you catch up with it again at Glens Falls.

In one way the river was more colorful a hundred years ago: It swarmed with sloops and schooners of varied types of sail, and paddle wheelers of every description. Today an occasional tanker, a barge or a white excursion steamer are the only craft enlivening its calm surface. But as a century ago, a steamboat excursion upstream is still an exhilarating experience, particularly on a clear spring or fall day.

Storm King Highway is one of America's picturesque river roads.

AN AMERICAN EPIC. The history of the valley is not exactly one of "Riches to Rags," but it began with a string of great land holdings in the feudal Old-World manner, and ended with a string of public parks along the lower river, and of public camps in the upper river country where people swim and play baseball, cook and picnic, relax for a day or vacation for a week. The democratic trend is new, though. For more than 200 years the aristocrats dominated the Hudson River scene; the Dutch patroons, people like the van Cortlandts and van Rensselaers, and the British lords of the manor who succeeded them, like the Livingstons and Morrisses, built themselves imposing castles and ruled like absolute monarchs over their crude and not always compliant peasants. When the latter wasted their time by racing horses on the streets and their money by loitering in the low-ceilinged, small-windowed stone taverns, instead of paying their rent, they were quickly thrown into debtors' prison. After the Revolution this feudalism vanished, and the wealthy merchants of New York built their fine country houses along the Hudson, large Victorian villas with superb views and patrician gardens. Most of these houses are still there, though no longer appreciated by their modern heirs, and often the mansions have been converted into schools, clubs or hospitals,—institutions which together with the new parks finally turn the river's beauty over to the common man.

The white "Day Liners" ply the waters where Fulton's "Claremont" was launched.

PRIMITIVE NEW YORK. That a mountain wildnerness should be found at the backdoor of the world's greatest city seems strange to European visitors, and quite normal to Americans who prize highly the side-by-side of urban civilization and untampered nature. North of New York City, around the headwaters of the Hudson, the 5½-million-acre Adirondack State Park contains five mountain chains which run parallel, about 8 miles apart. The main Adirondack Range extends 100 miles from Lake Champlain to the Mohawk River; it is crowned by Mt. Marcy, with 5,344 feet, the highest peak in the state; 2.2 million acres of the park have been set aside as the Adirondack Forest Preserve, to "be forever kept as wild forest land." A favorite hunting and fishing area in the very heart of the Adirondacks is the region of Blue Mountain and Raquette Lakes, along Highway 28 which touches the 150-mile canoe route from Old Forge to Loon Lake. Here the Reverend William Harrison Murray wrote his "Adventures in the Wilderness" in 1869, the first book to propagandize the wild beauty of the Adirondacks; it was so convincing that it resulted in the so-called Murray Rush, the beginning of the influx of tourists and sportsmen. In this area also a popular American ballad originated, the Blue Mountain Song: "The truth I will tell you/ Without a mistake/ About the rackets we have/ At Blue Mountain Lake."—In the deeper recesses there are

The fishing streams of the Adirondacks have a rugged beauty of their own.

tracts so rugged that they could not be exploited by the lumber companies, and stands of hemlock, birch and spruce tower on the ridges still in their primeval splendor.

THE ST. MORITZ OF AMERICA. In the northern part of the Adirondacks a number of attractions draw thousands of visitors. Near Lake Champlain the Ausable Chasm is a deep gorge, where for a fee, walks may be enjoyed on galleries cut into the rock high above the Ausable River, or boat rides in the rushing current. To the west at Jay the Adirondacks present themselves in all their grandeur: Their highest peaks—Whiteface, Wilmington, Marcy and MacIntyre—are towering around you. At Wilmington a serpentine tollroad will take you to the top of Whiteface Mountain; on a clear day the view encompasses Lake Champlain and the Green Mountains, and the whole northern section up to Mt. Royal in Canada; the pall of smoke in the sky marks Montreal. At the foot of Whiteface, Lake Placid is a famous all-year resort; because of its fine hotels, its exclusive Lake Placid Club, and its ideal wintersports facilities it has been called the St. Moritz of America. During the cold months Mirror Lake, in the center of the village, is a sight to behold: Its skating rink is surrounded by a row of Christmas trees which in turn are connected by evergreen garlands, in a mountain landscape of white snow and dark-green forests. Conditions for skating, skiing, dog sledding and skijoring are excellent, and the Mount

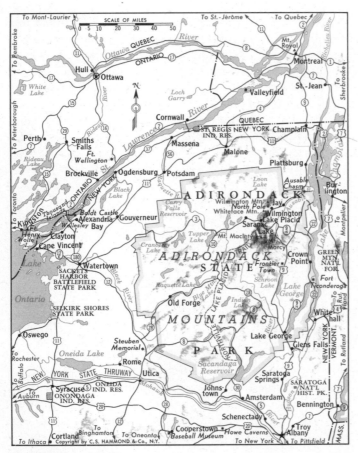

See sectional map, page 18

Van Hoevenberg Bobsled Run, the only one in this country, is a unique feature. Constructed for the Olympics and maintained by the state, it descends for a mile and a half, with 26 curves, some with almost vertical banks. At times a speed of 90 m.p.h. has been approached.—Saranac Lake is internationally known as a resort for TB patients; it owes its reputation largely to Dr. Edward Trudeau, a New York physician who was himself a TB sufferer. In 1876 he went to Saranac Lake to die; instead he recovered and organized both the first open-air sanatorium and the first research laboratorium for the study of the disease.

NOT 1000, BUT 1692. West of the Adirondacks, where Lake Ontario merges with the St. Lawrence River, there is a 60-mile archipelago of forest islands which enchanted even the Indians: They called it Manitonna, "Garden of the Great Spirit." The French named it "Les Milles Isles," which survives in "Thousand Islands," although officially there are 1692. Even that number is debatable. Is a rock with a single tree an island? Is a boulder with one nest of terns an island? In contrast, islands like Wolfe and Wellesley contain estates, clubs, and golf courses. This is a great summer playground for lovers of boating, and from the hundreds of island homes visiting and shopping has to be done over the intricate net of channels. It is also a paradise for anglers who fish

Ausable Chasm may be explored on foot, on galleries cut into the wall, or by boat.

for small-mouthed bass, pike, or muskellunge. The currents here are the world's purest river water; for the St. Lawrence has a granite bottom and so many fresh underwater springs that its waters are renewed every six hours. Visitors enjoy the Islands from excursion boats out of Alexandria Bay, Clayton, or Cape Vincent. They get a magnificent view of the archipelago from the 150-foot-high International Bridge. Also Kingston, on the Canadian side, offers wonderful land-and-water vistas. At this former capital of Canada, the Royal Military College, Canada's West Point, and restored Fort Henry are interesting.

ROMANTIC RUINS. Late in the 19th century the Thousand Islands were an exclusive playground for millionaires. But since the great democratization, many of their castles have been converted or boarded up. The most famous one, Boldt Castle, which looks as if it had been transplanted from the banks of the Rhine, is actually falling into ruins. It was built though never finished by George Boldt, a hotel tycoon who liked to cruise between the islands on his yacht. On board he had a steward with a talent for new creations in cooking; one day the latter pleased his master's taste with a newly-invented salad dressing, and Mr. Boldt had it introduced at his luxury hotels. The names of both the concoction and the steward have become famous: Thousand Island Dressing and Oscar of the Waldorf.

From Whiteface Mountain you can see as far as Vermont and Canada.

THE MEASURE OF ALL CATARACTS. When Father Louis Hennepin returned in 1678 to his native Belgium, he was asked what in the New World had impressed him most. For answer he showed a sketch he had made of a gigantic double water fall which, he said, the Indians called Niagara, i.e., "Thunderer of Waters." The sketch was reproduced in a book some years later, and the fame of Niagara spread. Later visitors were even more vociferous, and the Niagara Falls became, to the world at large, America's best known natural phenomenon. It also became the world's standard to measure all other cataracts, no matter where they were. In such comparisons Niagara often seemed to emerge a poor second; the Yosemite Falls, for instance, were discovered to be 11 times as high. But it was never the height that made Niagara great, but its volume and the fantastic power behind it; one somehow can feel that America's inland sea presses on these silent masses of water that suddenly burst into thunder and transform themselves into sheets and columns of spray as they crash into the cauldron 157 feet below. Touched by the sun into rainbow tints, they have stood the test of time and exploration. Many an eastern sightseeing attraction faded away when such wonders as Yellowstone and Grand Canyon were discovered. But the Niagara Falls have remained a wonderful sight, unmatched and close to our hearts.

Seneca Lake's motorboat races are said to rank first, east of the Mississippi.

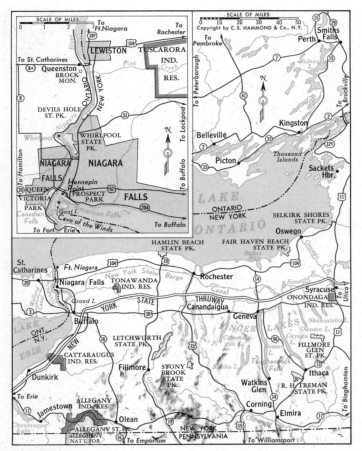

See sectional map, page 18

AN INTERNATIONAL PROJECT. Throughout most of the 19th century land-owning interests exploited the sightseeing public, and not until 1885 did the State of New York succeed in creating a state park around the American Falls. Today the U.S. and Canada have cooperated in presenting Niagara as exhaustively and attractively as possible. On the New York side Prospect Point is the spot from which most visitors have their first look at the 1000-foot-wide American Falls directly below the ledge, at Goat Island, and the 2,500-foot-wide Canadian Falls beyond. Few realize how much bigger the latter are: 94 per cent of the flow passes over them, and only 6 per cent over the former. From the parking area elevators descend to a network of trails and bridges. The "Maid of the Mist," a small steamer, takes visitors to all vantage points on the river, and the spray, the mist and the thunder are a good part of the fun. Hennepin Point where Father Hennepin is said to have drawn his sketch, is the top of a 187-foot precipice, and Goat Island is a 70-acre public park between the American and the Canadian Falls. From Goat Island you can reach the Cave of the Winds, at the bottom of the cataract; rented rubber clothing—coat, hat and boots—will keep you from being drenched.

QUEEN VICTORIA PARK. As nature has laid out the landscape, the real vantage point to view the spectacle is the Canadian shore of the river, and its man-made facilities are superior to those on the American side. From here you have a magnificent view of both falls, and you enjoy that view from a beautiful park with groves of tall trees and beds of fragrant flowers. At night floodlights of various colors play on the falls, which might seem a doubtful attempt at improving on nature, but it is done in a restrained, non-gaudy way, and is quite effective. Three miles below the falls, the sharp bend of the river creates a pothole whirlpool 1,754 feet wide. An aero car suspended on six cables takes passengers across the pool, in a thrilling ride. Another vantage point to view the whirlpool is the Whirlpool State Park on the American shore. The road along the Niagara River, on the American bank, leads to Fort Niagara which was restored authentically in 1934 to its early 18th century splendor. Over a drawbridge is a gate house which bears the French coat of arms. The restoration followed the original plans found in the Colonial Archives of France.

THE HAND OF THE GREAT SPIRIT. On the way from the Niagara Falls to the Atlantic Coast you cross the Finger Lakes region, one of the most attractive sections of New York State. According to Indian lore the Supreme Being pressed the fingers of his hand into the soil, and the cavities filled with pure water. Appropriately, the five lakes still keep their original Indian names: Canandaigua, Seneca, Cayuga, Owasco, and Skaneateles.

View from Goat Island, a public park between the American and the Canadian Falls.

205,000 cubic feet of water plunge over the ledge of Niagara Falls every second.

This is not a lakes-and-forest wilderness but a lush cultivated farm country of green hills and lovely valleys. Fields, pastures and vineyards descend to the broad blue ribbons of the lakes, the green-yellow pattern punctuated by long, bushy hedges, groves of trees, the thin threads of country lanes, and summer camps ashore. One feature of the area is the abundance of gorges, ravines, and waterfalls. Ithaca, for instance, at the head of Cayuga Lake and the seat of Cornell University, has two splendid chasms with cascades within its city limits, and nearby the Taughannock Falls make a 215-foot plunge. At the head of Seneca Lake, Watkins Glen State Park offers a 1½ mile climb up the Gorge Trail, over 700 steps and numerous bridges to an altitude of 600 feet above the starting point. For the summer visitors, watersports are the main attraction, and both the sailing regattas on Skaneateles and the motorboat races on Seneca are among the largest contests of their kind in the world. Sailing is dangerous on all the lakes, and squalls, "crosspuffs" and "catspaws" require expert seamanship. A number of years ago a regatta of the Star Boat class was held before a large assembly of spectators. Everything seemed to proceed smoothly when a strong gust of wind swept over the water with such suddenness that every single boat was toppled over, each on its beams ends. In a scene of excited shouts the motorboats scurried around to restore calm and order.

MORE THAN MERE BEAUTY. The beach of New Jersey finds itself in the position of a plain country maiden who, guided by the shrewd advice of her knowing mother, has become the most popular girl in town. The 125-mile-long shore from Sandy Hook to Cape May is neither the most glamorous nor the most picturesque coast in America; no palms or cypresses line the crest of its dunes, no granite rocks transform the onrushing breakers into spray. Yet, if blue water, white sand and pure ocean air were its only resources, it would probably not lure fifty million visitors and vacationists each year. It has other assets. One is its climate. The Gulf Stream, the great equalizer, flows by at a short distance, and especially those resorts which, like Atlantic City, lie on an island or a peninsula, know no extremes in cold or heat waves. Another advantage is the mid-Atlantic location: It is the oceanic picture window for America's most populated region which extends from New England and New York to Pittsburgh and Philadelphia to Baltimore and Washington. From that multiple-metropolitan area millions of visitors are siphoned to New Jersey beaches by a network of excellent highways; the N.J. Turnpike and the Garden State Parkway eliminate most of the bottlenecks from the shore traffic. All the other attractions are man-made, and everyone finds everything to his taste: Amusement parks and taffy stands, luxury hotels and beach clubs, miles of boardwalks and saltwater swimming pools, first-run movie houses and steel piers with the most famous variety acts, name bands and night clubs, and race tracks at Monmouth Park and Atlantic City. The centers of this resort life are Long Branch and Asbury Park, the metropolis of Atlantic City with its surging beach front of skyscraper hotels, Wildwood, and the quieter Cape May which has the charm of an old New England seaport; on the northern third of the shore some twenty resort towns have expanded so vigorously that they now form one continuous beach area, from Atlantic Highlands to Seaside Park. Everywhere the atmosphere is democratic and without social snobbery; relaxed good-will is in the air, and the sea breezes inject zest into life.

PRESIDENTS AND QUEENS. The Jersey shore claims to be the country's oldest seaside resort. When Henry Hudson sailed along this coast in 1609, vacationists could already be observed on the beaches: The Leni-Lenape Indians spent the warm season there, clamming and fishing. Philadelphia society summered in Cape May before George Washington was inaugurated president. Since the Cape lies below the Mason-Dixon Line, southern aristocrats poured in, too, and in 1847, when Henry Clay dazzled his female admirers on the beach, Cape May was America's leading resort. Presidents Lincoln, Grant, Pierce, Buchanan and Harrison vacationed there, but later in the century Long Branch, at the northern end, took over the distinction. It actually became the summer home of Presidents Grant and Garfield, Hayes and Harrison; Woodrow Wilson was the last political celebrity to honor the Jersey shore as a summer resident. After that the Jersey coast turned from presidents to queens, with a sigh of relief, and for more than thirty years the country's beauty queen has been crowned there with the title of Miss America, during a September pageant in Atlantic City. This ceremony has become an important American event, covered by more press photographers than a meeting of the United Nations or the final game of the World Series; the contest is managed smoothly and in good taste; charm and loveliness are not enough to win the prize, there has also to be talent, and the judges—usually responsible leaders in the world of music and drama—hear a great deal of good singing and see bits of acting, creative dancing, and skills in sports. For the winner the material rewards are considerable, but the core of the prizes are scholarships, stepping stones to advanced education and careers. Asbury Park staged a similar pageant, crowning "Mrs. America," a blend of beauty and domestic virtue.

THE DEEP SEA AND THE HIGH SKY. Sportsmen and nature lovers will find the New Jersey shore with its numerous inlets and bays, its canals and islands equally rewarding. Bass fishing is popular, and off the Manasquan Inlet a famous "mudhole" is the place to troll for bluefish, tuna, and bonita. Along the sheltered waters of

See sectional map, page 18

There is magic in Atlantic City's skyline-shoreline, during a calm summer night. Even during the winter months the city attracts many visitors. It is one of the biggest convention cities, its convention hall being the largest of its kind in the world.

the center where the tall red-and-white Barnegat Light towers above the sea as New Jersey's premier landmark, duck hunting is good in season. Toward the south the professional or amateur naturalist will encounter lovely landscapes among the dunes where the white, untouched sand has been ruffled by the wind into varied, artistic, imaginative and ever-changing patterns. There is a great traffic of birds, with red-winged blackbirds rising from the marshes, ospreys building clumsy nests on poles, sandpipers inspecting the surf, and terns darting over the crests of the waves. There is even virgin land left at the coast, a nine-mile strip of the Barnegat Peninsula called Island Beach. Here yellow dunes contrast with dark cedars and pines, and the bright green of the holly. Dune deer nibble at the beach heather and ocean birds congregate in masses. For years efforts were made to persuade Congress to create a national monument there, but in vain. Now the state of New Jersey has acquired Island Beach and is turning it into a wildlife preserve. The southernmost tip of the shore is another haven for ornithologists; it is one of the foremost observation points for the migration of hawks, and in season thousands of these magnificent birds pass by on their semi-annual migration. At Cape May Court House the Audubon Center offers special trails for the study of bird life.

SCRAPPLE AND BIDDLE. John Adams called Philadelphia "the happy, the peaceful, the elegant, the hospitable city," with the accent on the latter adjective. For there he "drank Madeira at a great rate and found no inconvenience in it." Thackeray thought the town "grave, calm, and kind." To Edward VII it was slightly confusing. "I met a very large and interesting family named Scrapple," he reported, "and I discovered a delicious native food they call Biddle." More factually, Philadelphia is one of the world's great ports, and so many factories are operating there that it is called the Nation's Workshop. Like every large city it has sorry tenements and endless rows of cheerless houses, all built in the same, dreary style. But it has also Fairmount Park, and a magnificent boulevard that connects the city hall with one of America's great art museums. It is an insurance and banking center and the publishing point of mass-circulation magazines. The late editor-publisher of the Poor Richard Almanac would probably be intrigued by that development. But the foremost reason why Americans have a friendly and respectful feeling for Philadelphia is historical: At the birth of the young republic the city acted as its godfather and godmother.

"FOR THE PURPOSE OF A BONFIRE." On the 8th of July, 1776, a boy climbed up a ladder and tore from Philadelphia's government building the coat of arms

Late afternoon on Independence Square, origin of America's greatest documents.

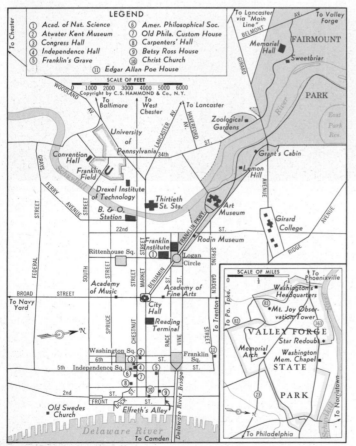

See sectional map, page 18

of the British King. With a shout of joy he threw it to the cheering crowd who in turn cast it into a fire while the Liberty Bell rang, summoning all citizens to the first public reading of the Declaration of Independence, and proclaiming "Liberty Throughout All the Land Unto All the Inhabitants Thereof." The building, known today as State House or Independence Hall, stands between 5th and 6th on Chestnut Street, on a small park that had been declared "a publick greene and walke forever." There everybody is welcome to enter and to see the fine, dignified room with the white panels and the crystal chandelier where the Second Continental Congress held its sessions. George Washington sat there, the only member wearing a military uniform, although Lexington and Concord had demonstrated that the fighting had started and that there was a war on. Jefferson squirmed in his seat while his colleagues picked at words, meanings and phrases in his masterpiece. His ruffled nerves were calmed by the jokes of old Dr. Franklin.

In the same room the Constitution of the United States of America was written, eleven years later. Here Alexander Hamilton pleaded for a strong central power, and James Madison proposed a government of three equal branches which would balance each other. In a world that has seen constitutions adopted and abolished, changed and disregarded, the work of the men at Independence

Hall has endured. We still uphold and cherish its original tenets. The prize exhibit of the house is the Liberty Bell whose ringing accompanied the birth of the nation.

The streets around Independence Hall yield memories of the same era. Carpenter's Hall welcomed the First Continental Congress in 1774, and very appropriately so; for it was erected as an assembly place for "builders." The Betsy Ross House, charming in its smallness and tidiness, saw the birth of the Stars and Stripes, at least according to tradition and to Mrs. Ross herself. In Christ Church on Second Street the pews of George and Martha Washington may be seen, of Betsy Ross and Robert Morris. Elfreth's Alley retains much of its colonial flavor and many of its colonial houses; it was a busy harbor street in the 18th century, full of the rattle of carts and the smells of rum, tea and spices. Even the open gutter in the center is preserved, a reminder of the yellow fever plagues that at times decimated the town's people. Finally, there are the city-owned mansions in Fairmount Park along the Schuylkill River, gems of architecture like Sweetbriar and Lemon Hill.

THE PRACTICAL PHILOSOPHER. To a surprising degree Philadelphia is still the city of Benjamin Franklin, America's first figure of international stature. If he could visit his city today he could still enter his pew in Christ Church; he would, of course, love the Franklin Institute; he would be surprised (or perhaps he wouldn't)

Valley Forge symbolizes the miracle of turning despair into victory.

at seeing his Saturday Evening Post grown into an American institution, and at observing his lightning rods on the skyscrapers, and his chairs, with small tables attached, in all schools, and his bifocals on the noses of distinguished elderly gentlemen who attend the meetings of the American Philosophical Society on Independence Square. He founded that oldest learned body himself, just as he organized the first fire company and the first public library.

THE VALLEY OF DESTINY. On the road from Philadelphia to Pittsburgh the old residential area called "The Main Line" has become so well known for pleasant, prosperous middle class living that it is now a veritable symbol of "suburbia" everywhere. In its western part lies one of America's great shrines, Valley Forge, now a state park where visitors may see the breast works of the camp, the reconstructed huts of the Continental Army, and the small, rural stone house where General Washington had his headquarters. Perhaps it is maturely human that we should have preserved this monument to an American defeat, and to the darkest hour in the life of the nation. For we feel that nothing will endure and stay dear to our hearts that is not born in agony and sacrifice. And there is another thought: Not only Washington was at Valley Forge but also von Steuben, and nearby were Lafayette and Pulaski; they showed the way: This was to become, in time, a Nation of Nations.

Meeting Room in Betsy Ross House, birthplace of the American flag.

A **PATTERN OF ITS OWN.** If you draw a map of Pennsylvania showing nothing but her rivers, your drawing looks like a Japanese screen on which three bizarre but pleasing willow trees are painted: To the left the Allegheny and Monongahela unite in the Ohio; to the right the Delaware winds its course; and the center is filled by the meandering branches of the Susquehanna. With their numerous tributaries these rivers form a cobweb of bright and friendly waterways which embrace tree-clad mountains in a rugged landscape or irrigate immaculately kept farms. Lakes and waterfalls are judiciously distributed here and there, with the result that the whole state is a grand vacation and resort country, not in the spectacular sense of our western scenery, but as a beautiful, quiet, prosperous hill-and-valley land with rich traditions and a great history, and a harmonious integration of the works of man with the creations of nature. The inscription of the old Swiftwater Inn which has been in business since 1788, seems to summarize the pleasant vacation atmosphere of the area: "Rest ye Bones/Tickle ye Palate/and nae/Rob ye Wallet." As mere samples, some highlights from the eastern part of the state are presented here.

THE SUSQUEHANNA. The river's upper reaches where it rushes through mountain gorges is a stretch highly prized by fishermen, because of its bass, perch, and wall-eyed pike. The current meanders southward, and at

The Susquehanna passes coal country and capital, in the heart of Pennsylvania.

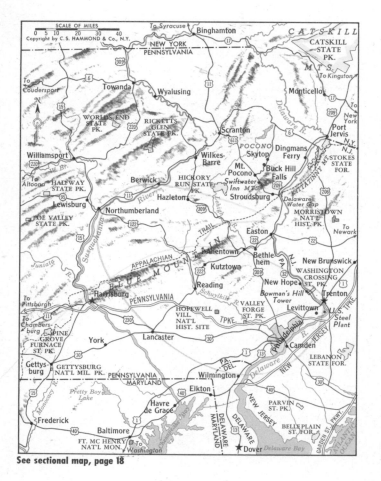

See sectional map, page 18

Wyalusing flows around a fascinating piece of history: The French Asylum. A colony of aristocratic refugees from the French Revolution was established here in 1793 in grand style. It's center, La Grande Maison, was probably the largest log house ever built in America, with two stories and 16 fireplaces, large glass windows, broad piazzas, and French furniture. There were 60 similar houses, all overwhelmingly elegant for the American backwoods, and occupied by such celebrities as Louis Philippe, later king of France, and Talleyrand. The site, selected for its natural beauty, can be seen from Highway 6; a marker overlooks the settlement of which nothing remains but the foundations of La Grande Maison. The river proceeds through the anthracite country of Wilkes-Barre and Berwick; some of the largest collieries are open to visitors, an interesting experience. At Northumberland the West Branch of the Susquehanna joins the main stem after having traversed a stretch of excellent grouse, quail, and pheasant country. At Harrisburg you will have a magnificent view of the river while crossing it on the turnpike bridge: Its blue waters flow around tree-covered islands, one of them a ball park, with the state capitol in the background. From now on the river broadens out into a string of wide, glistening lakes.

THE DELAWARE. Pennsylvania's eastern boundary river tumbles down from the Catskills in many lovely cascades, and between Port Jervis and the Delaware Water Gap, where it rushes straight across the Kittatinny range, it parallels the Pocono Mountains. This is the heart of the resort area, with such well-known summer-and-winter vacation spots as Mt. Pocono, Stroudsburg, and Skytop. Both the Buck Hills Falls which plunge for 50 feet into a deep-green pool, and Dingman Falls near Dingmans Ferry which tumble for 177 feet over rocks and boulders between spray-drenched ferns and moss, are exquisite. Between Easton and Washington's Crossing the narrow road which squeezes its way between the old, abandoned canal and the steep mountainside is one of the most beautiful in the East, particularly in the fall. It leads through quiet villages, past colonial stone houses, and along the rows of old elms that form a line of Gothic arches on the dam between the green canal and the blue river; it rambles through the picturesque artists' colony at New Hope, offers a grand vista of the river valley from Bowman's Hill Tower, and proceeds to Washington's Crossing where a dramatic moment of our history is commemorated in state parks both on the Pennsylvania and the New Jersey sides. In contrast to this rural serenity, the new Fairless Plant of the U.S. Steel Corporation, a few miles downstream, is a giant of modern industrial production, surrounded by a brand-new large city planned from scratch and incorporating the latest techniques of making life pleasant.

The Buck Hills Falls, of the Pocono Mountains, plunge into a deep-green pool.

"BUMP, THE BELL DON'T MAKE." This is supposedly the sign a Pennsylvania-Dutch housewife will hang at her door if the bell is out of order. "The off is all" means "vacation is over". It's funny little phrases like these through which the Pennsylvania Dutch have become widely known and, since they are the first ones to relate such gems, have endeared themselves to the American sense of humor. But it is also worth-while to visit their rolling country in southeastern Pennsylvania where on the world's second best soil (the best is in Belgium) they have erected impressive, spic-and-span farms with huge red barns that bear white hex-wheels for decoration. The district extends around Bethlehem, Allentown, Reading and Lancaster; the latter's central market is a famous institution where Amish farmers, with beards and black hats, and less conservative Mennonites sell schnitz and shoefly pies, scrapple and calves' heads, dandelion greens and sticky buns. The Pennsylvania Dutch, really Pennsylvania Germans, began to arrive in the late 17th century and continued coming during the 18th. They are hardworking, God-fearing, prosperous, and do not need the tourist trade. Therefore the best way of getting acquainted with their country is to join the weekend tours organized by the Brunswick Hotel in Lancaster, or the Bingler Tours of New York. The excursion includes a delightful evening of Pennsylvania Dutch stories, ballads, and songs.

Old household skills like soap-making are still practiced by the Pennsylvania Dutch.

BRIGHTEST STAR OF THE CONSTELLA-TION THAT ENLIGHTENS THE WORLD." With these words the Marquis de Lafayette referred to the City of Washington when he visited there in 1824. His listeners smiled skeptically. French *politesse,* they decided. For Washington was a wretched village, its few big buildings far apart, its Greek temple façades unfinished, its streets impassable after a rain, and its swamps breeding mosquitoes. And the world at large paid no attention whatever to any enlightenment that might have originated in the American capital. But the Marquis was a better prophet than his listeners. Washington did become a bright and beautiful city, and it did assume world leadership, although that pre-eminence was never sought. The eyes of the world are on it, and so are the eyes of America. Particularly in spring, around cherry blossom time, everybody seems to be there, and the thousands of parents who take their wide-eyed offspring from one hallowed place to another, are a reassuring sight; high school youngsters arrive by the busload, from as far away as Missouri and Wisconsin. They find the city a thrilling, concrete illustration to school books and civics lessons.

LEGISLATIVE, JUDICIAL, EXECUTIVE. The sightseeing excursion usually begins where the nation's laws are made, at the Capitol. After inspecting the Victorian splendor of the building itself, a visit to the

gallery of either the lower or the upper house of Congress offers the familiar sight of a speaker before empty seats, with two or three congressmen chatting casually, and a few others reading the morning paper. This sight shocks foreign visitors, but in the U.S. everybody knows by now that Congress does its work not on the floor but in committee rooms and in its office buildings reached by miniature subways. To the east, the Library of Congress is not only a fantastic collection of 16 million printed items, but also a historical museum where the originals of the Declaration of Independence, the Constitution of the U.S., and other priceless documents may be viewed.—Next to the library the judicial power of the land has its seat and symbol. Built in gleaming white marble, the Supreme Court Building has been called Washington's best adaptation to the classical style. The public is admitted to most rooms, and if you can attend a session of the court, the personalities of the judges and the splendid surroundings will probably interest you more than the trial on hand. From the Capitol, Pennsylvania Avenue leads to the White House. You will walk through the East Room where Mrs. Adams, first occupant of the premises, used to hang her wash, and where now formal receptions are held while Gilbert Stuart's Washington looks solemnly down from the wall. You will see the State Dining Room, the Blue, Green, and Red Rooms, and you will conclude that the elegant simplicity of the White House has stood the test of time better than the 19th century pomp of the congressional rotunda and wings. When George Washington discussed the executive mansion with Major L'Enfant, creator of the city's plan, the general specified for it "the sumptuousness of a palace, the convenience of a house, and the agreeableness of a country seat." And certainly it has all of that, to this very day.

3 MEN—3 SHRINES. Three outstanding attractions of the Washington scene are the Washington Monument, the Lincoln Memorial to the west, and the Jefferson Memorial to the south. It has been said that all three shrines somehow seem to reflect the personalities of the great Americans they honor: Washington's 555 foot column is solid, reliable, unshakeable; it hardly ever sways, even in a gale; the view from its top embraces the city, the Potomac, Arlington Cemetery, the Pentagon,—an excellent orientation point.—The Lincoln Memorial is the most touching of the three; its statue is a masterpiece by Daniel Chester French; perhaps Lincoln's face and figure are idealized, but no visitor can escape the hushed feeling: I am in the presence of a great man, the American who lived "with malice toward none, with charity for all . . ."—Jefferson Memorial is a creation of beauty, especially at cherry blossom time; it is as urbane and gentlemanly as the liberal aristocrat it glorifies, a symbol of the statesman who swore "eternal hostility against every form of tyranny over the mind of man."

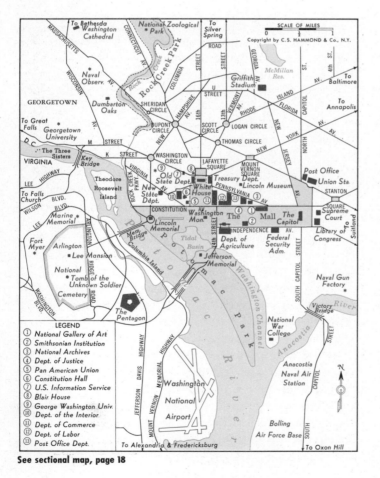

LEGEND
① National Gallery of Art
② Smithsonian Institution
③ National Archives
④ Dept. of Justice
⑤ Pan American Union
⑥ Constitution Hall
⑦ U.S. Information Service
⑧ Blair House
⑨ George Washington Univ.
⑩ Dept. of the Interior
⑪ Dept. of Commerce
⑫ Dept. of Labor
⑬ Post Office Dept.

See sectional map, page 18

Designed by John Russell Pope in the classical style so beloved by Jefferson, the Jefferson Memorial is one of Washington's most beautiful buildings. It is a fitting monument to the statesman who had sworn "eternal hostility against every form of tyranny over the mind of man."

ALONG THE MALL. On the Mall, the boulevard between the Capitol and Washington Monument, so many museums and sightseeing attractions are located that you will have to make a choice according to your taste. On the north side the National Gallery of Art presents a superb collection of paintings and sculptures in a magnificent setting; the entrance hall with its fountain and dark marble columns is especially striking. Two blocks down the Mall, at the Dept. of Justice Building, an F B I tour begins every half hour, and no show in Washington is more dramatic and thrilling; the 2-hour tour leaves you reassured our spy and crime detective apparatus is in prime working order. Around the corner

on 10th Street, the Ford Theater where Lincoln was murdered is now an interesting Lincoln Museum. Back on the Mall and across the avenue, the Smithsonian Institution is the number one attraction for all teen-agers who love to see the historical exhibits of outmoded machinery, the original "Spirit of St. Louis," the thousand inventions and relics, the wax statues of all first ladies wearing their inaugural gowns, the ship models, and the army uniforms since the Revolution. Finally, on the Ellipse south of the White House, the Building of the Pan American Union is a great show place. Spectacularly it makes us aware of the huge double continent on which we live.

HIGHWAY WITHOUT PARALLEL. Between two broad plains the Blue Ridge Mountains lie like the skeleton of a huge prehistoric monster, and the Skyline Drive finds its way along the crest of the backbone. Ordinarily automobile roads hug the valley, and if in mountainous country they climb over passes, they wind their way down again as fast as they can. Not so the Skyline Drive. Whether it is the world's only exception to the rule, is difficult to determine, but its more than 100-mile-long course, from Front Royal to Jarman Gap along the very backbone of the Blue Ridge Mountains is unique. There is a succession of wide views from "overlooks," now to the left, now to the right, and sometimes one turnout offers a grand panorama both to the east and to the west. The continuation of the Skyline Drive, the Blue Ridge Parkway, is also a mountaintop road, but there is a marked difference. The latter leads into the lonely hills and old forests that culminate in the Great Smokies. But the former is a small oasis in the busy expanse of Atlantic civilization. Whether you look into the Piedmont Plateau toward the ocean, or into the fertile Shenandoah Valley to the west, you see a carpet of green and yellow squares, the fields and pastures of rich farmlands. Villages and church steeples, a bridge over the silver band of a river or the smoke thread of a railroad indicate the presence of busy human life. At night the twinkling lights of the valley floor look like

Wide vistas may be enjoyed on both sides of the Skyline Drive.

reflections of the starry sky, and the Indian word Shenandoah becomes a most appropriate name. It means "Daughter of the Stars." On clear days the outlines of larger cities can be distinguished, and some maintain that from a certain point the Washington obelisk in the nation's capital can be spotted. It is about 75 miles away, and from New York and the large cities of Pennsylvania and Ohio the park can be reached in a day. Shenandoah National Park is about 75 miles long but only 2 to 17 miles wide. Its mountains are of medium height (3,000 to 4,000 feet), and the pines, cedars, beeches and maples are mostly second growth. But there are some virgin hemlock groves, some huge ancient oaks, and the grey skeletons of dead chestnuts. In spring the blossoms of the dogwood and the redbuds seem to cover slope after slope, and in the fall the blazing colors of the foliage seem especially rich and warm.

"HEART OF THE WORLD." The National Park, which did not come into existence until 1935, was created by buying privately owned lands, and about six hundred mountain families had to move out of the area. They sold their quit-claims willingly, for nobody had to wander far; there were more of the beloved hills near by. Freeman Tilden reports the reaction of an old mountaineer named Hezekiah who could tell by the smell in which valley any batch of "corn likker" had been made. He would have liked to stay but "never believed in bein'

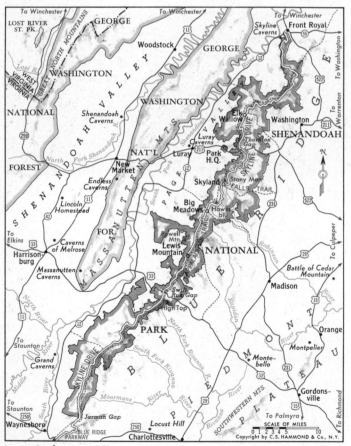

See sectional map, page 18

Shenandoah National Park and Its Road of Double Vistas

agin' the government." Signing the transfer papers, he admitted that he had not read them. "I reckon I could of," he said, "if I hadn't lost my specs. I allus said these hills would be the heart of the world." A few old mills and mountain cabins are preserved in the park, and occasionally a marker points out the name of a family that had lived in a certain "holler," and how many children they had raised in their circular little valley. But all this is not just history; a short drive along one of the side ridges, or still better a horseback ride or a hike will soon bring you to log cabins perched on steep hillsides, friendly country stores with a round iron stove in the center, and berry patches where blue-eyed children gather supplies for the canning season. There is an excellent network of trails, easily accessible from the Drive. A section of the Appalachian Trail, by the way, runs through the park the whole length of the Skyline Drive often crossing and recrossing it. Horses can be hired at Skyland or Big Meadow and the bridal trails, too, are well laid out.

STORY AND HISTORY. Ever since Governor Spotswood and his Knights of the Golden Horseshoe rode over the ridge to get a glance of the unknown West beyond, American history has circled around these mountains. In whatever direction the traveler may look, there are mementoes of George Washington and Thomas Jefferson, James Madison and Patrick Henry, George

Grand Cavern, one of many limestone caves of the area. Those of Luray are famous.

Rogers Clark and Sam Houston, Stonewall Jackson and Phil Sheridan. The villages and towns of the whole region abound with local history and mountain lore, and such characters as Governor Taylor's Bert Lynch, the bully of the mountains, and Brother Billy Patterson, the new preacher, are wonderful protagonists of the tough and gentle life in the hills of bygone days. The two had quarreled, and before fighting it out in the open, Brother Patterson pleaded for a reconciliation. It was rejected; all the bully conceded was time for a short prayer. So the parson knelt down, and with a loud voice addressed himself to the great Father: "O Lord, Thou knowest that when I killed Bill Cummings and John Brown and Jerry Smith and Levi Bottles, that I did it in self-defense. Thou knowest, O Lord, that when I cut the heart out of young Slinger and strewed the ground with the brains of Paddy Miles, that it was forced upon me and that I did it in great agony of soul. And now, O Lord, I am about to be forced to put in his coffin this poor, miserable wretch who has attacked me here today. O Lord, have mercy upon his soul and take care of his helpless widow and orphans when he is gone." The parson concluded his service with a vigorous song:

"Hark from the tombs a doleful sound;
Mine ears attend the cry."

He looked around. Bert, the Bully, was disappearing in a cloud of dust.

Falls Trail has a fairyland look when the dogwood is in bloom.

ORIENTATION. Historic shrines are so abundant in the state of Virginia that for travel purposes a certain organization seems advisable. Three areas are particularly close to the heart of all Americans: (1) Mount Vernon which is usually visited from Washington D.C.; (2) The tidewater area of Williamsburg, Jamestown and Yorktown; and (3) in the foothills of the Blue Ridge Jefferson's Monticello, Ash Lawn, and the University of Virginia at Charlottesville.

WASHINGTON'S REALM. Those of us who for the first time see the fine colonial mansion of Mount Vernon, with its elegant cupola and curving arcades, in a splendid hill setting with broad lawns sloping down to the Potomac, think of this estate as the home of the great general, statesman and father of our country. Yet it was rather George Washington the farmer who lived there, whose ambition it was to become the leading agriculturist in America; he kept elaborate notes, corresponded about his experiments with other farmers, for instance one Thomas Jefferson, introduced crop rotation, operated a smokehouse, dairy, distillery and grist mill, and had his products shipped, in his own schooners, to the market ports. When Frederick the Great sent him a sword, and Lafayette presented him with the keys to the Bastille, he felt honored. But he enjoyed it just as much when the Agricultural Society awarded him a prize "for raising the largest jackass."

This church ruin is all that is left of Virginia's first capital, Jamestown.

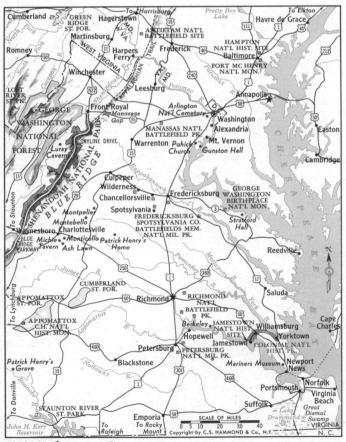

See sectional map, page 18

WILLIAMSBURG: MUSEUM OR LIVING PAST? Among European journalists who visit America, it is the fashion to call the restored capital of Colonial Virginia "just a replica." Such an opinion is based on a misconception. For the layout of the streets and some of the town's finest colonial houses, like the Wren Building of the College of William and Mary and the lovely Bruton Parish Church are originals. The other structures are erected, with absolute authenticity, on the original foundations. The result is as genuine as many of Europe's often repaired and restored historic shrines. Another complaint states that Williamsburg is commercialized. Also to this point there is an answer: The men who planned the restoration had to decide whether they wanted a hushed museum, or a living recreation of the past where visitors could not only see how the governor lived and where the bigwigs of the Council met, but also how 18th century boots and peruques were made; where modern Americans could sample the delicious foods of old Virginia and smoke the long colonial clay pipes. The latter course was chosen and millions of Americans have responded enthusiastically.

ALONG DUKE OF GLOUCESTER STREET. When you arrive at Williamsburg, you are advised to visit first the official orientation center where by means of films and slides you will be shown the role of the

52

capital in American history, and the fascinating story of the restoration. After that you will inspect the Governor's Palace (which in some ways is more sophisticated and elegant than the White House), the dignified Capitol, the Raleigh Tavern (where Phi Beta Kappa was founded) and the fine private homes, the Guardhouse and the Jail, always guided by well informed local ladies or gentlemen in the proper costume of the day. You will visit the apothecary and the other shops, and perhaps attend a service at Bruton Church or eat Brunswick Stew at Chowning's Tavern.

JAMESTOWN AND YORKTOWN: DEFEAT AND VICTORY. Easily reached from Williamsburg are Jamestown, one of the points where America began, and Yorktown, where the Revolutionary War ended with our victory. It is quite true that there is little to be seen on Jamestown Island: the ivy-clad brick ruin of a church tower of 1654, a cemetery of that era, the foundations of many of the earliest homes, and some modern monuments. Yet a visit is worthwhile, if only to get a feeling for the world's lack of permanence. For 92 years this was Virginia's capital; the floods of the James River did away with it. Not until 1901 a sea wall was constructed to secure the shore. To the east of Williamsburg, Yorktown lies picturesquely on a 50-foot bluff on the south side of the York River. Grace Church, the restored colonial Custom House, several

The Governor's Palace in Williamsburg once was America's most elegant building.

other historical buildings and the Colonial National Historical Park are worth visiting.

JEFFERSON'S GREAT LOVE. At the western end of the state where the Blue Ridge looms in the distance, near the pleasant town of Charlottesville, the spirit of Thomas Jefferson lives on in his beloved Monticello. It is a delight to visit because more intensely than any other great estate it bears the personal imprint of its owner: The hilltop view and the decorations betray his artistic-aesthetic taste; the classical touches on the house and formal gardens reflect his classical education; the well balanced and thoroughly thought-out organization of the plan are an image of his orderly mind; the clever devices and inventions which fill the house (a pulley clock indicating even the days of the week, a disappearing bed, dumb waiters, a duplicate writing machine, unusually designed chairs and tables, and others) indicate his American predilection for gadgets and improvements; and the fields, pastures, orchards, the brickyard, carpentry shop and nail factory were the fruits of his enterprising spirit. To the visitor the estate reveals the real and human side of a man who, as the author of the Declaration of Independence, has become a legendary figure. Near Monticello, Monroe's mansion Ash Lawn is much less pretentious; Michie Tavern built prior to 1740 is nearby. In Charlottesville the University of Virginia has one of the finest campuses.

In the Williamsburg Capitol the Council and the House of Burgesses used to meet.

53

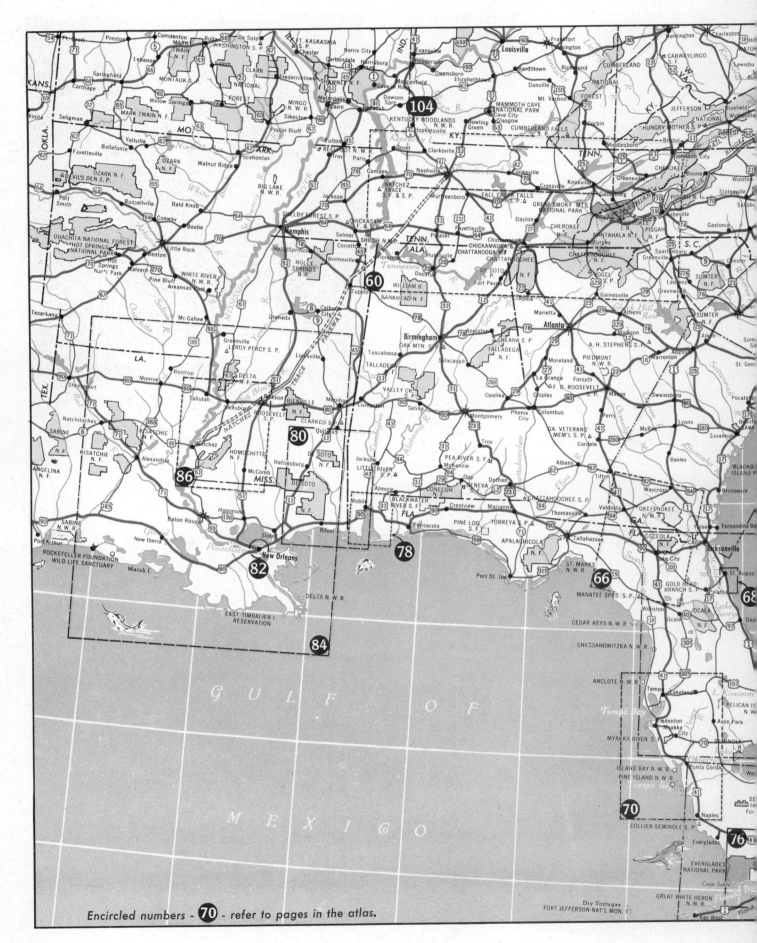

Encircled numbers - ⑦⓪ - refer to pages in the atlas.

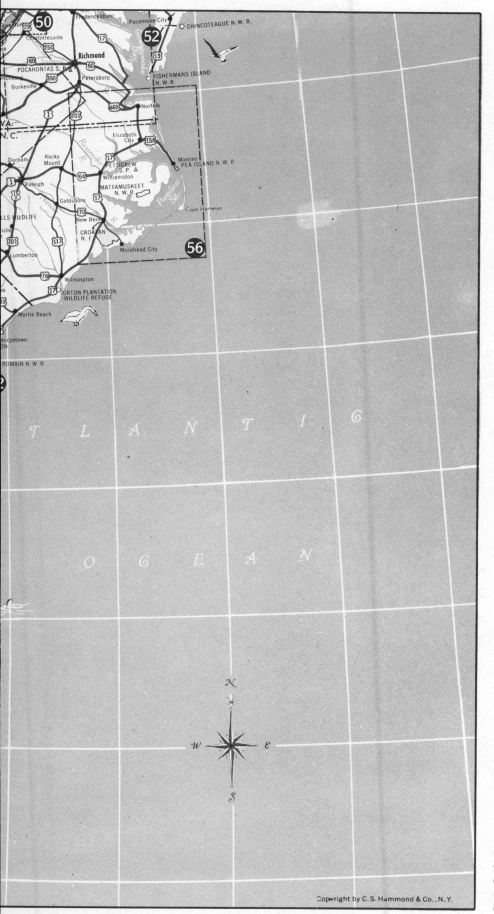

6-DAY TRIP THROUGH HISTORIC VIRGINIA. See pictures and maps on pages 48 to 54; also the Sightseeing Gazetteer.—Suggested stops: Washington, D. C. — Williamsburg with Jamestown and Yorktown—via Richmond to Charlottesville with University of Virginia and Monticello—via Waynesboro over Skyline Drive to Luray Caverns—Washington, D.C.—Three overnight stops in 6 days allow for 2- or 3-day stopovers in Williamsburg, on Skyline Drive.

10-DAY TRIP THROUGH BLUE RIDGE AND GREAT SMOKY MOUNTAINS (see also map on p. 18). See pictures and maps on pages 58 to 61, also the Sightseeing Gazetteer.—Suggested stops: Winchester or Front Royal, Va.—via Skyline Drive and Blue Ridge Parkway to Linville, N.C.—via Mt. Mitchell to Asheville—Cherokee with pageant "Unto These Hills"—Gatlinburg, Tenn., Headquarters of Great Smoky Mountain Nat. Park—Oak Ridge area with Atomic Museum and Norris Dam—White Sulphur Springs, W. Va., the fashionable resort with its medicinal springs—Front Royal, Va.—6 overnight stops in 10 days allow 2- or 3-day stopovers in Great Smoky Mountains, White Sulphur Springs, or elsewhere.

15-DAY TRIP THROUGH FLORIDA. See pictures and maps on pages 68 to 77, also the Sightseeing Gazetteer.—Suggested overnight stops: Jacksonville — St. Augustine with Marine Studios — Daytona Beach — Ocala with Silver Springs — Orlando — Winter Haven with Cypress Gardens and Bok Tower—via Vero Beach and McKee Jungle Gardens to Palm Beach—Miami and Miami Beach—the Everglades—Ocean Highway to Key West—back to Miami—via Tamiami Trail to Sarasota, with famous museums and circus winter quarters—over new bridge to St. Petersburg, with Tampa and Tarpon Springs Sponge Fisheries—Jacksonville.—11 overnight stops in 15 days allow for 2-day stopovers in Miami, Key West, Sarasota, or elsewhere.

The South is magnificently beautiful in March and April when the magnolias, azaleas and camellias are in full bloom. At that time many old mansions and plantation homes are opened to visitors. Famous and popular centers at blossom time are Charleston, S.C., with its spectacular Magnolia, Middleton and Cypress Gardens; Mobile, Ala., with the Bellingrath Gardens and the splendid Azalea Trail; the Gulf Coast resorts around Biloxi; Louisiana's Bayou Country which has its own Azalea Trail at Lafayette, and Natchez with its Pilgrimage; in Natchez the romantic Old South is recreated each spring. Both New Orleans and Mobile are great attractions during Mardi Gras. See pictures and maps on pages 62, 63, and 78 to 88, also the Sightseeing Gazetteer.

THE VIRGINIA DARE TRAIL. Two events of world history took place along this scenic highway, one a tragedy: the first English settlement in America, and the other a modern achievement: the first flight of an airplane. The trail starts at Elizabeth City, a pleasant town at the eastern edge of the Great Dismal Swamp which at one time was the spooky refuge of run-away slaves and desperate fugitives from justice but now is rather a haven for wildlife. Over the so-called floating road the highway proceeds through swampy woodlands which in spring are fragrant with honeysuckle and yellow jessamine, and then runs in a southeasterly direction along Currituck Sound. This body of water is a favorite spot for migratory waterfowl; the whistling swan which breeds in Alaska, winters here. At Point Harbor you cross the Wright Memorial Bridge, the spot of confluence of four great sounds: Roanoke, Croatan, Currituck, and Albemarle; you are now on "the outer islands."

MAN LEARNS TO FLY. Behind the dunes, shaded by wind-twisted trees, there is a village with the strange name of Kitty Hawk, possibly referring to the mosquito hawks that are frequent there in season. It was in the summer of 1900 that the postmistress of the village received a letter postmarked Dayton, Ohio, in which one Wilbur Wright and his brother Orville Wright inquired about the topography of the Kitty Hawk dunes because they planned to carry out a number of "kite-flying experi-

The Wright Memorial at Kitty Hawk where the first airplane flew for 59 seconds.

ments." The postmistress's husband, Captain W. J. Tate, gave all the requested information and later, when the Wrights arrived, acted as their host. For three years the two brothers worked at their experiments; the great moment came when they equipped their glider with a gasoline motor. Four epochal flights followed, on December 17, 1903, the brothers alternating as pilots; the first covered 120 feet in 12 seconds, the fourth 852 feet in 59 seconds; the news made headlines all over the earth.—To commemorate this feat, the Wright Memorial Monument was erected on top of Kill Devil Hill, surrounded by a park. It is an impressive 60-foot-high tower of granite from Mount Airy, with an inner room that contains a model of the original plane and the busts of its inventors. The incription honors the Wrights' genius, resolution, and unconquerable faith. To the north a granite boulder marks the exact spot where the first heavier-than-air flying machine left the earth and actually flew. The unusual name of the dune on which the monument stands is connected with the "Ballad of Kill Devil Hill"; this ballad deals with the abominable quality of New England rum which is capable of killing the devil.

THE LOST COLONY. The road now describes a hook, passes through the hunting and fishing resort of Manteo, and ends at Fort Raleigh, "the Citie of Ralegh" in what was then the colony of Virginia. After an abortive attempt in 1584, Governor John White arrived there in

See sectional map, page 54

1587, established friendly relations with the Indians, and prepared a settlement. On August 18th of that year the governor's daughter who was married to Ananias Dare, gave birth to a child which was appropriately christened Virginia Dare, the first white child of English parents born in America. A week after the christening, White sailed back to England for additional supplies, but because of the wars with Spain could not return until 1591. He landed at Fort Raleigh, prepared to celebrate the 4th birthday of his granddaughter, but to his horror found the colony of 116 men, women and children deserted. The place was still "very strongly enclosed with a high palisade of great trees." On a large tree he discovered a spot where the bark had been removed, and the mysterious word CROATOAN was carved in capital letters, "without any sign or cross of distress." The governor was puzzled, as there was no evidence of a violent struggle, and to this day we are puzzled about the fate of the first Anglo-Americans. John White, by the way, was a careful official who returned to England with minute drawings of what he had seen, so that the present reconstruction of blockhouses and palisades is an authentic reproduction of the 1587 original. A great attraction during the summer months is the picturesque pageant "The Lost Colony," performed in an open-air theater.

SHIPS' GRAVEYARD. The Southward continuation of the ride to Cape Hatteras used to be a perilous under-

The colorful pageant "The Lost Colony" draws thousands of spectators to Fort Raleigh.

Cape Hatteras, formerly known as "the graveyard of the Atlantic," is still dangerous.

taking for adventurous automobilists only. But all that is being changed now. For here a new kind of National Park is in the making, the Cape Hatteras National Seashore, to include the Outer Banks islands of Bodie, Hatteras, and Ocracoke. It will preserve, for the people's enjoyment, sixty miles of "virgin beach," white dunes shifting into fantastic shapes and throwing strange shadows, and of blue or green waters lining the narrow strip of sand on both sides. Ferry service across Oregon Inlet has improved greatly, and a highway now runs all the way south to Hatteras Light, the 193-foot tower that is spirally painted in black and white. No longer in service, it stands at the most treacherous spot on the Atlantic Coast. Even now, numerous ship skeletons can be seen protruding from the sand. During the sailing ship era this beach was a veritable graveyard, feared by sailors throughout the world. Salvaging was an important business, and there are gruesome tales from the early days when some salvagers were not above interfering with fate: A stormy night, a misplaced lamp, a shipwreck—and plunder.

WEATHERED, BRONZED, INDEPENDENT. On the cape the largest community is Hatteras, a picturesque fishing village. Some of its inhabitants believe themselves to be the descendants of shipwrecked English sailors. Their speech is strange. "If you're scunnered, don't fault me," means "If you are angry, don't blame me."

OUR GREAT HARDWOOD TRAIL. A green forest sanctuary, which used to be familiar only to the southern mountain people, has been opened to all Americans by the Blue Ridge Parkway. When this mountain-top route is fully completed—at present some stretches are still filled out by regular highways, at little or no inconvenience to the traveler—it will connect, in combination with the Skyline Drive, Shenandoah National Park and Great Smoky Mountains National Park, as the gateway to the very heart of the southern hills. In a world of valley roads the drive over 500 miles of breezy ridges with broad vistas is an exhilarating experience. On the southward journey you enter the Blue Ridge Parkway and after passing Roanoke, Virginia, you will realize at once that the wide valleys of farms and towns that follow the Skyline Drive on both sides, have receded into the distance. Instead, the "hollers" your eyes meet here are deep and often narrow, and from their green funnels a bluish mist will rise in the morning. The soil here is a sandy carboniferous loam, and in it the finest stands of hardwood in the United States are growing. White oaks and poplars, tall tulip trees and fragrant basswood, gum and buckeye, sourwood, persimmon, and dozens of other species produce an arboreal variety not known elsewhere. Various types of pines and hemlocks, while in the minority, are by no means absent, and the cuts and fills of the parkway have been planted with native shrubs. From early spring into summer a splendid parade of blossoms accompanies the traveler: The beeches show their tan and the maples their red flowers early; the redbuds, the dogwoods, and the azaleas follow suit; the mountain laurel blooms brightly in June, and the rhododendron may be admired even in July and August. Another popular travel season is the fall when the gold and scarlet of the slopes rivals with the autumn foliage of New England. All this natural beauty can be enjoyed from an excellently engineered modern highway unspoiled by advertising posters and hot dog stands. However, it is suggested that upon entering the parkway you should secure a guide-circular which will inform you on motels and restaurants on crossroads just outside the parkway.

GIANT OUTDOOR CONCERT HALL. By statistics it would be difficult to prove that per square mile more songbirds live in our southern mountains than elsewhere on this continent, but on the strength of subjective experience there seems to be no doubt about it. Bluebirds and thrushes, orioles and mockingbirds fill the forest with exuberant song, and of bright-red cardinals—year round residents in the hills—there are so many that both of the states sharing the Blue Ridge Parkway, Virginia and North Carolina, have honored the cardinal as their official state bird. The mountain people love the birds, too, and Jean Thomas tells of an old lady who lived alone in a cabin and refused to sell her stand of black walnut trees. "Be gone," she told the agent of the lumber company, "I don't want to be scrouged by your racket-makin' contrapshuns under my very nose." When promises and concessions were proposed, she came out with her most important reason for refusal: "Such as that skeers off the birds in the forest," she stated.

"DOVE-IN-THE-WINDOW" and **"SWING YOUR CORNER LADY."** The farther south the parkway takes you, the higher the mountains become, and wilder the scenery. On the toll road to Mt. Mitchell, with a height of 6,684 feet the tallest peak east of the Mississippi, you pass through landscapes of Alpine character. At the foot of the mountain the Craggy Gardens should be seen in spring when their huge rhododendron displays are in bloom. At the end of the parkway the pleasant resort city of Asheville will greet you; there every August a mountain folk festival keeps alive the old songs and square dances, and displays the artful crafts and century-old skills with ax, saw and knife that have flourished in the hills as a matter of necessity and self-sufficiency, from the carving of wooden bowls and trays to the shaping of utensils and pieces of furniture. Also the handwork of the women is still very much a living art; lace is crocheted in the sea-shell pattern or the acorn or the clover-leaf pattern and as to home-made quilts, you may choose from such famous models as "nine

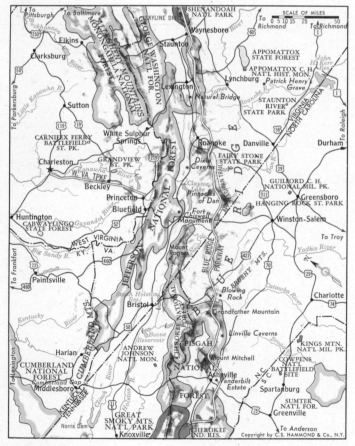

See sectional map, page 54

The Blue Ridge Parkway has opened to all Americans the green world of the mountaineers. With the Skyline Drive it presents 500 miles of road over breezy ridges offering broad and spectacular vistas.

patch" or "dove-in-the-window," or "double wedding ring." For 200 years the mountain people had lived in their own, isolated world, simple and proud, poor and self-assured, illiterate and hospitable, and above all independent and freedom-loving. So fond were they of their mountain forests that they did not take part in the great American westward trek of the 19th century. But now the parkways and singing contests, the folk dance festivals and handicraft fairs are establishing the contact between their small world and the great outside. That does not necessarily mean a loss. There is a good chance that many of the old traditions will survive; ballad-making and ballad-singing, for instance, has not died but has adjusted itself to a new century. There is even a ballad now on the great artery that opened the heart of the green hills to the American people at large, the Skyline Drive and the Blue Ridge Parkway. The poem does not claim to be literature, but with the simple clarity of a backwoods ballad it sets forth the purpose of the ridge-road system more forcefully than an engineer's report; here is a sample of it: "The builders of this skyline drive / Have filed no patent right / That they improved upon God's plan / Nor have more power and might; / But they have seen His handiwork / This panoramic view, / Have paved this road to ease the load / Of all the world and you." (George A. Barker).

BLUE HAZE OVER VIRGIN WOODS. Although the Great Smoky Mountains, the southern end of the Appalachians, lie within 600 miles of the population centers of the United States, they remained an unknown wilderness, as far as the world at large was concerned, until the first decade of the 20th century. That was a strange accident to which we owe a fortunate fact: To this day 40 to 50 per cent of the forests in the Great Smoky Mountains National Park are virgin timber. They are a sea of trees of incredible variation— 130 native species, and 1,300 varieties, as compared with 85 species in the whole of Europe; mountain laurels and rhododendrons, magnificent at blossom time, form impenetrable thickets called "slicks" or "hell." To enter Joyce Kilmer Memorial Forest, under ancient, sky-high hemlocks and tulip trees 6 feet thick, with green Gothic arches high above and no underbrush to block the view, is like walking through a cathedral. The mountains themselves are the highest east of the Rockies, with 16 peaks taller than 6,000 feet; yet the finest lookout points are easily accessible. Clingmans Dome, with 6,642 feet, the roof of the range, can be reached by a scenic highway, and with hikers Mount Le Conte is most popular. From these vantage points the blue haze, the "smoke" of the Great Smokies, can be observed. Copious rainfall, up to 80 inches annually, wets the ground from which light mists rise here and there in curving wreaths.

Pleasant mountain lodges offer views of valleys from which the "smoke" rises.

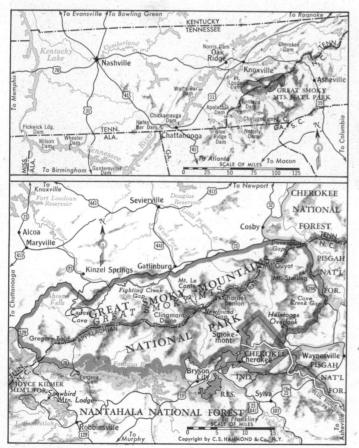

See sectional map, page 54

If a sudden burst of sunlight strikes the forest floor, a column of steam swirls up as if released from a boiler. Another unusual aspect of the landscape is the existence of "balds," treeless spots on the ridges.

THE CHEROKEE TRAGEDY. This green sanctuary is the ancient home of the Cherokees, one of the most intelligent and advanced of all Indian tribes. Already De Soto reported that they lived in log houses and farmed the soil; they were friendly with the early white settlers, and their great chief Sequoyah created a Cherokee alphabet of 86 characters. Many of the tribe learned to read and write. But in spite of their peaceful ways the shout "Run the Redskins out!" grew louder and louder, especially when a gold rush occurred in 1815. It was largely a false alarm, but the gold diggers and land grabbers succeeded with their scheme. In 1839 the U.S. Army drove the Cherokees from their mountains westward to Oklahoma, during the coldest winter months. One-fourth of the Indians perished on the march. But large numbers did not obey and for years hid in the mountains, outcasts in their own land, until they were finally granted permission to stay, and an eastern Cherokee Reservation was organized. Their descendants still live there, and their fine handicrafts are a tourist attraction. Near their town of Cherokee there is a great open air theater where, on a background of native hills and trees, the drama of the Cherokees is enacted skillfully and colorfully, during the balmy evenings of the summer.

THE LONG RIFLES. The drama of white man in these mountains is equally stirring. The English, Scotch and Scotch Irish peasants who drifted into the valleys in the 1700's, thought they had reached paradise: Here complete freedom reigned, without tax collectors, police sergeants, recruiting officers, or poaching laws. They could fish and hunt and talk and sing to their heart's content; life was poor but free, and corn, they discovered with joy, made both good bread and good whiskey. Their descendants are still there, all around the edges of the park, and they have changed little. They still live in log cabins that often can be reached only on foot or horseback; their tools and utensils are mostly home-made; in spite of that they are masters in woodcraft, and they are by no means restricted to their own simple needs; the Snowbird Mountain Lodge, for instance, has every room furnished in a different native wood, done by local craftsmen with excellent workmanship; they are expert marksmen and like to use the "long rifles" of their ancestors; many do not know how to read and write but they are natural-born story-tellers and ballad singers, fiddlers and folk dancers. To call their speech Elizabethan is perhaps an exaggeration, but they certainly talk a colorful, archaic English. The name of a local flower is Hearts-a-bustin'-with-love, and the surrounding landscape abounds with imaginative appella-

Fontana Dam symbolizes the mountaineers' new way of life.

tions like Charlies Bunion (bunion = big toe), Chunky Gal Mountain, and Fighting Creek Gap.

NEW WAY OF LIFE. Six thousand tons of water fall annually on every acre of the Great Smokies. In a thousand creeks the water rushes down to form the Tennessee River, and in the process carries along good soil. Erosion and floods used to be the characteristics of the river. Then a grand network of dams was conceived to end the waste and the damage, and during President Roosevelt's first term the Tennessee Valley Authority was created for the purpose of "maximum flood control, maximum development of the river for navigation, maximum generation of electric power—proper use of marginal lands, proper methods of reforestation—and economic and social well-being of all the people." The valley was turned into a huge technical, economic and social laboratory, and on the whole the experiment seems to have succeeded. When TVA began, less than three per cent of the farms of the region used electricity; now the electrification is almost complete. Kerosene lamps and wood stoves are disappearing, and with them many fine old folk ways and traditions. Whether the march of progress is always a blessing, is a purely academic question; it can't be stopped. But the traveler to the Great Smokies will find it interesting to visit Fontana Dam, the largest east of the Mississippi, and Oak Ridge with its atomic energy museum.

Some mountain streams form natural swimming pools of granite.

RICE AND ANCESTORS. Those northerners and westerners who from novels and stories have formed a romantic and picturesque concept of the South, should visit Charleston. There, more than anywhere else, their vision will be confirmed. The stately 18th century homes, the balconies of wrought iron and the French windows; the graceful porticos and the carved doorways; the waving palmettos and the moss-draped live oaks; the slave quarters and the old wharves,—all these ingredients blend into a charming, colorful picture of the historic South. The spirit is there, too; for the people of Charleston feel a deep love and fervent loyalty toward their city. They have been compared to the Chinese; for "they eat rice and worship their ancestors." Rice, by the way, was the crop that made Charleston rich.

There are fine patrician homes along the Battery, with a broad view of the harbor. Rainbow Row looks like a stage setting; it is a row of delicately tinted houses along the East Bay waterfront, once a street where sailing vessels from the seven seas tied up. There are various fine churches in town, and the oldest ones have experienced incidents of story-book quality. St. Philip's, for instance, famous for its tall, octagonal tower, once had a pastor who solemnly christened a bear. At St. Michael's the church bells attained celebrity status: They crossed the Atlantic five times. Cast in London and installed in Charleston, they were pillaged by the British during the

These old Bay Street houses are called Rainbow Row.

Revolutionary War and shipped to England. Later a loyal Charlestonian discovered them in London and sent them back to Charleston. During the Civil War the Confederates, desperately in need of metal, broke the bells as raw material for ammunition; before the metal was used, the war ended, and the pieces were dispatched to London to be recast in the original forms. In proper time they were returned, and ever since have been a part of Charleston's life.

Lovers of antiques and artistic interiors, particularly of the pre-Civil War period, will find a visit to the Charleston Museum rewarding. During the spring festival, 25 old mansions are opened to the public, and three houses may be visited throughout the year: The Manigault Mansion, the Heyward-Washington House, and the Pringle or Miles Brewton House.

THE SHOT THAT WAS HEARD AROUND THE WORLD. The historical background of this cultured American scene is as cosmopolitan as can be imagined. The first settlers were small sugar planters from Barbados; then a number of capitalists arrived, and with the help of intelligent, specially trained Gullah Negroes introduced the highly profitable rice culture and a truly baronial plantation system. French Huguenots, among them excellent artisans, found refuge and prosperity in the city. Life was not always a bed of roses, though. Storms, hurricanes, and at least one earthquake hit the town and the sur-

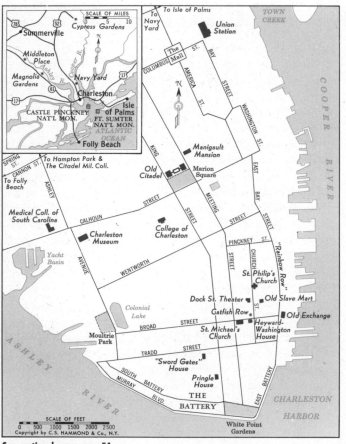

See sectional map, page 54

rounding countryside. The Spaniards attacked, the French were repulsed, and the British invaded the stronghold. Pirates boldly displayed the skull and crossbones in the harbor but did not fare so well on other occasions. For their benefit a row of gallows once stood on the Battery, and their bodies swayed in the breeze as a warning. During the years before the Civil War the "Charleston Civilization" was at its height. Its people looked down on New York and Boston as rather barbaric settlements, and oriented their lives toward Paris. A good deal of French was spoken in town, and exquisite art objects and elegant gowns were imported from France. Here the War between the States began when, as everybody knows, the Confederate cannons fired their shots at Fort Sumter in Charleston Harbor.

PORGY AND BESS. But Charleston has never been just a white man's town. Once the Negro population was its largest segment, and to this day it exercises a far-reaching influence. Remarkably uniform in appearance, the Charleston Negroes are descendants of the Gullahs, and in the main they speak what is called a Gullah dialect. It has a soft charm of its own and quite a strange vocabulary; to outsiders it is often unintelligible,—a fact which adds an exotic touch to the scene. The numerous Negro street vendors will not only sell their flowers, fishes, and other wares, but advertise them loudly in a colorful singsong: "Porgy walk, Porgy talk, Porgy eat wid knife and

Country church in Summerville, once a resort of the wealthy rice planters.

fawk; Porgie-e-e." To keep alive this picturesque Charleston tradition, a hucksters' street-crying contest is held during Azalea Festival in April. Porgy's Catfish Row was immortalized by author Du Bose Heyward; and Gershwin's classic folk opera Porgy and Bess, performed by excellent Negro casts, took the fame of this Charleston street to New York and London, Berlin and Paris. Charleston's old Slave Mart is unique.

THE MAGNIFICENT GARDENS. One of the first projects carried out by the early settlers of Charleston was a community garden. This love of bright flowers has survived, and today thousands of visitors descend upon the Charleston region, every spring, for the purpose of enjoying its famous plantings; the thickets of white, yellow, pink, red and purple azaleas, the 500 varieties of camellias, the magnolias and other blossoms. Among the various old plantation gardens that are open to the public and can be reached easily by car from Charleston, three are outstanding, and are classed among the loveliest in the world: Magnolia Gardens with its 25 acres of azaleas and camellias; Middleton Place, the first landscaped gardens in America, laid out in 1741 by a European architect with the help of a hundred slaves on the 8,000-acre plantation of Henry Middleton, president of the Continental Congress; and Cypress Gardens, a former rice plantation, where visitors may ride in boats through the arched avenues of tall trees.

A marble nymph graces the aristocratic Middleton Gardens.

THE CLASSIC TOUCH. Green is Savannah's color if seen from the air, and the name of Forest City is well justified. For there are trees everywhere, and—a unique urban feature—24 little parks called squares are strewn throughout the old section of this lovely city. General Oglethorpe wanted it that way when he laid out the town in 1733, in accordance with a sketch he found in the book "Villas of the Ancients;" the latter was written by an Englishman named Robert Castel who died in a debtor's prison,—ironically so because the Georgia experiment was supposed to relieve the lot of men thrown into that type of jail. The regular layout, inspired by Roman models, is not the only classical touch; the city also boasts of a number of fine old residences erected in the style of the Classical Revival: The Telfair House, for instance, which as the Telfair Academy of Arts and Sciences contains one of the finest art galleries in the South. The Low House, another Classical Revival structure, was built by a family of great Savannah cotton factors. Thackeray the poet stayed in that house twice, in 1855 and 56; Robert E. Lee visited there in 1870, and in 1912 Mrs. Juliette Gordon Low founded, in the same building, a movement which grew into the Girl Scouts of America. In the old days a popular construction material was rough, red bricks brought as ballast in sailing vessels, or the gray bricks from the kilns of the Hermitage plantation nearby.

Shrimp Boats are a fixture of Savannah's many waterways.

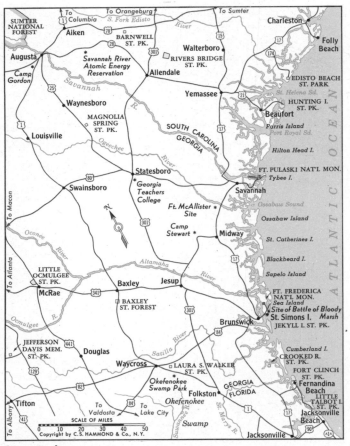

See sectional map, page 54

A SISTER OF CHARLESTON. In many ways Savannah seems related to her northern neighbor, Charleston. It has the same old magnolia trees, the exuberantly blossoming azaleas, and great mansions that blend into the "Romantic South" of the story books, together with the same ancestor-worship, social exclusiveness, cultivation of good manners, and friendliness. And if Charleston for two centuries preserved an ancient African civilization in its Gullah dialect and traditions, Savannah did the same with its 'Geechee Negro speech and songs. Both cities have their picturesque colored street vendors who with a loud sing song, intelligible only to the native residents offer their glistening fish, southern vegetables and bright flowers. In one point, however, there is a difference: Savannah has not "gone overboard"—as its leading citizens put it—to turn itself into a tourist attraction, as Charleston supposedly has done for some time.

LIKE THE DECK OF A SQUARE RIGGER. To many visitors the most intriguing section of Savannah is the waterfront portion called Factors' Row. Here a line of old red-brick warehouses face the Savannah River as four-or-five-story buildings; on the land side they appear as two-story structures on a broad, tree-shaded esplanade that runs on a high bluff. However, between the avenue and the warehouses a narrow alley or court ambles along, about halfway between the street level and the river level. It has a cobblestone wall on the avenue side, and little wooden bridges cross above the alley from the storehouses to a wooden walk running along the Row and connecting the small bridges. The whole arrangement is reminiscent of the catwalks of the large vessels of the late sailing ship era, and revived on modern tankers. In its heyday, Factors' Row was a center of world commerce, and from there the first sea-going steamship, the Savannah, crossed the Atlantic Ocean in 1819. Also the City Market on Barnard Street is worth seeing; it is a scene full of southern life and color.

OYSTER ROASTS AND SAND SAILING. From the Savannah River to the Florida state line a string of islands separates the mainland from the ocean; all have the same scenic character: They are flat, covered with fine stands of live oaks, magnolias, cedars, and pines, and are crossed by saltwater creeks. The Spaniards under Menéndes de Avilés, founder of St. Augustine, discovered the isles, took possession of them and after the local Indian chieftain Guale they called them, euphemistically, "the Golden Isles of Guale." Early in the 18th century the pirate Blackbeard had his hideout there, and a generation later the Battle of the Bloody Marsh decided that the British would rule in that part of America instead of the Spaniards. In contrast to this martial past, the islands' present is peaceful and wholly dedicated to recreation and pleasure. Tybee Island is the favorite beach re-

New Savannah: Modern apartment buildings fit well into the colorful southern scene.

sort of Savannah, and on its broad white sands a local specialty flourishes: The oyster roast. In a small oven or in a pit the oysters are roasted, opened speedily, dipped into a sharp sauce, and eaten without the benefit of a fork. All islands to the south are in private ownership and not open to the public except St. Simons Island and its close neighbor, Sea Island. Both are wonderful blends of old live oaks (the first fleet of the U. S. was built of St. Simons oak, including "Old Ironsides," the frigate "Constitution"), of white oleanders and pink crepe myrtles, with gleaming beaches and stretches of the deep-blue sea. The overgrown ruins of the British Fort Frederica, also on St. Simons Island, tell a pathetic story: The fort once protected a seaport of 1000 inhabitants,—a town which has vanished without traces. On Sea Island "The Cloister" is one of America's well-known all-year resort hotels, with a lively early spring season; there the guests enjoy, besides all the usual sports, a pastime carried out on especially designed craft; it is sand-sailing, a favorite of the numerous honeymooners who start their married life in the non-monastic atmosphere of the Cloister. South of St. Simons Island, Jekyll Island is in process of democratization; it is being transformed into a state park after it had been the property of an ultra-exclusive winter-resort-club of such fabulous millionaires as J. P. Morgan, William Rockefeller, William K. Vanderbilt, and Cyrus McCormick.

Old Savannah: The Iron Lace House is now an antique shop.

A LOST WORLD. America has her massive mountains, her big rivers, her great desert. She also has her huge swamp, properly called "Okefenokee," that is "Trembling Earth," comprising 660 square miles in southern Georgia and northern Florida; most of it is a National Wildlife Refuge accessible from the north at Waycross (Okefenokee Swamp Park), from the west at Fargo, and from the east at Folkston; guides and boats are available and, at the Swamp Park, also electric boats. As a rule swamps are dismal places, and hardly an attraction for travelers, but Okefenokee has a different character. It lies at an altitude of 120 feet; its waters well up from hundreds of springs and are pure and transparent until they reach the cypress groves which color them dark; the swamp is not stagnant but has a slow, steady flow, and therefore it does not breed malaria, and few mosquitoes will annoy you. To penetrate into the thicket in one of the shallow, light pole boats, is an experience without parallel. Wherever you look, there is around you a motionless mirror of water which reflects the blue sky, the white clouds, and the tall, unkempt trees. In this scene of untamed, unfinished wilderness thousands of water lilies float in splendid perfection. Or you will ride on one of the "boat runs," i.e. the channels meandering between clumps of trees and underbrush; in the veritable maze of these runs you could lose your way easily. One phenomenon of Okefenokee is the so-called "blow-up":

Okefenokee is a huge, primeval swamp refuge of American wildlife.

Decaying vegetable matter frequently generates gases which force a stretch of bottom vegetation to the surface; there it becomes a floating island of perhaps 100 square feet, and on its travels gathers grass, briars, weeds and seeds. The journey continues until the float is anchored by a clump of trees; sometimes it becomes firm, but just as often it never solidifies and sways and trembles at the slightest provocation. However, there are also firm islands with a sandy base, and one of them is even enchanted. A party of Indians once landed there and was welcomed by beautiful girls who treated them to marsh eggs, corn pones, and fancy grapes. When the banquet was at its height, the girls announced that now their jealous husbands would drown the visitors in the swamp. The Indians left hastily, and ever since parties of Seminoles have tried to rediscover the island; but they have never succeeded.

A SAFE RETREAT FOR BIRDS AND BEARS. Around noon the silence is almost incredible, yet there is life. Alligators float in green bays like ten-or-twelve-foot logs; turtles sun-bathe on a stump; a raccoon sleeping in the fork of a tree seems to wink at you; on a tangle of roots and cypress knees a cottonmouth water moccasin lies neatly coiled; an egret stands in the center of a small "prairie," motionless, and a heron rises from a cove with a quiet grace. At sundown, however, a nightly concert begins. The frogs account for the upper registers, the

See sectional map, page 54

bull alligators roar the basso parts, and additional sound effects are provided by splashing waterbirds, hooting owls, and the occasional spine-chilling screech of a wildcat. All this night music blends into a rumbling symphony called "the booming of the swamp." You will probably not encounter any panthers or otters, but you may meet one of the Okefenokee bears. One of the park patrolmen had the same humorous experience on more than one occasion: A bear had climbed high up in a tree, picking berries or grapes from vines. The ranger would glide nearer, avoiding all noises, and then suddenly burst out with a startling yell. Each time the same thing happened: The bear let go and dropped through the crashing branches into the water with a huge splash, drenching the boat. Then he would stumble ashore and vanish in the thicket. Former park manager Bill Edwards reported how he and a ranger spent a night in a swamp shack which they suspected to be the hide-out of alligator poachers. For hours they waited silently in their ambush, then they noticed a paddling noise; footsteps were heard, and finally a black outline appeared in the door. Confident of having trapped an illegal hunter, the ranger cocked the pistol and switched on the flashlight: There stood, on its hind legs, a huge black bear filling out the whole frame. It was difficult to say who was more tensely excited, the bear who ejected threatening grunts, or the men who crouched breathlessly in the corner. Finally

Fort Frederica (see page 65), where English and Spanish power clashed.

the beast turned and sauntered away, slapping angrily the bushes in front.

"WAY DOWN UPON THE SUWANNEE RIVER." In 1889 a lumber company built a canal into the eastern part of Okefenokee in order to float out cedar and cypress logs. After the waterway had been completed at great cost, it was discovered, to everybody's consternation, that the logs floated the wrong way, i.e. to the west. The company went bankrupt, and upon investigating the phenomenon it was found that Okefenokee is the source of the Suwannee River which drains the swamp waters off in a southwesterly direction. A number of boat-runs unite and form the riverbed; at first the pace of the new stream is slow, but when it crosses into Florida it becomes a swift current, its boulders almost suggesting a mountain brook. The banks are high limestone ridges covered with cedar forests. After flowing through a lonely wilderness for many miles, the river touches a very civilized spot, the old Florida spa of White Springs. This is a shady village of late Victorian overtones, at one time known as "Rebels' Refuge," because during the Civil War a number of planters from Georgia found a safe haven there for their families and slaves. White Springs boasts of a new Stephen Foster Museum, for "Old Folks at Home" made the Suwanee one of America's famous rivers. Oldtimers insist that Stephen Foster visited the region in the 1850's, but history knows that he didn't.

The fashion of egret feathers on hats almost spelled extinction for the egret.

THE FOUNTAIN OF YOUTH AND SIR FRANCIS DRAKE. In the pageant of American history the City of St. Augustine plays a small but spectacular part: It is our country's contact with the Spanish Main. It has the same kind of Castilian fortress, with moat and steep walls and corner turrets, that is encountered in Puerto Rico's San Juan and Cuba's Habana, and the same type of cathedral and patio. It also can boast of all those swashbuckling deeds and events that made the Spanish Main a colorful corner of the earth. St. Augustine had its conquistadores: In 1513 Ponce de Leon landed there and spent five days searching for the miraculous Fountain of Youth, and the Spanish admiral Menéndez de Avilés took possession of the land for Castile in 1565; he founded the settlement on August 28th, St. Augustine's day, hence the name. Like so many towns of the "Main," St. Augustine had its own massacre: A French fleet under Jean Ribaut approached to attack and sack the city when a hurricane blew it out to sea, and the majority of the 300 Frenchmen found themselves shipwrecked nearby at Matanzas Inlet. When the Spaniards arrived, the French surrendered unconditionally and were executed promptly, not for being French but for being Protestants. The town suffered from pirates: The worst of them was Sir Francis Drake who plundered and burned it; the Spaniards had fled to the woods, then returned and rebuilt

Practically the whole 1,300-mile coastline of Florida is broad, palm-fringed beach.

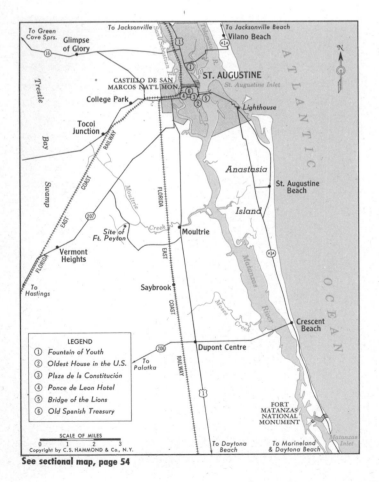

LEGEND
1. *Fountain of Youth*
2. *Oldest House in the U.S.*
3. *Plaza de la Constitución*
4. *Ponce de Leon Hotel*
5. *Bridge of the Lions*
6. *Old Spanish Treasury*

SCALE OF MILES
0   1   2   3
Copyright by C.S. HAMMOND & Co., N.Y.

See sectional map, page 54

their settlement. One integral part of the Spanish colonial system was the establishment of Indian missions, and St. Augustine became the headquarters of a chain of 40 of them, reaching as far west as Pensacola. In the middle of the 18th century the British moved in; the next flag to fly over St. Augustine was that of the short-lived Republic of Florida. In 1821 the United States took over, and has stayed there ever since, with the exception of the Civil War years which furnished the city with its fifth official flag, that of the Confederacy.

CATHEDRALS AND PATIOS. This wonderful story-book history has not vanished from the face of the city, and many relics of the days of the Spanish Main's glory are preserved. One fortunate circumstance was the occurrence of a building material more durable than timber: coquina. As this is a limestone composed of prehistoric sea shells, it is readily available along the coast and has helped to preserve a unique heritage. St. Augustine's most photographed item is the Oldest House in the United States, on St. Francis Street, built in the late 1500's. On a thick coquina wall the wooden second story rests, and the crushed coquina floors, the hand-hewn cedar beams, the low ceilings and the massive fireplaces are reminiscent of the Middle Ages. At Treasury and St. George Streets the Old Spanish Treasury is most interesting; the original building was erected about 1600, and the patio contains a collection of rare plants, including frankincense and Mexican coral trees. Inside there are fine old mahogany furnishings, carved four-poster beds, ancient oil paintings; the treasury room preserves two relics that reflect medieval barbarism pure and simple: Two horrible figures, half ghouls, half apes, were used by the Spanish court of inquisition to intimidate the poor wretches before the tribunal. The Cathedral of St. Augustine, begun in 1793, has a coquina front and a gable extended into a belfry, in the style of the missions of our Southwest. At the Plaza de la Constitucion, in the center of town, the Slave Market is a "new" structure, dating from 1824; the "old" building has stood on the same site since 1598. Also the Ponce de Leon Hotel, which introduced St. Augustine to the country at large as a winter resort, is a kind of historic shrine by now.

THE SPANISH CASTLE. Castillo de San Marcos, formerly Fort Marion, so called in honor of General Francis Marion, "the swamp fox," was started in 1672, and Negro slaves and Indian hostages, soldiers and citizens dug the moat, ferried the coquina blocks from Anastasia Island to the building site, and labored for two generations before the fortress was completed. The "hot shot oven" is still preserved in the eastern earthworks; in it cannon balls were heated and fired red hot into pirate and enemy ships, causing spectacular fireworks. Although there are hardly any descendants of the Spanish builders of the fort alive today, the Spanish

A porpoise-acrobat leaps 6 feet for his dinner.

tradition has been carried on by a large group of Spanish immigrants from Minorca who arrived in 1767, almost 200 years ago. Local guide books refer to them as the town's "largest foreign group." How long does one have to live in St. Augustine to become a native son?

THE HIGH-JUMPING PORPOISE. The coast road to the south leads over the Bridge of the Lions to Anastasia Island; at St. Augustine Beach the "new" lighthouse dates from 1874; the "old" signal tower was reported by Sir Francis Drake as standing at the same spot in 1586. The Alligator Farm with 6,000 specimens of all sizes is a local curiosity. Seventeen miles south of St. Augustine the Marine Studios of Marineland are a great coastal attraction. Deep-sea life is maintained in two great tanks, and through portholes the daily routines of sharks and porpoises, sawfish and devil fish, giant green turtles and shrimps may be observed. As the water is changed 6 times every 24 hours, and cleaning crews in divers' suits are permanently at work, the water is wonderfully clear. At 11 A.M. and 4 P.M. a dinner bell sounds, and the whole fish population rushes to the hand-out. Porpoises leap out of the water for six feet to snatch bits of fish from the keeper's hand. There are also splendid sea gardens where brilliant tropical fish swim between corals and algae, and on the surface penguins walk around as if they were the duly appointed inspectors of the establishment.

A piece of the Middle Ages: The oldest house in the U.S., built in the late 1500's.

RINGLING AND RUBENS, TIGHTROPE AND TITIAN. The general assumption that the central west coast of Florida is an "activity area" for retired couples rather than a region of spectacular scenery, is correct to a certain extent. Yet many a sight to be seen there can safely be called "picturesque." If Al Hine presents "that magnificent municipality, that balmy abode of baseball, that scintillating sanctum of the circus, Florida's begemmed, bejeweled bijou, the one and only Sarasota,"—he just tells the truth. It is an attractive town, with its municipal pier, its causeway to Longboat and Lido Keys, and its lovely white beaches where the trees creep up almost to the water's edge. You also see big league baseball players downtown, for the Red Sox make Sarasota their spring training center. And, as almost everybody knows, the town is the winter headquarters of the Ringling Brothers-Barnum and Bailey Circus, the Greatest Show on Earth. East of the city a large fenced-in plot is open to the public, for a single admission, and there people from 48 states walk around leisurely and admire the long lines of shiny railroad cars that take the circus all over the country, look at the tigers and lions of the menagerie, watch 30 elephants going through their routines, observe a 10-horse act in training, pass some circus folks conversing in German or Italian or Siamese, and spend a whole afternoon with the pleasant feeling of having seen the circus "backstage."

The Sarasota Jungle Gardens recreate the virgin forest seen by Spanish explorers.

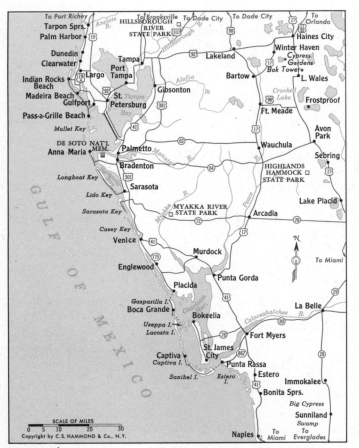

See sectional map, page 54

The Ringlings, and especially John Ringling, left their mark on Sarasota, sometimes in surprising ways. In an area of shuffleboard and trailer camps there is suddenly the John and Mable Ringling Museum of Art, one of the world's great collections of baroque paintings, with works by Titian and Tintoretto, Raphael and Rembrandt and many others. Its larger-than-life-size Rubens sketches which were patterns for tapestries, are a treasure that only the Louvre at Paris can match. Don't fail either to visit the John and Mable Ringling residence, overlooking Sarasota Bay. It's a palace, the vision of a flamboyant circus man's castle come true. Finally there is the Museum of the American Circus, a unique and exciting exhibit of Circusiana, among them two miniature scale models of the Ringling show, one set up under canvas, the other packed up in the train and ready to travel. The specimens of retired old parade wagons with their guilded carvings are as baroque as the Rubens paintings; one of the former, the "Two Hemispheres," used to be drawn by a team of forty horses.

THE GREEN BENCHES: A UNIQUE OUTDOOR CLUB. One city that does not want to be baroque, is St. Petersburg. Quiet and pleasant, it caters to those who have done their life's work and wish to enjoy their declining years, and in doing so the town fulfills a real mission. Its principal commodity is sunshine, and any day on which the sun fails to appear before 3 o'clock, the whole edition of the afternoon paper is given away free. That happens about 5 times a year. The prettiest parts of the Sunshine City are the parks and boulevards along Tampa Bay, with harbor, yacht basins, and the famous Municipal Pier. Here fishermen try their luck from special balconies, and pelicans and gulls wheel around screaming for tidbits. In the late afternoon the fishing boats return, the prize catch—perhaps a mighty tarpon—proudly displayed hanging from the mast. But St. Petersburg's most famous institution is that of the green benches, thousands of them, inviting visitors to rest not only in the parks but also on the sidewalks of the principal business streets. These green benches have become a sort of outdoor club where "members" may strike up a conversation without formal introduction, discussing the weather, operations, or politics. Promoters of good causes and real estate salesmen find the benches a profitable hunting ground, and often the green seats serve as an open-air matrimonial office. No one ever really gets old in "St. Pete," and the Three-Quarter-Century Club (all members are at least 75 years old) organizes dances, theatricals, and contests.

A BIT OF GREECE: THE SPONGE CAPITAL OF THE WORLD. Driving north, past the attractive waterfront of Clearwater, you will soon find yourself in one of America's most interesting towns, Tarpon Springs. Here the descendants of Greek sponge-fisher-

Tarpon Springs sponge fishermen carry on an ancient Greek skill.

men who for thousands of years had practiced their difficult trade in the Aegean Sea, carry on the ancient craft in the New World. On the docks of the Anclote River the colorful boats and the Greek waterfront life may be watched; the Greek language is heard here, delicious Greek honey-and-almond confections may be sampled, and a demonstration-boat-trip down the river with a diver descending to the bottom and emerging with a cluster of sponges, is an interesting excursion. If you are lucky, you may witness the return of the sponge fleet, for instance at Easter time. The whole community is assembled to greet the brightly painted boats that bear the names of Greek gods and goddesses or of Greek national heroes; the Stars and Stripes and the blue-white Greek pennants flutter in the wind, the diving suits dangle from the masts like grotesque scarecrows, and the decks are piled high with the harvest of sponges. There is the laughter of welcome on the wharves, and music and excitement. The sponges are sold at auction in the Cooperative Warehouse which looks like an old southern slave market. The community preserves many colorful Old-World ceremonies, like the blessing of the departing boats, or Greek Cross Day when a priest of the Greek Catholic Church releases a white dove and throws into the water a gold cross which is retrieved by young divers; or the Easter festival with its candlelight service and roast-lamb-and-rice dinners.

The John and Mable Ringling Museum of Art contains famous baroque masterpieces.

ACRYSTAL COVE OF 150 SPRINGS. "Florida Cracker" is a very respected name in the central part of the state. It implies the genuine, original, native Floridian spirit, in marked contrast to that of the southern part of the peninsula where the Yankees prevail. This "heartland" comprises the citrus belt, with lush orange and grapefruit groves rising to little hills, descending to small lakes and climbing back to gentle ridges. These plantings are clean and neat, and beautiful and fragrant at blossom and at harvest time. Occasional stretches are monotonous, but then again there are breath-taking spots where deep-blue lake views are framed by tall live oaks or cypresses decorously draped with Spanish moss. Much of this section lies on top of a thick layer of porous limestone which stores huge masses of water; consequently there are 27 big and numerous small springs in that area, but Silver Springs, near the town of Ocala, surpasses them all. Here 150 natural springs flow into a common basin, and from an easily visible cove 65 feet long and 12 feet high up to 800 million gallons of water gush to the surface every day. Visitors may swim there and admire the limestone-filtered water which is so clear that light is broken into prismatic colors. In 80 feet of this iridescent current all bottom plants are clearly seen from glass bottom boats, and not only the life of numerous fishes, turtles and shrimps can be observed there but also a graceful water

At blossom time orange groves hum with bees, a fragrant drowsiness engulfs the area.

See sectional map, page 54

ballet or occasionally the filming of an underwater movie.

THE CITY THAT IS A GREAT PARK. Southeast of Ocala, Orlando is one of America's most attractive residential cities. Subtropical gardens, parks and boulevards display their camphor trees and live oaks, palms from many corners of the earth and winter-blooming flowers. The foliage is green, the brick pavement red, the surface of the lakes sparkling blue. The town has also a surprising number of cultural attractions: Fine theaters with Broadway plays, excellent book stores, and the widely acclaimed Central Florida Symphony Orchestra. Academic life centers around nearby Rollins College. No wonder that proud Orlandians derive the name of their city from Orlando, the hero of "As You Like It."

CINERAMA SCENERY. When the producers of the first giant screen motion picture looked for samples of spectacular American scenery, they went to the Florida Cypress Gardens near Winter Haven, south of Orlando. There a wild swamp adjacent to Lake Eloise has been turned into a tropical park; its masses of blooming azaleas, camellias and gardenias are planted around placid lagoons in which old, moss-festooned cypresses are mirrored. Pretty girls in period costumes help to create a make-believe atmosphere of the Old South, and a boys-and-girls performance of water-ski acrobatics is a great drawing card.

Blossoming Groves and The Singing Tower

CARILLONS AND NIGHTINGALES. A few miles to the south, near Lake Wales, a 325-foot hill called Iron Mountain rises above the surrounding valleys. There the early settlers discovered a large boulder surrounded by 13 smaller stones, a symbol of the sun and the 13 moons of the Indian year. Since time immemorial this crest had been a sanctuary, and it still is, thanks to a thought of the Philadelphia editor and publisher Edward Bok who established here his Mountain Lake Sanctuary. The Bok Singing Tower is probably the most famous single sight in Florida, and rightly so. The far-away loneliness of earlier years is gone now, with an ever increasing influx of visitors, but the spire itself is the same work of beauty and dignity, "its feet in flowers and its brow in the sun." Built of steel and faced with coquina rock from the coast and grey and pink marble from Georgia, it rises for 230 feet overlooking 30 lakes. Its metal work, its marble carvings, its friezes and its colorful ceramics blend into a perfect setting for one of the finest carillons in existence. The 71 bells—the smallest weighing 12 pounds and the largest 11 tons—are tuned in a chromatic scale ranging over 4½ octaves, and their music sweetly and peacefully merges with the breeze. In the surrounding garden a profusion of azaleas and callas, iris and amaryllis blossom among the trees, and more than a hundred species and varieties of birds have found a safe home there. Especially introduced are European

Bok Tower, 555 feet above sea level, is Florida's most famous single sight.

nightingales which even outsing our mockingbirds. A 12-by-24-foot reproduction of Leonardo da Vinci's "Last Supper," done in mosaic by German artisans, preserves the fine color shades which in the original are fading.

CITRUS FRUIT AND BRAHMA COWS. Lakeland, to the southwest, is the busy center of large groves which produce one third of the state's citrus fruit. Visitors soon discover that the connoisseur does not just buy oranges but Temple or Parson Brown, Pineapple or King or Valencia, Satsuma or Lue Gim Gong. It is interesting to visit a packing house and watch the cleaning and sorting. East and south of Lake Wales and the Bok Tower the cow country of Florida begins. There in the palmetto flatlands with a scanty growth of grass a sturdy breed of cattle with an outlandish ancestry has been bred. The original European stock had been imported by the Spaniards long before the Pilgrims landed at the Rock. The cows were so scrawny that as late as the turn of this century they only reached the size of a small donkey and were the laughing stock of the western cattlemen. Then hump-backed Brahma bulls from the East Indies were introduced, and the resulting Florida strain is a healthy meat animal. In the cattle town of Kissimmee the advertising runs to leather, saddles, and the Silver Spur Rodeo. One local invention has been widely imitated in the West: A bar where a cowboy on horseback can have a drink without dismounting.

AMERICA'S MAN-MADE GOLD COAST. Sixty or seventy years ago, when the U.S. was quite settled and even the Pacific shore cities had passed their early youth, the southeastern coast of Florida was a wilderness of lonely dunes and palmetto thickets, mangrove forests and swamps infested with snakes, alligators and mosquitoes. Then suddenly that force appeared which is called American enterprise. The railroad pushed south, engineers built canals, dams, causeways, bridges and artificial islands, and architects laid out new cities. To this day the photogenic beauty of the Gold Coast—the pastel-colored, palm-shaded villas by blue canals, the city skyline above the flat shore, the white yachts in the basin—is man-made although, of course, the basic ingredients have always been there: The sun, the crystal-clear air, the white beaches, the azure-blue Gulf Stream. Beside the builders, the botanists and horticulturists were at work; they imported brightly blossoming, decorative plants and fine tropical fruit trees, adapting them to the climate and improving them until today Florida's royal palms are taller and straighter than those of Brazil, and her mangoes surpass their progenitors in India. This collaboration of nature and man resulted in attracting such numbers of winter residents and tourists that statistically speaking the Gold Coast has become the greatest resort playground on earth.

THE OLD RICH: STARS OF SOCIETY. In 1878

Palm Beach is closer to the Gulf Stream than any other spot on the Atlantic.

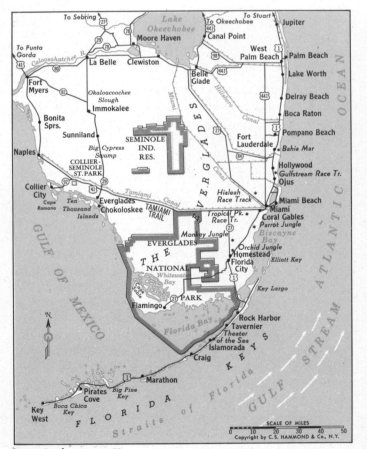

See sectional map, page 56

74

stars, successful producers, TV comics, radio commentators, gossip columnists. The row of hundreds of sybaritic waterfront hotels in Miami Beach is not duplicated anywhere else on this planet; each hotel has its swimming pool, private beach, terrace, sundeck, cabanas, sea-view platform for midday dancing outdoors, and often its own night club. Rates are fantastic, but so is the service, and in some of these palaces elegant stationery with your name engraved on it is delivered a few hours after your arrival. On the whole, resort life does not lean heavily on sports but runs to sun-bathing, swimming, long siestas, elaborate dining, extensive night-clubbing and romancing. The nightclubs are gay and gaudy affairs with swarms of pretty girls and the world's most famous entertainers. Sight-seers will find the Miami Bayfront Park and the Municipal Yacht Basin interesting. Excursion boats will take you over Biscayne Bay to lush, artificial islands and through quiet man-made canals where the estates of the millionaires will be pointed out; glass-bottom boats will show you the "sea gardens" where brightly colored tropical fish dart from coral formations and sea plants; and deep-sea fishing boats are available to those who would like to write home about catching a sailfish or a barracuda. In Coral Gables the ultra-modern campus of the University of Miami is in tune with the area. In Hialeah Park the race track is famous both for the huge sums of money placed there in bets and for its

The Overseas Highway to Key West connects 100 miles of subtropical islands.

beauty; 300 pink flamingoes wade placidly through an artificial lake, in plain view of the grandstand.

VENICE OF THE SPORTSMEN. Between Palm Beach and Miami resorts like Hollywood and Boca Raton are fashioned after the Miami pattern while the City of Fort Lauderdale is a watersports Eden. Natural and man-made islands are surrounded by 150 miles of rivers, inlets, canals and waterways, and the effect is that of a bright, modern Venice. Bahia Mar, the luxurious yacht basin of the Inland Waterway, is the last word in yachting comfort. While approaching it by boat, you may radio ahead and order a steak dinner to be served on deck, an engine repairman, and a baby-sitter.

THE KEYS TO PARADISE. Between Miami and Key Largo there are only 50 miles, but they lead from Florida at its gaudiest to Florida at its quietest, to fishing coves, rickety piers, rusty anchors, wind-blown beachcombers' shacks, and old-time saloons. The 100-mile-long chain of islands called Florida Keys is connected by the Overseas Highway, and a ride to Key West is one of America's outstanding travel experiences. Key West is a picturesque "Caribbean" city that in the early 1800's prospered on vessels shipwrecked on the outlying reefs; salvaging the cargoes was a profitable and adventurous business. Of particular interest on its present-day waterfront are the "turtle crawls."

A **PRIZE EXHIBIT.** That our countryside prides itself in towering peaks and glistening glaciers, in blooming deserts and huge canyons, in primeval forests and rugged coasts, is taken for granted. But that among the sights to be enjoyed there is also a huge tropical jungle, with a fantastic fauna and flora, and with the largest mangrove forest in the Americas, is a crowning glory. Since the Everglades has become a National Park, this jungle will retain its unusual personality and develop according to its own laws. The nucleus of the park was Royal Palm State Park, established as a wildlife sanctuary by the State Federation of Women's Clubs.

The geographers will object to the term "tropical," and the forestry experts to the word "jungle." Yet in the layman's mind the Everglades is just that, and the laymen receive a good deal of support from the meteorologists who consider the climate tropical, and from the botanists and zoologists who find that its plant and animal life is, to a considerable extent, tropical rather than sub-tropical.

THE RIVER OF GRASS. To classify the Everglades is difficult; to describe them is easy. The southernmost part of the Florida peninsula consists of two mildly elevated ridges along the two coasts where the great resorts have been built with their skyscraper hotels and luxury stores. Between these two narrow ridges there is a broad groove extending from Lake Okeechobee to Florida Bay, at the southernmost tip of land, a wide expanse of untouched,

The Anhinga Trail and the Gumbo Limbo Trail offer fascinating sights.

empty wilderness, half dry and half wet, half soil and half

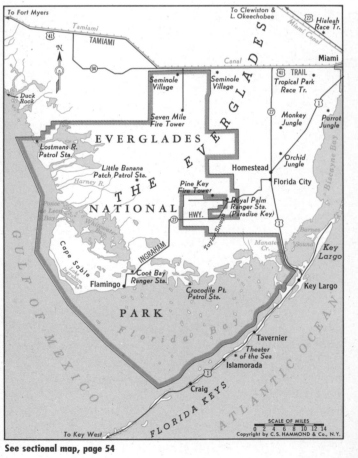

See sectional map, page 54

76

American egrets, their snowy-white bodies and S-shaped necks balanced on thin black legs; some stately herons and cranes wade through the shallows in search of their dinner; an anhinga and a white ibis with black wing tips fly by, with a clumsy, primeval grace. There are also crocodiles in the park, distinguished by their long, tapered noses from the blunt snouts of the alligators.

The Everglades is one of the last refuges for another creature of antediluvial appearance, the sea cow or manatee, a large, harmless mammal; it grows to a weight of a thousand pounds on a diet of sea grass plucked from the bottom of shallow bays; as the female nurses her baby upright in the water, exposing head and shoulder, clasping her infant with her flippers and nursing it serenely, such a scene is said to be the origin of the ancient mariners' tales of mermaids in Florida waters. Along the ocean huge loggerhead turtles, weighing up to 300 pounds, build their nests, especially on the beaches toward Cape Sable where also some of America's most magnificent shells may be found. Snakes abound, and with their flaming colors and strange patterns offer a weird beauty of their own: diamond rattlers and cottonmouth moccasins, blue indigo and green water snakes, king snakes and bright corals. But no cautious visitors will be harmed.

It seems strange that the low, warm and watery Everglades should shelter the same group of animals that inhabit the high, dry, and cold regions. Deer, bears wildcats

Outside the park Brahma cattle from India have adapted well to the Everglades.

and panthers splash through the tepid streams, raccoons climb into the tree tops to catch the cool trade winds, and otters, playful, nonchalant and unafraid, have a wonderful time. Those interested in fishing may take the marl-surfaced Ingraham Highway which traverses the park to Coot Bay Station. There and in neighboring Flamingo boats may be rented. Fishing is fine, and the varieties are endless, but the coveted prize is the tarpon, the large, spirited game fish with the shiny, silvery scales.

BIRDS THAT BUILD A TOWER AND TREES THAT KILL. Large areas of the park are and should be practically inaccessible, to leave undisturbed the haunts of rare, beautiful birds like the bald eagle, the roseate spoonbill, the bronze turkey, and others. The huge rookeries of the more common pelicans and cormorants, limpkins and ducks, egrets and gallinules are an incredible bedlam of noise and excitement during the nesting season. A mass of white ibises rising from their nests in a circling flight and forming a "tower" is a sight to behold. At Duck Rock, a little key just north of the park on the Gulf, as many as 50,000 of these ibises may be seen roosting during the summer months.

Tree lovers will enjoy the Gumbo Limbo Trail, also near the Royal Palm Ranger Station, to study the vegetation of a typical hammock, from the tamarind tree and the wild coffee bush to the cabbage palm and the strangler fig which embraces a "host tree" and strangles it.

Bears and even panthers live and hunt in the Everglades.

THE GRANDMOTHER OF NEW ORLEANS. On the first document to bear the name "America," Waldseemüller's map of 1505, the outline of Mobile Bay is clearly drawn. De Narvaez landed there in 1528, and the first settlement was organized in 1559. Had it lasted, Mobile would have the tourist trump card in her hands which now is played by St. Augustine: "We are the Oldest City in the U.S." But the town on Mobile Bay was abandoned, and not until 1699 was a new colony established. It was there that the first cargo of Cassette Girls arrived, 23 poor but good young women from Canada. Within a month 22 had husbands; one was hard to please. In 1710 the settlement was transferred to the present site of Mobile and in 1721 received her first slaves: 600 Africans. All these data make it abundantly clear that Mobile is not, as is sometimes stated, the little sister of New Orleans. It is rather the old lady across the bay who taught the growing infant on the Mississippi how to be a southern gentlewoman.

NO LONGER POOR, AND GLAD OF IT. Indian troubles, hurricanes, conflagrations, yellow fever epidemics,—Mobile had its share in all of them. But, while after the Civil War many southern centers languished, Mobile shipped cotton to the world at large and organized the lumber industry in its hinterland. Later the steel and iron from Birmingham floated down the river in barges and was reshipped from Mobile to foreign ports. Paper

Bellingrath Gardens are a memorial to Coca-Cola tycoon Walter Bellingrath's wife.

See sectional map, page 56

mills moved in, shipbuilding flourished, and the Bankhead Tunnel under the Mobile River facilitated communications to the east. Today Mobile is a prosperous international port with a future, and because it is well-to-do, it proudly preserves its past. It has a unique method of doing so: Whenever an ancient structure is demolished, the weathered old bricks and particularly the iron lacework are saved and used again in new construction. This adaptation of the old and the new works very well, and the modern city preserves many a genuine French and Spanish touch. On Mobile's famous Bienville Square the live oaks, the bright flowers and the splashing fountain suggest relaxed leisure; the tall office buildings and hotels, the mid-20th century.

BOEUF GRAS, JUG BANDS AND JUBILEE. Where was carnival first celebrated in America? Why, in Mobile. The Gulf coast was a howling wilderness in 1704, but the Cassette Girls had just arrived, and so everybody dressed in fancy clothes for the Masque de St. Louis. In 1711 this annual affair was renamed Boeuf Gras. When it shifted from New Year's Eve to Shrove Tuesday, it became Mardi Gras. It is still the great event of community merry-making, with parades, floats, and balls presided over by Emperor Felix. The colored people have their own picturesque procession, and the jug bands that appear all over town on that occasion, are a local curiosity: Two boys accompany their street singing with a guitar and a contraption consisting of a washboard, a frying pan, a coffee pot and an ancient auto horn. One "Jubilee" is provided by nature, usually on the eastern shore of the bay in late summer. Early in the morning a cry is heard along the bay: "Jubilee! Jubilee!", and as the news travels up the streets, people appear with baskets and wheelbarrows, and laughing and shouting they race to the bay. What happened? Jubilee means that hundreds of thousands of fish of all descriptions, from flounders to shrimps, have flung themselves on the shore, and innumerable sea food dinners may be had for the picking. There is no scientific explanation for the phenomenon, just the complicated theory of a "tidal spasm." According to James Street, "some say the fish just go crazy. Anyway, the people do."

BLOSSOMS BY THE BAY. The question "Who started the southern flower craze?"—if craze is the right word for so pleasant an enthusiasm—is difficult to answer. But Mobile has an excellent claim to the crown. For it was Mobile that imported the first azalea from France, in 1754, and has pampered, improved and crossbred the plants until today you can admire there every imaginable type from 120-year old azalea trees that are giants 35 feet tall, to oriental miniatures that are midgets. For one March week every year thousands of visitors descend upon Mobile to enjoy "the Azalea Trail," 17 miles of streets blazing with flowers, with all gardens

The first azaleas in America blossomed in Mobile which imported them from France.

along the route open to the public. The trail starts out from Bienville Square, and the markers are followed easily. For a consideration official guides are available, usually pretty girls from town; to outsiders their lush Alabama accent alone is worth the fee. The next goal of all visitors lies about 20 miles to the south: the magnificent Bellingrath Gardens, where a quarter of a million azaleas cover 800 acres. Owner of this paradise is the Coca-Cola tycoon, Walter Bellingrath, whose mansion emphasizes the Gulf coast style with wrought-iron railings and an iron-lace patio. The gardens are in bloom all year, with a succession of roses, laurel, sweet olive, gardenias, crape myrtle, oleander, allamanda, hibiscus.

THE HAUNTED BAYOU. Not far from Bellingrath, near the village of Irvington, it is a fascinating short trip to follow the road along Bayou la Batre; this is the old Spanish highway that was paved with white, crushed shells; the oaks shading the dark waters stood there already when the Spaniards came, when Lafitte used the inlet as a hideout, and when the buccaneer La Mas spent his last years in a cabin by the bayou. He had "waded the decks knee-deep in gore," and was the source of gruesome tales. His final days were sometimes disturbed by the phantom of a mounted Spaniard galloping over the oyster shell road, red sparks pouring from his mouth. The rider had seduced a French girl, and with his sword her father had pierced the Spaniard's throat.

Mobile's "Mardi Gras" goes back to "Boeuf Gras" which started in 1711.

THE LUSH AND BREEZY SHORE. Through arches formed by oaks and cypresses, catalpa and tulip trees you look out on the calm, glistening Gulf. The scent of magnolia and oleander is in the moist, mild air. Mockingbirds sing in the crepe-myrtle trees, and pelicans land on the water's mirror with a splash. Lilies, roses, honeysuckle and jasmine blossom in sight of the beach, and the smell of the sea and the fragrance of the flowers blend into a rich, exuberant atmosphere. The white 40-mile sea wall and the ancient live oaks where Indian tribes used to hold meetings, the shore road that used to be the Spanish Trail, the stories of pirates and adventurers, of French blades and Spanish poniards, the small shipyards where wooden craft are built, the food stands that advertise giant shrimps, gumbo and jambalaya, and the Negro street vendors singing "Oyster má-an from Pass Christi-á-an"—all this is Mississippi's Gulf Coast. It consists of seven cities, six of them pleasant resorts: Pascagoula, Ocean Springs, Biloxi, Pass Christian, Bay St. Louis, Waveland; and one, a new, shiny commercial emporium: Gulfport.

BEES AND CRABS. The waters of the Mississippi Sound are calm because a row of islands several miles off shore break the pounding waves; the only winds they cannot mitigate are the hurricanes. The islands themselves are low sand bars, with patches of an evergreen shrub called *titi;* when the latter blossoms, in April,

there is such a heavy sweet fragrance in the wind that the fishermen can smell it far out on the Gulf. The myriads of honey bees and the white sand crabs that race over the lonely dunes seem to be the only living creatures there. Opposite Pass Christian, some islands are completely covered with shells and produce small, sweet oysters. Ship Island, opposite Gulfport, is rich in history and legend and site of Civil War Fort Massachusetts.

THE SINGING RIVER. It sounds like a swarm of bees, or like a honey locust, and can best be heard on a hot summer evening. In front of the fish docks of Pascagoula, the old Gulf town, the river of the same name has been singing this strange song for time immemorial. Spanish records of the 17th century mention it, but it is as much of a puzzle today. Scientific explanations do not exist, only theories: It may be natural gas escaping, or the rolling of sand on the slate bottom, or a cave sucking in a current. Only the Indians know the true reason: Once upon a time the Pascagoulas found themselves hopelessly surrounded by the Biloxis, their arch enemies. They would not think of surrender but chose suicide instead. From a great water oak on the shore they walked into the river with joined hands, chanting their song of death until the last body had vanished in the dark current. But their voices were never hushed; they are humming on, just as the old water oak still stands on the river bank.—In American naval history, the "battle of Pascagoula" turned out to be a brilliant victory of good sense for all concerned. A local boy, David Farragut, who had grown up on a plantation near the Singing River, returned as a famous Yankee admiral during the War Between the States, took New Orleans, and approached his hometown to effect a military occupation. Outside the port he was met by a fleet of small craft of every description, manned by the admiral's old playmates and school friends. The reception was terrific; joy and emotion ran high, and what might have been a bloody encounter, ended as the biggest fish fry in the history of the Gulf Coast.—West of Pascagoula the restful village of Ocean Springs is the original Biloxi, first capital of French Louisiana.

TORCHES AT EBB TIDE. During dark spring evenings the shallow waters at Biloxi are aglow with lights; you'd think of fireflies in a pasture rather than of torches on the sea. Men are "gigging" here for flounders. Two by two, they wade through the water, the light in one hand, a spear with a long, narrow tip in the other. Heads bent, they look for flounders half-buried in the sand, spear them, throw them into a basket, and late at night return in a torchlight parade. The fishermen here are mostly Slavonians, Austrians, Poles and Yugoslavs, and as they all possess a certain natural gaiety, they fit well into this country of French, Spanish, and Negro traditions. A fiesta atmosphere hovers over Biloxi which once was the fashionable rendezvous of the southern *haute*

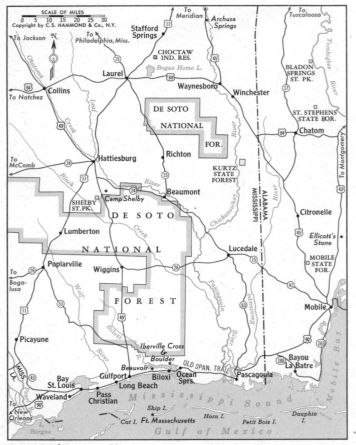

See sectional map, page 54

Historic Biloxi Lighthouse was built in 1848. Although they were loyal Confederates, the people of Biloxi painted their lighthouse black when they received the news of President Lincoln's assassination. Later, of course, the government had it painted white again.

monde and still is a lively resort with a Victorian charm.

THE WHITE CROSS. In 1699 the French, under D'Iberville, landed near Biloxi in a quiet cove, erected a white cross, and under that symbol took possession of the land for their king and their God. On that same bay a white cross is still erected every year, the Sunday preceding the 15th of August. All the deep-sea fishing boats of the region are anchored there for the occasion, freshly painted and bedecked with gay pennants and flags. The chants begin at midnight, and mass is held with all the magnificence of the church; priests visit each boat to bless the crew, sprinkle drops of holy water on the planks, and pray for the men's safety and prosperity dur-

ing the new season. At dawn the boats set out for the open sea.—Near Biloxi the shore estate of Beauvoir was the last home of Jefferson Davis, the Confederate President. Gulfport is a planned city of 20th century vintage, a busy port. The most beautiful of "the Seven Pearls" is Pass Christian, an aristocratic summer town of Greek Revival homes, white pillars, wrought-iron balconies and exuberant gardens. Bay St. Louis used to be as exclusive as Pass Christian across the bridge, but is now a gay, popular middle-class resort. Waveland, near the Louisiana state line, is a haven for summer commuters from New Orleans. Its "pirate house" is linked, though somewhat indistinctly, with Jean Lafitte, the buccaneer.

A FRENCH CITY? Mark Twain called New Orleans "Paris in America." So did Thackeray. Yet many visiting Frenchman do not perceive there any Franch atmosphere. Architects confirm that the old homes in the Vieux Carré with their patios and iron grill-work, are Spanish rather than French. Gastronomes assert that the city's famous cuisine is based on the spices of the Delta and the bounty of the Gulf; it is Creole, not French. Connoisseurs of fine wines discover that New Orleans prefers mint juleps and Ramos gin fizz to the vintages. And entertainment experts find the burlesque night club shows as American and un-Parisian as apple pie. All that is a tribute to New Orleans. It does not imitate; it is fascinating in its own right.

LIVE DANGEROUSLY. That a great and gay metropolitan city should have grown on the lower Mississippi, seems a miracle. You visit one of the cemeteries with their above-ground crypts, and you realize that any grave or hole 2 feet deep used to fill up with black swamp water immediately. You see the pumping stations at various points of the city, and realize that they are necessary to keep streets and cellars dry. You approach the levee and see the steamers tower high above you: The level of the Mississippi may be 20 feet above the level of the town. Obviously, only a community could survive which was willing to re-conquer anew and anew what it possessed, often doing so while floods, conflagrations, tornadoes and

The Court of the Two Sisters is a well-known restaurant in a 120-year-old patio.

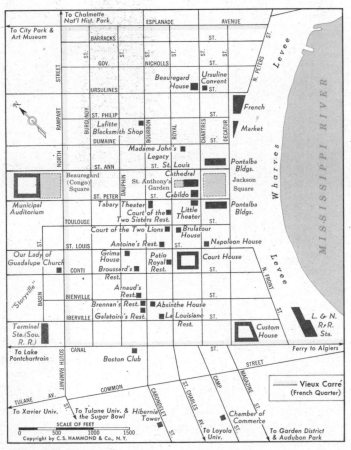

See sectional map, page 54

epidemics played havoc with it. Yet this dangerously-built city became America's gayest. At the levee, by the way, you should take a harbor trip on an excursion boat; you will meet the New Orleans of the modern port, the coffee steamers, the banana boats, the rice mills, the factories.

THE PAST AND PRESENT MERGE. The French Quarter is but a small part of the metropolis, but for the traveler it is the greatest attraction. You can see it all on foot; you walk through narrow streets and alleys, look into patios and courtyards where banana and oleander bushes thrive around 150-year old staircases, pause for a moment in St. Louis Cathedral, look at the stately Pontalba Buildings, visit the Cabildo which used to be the Spanish government house and is a most interesting museum now, admire the iron-lace balconies, and watch the numerous artists perpetuate the treasured sights in paintings and drawings. And you will get the feel of history: This is the square on which the French flag was lowered and the Stars and Stripes rose high when the world's greatest real estate operation was consummated. Up to that time empires had been conquered. Here, in 1803, an empire was purchased, at 4 cents an acre. At Bourbon Street on the second floor of the Absinthe House Andrew Jackson and Jean Lafitte planned the defense of New Orleans in 1815, and a small but clever American army beat a large and rambling British one brilliantly but unnecessarily, as the peace had been signed two weeks before the battle. You will feel the continuity from the past to the present. There is no restoration as in Williamsburg which in parts is too spick-and-span to be convincing. The French Quarter is in a good, habitable condition, and if some edges are frayed a little, they are not hidden.

CULTURE AND BURLESQUE, MARDI GRAS AND SPRING FIESTA. During the day Royal Street will intrigue you. It is the antique capital of the United States where you may furnish a home with a complete set of genuine antiques of any given period. Purchasers like to think that the chandelier they bought had once graced a great Louisiana plantation home, but that is almost certainly not so. Antiques is an international business with its main sources of supply in Europe. There are also numerous book and art shops which lend a cultural touch to the street and where fine etchings, old maps and rare books may be bought at modest prices. At night the scene shifts to Bourbon Street where bars and night clubs flourish in profusion, for almost nine blocks. The air is most festive around midnight when cars move slowly, people fill the sidewalks, and jazzy music resounds from everywhere. You look around and are not at all sure whether that elegant gentleman is a banker or a gambler, whether the pretty young lady in front of you might be a debutante or a night club "hostess." Surely all these categories are represented. The core of every nightclub performance is

The Mardi Gras is matched only by the carnivals of Nice and Rio de Janeiro.

the strip-tease which in vigor and liberality has been brought to perfection here. The annual climax of this wine-women-and-song trend is, of course, Mardi Gras; since its joys are well known and often described, it is mentioned here only in passing. A newer institution is the yearly Spring Fiesta with tours through the Vieux Carré and the antebellum houses of the Garden District.

THE HEAVENLY FOOD. There is no doubt that New Orleans is America's gastronomic capital. The names of such restaurants as Antoine's, Galatoire's, Arnaud's, Broussard's, and Brennan's are nationally or even internationally known; fine food is served in practically every restaurant in town. Even the sandwiches ordered by the dockworkers in little eating places are works of art: crusty French bread, hollowed out, with delicious fillings. The town's specialty is seafood which the bayous and the Gulf furnish in prime quality: crawfish and crabs, shrimps and oysters, and the splendid pompano. Flaming deserts are cultivated by all the luxurious restaurants; shortly before the cherries jubilee, the café brûlot or the crêpes Suzette flare up, touched by the captain's match, the lights are dimmed and everybody enjoys the spectacle. A night of merry-making, by the way, should end with an old New Orleans tradition, a visit to the French Market on the water front where French-type café-au-lait and fresh doughnuts are served to dock hands and tourists, market vendors and socialites during the hours of dawn.

The iron-grillwork balconies are the work of blacksmith-slaves, masters of this art.

RIVERS THAT FLOW THE WRONG WAY.
The early explorers of the lower Mississippi were
surprised to discover a number of "tributaries"
which did not flow into but away from the big river,
ambling southward into the Gulf of Mexico. They called
them "bayous," after the Indian name. The bayous
formed a cobweb of waterways, a wet and tangled wilderness that remained practically uninhabited until the latter part of the 18th century when the Acadians arrived
and settled there. The Acadian pioneers would be relatively unknown today were it not for Longfellow's
"Evangeline," a literary staple diet of all American high
schools. Consequently almost everybody is aware of the
heartbreaking odyssey of the French peasants expelled
by the English from Nova Scotia (then part of a vague
territory called "Acadia") who finally found their way
into French-speaking Louisiana. Their country is not
exactly a tourist center in the sense of big hotels and
motor courts at every corner, but it will have a two-fold
appeal to many: First, the landscape of tangled streams
and live oaks, bright-green sugar-cane fields and somber
cypress swamps has an unusual tropical charm. And second, the people are one of America's most interesting
ethnic groups.

"RIDING ON A DEW." The Acadians have become
an integral part of the landscape. Gentle, gay, religious
and prolific, they have grown deep roots in their new

From the state capital high above the bluffs of Baton Rouge there is a 30-mile view.

See sectional map, page 54

homeland: About 4000 arrived, and now there are more
than 300,000 of them. They settled along the bayous, and
made Bayou Lafourche the longest village street on
earth, lining it on both sides with farm houses and country stores for 120 miles. The Acadians never owned slaves
and are content to cultivate their small patches of corn,
sugar-cane and vegetables, to fish and to trap. Adapting
themselves to local conditions they invented the pirogue,
a canoe hand-carved from a single cypress log and able
to "ride out a flood and travel on a dew." The pirogues
are difficult to manage but develop incredible speed.
The annual pirogue race held on Bayou Barataria over
a five-mile course is a unique event. Fishing is wonderful
in the bayous, swamps, and lakes, and this same area is
also, contrary to general belief, America's greatest pro-
vider of furs, because of its enormous muskrat population. In such a setting the Acadians preserved their old
ways, created a colorful French patois, and a rich folklore. Imaginatively they peopled the bayous with strange
creatures, for instance the loup-garous, cousins to the
European werewolves; these monsters, half wolf and half
man, are cursed souls or wicked humans turned vam-
pires. They hold their annual witches' ball, a wild orgy,
on Bayou Goula.

EVANGELINE LAND. Center of the Bayou country
is St. Martinville; there on Bayou Teche, at East Port
Street, the Evangeline Oak commemorates the landing

of the Acadians. According to local tradition this spot also marks the meeting of Emmeline Labiche and Louis Arceneaux, the Evangeline and Gabriel of the Longfellow epic. Unfortunately, and contrary to the poem, reality had a sad ending. The lover had not been faithful, had taken another wife, and Emmeline-Evangeline broke down with grief, lost her mind, and died shortly afterwards. The heroine's grave, in the cemetery of the local Catholic church, is marked with a statue posed and donated by Dolores del Rio who once played the part of Evangeline in a motion picture. Nearby in the Longfellow-Evangeline Memorial Park the traditional home of Louis Arceneaux is an Acadian Museum now; it is an interesting relic of pioneer life in the subtropics.

TABASCO AND EGRETS. Starting point for the trip to St. Martinville is the busy town of New Iberia, originally a Spanish settlement. Here "The Shadows" is a famous plantation manor; so solidly was it built in 1830, that its blinds of cypress wood are still the original ones. The beautiful garden with its marble statues and boxwood, bamboo hedges and thriving flowers faces Bayou Teche and may be visited. New Iberia's other great attraction is Avery Island, a solid circle surrounded by sea marshes. It has been in the hands of the Marsh-Avery-McIllhenny family since the 18th century, and has been kept for good reasons. For the island contains a rock salt dome more than a mile deep, its exploitation being

"The shrimp boats are coming" is electrifying news at Morgan City.

The folk costumes of the Acadians are as pretty as their wearers.

leased to the International Salt Company. The island also produces the peppers from which the famous McIllhenny Tabasco Sauce is made; the factory which produces the sharp sauce and exports it to many parts of the world, may be inspected. The McIllhenny Mansion lies in 200 landscaped acres called Jungle Gardens which, for a fee, are open to the public. The variety of plants, native and exotic, is stupendous; among the latter, varieties of bamboo range from fern-like dwarfs to Chinese giants 60 feet tall. Chinese lotus grows on the lagoon of the Temple Garden, and the Sunken Fern Garden contains 80 varieties. But the most see-worthy spot of the Jungle Gardens is the southeast corner where Bird City is located. This is a great colony of the American egret or snowy heron, a rookery established in 1893. In those days egret plumes were in such demand for ladies' hats that plume hunters had practically exterminated the species. When, after a prolonged absence, Edward McIllhenny returned home, he found the beautiful birds extinct even on Avery Island. Taking along two young Negroes, he prowled through the swamps for days until he found seven young birds in a thicket. He took them to his Willow Pond, and they nested and multiplied. Around the edges of the lake he had "apartments" built of bamboo, perched on stilts; the egrets loved the convenience, and more than 150,000 live there now, in the country's largest colony. If you can, visit it in spring.

PILGRIMAGE CITY. "Why not let some less fortunate folks, even if they are Yankees, see the wonderful heritage we have here in our refined, old homes?" That was the convincing argument with which the Garden Club of Natchez persuaded the owners of the lovely old plantation houses to open their gates and display their treasures to the public, during the Natchez Pilgrimage each March. The year was 1931, the depression hitting the bottom, and many of the old estates were in a state of delapidation; so the idea of the Garden Club was gladly accepted as both idealistic and practical; the admission fees were to be used for the purpose of restoration and maintenance. The project turned out to be a great success, and today the Natchez Pilgrimage is almost a national institution. There you will not only see the actual settings of our southern novels, but ladies in ante-bellum hoop skirts will greet you at the door. Acres of azaleas are in bloom, a Confederate Ball is celebrated, and in tableaux crinolined southern belles with Dresden-china complexions accept the adoring smiles of dashing young officers of the Confederate Army. Every year in March, Natchez offers the most spectacular revival of an era in which slaves sang spirituals in the cotton fields, planters were colonels, young women had a romantic bend and at the drop of a pin men defended their honor on the dueling ground.

ROYAL SPLENDOR. The mansions which in Nat-

Dunleith, built in 1847, is a typical square plantation house with Greek Doric columns.

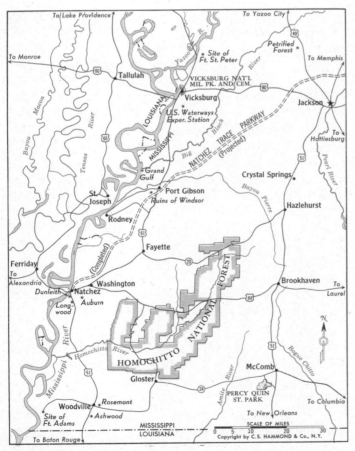

See sectional map, page 54

chez and surroundings were completed just before the War Between the States, are of a magnificence that is not matched by other southern cities with similar traditions, like New Orleans, Savannah or Charleston. Stanton Hall, for instance, has ceilings 22 feet high, mantles carved of Carrara marble, and huge doors of mahogany. Tall mirrors, bronze chandeliers and exquisite furniture were purchased in France and Spain, and a sailing vessel was chartered which brought the treasures across the Atlantic and up the Mississippi directly to the Natchez water front. On the other hand, the homes built before 1800 under the Spanish regime, like the Conti House on Wall Street, are of a simple, Latin character. Most homes take a middle course. Of the numerous showplaces only a few can be mentioned here: Rosalie, on the site of the Indian massacre of 1729 and Old Fort Rosalie, its living room furniture appropriately carved of rosewood; Buntura (private) with its lovely lace ironwork, erected by a wealthy Portuguese merchant; Greenleaves, the Elms, Arlington, Dunleith, and Auburn. Outside of Natchez to the south, Longwood is an unfinished monstrosity of oriental splendor; the eight-sided six-story structure was under construction when the War Between the States began; the workmen dropped their tools to join the army, and the house was never completed. If you cannot visit Natchez in March, come at any other time; quite a few houses are open the year round.

PLANTERS, GAMBLERS, RIVER PIRATES. On Jefferson Street the King's Tavern (the oldest house in the city) and Ellicott's Inn (also called Connelly's Tavern) are mementoes of another Natchez. That the town on the bluffs should have developed into one of the country's most refined and cultured centers of well-mannered and gracious living while below along the waterfront Natchez-Under-the-Hill carried on at its gaudiest and wickedest, seems an ironical coincidence. For many years during the flatboat and steamboat eras the lower town swarmed with flatboatmen and deckhands, Kentuckians and Acadians, Indians and half-breeds, highwaymen and river pirates, perfumed quadroons and gay women, imposters and gamblers. Bars and gambling houses did a booming business while flatboats were tied to the shore twelve or fourteen deep, for a two-mile stretch. Sailing vessels from Liverpool or Genoa docked at the wharf. But only part of the customers arrived on the river; even more men gallopped into town on horseback, their money belts bulging, their arms ready, the groups keeping close together to discourage holdups. For all flatboatmen sold their cargoes downstream together with the boat itself, and traveled back on the notorious Natchez Trace. King's and Connelly's Taverns both stand where that trail passed by.

HIGH BLUFFS ABOVE THE MISSISSIPPI. On the way north you will ride through the old plantation

Vicksburg Park commemorates the "Campaign, Siege and Defense of Vicksburg" in 1863.

country. Near Port Gibson, on a bluff overlooking the Mississippi, the spectacular ruins of Windsor stand out against the sky: 22 tall stone columns of Corinthian elegance, deserted, overgrown, a sad memorial. Seventy-one miles north of Natchez, the City of Vicksburg is a spot of great scenic beauty. Built on high bluffs that rise 200 feet above the river, it lies in a countryside of terraces, ravines, caves, and a tangled vegetation that is almost jungle-like. It's a lively commercial center, but looking down its busy, steep streets you'll have enchanting vistas of the broad Mississippi and the green lands beyond. The city's great moment in American history had been, of course, the siege and defense of the town in 1863, an event that is remembered in the Vicksburg National Military Park, organized "to preserve the history of the battles and operations on the ground where they were fought." The park of 1,324 acres is well laid out and marked, and the military leaders are honored in 3 equestrian statues, 19 memorials, and about 150 busts and relief portraits. Another interesting institution near Vicksburg is the U.S. Waterways Experiment Station, a hydraulic research laboratory investigating problems of drainage and flood control. Most interesting is a scale model of a 600-mile stretch of the Mississippi River, including all tributaries. The model is 1,055 feet long, and all natural conditions like the flow of water and the run-off from rainfall are authentically recreated.

Auburn, famous for its spiral staircase, is now owned by the city.

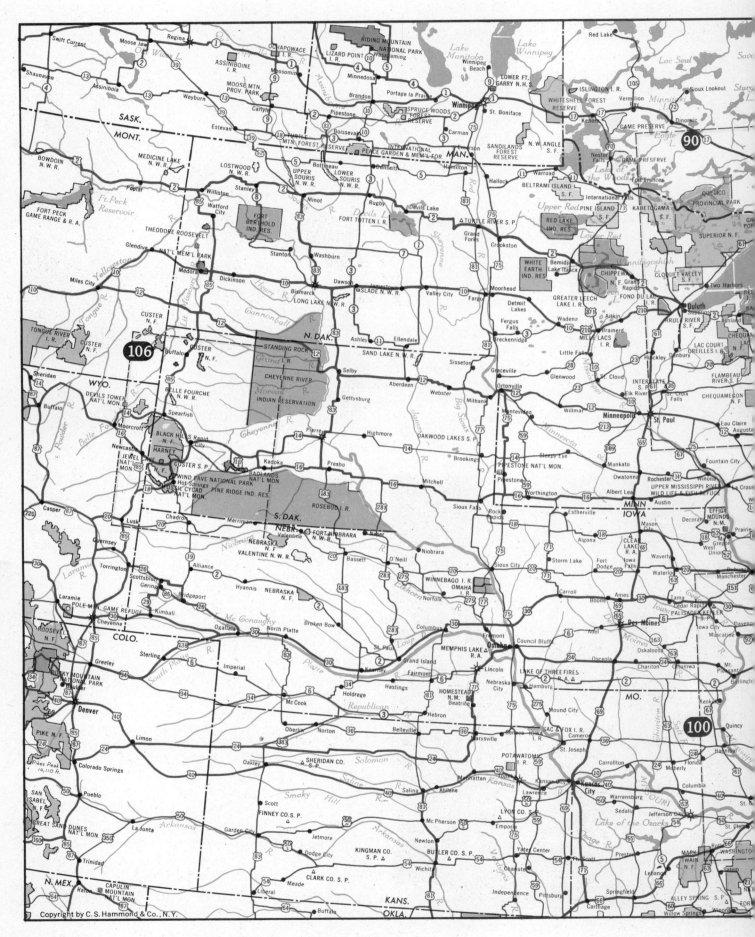

Copyright by C.S. Hammond & Co., N.Y.

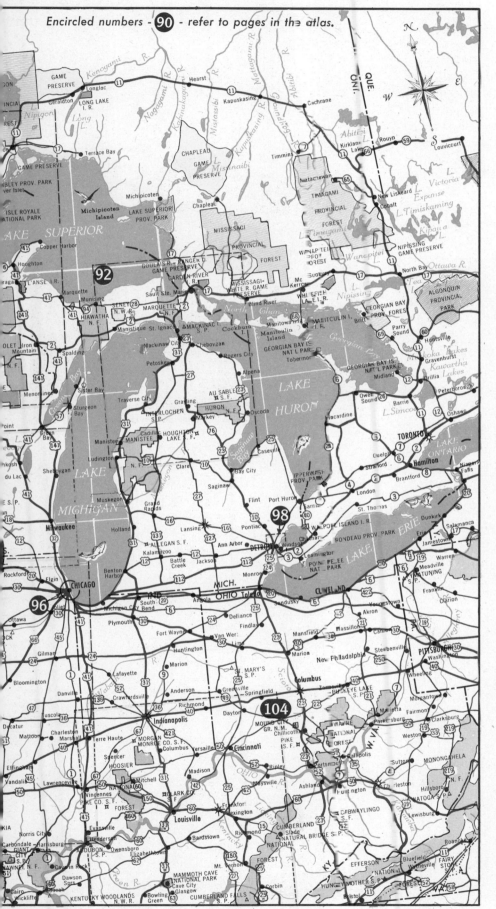

Encircled numbers - **90** - refer to pages in the atlas.

6-Day Trip Through the Bluegrass Country to Kentucky Lake. See pictures and map on pages 104 and 105, also the Sightseeing Gazetteer.—Suggested stops: Louisville, Ky., with Churchill Downs—Lexington with Bluegrass Country—Cumberland Falls State Park—Mammoth Cave National Park, with excursion to Lincoln's Birthplace near Hodgenville and Bardstown with "Old Kentucky Home"—Kentucky Lake—Louisville.—4 stops in 6 days allow for 2-day stopovers in the Bluegrass Country, Mammoth Cave National Park, Kentucky Lake, or elsewhere.

10-Day Trip Around Lake Michigan. See pictures and maps on pages 92 to 97, also the Sightseeing Gazetteer.—Suggested stops: Chicago, Ill.—Milwaukee, Wis.—Wisconsin Dells—St. Ignace, Mich., with Mackinac Island—Sault Sainte Marie with Soo Canal and Tahquamenon Falls—Traverse City resort area—Indiana Dunes State Park near Michigan City—Chicago.—6 stops in 10 days allow for 2-day stopovers at Wisconsin Dells, Mackinac Island, Traverse City or elsewhere.

7-Day Trip Along North Shore of Lake Superior. See pictures and map on pages 90 and 91, also the Sightseeing Gazetteer.—Suggested stops: Duluth, Minnesota—Grand Marais with Gun Flint Trail and canoe country—Fort William and Port Arthur—steamboat trip to Isle Royale National Park—Nipigon; Nipigon offers Kama Lookout, 18 miles away, with a magnificent panorama of island-studded Nipigon Bay, and Orient Bay, 28 miles north on Lake Nipigon, in wild north country with excellent fishing. Return to Duluth on the same North Shore Drive.—4 stops in 7 days allow for 2-day stopovers in Grand Marais, Isle Royale, Nipigon, or elsewhere.— If a different return route is desired, route 17 can be taken from Port Arthur to Kenora, then south to Fort Frances and International Falls. But the distance is great (456 miles).

5-Day Trip Through Northern Minnesota. See Sightseeing Gazetteer.—Suggested stops: Minneapolis — Bemidji with Paul Bunyan country — International Falls at Rainy Lake—Hibbing and the open pit iron mines of the Mesabi Range — Duluth — Minneapolis.

5-Day Trip Through the Black Hills of South Dakota. See pictures and map on pages 106 and 107, also the Sightseeing Gazetteer.—Suggested stops: Hot Springs with Wind Cave National Park—Sylvan Lake with Mt. Rushmore Memorial—Rapid City with excursion to Badlands—Deadwood with Homestead Mine at Lead—Spearfish with Passion Play and excursion to spectacular Devils Tower National Monument in Wyoming, 57 miles to the northwest.

BENJAMIN FRANKLIN'S ISLAND. Like a giant battleship at anchor, the rock Isle Royale stands firmly in Lake Superior, 44 miles long and up to 9 miles broad. That Isle Royale should belong to the United States although it lies much closer to Canada, is due to Ben Franklin's obstinate insistance, when negotiating the Treaty of Paris, that the island should be ours. His reasons were quite personal: He had carried out extensive experiments with electricity; he suspected that the new power would play an important part in the life of his country; he knew that copper was a good electric conductor, and he had heard of great copper treasures on Isle Royale. He had his way, and he was right about the future of electricity. The copper, however, turned out to be a matter of pre-history rather than actual wealth. Hundreds of primitive pits had been worked by ancient Indians who had separated the rock and the metal by alternately applying fire and water. But while the archeologists were intrigued, the miners who flocked there were disappointed; the island deposits could not compete with richer mines on the mainland. So, instead of becoming an industrial giant, Isle Royale has been turned into a National Park, which would suit well the public-spirited Mr. Franklin.

LAKE WITHIN LAKE, ISLAND WITHIN ISLAND. The shortest trip to Isle Royale is that from Port Arthur, Canada; on the American side it may be

Washington Harbor of Isle Royale, a park where boats are the only transportation.

reached from Eagle Harbor or Copper Harbor, Michigan, and Duluth, Minnesota. Cars have to be left at the mainland port, since nothing with wheels is allowed on the island, and all excursions are made by hiking or canoeing, or a combination of the two. Limited accommodations are available. Of all our national parks this is one of the wildest; its beauty is found in its groves of white birches and dark balsams, its wildflowers and mosses, its wooded hills and deep fjords, picturesque bays and excellent harbors, its myriads of small islands and reefs that surround the big "fortress," and its many lakes teeming with fish; in Lake Siskiwit, Ryan Island is "an island within an island." Among the fauna of Isle Royale the moose is its most spectacular inhabitant. During the winter of 1912 a small herd crossed over the 14 miles of ice from Canada and multiplied until they are now about 600 strong; since the food resources of the island are limited, considerable numbers have to be trapped and transplanted to the mainland.

A SCENIC HIGHWAY BY AN INLAND SEA. The road that crosses the map diagonally along the north shore of Lake Superior, No. 61, is to Midwesterners what the Maine coast is to New Englanders and highway 101 to Oregon. People unfamiliar with the territory, imagine it to be low and flat. That is, however, not the case. Port Arthur and Fort William, the two modern Canadian ports, are built at an altitude of over 600 feet, and at

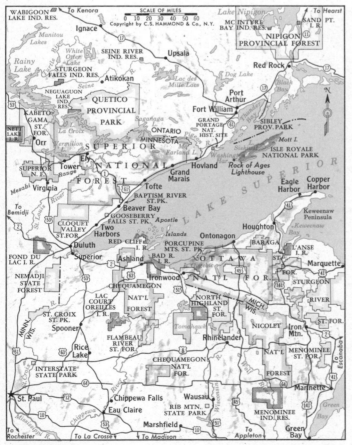

See sectional map, page 88

90

A Corner of Virgin America

the International Border the highway even climbs to a height of 900 feet. The boundary is a strikingly beautiful spot: The International Bridge spans a deep canyon through which the white water of the Pigeon River rushes over the rapids. The river was named for the thousands of passenger pigeons that used to visit this valley before they were exterminated. Five miles to the south, the Grand Portage Trail Crossing was traveled by voyageurs and fur traders 200 years ago, and for centuries by the Indians; it crosses the highway. At Grand Marais don't miss the Forest Lookout Tower, on the rose-colored rocks of a point shaped like an arrow, near the fine harbor. Along the highway there are several attractive parks, for instance, Gooseberry Falls State Park; and don't forget to sample the culinary specialty of the region, excellent smoked fish.

THE UNTOUCHED WILDERNESS. To the west of the North Shore Highway, Superior National Forest together with the adjacent Quetico Provincial Park of Canada is one of America's great wilderness areas, of picturesque forests (virgin toward the north), 5,000 lakes ranging from little ponds to a size of 70 square miles, crystal-clear, cold streams and tumbling rapids, of soft grass and countless wildflowers, and the clean smell of pines. Within the National Forest there is a large "primitive area" without roads, electric wires, telephone, telegraph; not even planes are allowed to fly over it so

Superior National Forest contains 5,000 lakes, and many more are in adjacent areas.

as not to disturb the game in the virgin timber. In a way this country is more "untouched" now than 200 years ago when the fur traders blazed the portages from lake to lake, and the Hudson's Bay Company and the Northwest Company struggled ruthlessly for supremacy. Today it's a peaceful heaven for fishermen, and the only way to enjoy it is by canoe. Such canoe trips may start from Tofte, Grand Marais or Hovland on the North Shore Highway, or from Tower or Ely (a town with an interesting frontier atmosphere) in the western part of the forest, and have to be carefully prepared in advance. Maps and detailed information may be secured from the Federal and State Forest Service in Duluth, and the Chamber of Commerce and Minnesota Arrowhead Association in Duluth. The range of possibilities is wide; you may choose a one-day trip from Ely, with 13 miles of paddling and 4 miles of portaging, or take a 17-day trip with 235 miles of paddling and 9 miles of portaging, starting at McFarland Lake, in the so-called Gunflint Area, to be reached from Grand Marais, and following the International Boundary Route. Lake scenery and portages around rapids and water falls are picturesque, the currents are varied, and the fishing is fine. While crossing Lac La Croix you will view the Painted Rocks where ancient Sioux or Algonquin artists painted a number of pictures in reddish ocher, representing such varied objects as hands and bear paws, a moose and a goat.

Rock of Ages Lighthouse is built on one of many reefs that surround the island.

REEN TURTLE AND RED-PLUMED HORSES. The state ferry which connects the lower with the upper peninsula of Michigan is jammed with automobiles, but the island to the east of the ferry route is strictly car-less. It can be reached only by small steamer, either from Mackinaw City or St. Ignace. Rising from the blue waters between Lake Michigan and Lake Huron, with its gently curved green hills, it looks like a great turtle; that's what the Indian name Michilimackinac, abbreviated to Mackinac, means. Upon arrival at the harbor which resembles the small British towns of Bermuda, you will find a long line of horse-drawn carriages waiting to take the visitors on an all-island excursion. Or you may board the Victorian hotel bus whose coachman wears a splendid red jacket and whose horses balance their red plumes above arched necks. Of course, such colorful trappings smack of the circus, but never fail to evoke pleasant smiles on the riders' faces. The Grand Hotel, once presided over by Cornelius Vanderbilt, is one of America's famous hostelries. From its white-columned porch—"the longest hotel porch in the world"—an enchanting vista encompasses the bright town, the busy harbor, and the wide waters of the inland sea. Since the island is free of polluted waters, swamps, mosquitoes, and hay-fever-producing pollens, it is an ideal resort; add to that a wonderful climate, fragrant woods, flowering gardens, white beaches, superb views

Mackinac Island, once the scene of battles, is a placid, beautiful resort now.

which in places have a Mediterranean character, and such attractions as the Old Fort, Arch Rock and Chimney Rock, Devil's Kitchen and Scott's Cave.

A DAREDEVIL PRANK AND A FUR EMPIRE. The island was discovered in 1634 by Jean Nicolet on his search for China, and passed from French to British to American hands. In the War of 1812 the British reconquered it, and the two American warships Tigress and Scorpion were charged with blockading the island and forcing its surrender by cutting off the food supply. But one dark and blustery night 70 British soldiers rowed stealthily to the Scorpion, boarded the ship with scaling ladders in a surprise attack, and overpowered the crew. Then they sailed around the island, the American flag still flying, and approached the Tigress which was unaware of what had happened. A few well-aimed cannon shots demolished the second American warship, and the blockade was ended. When, after the conclusion of the war, Mackinac Island returned to the U.S., John Jacob Astor set up shop there, with his 2000 voyageurs and 400 clerks. For the island was a convenient "bottleneck" through which most of the north-western fur trade had to pass. Those were Mackinac's hey-days when wigwams and tepees lined the beach three rows deep, swarming with 3000 Indians; when millions of pelts were dried, beaten, sorted, counted and repacked there, and the nights resounded with drunken revelry. By the middle

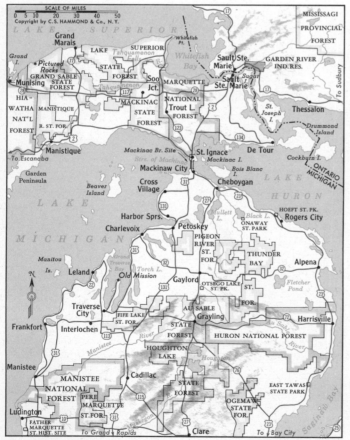

See sectional map, page 88

of the century the fur trade collapsed, and after the Civil War the summer guests and tourists moved in.

SOO CANAL = PANAMA + SUEZ + KIEL CANALS. From the ferry and fishing town of St. Ignace whose Indian Village is patterned after the Indian encampment found there by the French explorers in the 17th century, you proceed northward to Sault Ste. Marie. This colorful city was once described by Henry Clay as the remotest in the country, "if not in the moon." Yet it is the third-oldest surviving community in the U.S., founded in 1618. It is a great hunting and fishing town; but to the summer visitor the federal Ste. Mary's Locks, also called the Soo Canal, are the most fascinating attraction. The difference in level between Lake Superior and Lake Huron is about 19 feet, and the connecting rapids, the Sault Ste. Marie proper, can be seen beside the locks, although the locks and the power plant have greatly diminished the volume of the falls. The spectacle here is interesting for more than one reason: it gives you a close-up view of the long, big ore ships that dot the horizons of the Great Lakes as symbols of the steel age; they are steered into the locks on the Superior side, the gates close, the water level and the ship sink slowly to the Huron level, the opposite gates open, and the steamer glides out quietly. Even more interesting is the ease and efficiency with which the operation is performed; no tolls are levied, no inspectors board the boat,

This is the land of Longfellow's Hiawatha, cedar groves and birch bark canoes.

no forms are filled; but the purser receives the boat's mail, and the crew members exchange greetings and news with visiting friends, sweethearts, and relatives ashore. All over the locks curious tourists are swarming and watching, at a spot which in Europe almost certainly would be labeled strategic and "verboten" to the public. It's a very American sight. The procession of ships is continuous and the Soo Canal handles more freight than the world's next three canals, the Panama, Suez and Kiel canals, combined.

CASCADES IN THE NORTHWOODS. To the west of Sault Ste. Marie an excursion to the Tahquamenon Falls will prove a typical Northwoods experience. The upper falls can be visited by taking a side road from highway 28 to Soo Junction. There a narrow-gauge railway proceeds for five miles to the Tahquamenon River from where an excursion boat rides on to the upper falls, past fragrant cedar groves, and between 100-feet-high cliffs, along the bank where Longfellow's Hiawatha built his birch bark canoe. At the boat landing the low thunder of the falls can be heard, and a 3/4-of-a-mile trail leads both to the brink of the cascades and the bottom of the gorge. The lower falls may be reached by taking highway 123 to the mouth of the Tahquamenon River. From there a boat carries visitors over the 18-mile course up the river to the beautiful lower cascades which drop 43 feet in three terraces.

The Soo Locks, busiest in the world, offer a close-up view of the big ore ships.

INTER-LAKE ISTHMUS. Life Magazine once conducted an informal poll to determine the American city most pleasant to live in. Considering human tastes and individual values, the question could not be answered, but the city that came closest to winning a prize was Madison, Wisconsin. Visitors will easily discover the reasons. From wherever they approach, the first sight will be the conventional but stately state capitol which stands in the heart of the community on a hill; its public roofwalk offers a fine orientation view. From the capitol the open half-mile of State Street leads to another hill where the university stands. These two landmarks, the capitol and the university, are the two poles that create a lively intellectual and cultural life; their close and continuous collaboration has won national acclaim as "The Wisconsin Idea." Physically, the setting is equally attractive: The modern, tree-lined city is surrounded by three beautiful lakes with the musical names of Monona, Mendota, and Wingra. The seasons are very pronounced: During the summer the gardens sparkle with flowers, and the wooded bluffs and parks, the beaches and boathouses are alive with young people. Mendota's blue waters are dotted with white sails and red canoes. In the fall, when the leaves turn scarlet and yellow, and pumpkins and apple cider dominate the countryside, the football stadium of the university is the scene of excitement and holiday en-

The dome of the State Capitol looms high above city and countryside.

thusiasm. During the winter graceful iceboats swoop over the frozen lakes, tobogganers enjoy the campus slide, and students take off from the ski-jump, training for championships. The combination of legislative-political activity and scholarly academic work, together with the facilities of an all-year pleasure resort give Madison a special place among the cities of America. Ironically, the early settlers of Wisconsin considered the site "beautiful but uninhabitable," and it took a land speculator to sell to the legislators this isthmus wilderness.

MOUNDS AND ARROWHEADS. From Madison northward, highway No. 12 is a popular excursion route. Sauk City, once America's "Freethinkers' Heaven," may look like other midwestern towns, but it is an historic spot; for on Sauk Prairie the Great Town of the Saukie Indians was located, one of the most remarkable achievements of native Indian culture. The settlement consisted of about ninety houses, each sheltering several families. Jonathan Carver who traveled there in the 18th century, wrote of these homes that they were "built of hewn plank neatly jointed, and covered with bark so compactly as to keep out the most penetrating rains. Before the doors are placed comfortable sheds in which the inhabitants sit—and smoak their pipes—They raise great quantities of Indian corn, beans, melons, etc., so that this place is esteemed the best market

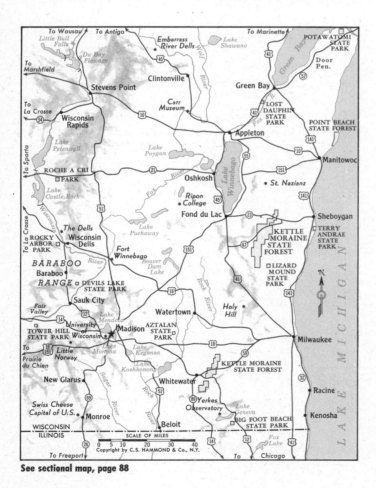

See sectional map, page 88

for traders—within 800 miles." In 1832 the Indians fought their last real battle with the whites and were, of course, defeated. One hill that comes to a sharp point, is still called Black Hawk Lookout, and country boys find arrowheads in the pastures. Indian mounds are also encountered in this region, particularly to the north in Devil's Lake State Park. It is a spectacular spot: The clear, cool oval of the lake has a horseshoe setting of cliffs that tower four to five hundred feet above its surface. There are tumbled piles of rocks, pot holes, glacial scratches and petrified sand waves, and the reddish and purple colors of the stone are set off by the deep green of the pines. The lake is a frequent goal of the field trips of geology students.

SCROLLS AND FLUTED COLUMNS. You are now approaching the stretch of the Wisconsin River where, according to a legend of the Winnebago Indians, a giant serpent smashed its way southward, battering and crushing the rocks on both sides and leaving them torn and broken in fantastic shapes. Driving toward the "scene of the serpent," today called the Wisconsin Dells, you will notice road signs that introduce the coming attraction as something like the 8th wonder of the world. That it is not, but it will be worth your while to visit the Dells, to look around from the bridge that divides the Upper from the Lower Dells, and to take boat excursions to each one of these two sectors. What

More than 8,500 counted lakes invite canoeing, sailing, and swimming.

you will see on your trips are a river channel carved deeply into solid sandstone; yellow ledges crowned with tufts of green bushes; narrow flumes with steep rocky walls from whose crevices flowers, ferns and vines protrude decoratively; beautiful rock islands; fantastic columns and seemingly sculptured rock formations, with names often employed for this type of scenery, like Fat Man's Misery, Sugar Bowl, Cave of the Dark Waters, Arrow Head; and a varied collection of gaily painted craft (the other sightseeing boats), many of them with an Indian in full regalia as guide. The town of Wisconsin Dells, called Kilbourn before 1931, is teeming with tourists during the summer months.

"A GATHERING OF WATERS." This is the meaning of the Indian word Wisconsin, and it expresses the pleasant fact that the modern seeker of recreation can find water sports in many parts of the state. Besides the 500 miles of Great Lakes shore, there are more than 8,500 counted lakes in Wisconsin, the largest being Lake Winnebago, with a surface of 215 square miles, and the most fashionable the spring-fed Lake Geneva. The latter is surrounded by large estates on wooded hills, and a fishing ground for bass, pike and cisco. At Williams Bay, near the summer resort city of Lake Geneva, the Yerkes Observatory of the University of Chicago is located. The lake resort area of northern Wisconsin is described in the Sightseeing Gazetteer, see page 208.

The fantastic rock formations of the Dells are carved by the Wisconsin River.

95

THE CENTER. Chicago's statistics are astonishing: In four generations it assembled 4,000,000 inhabitants, grew into the nation's biggest grain and livestock market, became the country's railroad center (1500 passenger trains arrive daily, and more freights than can be counted), and developed into the world's Number One convention town. It reversed the Chicago River so that its current would no longer flow into Lake Michigan but, eventually, into the Gulf of Mexico. It built scores of skyscrapers on huge, "floating" platforms of concrete because its soil was "unsuitable" for skyscraper construction. Are these reasons why any tourist should visit Chicago? They are, especially since there is an unmatched spirit of vitality behind the material phenomena. How else could it happen that 400 novels have been written about Chicago, and innumerable non-fiction pieces, that great minds like Dreiser, Hemingway, Anderson, and Cather expressed their fascination, and that Sandburg heard the young city "laughing the stormy, husky, brawling laughter of youth," and described it as "proud to be Hog Butcher, Tool Maker, Stacker of Wheat, Player with Railroads and Freight Handler to the Nation."

A BIRD'S EYE VIEW. Metropolitan cities are always a little overwhelming to the casual tourist, but it is easy enough to get acquainted with Chicago. The 25-mile-long lakefront is the town's splendid reception hall—

a multiple row of skyscrapers in a setting of green parks, white beaches, and ruffled blue waters. In the lakefront's center the Loop is the principal business district. South of it, the so-called South Side has features that are admirable (miles of cool, sandy beaches, tree-lined residential sections, lovely parks, outstanding museums, the University of Chicago, Comiskey Park and the White Sox) and others that are not so pleasant (the Negro slums, the stockyards, the sooty steel mills). North of the Loop, across the Chicago River, the North Side boasts of Chicago's swanky Oak Street Beach, the legendary Gold Coast, a group of great hotels, Lincoln Park and Wrigley Field and the Chicago Cubs. Everything that does not belong to the Loop, the South Side and the North Side, is called the West Side, the jungle of factories and the agglomeration of foreign sections.

THE MAGNIFICENT MILE. Michigan Avenue, the skyscraper-studded boulevard by the lake, is one of the world's famous streets, and Chicago's best-known. It has been compared with New York's Fifth Avenue because of its cosmopolitan glamour, or with Paris's Champs Elysees because of its monumental layout or with the waterfront of Rio de Janeiro because of its beach-park-skyline combination. Yet its setting—the quiet park-fringed lake on one side, and the noisy Loop with its steel ribbons of elevated tracks on the other—is truly Chicago. The stretch north of the Chicago River, running from the Wrigley Building of chewing gum fame to the elegant Drake Hotel, is the so-called "Magnificent Mile" although it actually comprises only three quarters of a mile. Its landmarks are the Palmolive Building and the old "Gothic" Water Tower which survived the great fire of 1871 and the attacks of architects who called it an eyesore; the Water Tower, by the way, is the only Chicago building supposedly plagued by ghosts; they are of the noisy, good-natured kind, so-called poltergeists; finally there is the Tribune Tower, home of the outspoken Chicago Tribune which calls itself "The World's Greatest Newspaper." Farther south, beyond the Public Library, the Chicago Art Institute is, on the outside, an Italian Renaissance palace; inside, it contains one of the nation's greatest art collections, predominantly classical and cautiously modern. Across the street there is the home of the Chicago Symphony Orchestra, and beyond that the world's largest hotel, the Conrad Hilton (every day 3,000 rooms to clean, 300,000 dishes to wash) is a marvel of organization. Finally Michigan Avenue runs near the campus of the University of Chicago, "the Harvard of the Midwest." Opposite the southern stretch of the avenue Grant Park is the sight-seer's happy hunting ground. Buckingham Fountain and the band shell will attract him at concert nights; Soldier Field has been the scene of great sports events; and the Field Museum of Natural History, the Shedd Aquarium and the Adler Planetarium are leading scientific institutions.

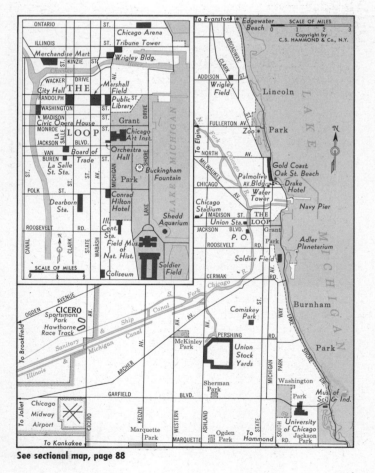

See sectional map, page 88

The 25-mile-long lakefront is Chicago's splendid reception hall—a row of skyscrapers in a colorful setting of green parks, white beaches, and ruffled blue waters. This is the fashionable Oak Street Beach.

THE CENTER'S CENTER: THE LOOP. The name "Loop" dates back to the 1890's when it was the section _____ by the cable cars. Today it is, in a narrower ___ f the city which is circled by the ele- ___ in a wider sense, the whole central ___ , "Downtown Chicago." Crowds are ___ d busy in this "nerve center of the ___ There is a challenge in the air also ___ you want to watch the world's busiest ___ d it at the crossing of the two principal ___ the Loop, State and Madison Streets. ___ s one of the nation's best-known de- ___ and a Chicago landmark. If you are

interested in economics, you may walk through La Salle Street, Chicago's Wall Street, to the Board of Trade. To watch the trading at the grain pit on a day of oscillating prices is a unique experience. What does the excited crowding and shouting mean, the waving of arms, the poking of fingers? It means that here the grain of the nation is sold and bought at auction, in split-second decisions often expressed in gestures only, and always carried out honestly. Beyond the northwestern corner of the Loop in the near North Side the Merchandise Mart is the greatest commercial building in the world, a monolith by the river bank; it claims to be big enough to hold the whole population of Chicago.

CADILLAC AND THE HAIR BUYER OF DETROIT.

Since one of America's luxury cars honors the name of the city's founder, the Sieur de la Mothe Cadillac, we are tempted to imagine Detroit's father as an aristocrat of the purest blood. That he was indeed, but in contrast to his swash-buckling grand-seigneur ways, his new town remained a poor and struggling frontier outpost for many years. When it became British, after the French and Indian War, Detroit acquired a horrible reputation. Its Governor Hudson incited the Indians against the American revolutionary patriots and paid the redskins a handsome reward when they brought him a scalp, but nothing when they brought him a prisoner. The American fighters called him "The Hair Buyer of Detroit." Even after the Revolution had succeeded it took years of negotiations and the Battle of Fallen Timbers to pry the British from Detroit. After that the frontier moved westward, to the prairies, the Rockies, the Pacific Coast. By the end of the century the most dynamic aspect of the young nation, the frontier, had vanished. Or so it seemed. But about that time America discovered that new frontiers were not merely geographical concepts but could be opened, even more promisingly, in other dimensions. The place which made this discovery first was Detroit.

REMAKING THE WAYS OF THE WORLD.
Detroit had grown slowly after the expulsion of the British, and

Greenfield Village, the Wright Brothers' Shop, where the first airplane was built.

LEGEND
① Art Institute
② Public Library
③ Wayne Univ.
④ Briggs Stadium
⑤ Fisher Bldg.
⑥ Lawrence Tech
⑦ Ford Rotunda

See sectional map, page 88

had become a fine provincial city of shade trees and Victorian mansions. Then suddenly, at the turn of the century, "beautiful Detroit" turned into "dynamic Detroit." For at that time a number of men like Ford, Durant, Buick, Olds, and the Fisher Brothers decided that Detroit was the ideal location for manufacturing the new-fangled automobile. The new movement had all the earmarks of a frontier boom. The leaders became millionaires quickly. The Ford Company was organized in 1903, and in 1908 the stockholders realized a profit on their investment that amounted to ten thousand per cent. It seemed a veritable Comstock Lode. And just like a western mining town Detroit became a giant magnet to draw men from all the neighboring states; from the Old World more Poles and Ukranians flocked there than lived in some of the large cities of Poland or the Ukraine, and tens of thousands of Germans, Italians and Hungarians, Greeks and Syrians. Almost all of them worked on the automobile which was not invented at Detroit but was mass-produced there for the first time, so that it could be sold cheaply all over the country; it remade the American way of life, and ultimately the life of the world.

TECHNOLOGICAL SIGHTSEEING.
The city grew so late and so suddenly that it did not acquire the quaintness of New Orleans which is 16 years younger, or the glamor of Chicago which is a hundred years younger. Consequently the most interesting sightseeing in Detroit

is of the technological kind. It shows how our automobiles are made, both actually and historically. Just name the make of car you are interested in—Chrysler, Hudson, Cadillac, Lincoln, De Soto, Packard, others—and you are welcome to inspect their plant. Guided tours for visitors are arranged every weekday at frequent intervals. Best-known is probably the tour of the Ford River Rouge Plant in Dearborn which starts at the Ford Rotunda, and offers a glance into a sequence of superbly planned manufacturing operations. Also in Dearborn are the Edison Institute and Greenfield Village, both educational enterprises of the Ford Company. The Edison Institute presents the history of agricultural implements of manufacturing and transportation, from wooden plows and hand looms to the latest inventions; of particular interest is, of course, the development of the automobile, as illustrated in a collection of actual models. Greenfield Village shows a good many of the places where this progress was achieved, like Thomas Edison's laboratory of Menlo Park, N. J., where the electric lamp was invented, the cabin of George Washington Carver, the great Negro scientist, the office of Luther Burbank, the genius in plant breeding, and the schoolhouse of McGuffey who wrote the first truly American schoolbooks. But there is also a copy of a 16th century cottage from the Cotswold Hills in England, Sir John Bennet's Jewelry Shop in London, a Cape Cod windmill, and many other structures, either in the recon-

The Cranbrook Foundation maintains various schools, among them the Academy of Art.

structed originals or in replicas. Among the non-technical sights of Greater Detroit the Art Center on Woodward Avenue, with the Institute of Arts on one side of the street and the Public Library on the other, is a cultural achievement. Belle Isle Park, about half a mile offshore in the Detroit River, is the city's recreation center, with 20 miles of driveways, swimming beach, a symphony shell (for summer concerts and folk dances by Detroit's racial groups), an aquarium, and other attractions. Twenty miles north of Detroit, Cranbrook is an artistic oasis, an endowed campus of schools and institutes, largely designed by Eliel Saarinen, of which the Academy of Arts has won wide recognition.

"OLD COON'S WOLF STEAKS." Besides remaking the world, Greater Detroit claims also the achievement of nick-naming the State of Michigan. In Dearborn, opposite the entrance to the Ford estate, a popular old inn was located which belonged to Conrad Ten Eyck, commonly called "Old Coon." His steaks were famous, and he himself kidded his guests by forever praising his "wolf steaks." Once a pretty Michigan girl approached the landlord after dinner, looked straight into his eyes, and inquired: "Have I really eaten wolf steak?" Seriously he replied: "Of course, you have." "Well," she said, "then I am a wolverine now.' All the guests laughed and the word was passed on along the highways and byways; ever since then Michigan has been the Wolverine State.

In the Detroit Zoological Park wild animals are confined by moats.

A 12-ROOM HOUSE OF OAK AND WALNUT, WORTH $2,800. In April, 1837, Lincoln arrived in Springfield on the back of a borrowed horse, with all his earthly possessions in two saddlebags. After 28 years of backwoods life the bustling state capital bewildered him, and progress in his new environment was slow. Even when he married Mary Todd in 1842, he was still so poor that the newlyweds lived at the Globe Tavern, at four dollars a week. But, in 1844, his practice and income increased, and at 8th and Jackson Streets a story-and-a-half frame house was purchased for $1,500. Twelve years later, while Lincoln was traveling on the circuit, his wife had a second story added, in the same solid oak and walnut construction, at a cost of $1,300,— so that their home had now 12 rooms. For a total expenditure of $2,800 the Lincolns had a fine sturdy house, —the same structure that thousands of visitors inspect today. It has survived well indeed, and would be a desirable residence even now. The interior arrangements and the furniture are the same as they were during the nearly 17 years when the Lincoln family lived there, when the master of the house sat by the fireplace, reading, or rested on the couch made extra long for his size, and when the Republican Notification Committee was received in the large double parlor.

MARBLE SHAFT ABOVE THE TREES. Four years and two months after the great native son had gone to

For nearly 17 years the Lincoln Family lived in here, the only house Lincoln ever owned.

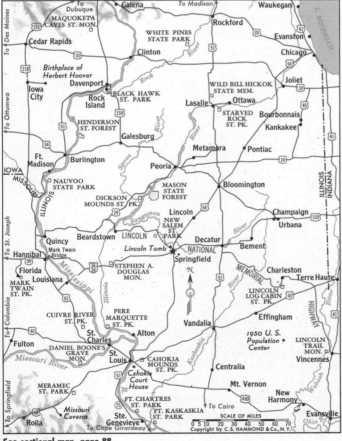

See sectional map, page 88

the White House, he returned, and tens of thousands sadly watched the arrival of the funeral train. 75,000 mourners passed by his bier at the Old State House. On his tomb a white marble shaft was erected; it rises brightly above the green, wooded hills of Illinois. The city of Springfield considers itself Abraham Lincoln's home town; street signs lead the visitor to the various Lincoln memorials, a huge collection of Lincolniana has been assembled in the Illinois Centennial Building, and the Abraham Lincoln Association which has just published the definitive edition of his writings, in many volumes, has its headquarters in town.

THE VILLAGE THAT VANISHED—LUCKILY. Twenty miles northwest of Springfield, the Lincoln village of New Salem has been reconstructed in a state park. On a ridge by the Sangamon River there stand again the log cabins with their primitive pioneer furniture, the country stores with their wares and the little mills and factories with their simple machinery. The cooper shop is original while the others are reconstructions, but the work has been done with scientific accuracy and the village gives an excellent picture of the country's way of life when young Lincoln tried storekeeping here, worked as surveyor and postmaster, was elected to the Illinois state legislature, studied law, and had his sad romance with Ann Rutledge, the innkeeper's daughter. After Lincoln had left New Salem, it went into a rapid decline, became a deserted ghost town, and vanished in the returning growth of the wilderness. Had it prospered, streets, squares and stone buildings would now obliterate the original site; as it happened, it was possible to find the old foundations on the abandoned ridge, and the village of young Lincoln could be reconstructed authentically.

TOM SAWYER'S FENCE. A little over a hundred miles west of Springfield across the Mississippi River, there is Hannibal, Missouri, Mark Twain's boyhood town. He gave a good-natured, amusing picture of it—"the streets empty—one or two clerks sitting in front of the Water Street stores—chins on breasts, hats slouched over their faces, asleep—a sow and a litter of pigs loafing along the sidewalk—a pile of 'skids' on the slope of the stone-paved wharf, and the fragrant town drunkard asleep in the shadow of them"— Then suddenly, "a Negro drayman, famous for his quick eye and prodigious voice lifts up the cry 'S-t-e-a-m-b-o-a-t a-comin!' and the scene changes. The town drunkard stirs, the clerks wake up, a furious clatter of drays follows,—and all in a twinkling the dead town is alive and moving. Drays, carts, men, boys, all go hurrying—to a common center, the wharf. Assembled there, the people fasten their eyes upon the coming boat as upon a wonder they are seeing for the first time And the boat is rather a handsome sight, too. She is long and sharp and trim—." Since then Hannibal has changed, of

To the boy across the street the Thatcher House seemed the essence of elegance.

course, but the neat little house that served Sam Clemens as headquarters for his explorations of the Mississippi country is still there, with the white-washed Tom Sawyer fence on one side, and a museum of Mark Twain memorabilia on the other. The furnishings of the house are not those of the Clemens family but they are early 19th century pieces from Hannibal and have a genuine look. Across the street, the Becky Thatcher House is now the home of a good restaurant and an excellent book shop; upstairs the rooms of the Hawkins family, the prototype of Mark Twain's Thatchers, are restored with all their crystal-and-mahogany magnificence. Even Becky's blue silk dress is still there, and her soft, long, white lisle stockings lie on the chair. It is easy to see here why Becky-Thatcher-Laura-Hawkins with her out-of-this-world elegance charmed the barefoot boy across the street. At the foot of Cardiff (now Holliday) Hill where in "Tom Sawyer" the Widow Douglas kept a lamp in the window at night, as a miniature lighthouse for the river steamers, here is a life-size double statue now of Tom Sawyer and Huckleberry Finn. Presumably that is the only monument in the Americas in which two fictional characters are honored. The Mark Twain Bridge which crosses the river, is new and paddle wheelers hardly ever call at Hannibal any more. But the banks of the Mississippi are as green and lonely with silent little bays and coves as they used to be, and small lads still splash in the river on hot summer days.

Mark Twain, from his third year on, lived in Hannibal in this neat, small house.

101

A METROPOLIS FOUNDED BY A 13-YEAR-OLD BOY. St. Louis is not a replica of Chicago or any other midwestern city. It is different, and therefore worth seeing and visiting. All typical representatives of our inland civilization are boosters. But not St. Louis. It does not care whether it takes the 7th or 6th place among America's cities. In fact, it once was our 4th, and now is our 8th largest metropolis, and is not at all excited about it. For in contrast to its great midwestern rivals it has a fascinating and important history of its own, and its own long traditions even in such esoteric fields as symphonic music and philosophy. Therefore St. Louis has the mental security and social poise of a "grande dame"; calm self-assurance is in the air; you can feel it. The very founding of the city avoided the commonplace. No heavily armed captain-generals, as in the south, or farmer-pioneers, as in the north, settled it; well-to-do cosmopolitan business men took the step. The great mercantile house of Maxent, Laclede & Co. of New Orleans acquired the fur trade monopoly in the Missouri Valley and sent a junior partner north into the wilderness. On this expedition his stepson, in temporary command, had the forest cleared at a certain spot south of the mouth of the Missouri, on February 14, 1764, and supervised the erection of a trading post which grew into the present metropolis of St. Louis. The boy's name was Auguste Chouteau. He was thirteen years old.

Mississippi Boat, Modern Style.

WESTERN SQUAW, SOUTHERN BELLE, GERMAN FRAU. During the decades that followed St. Louis became the brain and nerve center for conquering and civilizing the West. Financed and planned by its fur merchants, all western expeditions left from here, and under its guidance the trappers, *voyageurs* and *coureurs de bois* opened the trails into the great *terra incognita* beyond the wide Missouri. At that time St. Louis—to use the words of Hamilton Basso—"frolicked away the nights with wild, reckless men who had drunk from the headwaters of the Yellowstone, fought Shawnees and Blackfeet, and been lost in the snow of the Wind River Mountains." . . . Later, when the beavers were almost exterminated, the Astors and most others got out of the fur trade; but St. Louis stuck to it; it is still America's leading fur center. In the 19th century the French founders were joined by Americans, many of them from the southern states. The latter injected style and manners into the frontier community and harmonized well with the old French-Creole families. One of their joint contributions to present-day St. Louis lives on in the annual Veiled Prophet Ball and Parade, held each October, with its colorful costumes and imaginative floats a counterpart to New Orleans' Mardi Gras. Finally, from the 1830's on, there was a great German migration to St. Louis, an event which established *gemütlichkeit*, beer gardens, and Anheuser-Busch as landmarks of the town.

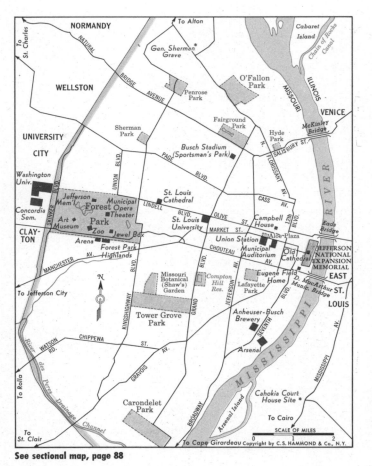

See sectional map, page 88

102

The "Dowager Queen" of the Mississippi

Of the beer gardens few have survived, but Anheuser-Busch is the world's largest brewery; it is open to visitors. Most of the German refugees of 1848 were intellectuals and liberals, and helped to found and lead the St. Louis Movement of Philosophy. For a quarter of a century this merchant's town was a world center of philosophic thought. Politically the Germans kept the city on the Union side, and its famous German leader Carl Schurz, who became U.S. Senator from Missouri, campaigned under the slogan "Right or wrong, my country. If right, to stay right; if wrong, to be set right." Also St. Louis' love of music is largely a German trait. The country's second symphony orchestra was founded there in 1880, and is outstanding today. Music outdoors—always a favorite pastime for summer evenings in Germany—is practiced on a grand scale. The Municipal Opera offers open-air performances, in Forest Park, to hundreds of thousands of residents and visitors.

OLD CATHEDRAL, NEW FOUNTAIN. Although St. Louis is not a sightseeing town in the sense of New Orleans or San Francisco, there is much of interest to the traveler. The Old Cathedral of St. Louis of France, for instance, dedicated to the city's patron saint, is erected on the exact spot (on the north side of Walnut Street) where in 1764 the first mass was celebrated, in the presence of the city's boy founder. Soon afterwards, a log cabin church was built there, and in the early 1830's the

Old Cathedral of St. Louis of France stands where the city's first mass was held.

Mississippi Boat, Old Style.

present limestone structure was erected. In keeping with the genesis of St. Louis, its inscriptions are chiseled into the stone in three languages, in French, Latin and English. Three very old religious paintings are a royal gift from France, and one of its church bells has a curious story: A Spanish soldier and landholder, Benito Vasquez, had the bell cast, as his present to the church; in order to sweeten the bell's sound, he provided 200 Spanish silver dollars which were melted into the bronze. Among the new sightseeing attractions Aloe Plaza presents one of our continent's famous sculptures, the Meeting of the Waters by Carl Milles. It symbolizes St. Louis' *raison d'être*, the confluence of the Missouri and the Mississippi: A young woman touching up her hair (the Missouri River) is eagerly approached by a young man (the Mississippi River) who in a friendly welcome stretches out his hand, offering a flower. They are surrounded by a dozen other bronze figures, sea creatures which spout water high into the air.

FAUNA AND FLORA IN THE ZOO AND AT SHAW'S. The Zoo of St. Louis is not unusually large, but no visitor to the city should miss it. It's chimpanzee act is sparkling and wonderful, and rightly famous. Shaw's Garden, which is the Missouri Botanical Garden, has splendid displays of lilies, iris, chrysanthemums, orchids and camellias. It is modeled after Kew Gardens of London.

PETER DIRT" AND ECHO RIVER. In the early days of our republic, America's two great scenic attractions were the Niagara Falls of New York and the Mammoth Cave of Kentucky. The latter seemed a bit out of reach, but by stagecoach and on horseback visitors from the Eastern Seaboard and even Europe found their way to the cavern and marveled at its stalactites and stalagmites. During the War of 1812 the cave became a major armament plant; "peter dirt" (as they called saltpeter in those days was gathered there; with the help of oxen and carts, pumps and vats, one of the essential raw materials for gun powder production was prepared, all underground, and then shipped to Philadelphia by wagon train. After the war the factory became a showplace again, with a long roster of famous visitors. In the so-called amphitheater the great actor Edwin Booth recited Hamlet on a stage of stone; in other chambers Jenny Lind, "the Swedish nightingale," sang to her companions, and Ole Bull, famous Norwegian violinist, played a recital. Therefore Mammoth Cave is not only a natural phenomenon but also a historical monument. In that sense it holds its own very well, although later discoveries like the Carlsbad Caverns in New Mexico are infinitely larger. Another unique feature of the Kentucky Cave is the abundance of water: There are, on the five levels of the cave, three rivers, eight waterfalls, one lake, and one "Dead Sea." A boat ride on the Echo River on

In Mammoth Cave there are underground rivers, waterfalls, and a lake.

the lowest level, 360 feet below the surface, is an interesting experience. The ceiling is rather low, and every spoken word echoes back and forth many times before it dies away. The river, 20 to 60 feet wide and up to 25 feet deep, has strange inhabitants. Adapting themselves to their ever dark environment, its small fish no longer have eyes, and their skin is white. There are also transparent crawfish in the cave, and crickets and beetles all of which are blind. Among the cave's stone formations the so-called Frozen Niagara is noteworthy.

HORSE HEAVEN. If there is an equine paradise to which good horses go after they have passed away, it must be patterned after Kentucky's Blue Grass Country, north of Mammoth Cave National Park and extending eastward with Lexington as its center. There are well-watered, lush pastures, groves of shady trees, white fences, and both the blue grass and the water seem to have a special stamina-giving quality. The barns are super-modern, sanitary, spacious, with cork floors and often with air conditioning. The product of this close collaboration of nature and man is the world's finest thoroughbred race horse. Not only in the United States but also in Canada, Mexico and Cuba a substantial majority of all open-stakes races are won by Kentucky-bred horses. No wonder, then, that horses are a tourist attraction; some of the great stud farms are open to the public, and even people without any interest in the turf will find it fasci-

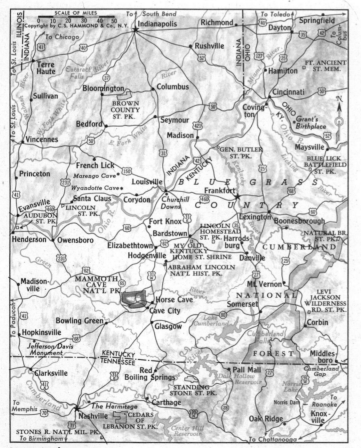

See sectional map, page 88

nating to watch the mares with their foals scamper over the velvety pastures, or to walk on broad tree-lined avenues to spick-and-span barns, or to see the last resting places, some of them crowned with bronze statues, of such celebrities as Equipoise and Fair Play. The grave of Man o' War draws considerably more visitors annually than the tomb of Henry Clay. Famous stud arms, producers of race-track winners, are Calumet, Coldstream, Beaumont, Walnut Hall and others, all of them circling Lexington. The great annual event of the Blue Grass Country takes place on the first or second Saturday in May when America's number one race, the Derby, is run in Louisville's Churchill Downs. There is probably nowhere else a spectacle like it, and therefore it is quite worthwhile attending. Even if thousands of visitors see hardly anything of the race itself, they share in the excitement and the festive mood.

"MY OLD KENTUCKY HOME." That famous ballad was written in 1852 when Stephen Foster and his wife, on their way from Pittsburgh to New Orleans, passed through Bardstown and stopped at Federal Hill, the estate of their cousin John Rowan. The Rowans were wealthy planters, statemen and diplomats, and life in the splendid, but not showy, house proved so pleasant that Foster immortalized it in his song. The building is now located in a state park, about half-way between Mammoth Cave and Lexington, a well-balanced two-

Thousands of caverns are in Kentucky; Mammoth Cave has miles of passageways.

story home of brick with large windows and beautifully carved mantels. Local tradition has it that John Rowan, Henry Clay, and their cronies played many a game of poker here, and emptied many a keg of bourbon. Quite near, in a southwesterly direction, is the memorial of Lincoln's birthplace, just out of Hodgenville. A flight of stairs, lined by trees and hedges, leads to a ridge where the memorial arises in Connecticut granite and Tennessee marble, with Lincoln's motto inscribed above the Doric columns: "With Malice toward None, with Charity for All." Inside there stands the log cabin that is said to have been Abraham Lincoln's birthplace, the cracks between the logs chinked with clay, and the clay-lined log chimney at one end. In December, 1808, Thomas Lincoln purchased this farm land, settled here with his wife and daughter, and on February 12, 1809, Abraham was born. Near Harrodsburg the Pioneer Memorial State Park also preserves a Lincoln shrine. The reconstructed Fort Harrod and the Pioneer Cemetery honor the first settlers of these "dark and bloody hills." Southeast of Mammoth Cave National Park, the Cumberland Falls are a popular attraction. Behind the sheet of falling water, 68 feet high and 125 feet broad, the rock wall recedes, and the visitor can walk through an arch which on one side consists of stone, on the other of water. This cataract is one of the few on our continent which show a moonbow in the spray when the moon is full.

This Green River Ferry serves an area that does not have a traffic problem.

DAKOTA CAMELS AND MIDGET HORSES.
No greater contrast could be imagined than
that between the Badlands and the Black Hills
in the southwestern part of South Dakota. The hills are
lush with woods and streams, the Badlands, to the east,
are an arid waste of 640,000 acres; they are a desolate
desert, but a fascinating and beautiful one that should be
seen in the early morning or toward evening when the
shadows of its thousands of pinnacles are black, and the
deep canyons are dark while the yellow, reddish and grayish towers sparkle in the sunlight. The landscape has an
eerie atmosphere, as if it were a part of another world,
and the traveler who has passed the wastelands and approaches Rapid City, and suddenly distinguishes, on a
ridge against the setting sun, the dark outlines of two
antediluvian monsters, is not too surprised. They are life-
size reproductions of the brontosaurus which roamed
these lands when they were swamps, in geological times.
More bizarre animals lived in these parts, and the beds of
vanished rivers preserved fossils and skeletons in abundance. The Museum of the South Dakota School of Mines
has a famous and excellent collection. Among the former
inhabitants of the region are midgets like a two-foot
camel, a nine-inch deer, and a twenty-inch, three-toed
horse. Among the giants there are a clidastes, i.e. a
twenty-nine foot marine lizard, and a titanothere, half
elephant and half rhinoceros. The museum also shows

The bare rocks of the Needles Highway contrast with the lush green of the Black Hills.

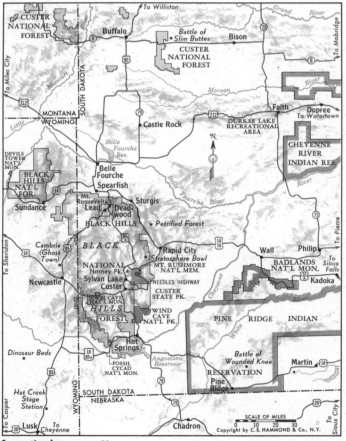

See sectional map, page 88

the great subterranean wealth of the area whose rocks
contain about 200 different minerals.

FOUR PRESIDENTS ON A GRANITE LEDGE.
The Black Hills are a veritable oasis in the hot prairies,
a cool retreat with shady trees and rushing water, and the
clear air of mountains 6 to 7 thousand feet tall. A prime
attraction is the Mount Rushmore National Memorial
where the great stone faces of Washington, Jefferson,
Lincoln and Theodore Roosevelt, carved into the solid
granite of a towering pinnacle, look down into the valley. This monumental sculpture by Gutzon Borglum is
carried out at a scale of men 465 feet tall; mountain goats
cavort on the rim of Roosevelt's spectacles, and every so
often hardy bushes have to be removed from Washington's chin. There is a modernistic school of art which
condemns the monument as "corny," but this visitor and
thousands of others have found it a truly inspiring memorial to four great Americans, a work as colossal as the
land they served so well and, we hope, as lasting as that
land. Geologists believe that the carvings will remain intact for a hundred thousand years. The technique is not
new; 3,000 years ago Asiatic sculptors chiseled huge figures into the mountain sides of the Near East. But it is
new for our day and for America, and a welcome change
from the all-too familiar. An even huger project is under
way at Thunderhead Mountain, near Sylvan Lake, where
the well-known sculptor Ziolkowski is carving out of the

106

mountain top the monument of Crazy Horse, great Sioux.

THE WHISTLING EARTH. In the southern part of the Black Hills, Wind Cave National Park presents a natural phenomenon different from the usual stalagmite-and-stalactite cavern. More than ten miles of passages are covered with fragile, beautiful box-work, where the calcite in the rock remained in delicate, interlacing shapes while the limestone dissolved. This cave was discovered by a deer-hunting pioneer named Bingham who heard a whistling sound coming from the earth, and found a hole in the rock from which a jet of wind was blowing. This puzzling adventure led to the exploration and naming of the cave. The wind current is due to barometric pressure and to the fact that the ten-inch hole is the only natural opening of the cave. The present entrance is artificial. Above ground the park has 27,000 acres of wildlife preserve where a buffalo herd of 400 heads lives.

GOLD IN THE HILLS, AND CALAMITY JANE. The cities of the Black Hills are not large but they are interesting. Lead (pronounced Leed) is a hilltop town that once had a gold rush and still has the gold. It is the seat of Homestake Mine, America's largest gold mine in whose underground passages a hundred miles of railroad are in operation. Visitors may inspect the surface installations, all on a grand scale, and see the gray, unimpressive ore two and a half tons of which produce one ounce of

A lonely elk; during mating time he will lead a harem of perhaps 10 or 12 females.

gold. Nearby Deadwood, ambling along a valley road, is one of the great centers of American folk history. Here some saloons of gold-rush days have survived, like the Old Style Bar of '76, where buffalo horns and elk heads adorn the walls, and anybody may sit on Wild Bill's favorite stool. The story of Deadwood's flamboyant past can best be read on Mount Moriah Cemetery, which perches precariously high above the town. On this unique hilltop there lie buried some of the most colorful figures of the West: Wild Bill Hickock's grave is fenced in and ornated with a small red sandstone statue whose head, unfortunately, has been chipped off. Potato Creek Johnny lies there, and Preacher Smith who was the victim of a Sioux killer; right next to Wild Bill, America's most famous frontier woman has found her last resting place, Martha Jane (Canary) Burke called Calamity Jane. She was a respected member of her society, a mule driver with a marvelous skill in handling the bull whip—she could actually take off a person's ear—, a dead shot, and an expert in the roughest language of the Old West. Remembering her fondly, the people of Deadwood buried her in a white dress with a gun in each hand. Presumably she still lies in her grave in that unorthodox fashion. At the southern end of the Black Hills, in the city of Hot Springs, the visitor may admire the bath tub which prehistoric Indians had carved into the rock to alleviate their aches, and the big spring-fed indoor pool.

The four faces are sculptured at a scale of men 465 feet tall.

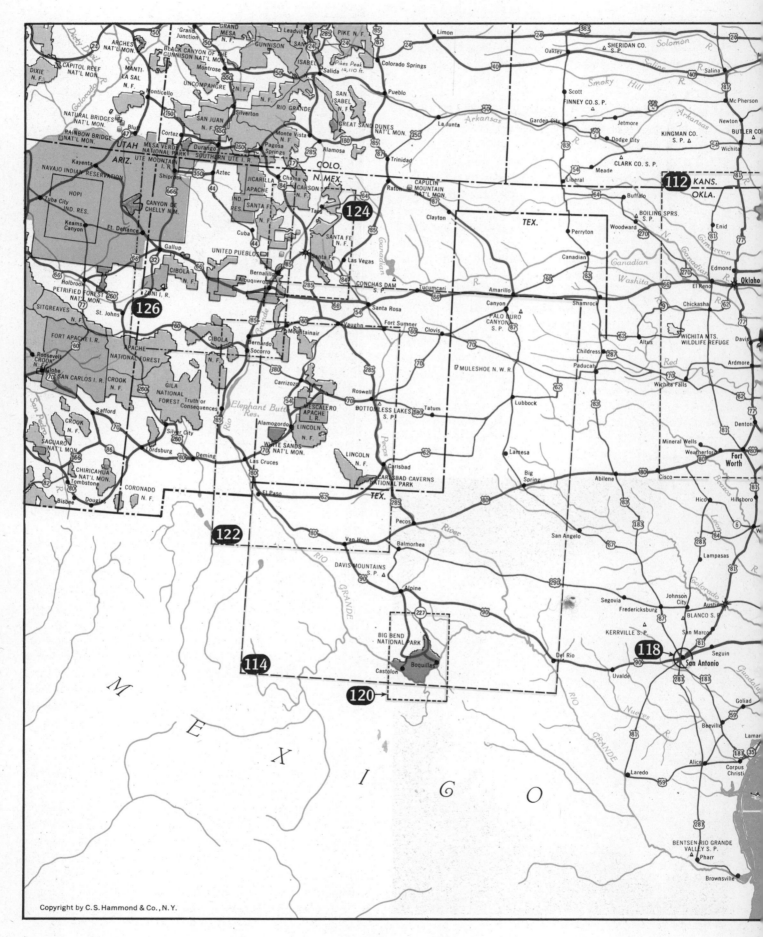

Encircled numbers - **124** - refer to pages in the atlas.

6-Day Trip Through the Ozarks and Ouachita Mountains, with an optional extension of a "floating trip" from Branson. See pictures and map on pages 110 and 111, also the Sightseeing Gazetteer.—Suggested stops: Hot Springs, Ark.—Fort Smith, gateway to both Ozarks and Ouachita Mountains—Eureka Springs, a spa in the mountains—Branson, Mo., on Lake Taneycomo; "floating trips" of 3 days to 2 weeks on the White River can be arranged there—Lake of the Ozarks—Van Buren, Mo., with Big Spring State Park—via Poplar Bluff, Mo., and Little Rock, Ark., back to Hot Springs, Ark.

5-Day Trip in Oklahoma. See pictures and map on pages 112 and 113, also the Sightseeing Gazetteer.—Suggested stops: Oklahoma City—Tulsa and Claremore with Will Rogers Memorial — Platt National Park — Wichita Mountains Wildlife Refuge near Lawton—Oklahoma City—3 stops in 5 days allow for 2-day stopovers in Tulsa with Claremore, Wichita Mountains Wildlife Refuge, or elsewhere.

8-Day Trip Through Gulf Coast Country, from New Orleans, La., to San Antonio, Texas. See pictures and maps on pages 84, 85 and 116 to 119, also the Sightseeing Gazetteer.— Suggested stops: New Orleans — New Iberia, heart of the bayou country, with Avery Island, St. Martinville and Longfellow-Evangeline State Park—Beaumont—via Port Arthur along coast to Galveston, cosmopolitan port and popular Gulf Coast resort—the fabulously rich and modern metropolis of Houston and the San Jacinto Battlefield—San Antonio with the Alamo, the Spanish Missions, and numerous other relics of its Spanish-Mexican past.—5 stops in 8 days allow for 2-day stopovers in New Iberia, Houston, San Antonio, or elsewhere. Fishermen may want to stop over at Beaumont for an excursion into the Big Thicket.

6-Day Trip Through Western Texas and Southern New Mexico. See pictures and maps on pages 114, 115 and 120 to 123, also the Sightseeing Gazetteer.—Suggested stops: El Paso, city of old traditions and of two nations—Alpine, a pleasant oasis in the desert country—Big Bend National Park, a fascinating wilderness of monumental proportions—via the Davis Mountains and Balmorhea State Parks to Carlsbad Caverns National Park, a 3-story network of caves, probably the world's largest—Alamogordo and White Sands National Monument—via Las Cruces to El Paso. 4 stops in 6 days allow for 2-day stopovers in Big Bend National Park, Carlsbad Caverns National Park, or elsewhere.

GHOST TOWN AT THE LAKE BOTTOM. Quite a few Old World legends report of bewitched towns at the bottom of the sea; if you drift on the surface on a clear day, you can hear the church bells ringing far below and see, in the deep water, the ghastly rows of houses. This is an experience you may also have in the New World, at the Lake of the Ozarks, and if no underwater church bells will mystify you, you may, while swimming, get your foot caught in the weather-cock of a church steeple. When Bagnell Dam was built, the people in a number of valleys had to move, but it seemed costly and unnecessary to demolish the buildings and trees. So when the great new reservoir of water, the Lake of the Ozarks, filled up, it retained its "sunken village." The tree skeletons and house ruins are shelters for young bass now. This lake, fed by the Osage River, has the shape of an octopus with a shore line of 1,375 miles. It is a recreation center of the Ozarks; the latter, a very ancient mass of hills and plateaus with a north-south span of about 200 miles and an east-west run of approximately 100 miles, is located in southwestern Missouri and northwestern Arkansas, spilling over into the neighboring states. It is a lovely, quiet hill country, a gentle wilderness, a green, pleasant backwoods area with blooming dogwood, redbud and hawthorn, with tall oaks and elms, cold streams and bubbling springs. Caverns abound, and in Bella Vista, Arkansas,

even a night club is operating 500 feet underground in a bright limestone cave with terraces and galleries. Around the Lake of the Ozarks and, to the south, Taneycomo Lake, there are modern cabins and hotels. Nearby Branson is the point of departure of the popular Ozark floating trips down the White River which wends its way, in innumerable oxbows, between wooded hills, farming country, islands, and narrows. On the shallow boat you may fish as you drift along, or knit or just rest. At night your guide will pitch tent at some picturesque bend of the river, and cook an outdoor supper.

THE GIANT SPRINGS. The central eastern edge of the Ozarks is the Big Spring country where clear, cold water rushes and gushes through the earth, bursts through fissures in the granite and porphyry, and swirls into "sinks," pools, streams, and rivers. There are hundreds of such giant springs, but the most impressive, one of the world's largest, is Big Spring, in a state park near the town of Van Buren, Missouri. At the bottom of a dark, 250-foot limestone cliff there is a great basin from which the pale-blue flow emerges, rebounding from the boulders. More than half a billion gallons of water rush over the ledge every day, enough to supply a city the size of St. Louis. At the end of a lonely road, this torrent of a spring will strike you as an unforgettable sight, whether you see it sparkling in the morning sun or in the blue magic of twilight.

FIDDLERS, CALLERS, WALKER HOUNDS. As interesting as the landscape are the people of the Ozarks. They are of pure English and Scotch stock, mostly mountaineers from Tennessee, Virginia and Kentucky who in the restless years after the War of 1812 migrated to this island of hills and have stayed there ever since. To call these well-mannered and contented, generous and gentle, intelligent and competent people "hillbillies" is a pathetic reflection on the caller. How long they will be able to keep their old ways, with huge hydro-electric dams arising and tourists swarming in, is another question. The frequent presence of visiting sociologists and folklorists collecting ancient ballads and tape-recording the Ozark speech is ominous. At present, folk life is still alive and strong; there are still many Ozark fiddlers who have whittled their own instruments, who cannot read a note but have a repertory of perhaps 300 tunes, and who can adapt to Saturday's dance music any new tune that may appeal to them on the radio. And there are square dance callers who can go on and on without repeating a figure, ordering innumerable patterns from a simple star to a rattlesnake glide, and stopping only when the dancers approach a collapse. The people are also great hunters and dog breeders. Their coon dogs are killers, trained for the practical purpose of securing raccoon hides, but the smaller Walker Hounds are genuine sportsmen kept and cared for as fox hunters, for the world's most gentle variety of fox hunting. Five or six

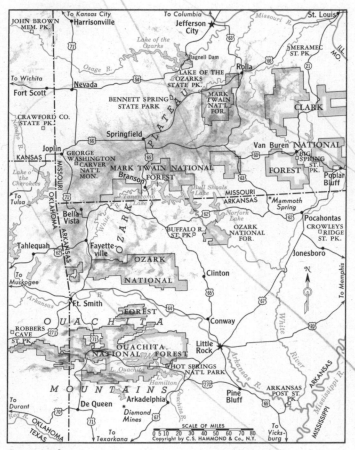

See sectional map, page 108

The Ozarks are a back-to-nature region of great hardwood forests, cool streams, bubbling springs, and the home of a people who have, as yet, managed to maintain their own unique way of life.

dogs are taken by truck to the neighborhood of the fox's burrow, and are released at night. The men settle under a tree and do their hunting by ear. Yipes, yelps, and little barks tell them the story of discovering the bacy smell of the fox, finding or losing the track, confronting the fox, and so on. The latter is never killed.

"TAKING THE WATERS." South of the Ozarks, in the Ouachita Mountains, Hot Springs National Park is an attraction not only for the sick. Its baths—the waters are heated by vapors rising through cracks in volcanic rock —are applied both as a cure and as a tonic-preventive and their fame goes back to Indian days. According to local tradition the Osages, Ouachitas and Cherokees used to fight for the possession of the health-giving springs but later came to a sensible accord and declared the spa neutral territory, open to all sick Indians. The first white man to enjoy a mineral bath there, is said to have been De Soto who indeed visited the spot. As early as 1832 the U.S. Government set aside as a national reservation about 1,000 acres surrounding the springs, so that the Hot Springs of Arkansas can claim quite rightly to be America's first National Park. Today a great Veterans' Hospital, eight bath houses built on leased government property, and about 250 hotels and cottages take care of the sick and the hale who come here in search of restoration and rejuvenation.

OKLAHOMA CITY: PILLARS AND DRILLS. Thousands of Americans have derived their knowledge of Oklahoma from the successful Rogers and Hammerstein musical of the same name. Accordingly, they picture it as an idyllic farming and ranching community, which indeed it is in large part. But early in the 20th century another factor appeared that added an accent of its own: oil. Particularly Oklahoma City, the capital, bears its imprint. The town is not a tourist attraction in the strict sense of the word, but if you happen to travel in its neighborhood, you will find a visit interesting. Imagine, for instance, the Oklahoma state capitol built in the style of an ancient Greek temple, and right in front of the classical columns the lacy steel tower of a modern oil derrick. The contrast is so striking that the derrick is probably the most photographed sample of its kind. There are derricks in frontyards of private homes and backyards of apartment buildings. The whole capital stands on top of a huge petroleum pool.

TULSA: OIL AND INDIAN LORE. Approaching Tulsa from the southwest, you will see one of America's dramatic city panoramas. Beyond the smokestacks and tank installations of a large oil refinery, and beyond the sandy carpet of the Arkansas River, there arises high on the ridge of the bluff the skyline of Tulsa. As a low cloud of mist and steam often hovers over the

The Will Rogers Memorial at Claremore honors the great American humorist.

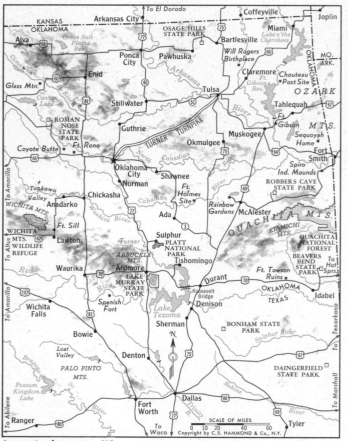

See sectional map, page 108

refinery while the air on the hill is dry and transparent, the clear skyline seems to emerge from the cloud like a dream city. The fact that Tulsa considers itself "the Oil Capitol of the World," that it is the home of several hundred oil companies and related enterprises, and the seat of the biennial International Petroleum Products Exposition, is only of mild interest to the sightseeing traveler; but Tulsa's two art institutions will be fascinating to many. The Philbrook Art Center is a splendid private mansion turned into a museum, but the more unique of the two is the Gilcrease Foundation, three miles north of the city. The latter contains the finest collection of Indian painting in existence. The art of 45 Indian tribes, beginning as early as the year 300 A.D., can be studied there, as well as the paintings of modern Indian artists and of such white painters as Russell and Remington, the classical recorders of the Old West. The priceless collection is supplemented by a library of 62,-000 letters, manuscripts, and books. Thomas Gilcrease, the oil millionaire who established this gallery, had a Creek Indian grandmother and lived in Indian territory as a boy.

A GREAT AMERICAN AT HOME. Northeast of Tulsa, the small city of Claremore is the hometown of Will Rogers, the homespun philosopher and humorist who was probably the best-loved American of his day and could have become President of the United States

112

if he had cared to assume that office. By descent he was truly an American. His father Clem, one eighth a Cherokee, served four terms as a Cherokee senator and helped to write the constitution that changed the Indian Territory into the State of Oklahoma. His mother was a one-quarter Cherokee, and Will remarked correctly that his ancestors "did not come over on the Mayflower—they met the boat." After he had won fame as an entertainer and had become a national figure, he returned to Claremore for a visit and bought twenty acres on a hill overlooking the town. There he planned to retire, build a home, and "just sit and whittle and gab" with his friends. He could never carry out his plan; for on a good-will mission to Russia his plane crashed in Alaska, in 1935. But he returned home, nevertheless. The State of Oklahoma built on that hill the Will Rogers Memorial, as Will's burial place. It looks like a ranch house he might have erected there himself. In the foyer his statue glances over the countryside in his friendly, casual way; millions of Americans have been there and given it a nod, and looked at Will's saddles and lassos, his hat and his typewriter, twisted and battered in the plane crash, and the small red bag "that packs itself." All who visit this shrine like to recall the whimsical, nail-on-the-head sayings of this "good Injun"; one of his own words is chiseled into the base of his statue: "I never met a man I didn't like."

The original buffalo preserve is the Wichita Mountains Wildlife Refuge.

The world's most photographed oil derrick in front of the state capitol.

SULPHUR AND BROMIDE. In the southern center of the state is Platt National Park whose attraction is an area of 31 large springs. They include 18 sulphur, 6 fresh water, 4 iron, and 3 bromide springs,—formerly a part of the territory of the Chickasaw Nation. Perimeter Boulevard describes an elongated circle in the park which abounds with bright wildflowers.

BISONS AND LONGHORNS. Sixty million buffaloes roamed this continent when white man arrived. In 1895 eight hundred were left, and there was danger that this great native animal might vanish like the passenger pigeon. So in 1905 President Theodore Roosevelt accepted a herd of 15 buffaloes, as a nucleus for survival, from the New York Zoological Society and, as the buffaloes' preserve, established the Wichita Mountains Wildlife Refuge in southwestern Oklahoma, near the city of Lawton. There the herd has grown to about 600, and additional refuges throughout the West and in Canada make it certain now that the buffalo (or bison) will not die out, although it survives only in a half-tame condition. Another, equally picturesque American animal saved here from extinction is the Texas Longhorn. Survivors of Spanish cows and bulls that had been brought to this continent 300 years ago, the Longhorns had run wild, inhabiting the prairies of Texas and the Southwest in great numbers.

FIFTY MILES TO GET YOUR MAIL. The Pecos River, a tributary of the Rio Grande, used to be the trail of the Spanish Conquistadores. But throughout the centuries it remained the lonely river of a frontier,—one of the roughest frontiers the 1880's experienced. "West of the Pecos" became a nationally known phrase implying that no law existed beyond that line. At one time there was even a verb derived from Pecos (either the river or the small cow town whose streets were lined with hitching rails); "pecosin' a guy" referred to a treatment in which a man was shot, his corpse filled with rocks, and the body dumped into the river. Of course, more civilized practices have reached the Pecos by now, but the whole western corner of Texas is still a vast and lonely country, and a landscape in grandiose style. Plains and mesas roll away to all horizons; the occasional goat or sheep ranches are huge domains because the grazing land is a semi-desert. Every so often wild, rugged mountain ranges appear, either shutting off a broad valley in a distant purple haze or crowding the highway with steep cliffs, their peaks rising to heights from 5000 to nearly 9000 feet. In some stretches the country seems to be entirely uninhabited, but let there be a Fourth-of-July celebration or a barbecue or a rodeo, and a surprising number of families appear from hidden valleys and distant mesas. Indeed the rodeo is said to have origi-

Indian Lodge offers modern accommodations in the rugged Davis Mountains.

nated here. Nobody minds spending untold hours in travel; to this day many a rancher has to ride fifty miles to reach the nearest post office or buy a bag of lemons in the general store. This is not really a tourist country, and no mid-summer visit is recommended. But crossing it in spring and fall, perhaps on your way to Big Bend National Park, is an exhilarating experience. This last frontier land has been called the "most barren and yet most scenically attractive section of Texas."

BALMORHEA: LUSH OASIS. Twenty-four million gallons of water every day,—that is one of the occasional surprises of the arid land. It happens at San Solomon Springs, and appropriately the pleasant Balmorhea State Park has been established around this clear flow. A 10,000 acre tract is irrigated by the spring water, with the small town of Balmorhea, five miles away, as its market center.

DAVIS MOUNTAINS: RUGGED BUT FOREST-CROWNED. Toward the southwest, the rangelands of sagebrush and yucca form undulating foothills where sudden gusts of wind blow dried weeds high into the air, into a brief whirling dance. Then the Davis Mountains arise, their ruggedness mitigated by a cover of refreshing green woods. In Davis Mountains State Park you may hike, swim, and ride horseback, and admire the beauty of upper Limpia Canyon; in season, a star-

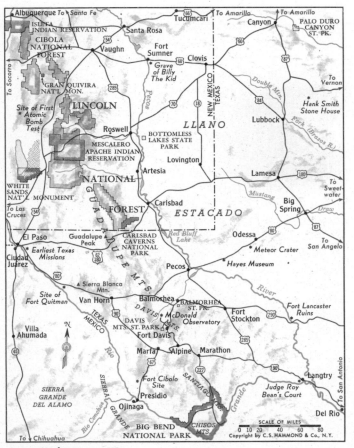

See sectional map, page 108

114

tling display of bright wildflowers, including orchids and cacti, will greet you. You may see deer, bears, and prong-horned antelopes, and although you may not encounter a panther, it is quite true that panthers live there, too. On one of the higher mountains of the range, Mount Locke (altitude 6,791 feet), the McDonald Observatory is located. One of the world's large observatories, it is open to the public at certain hours, and occasionally public "star-gazing sessions" are conducted at night.

AN OASIS AGAIN. Nearby, to the southeast, the picturesque town of Alpine lies in a green valley be-tween tall mountains. The shade trees in the streets, the large state parks to the north and south, the many dude ranches and the campus of Sul Ross Teachers' College are pleasant, but more interesting to the trav-eler is the western twang in the town's atmosphere: the high-heeled boots, the Highland Herefords (a famous prize cattle of the region), the cowboys and the cattle barons, the sheep herders and the goat ranchers. The town's Big Bend Historical Memorial, on the college campus, carries out the same theme of West Texas. It contains a unique collection of utensils of the prehistoric cave dwellers of that region, and of relics of Indian days and pioneer times.

EL PASO: BRIDGE BETWEEN TWO NATIONS
From a mountain top the great statue of El Christo

San Solomon Spring in Balmorhea State Park has a daily flow of 24,000,000 gallons.

Rey looks down upon the city. On the background of a white cross, the Savior's arms point to the north and south of the American-Mexican boundary, symbolizing the two-nation character of El Paso, and the two cul-tures united in the same religion. El Paso, western cornerstone of West Texas, has a history quite different from that of the cattle towns which sprang up over night. At the great throughway to the north, Cabeza de Vaca found flourishing Indian pueblos in the region of the present-day town as early as 1536. He commented on the Indians' strength and intelligence, and marveled at the huge buffalo herds. The town did not take part in the Texas Revolution; during the Mexican War it surrendered amicably to the Americans, in 1846. Ever since then it has been a city of two friendly nationalities, and its at-home-abroad atmosphere has a special charm for the traveler who, by the way, will also appreciate El Paso's fine winter climate. There are few actual sight-seeing attractions, but it is an intriguing experience to hear Spanish and English spoken with equal fluency; to watch the people pray to the same saints and celebrate the same fiestas; to visit Ciudad Juarez across the Rio Grande; to enjoy, on either side of the river, the adobe stores with their flamboyant displays of chili peppers, varied fruits, sombreros, and folk art souvenirs; and to buy, perhaps, a native piece of pottery or hand-tooled leather, or a hand-woven Mexican rug.

Highway 80 presents a view of the lonely Sierra Blanca Mountain.

FORTRESS AGAINST THE SEA. Gently the waves of the Gulf of Mexico ripple over a broad, white, sandy beach where a formidable gray wall towers 17 feet high like a medieval fortification. Behind that wall the City of Galveston gradually slopes down to the bay side of the island on which it is located. The huge wall structure, fifteen feet wide at its base and five at the top, was erected as a protection against the sea, after the hurricane of 1900 had swept over the city, had destroyed large parts of it, and killed about 6,000 people. Since then the bulwark has withstood several severe tests, and any visitor who happens to be in Galveston during a storm, should watch the spectacle at the Sea Wall, the battering of the waves and the spray that is sometimes thrown up into the air in sheets 50 feet high. Galveston proper is one of America's most interesting port cities, its landlocked harbor on the north side connected with the Gulf by a deep ship channel. Crowding the docks, dozens of steamers unload their Central American bananas, their Indian jute and Cuban sugar, and take in as cargoes hills of yellow sulphur and mountains of whitish cotton bales. Sailors from every corner of the earth saunter along the curio shops and the consulates of 27 foreign nations. To complete the cosmopolitan atmosphere, most of the town's Negroes converse in French patois, because originally they came from Louisiana or the French-speaking West Indies. But Galveston, the international harbor,

has another distinction; it is "The Oleander City." The story goes that in 1841 one oleander shoot was brought to the town from the West Indies, and that it has multiplied into more than a million oleander bushes which blossom gloriously. Poinsettias and bougainvillaea thrive with equal vigor.—With the Gulf at its front and quiet Galveston Bay at its back door, all watersports flourish, and the annual deep-sea-fishing "rodeo" is an outstanding event. Also Mardi Gras is celebrated in Galveston, and the sea wall is an ideal setting for dance pavillions, cafés, and night clubs.

500 MILLIONAIRES, AND A LEGENDARY SUCCESS STORY. To the west of Galveston Bay there lies the big modern city which likes to call itself "Houston, USA" rather than "Houston, Texas." The traveler will find there no 18th century mansions or quaint colonial churches to visit, but clusters of imposing skyscrapers, headquarters of oil companies whose gas he buys at the corner station; Foley Bros. Department Store is a marvel of modernity, with its own huge garage where cars may be serviced while customers shop; and flamboyant is the word for the Shamrock Hotel several miles from downtown, with its huge, lyre-shaped swimming pool and beach cabanas, clubs and elegant stores. While you do your sightseeing along ultra-modern lines, some proud resident will tell you that in 1940 Houston had 385,000 inhabitants; 850,000 in 1952; and that it will have a population of 3,000,000 in 1980. The latter figure is not the estimate of an enthusiastic local booster, but of Lloyd's of London. You will hear that this inland city 50 miles from the sea is America's Number 2 harbor, its link with the ocean being maintained by the ship canal of 1914. That there are 500 millionaires (most of them "oilionaires") in Houston, of whom some are poor (they just completed their first million) and some are rich (they have a daily income of $10,000 to $20,000). And that the city was founded as a real estate promotion of the Allen Brothers of New York; in 1837 advertisements praising the new metropolis to the sky appeared in dozens of American newspapers, but when the sternwheeler "Laura M." traveled up Buffalo Bayou to Houston, it never noticed the city and traveled past it for three miles. Nevertheless, the land speculation turned out to be a huge success, like almost every other venture attempted there. For Houston is the symbol of a stretch of America that has been enriched by nature with almost fantastic lavishness. The Golden Gulf Coast has rich, dark soil on top, and immense petroleum pools, sulphur mines and salt deposits below. It has a hinterland of excellent cotton fields and grazing lands for beef cattle, and it has great natural beauty besides all this. In the residential sections of Houston cypresses, magnolias and live oaks line the streets, and many mansions have a primeval setting of tangled woodlands draped with wild grapevines and Spanish moss. Roses bloom all year, and bright, subtropical flowers in season.

See sectional map, page 108

The tallest stone structure on earth, crowned with the Lone Star of Texas, is the fitting memorial of the Battle of San Jacinto which secured independence for Texas. It is located in a state park which surrounds the battlefield.

THE BATTLEFIELD OF TEXAS INDEPEN-DENCE. Twenty-two miles east of Houston a fierce battle was fought in 1836. By modern standards it was microscopic, involving 783 Texans under Sam Houston, about 1400 Mexicans, and three pieces of artillery. But it won independence for Texas. Besides, it was carried out with such vigor and elan, that it set the spirit and tenor of the Texas tradition. At a point when the cause of the Texas revolutionaries seemed lost beyond repair, when Santa Anna, the Mexican dictator, believed he was driving the remnants of the rebellious army into the sea, Sam Houston's men suddenly made a stand where the San Jacinto flows into Buffalo Bayou, at-tacked during siesta time, and in a furious 18-minute battle annihilated the Mexicans. Santa Anna was picked up in a swampy thicket the following day, and the Republic of Texas was born. Proud and grateful, the Texans of today established San Jacinto State Park around the battlefield and remembered the great victory of early Texas in the San Jacinto Memorial Monument, with a height of 570 feet the tallest stone structure on earth. Appropriately, it is crowned with the Lone Star of Texas. The tower contains a historical museum and an observation platform that is reached by an elevator. As an additional attraction of the park, the old battle-ship Texas has been anchored in a slip of Buffalo Bayou.

VILLAINS AND HEROES. A strange procession trekked laboriously from Mexico City to San Antonio, in 1718; the first Captain General and Governor of the Province of Texas arrived with 1000 sheep, 548 horses, 200 oxen, 200 cows, but only 72 human beings. The church, of course, was represented, and proceeded in its task with admirable vigor; within 13 years a string of famous missions was established. During the Mexican Revolution San Antonio seceded from Spain, but the Spanish General Arredondo recaptured it, smothered some citizens in an airless prison, shot others, and mistreated the women. The place where these cruelties occurred is still called "Dolorosa," the "Street of Sorrow." In the 1840's a few thousand German immigrants settled in San Antonio and added to the Spanish flavor beer gardens, *Sängerfests,* and the *Kaffeeklatsch.* During the Revolution of Texas, San Antonio witnessed both a triumph and a catastrophe. In December 1835, the Mexican General de Cos surrendered to the victorious revolutionaries, but on March 6, 1836, the tragedy at the Alamo occurred when 187 Texans fell heroically in defense of the mission-fortress, against an army of more than 3000 Mexicans. After the Civil War the Anglo-American population increased and changed the character of the town. Those were the days of the open range, of the mustangs and the cowboys, of the longhorn herds and the cattle drives, when San

Modern skyscrapers contrast with old Spanish buildings.

Antonio became the lusty capital of a cattle empire, a wide-open city teaming with professional gamblers, beautiful women, and trigger men. Toward the end of the century the railroads arrived, industries developed, and the modern city emerged. During most of its career, San Antonio was also an army post, and the large Fort Sam Houston is still chiefly located within the city limits. In our day so many service men from all corners of the U.S. have married Texas girls that the city has been called "the army's mother-in-law."

THE CROOKED RIVER. Modern visitors will discover that San Antonio is laid out like an irregular spider web, with most of the sightseeing attractions at or near the center of the web. One of the most pleasant features of the town is the San Antonio River which meanders along in such a crooked fashion, and with so many turns and oxbows, that it takes a course of 15 miles to cross 6 miles of city blocks. In a flash of good humor the early Indians of the town coined a name for the river which translated into English means "Drunken-old-man-going-home-at-night." The stream has been landscaped very attractively, with fountains and walks by the river edge, and a unique outdoor theater whose river-bank stage is closed by a water curtain.

THE TEXAS SHRINE. Of the once mighty fortress-mission of the Alamo only the small gray chapel and

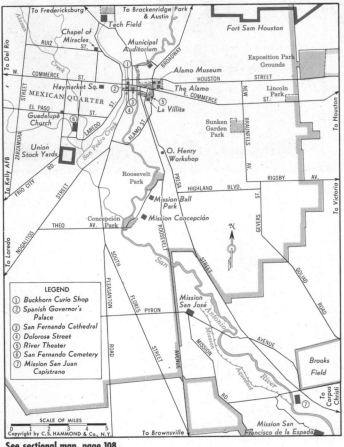

LEGEND
① Buckhorn Curio Shop
② Spanish Governor's Palace
③ San Fernando Cathedral
④ Dolorosa Street
⑤ River Theater
⑥ San Fernando Cemetery
⑦ Mission San Juan Capistrano

SCALE OF MILES
Copyright by C.S. HAMMOND & Co., N.Y.

See sectional map, page 108

A Blend of Old Spain and Modern America

some ivy-covered courtyard walls remain All missions had fallen into decay by the end of the 18th century, and by the time of the Alamo tragedy the buildings were roofless ruins filled with debris. But a high rock wall about three feet thick was still standing, embracing much of what is now Alamo Plaza. That was the enclosure defended by the Texans who made their last stand in the chapel. The latter is largely in its original state, except for the new roof; it is flanked by the Alamo Museum. In the center of the former fortress area the Cenotaph honors the Heroes of the Alamo. The figures of the Texas leaders, Bonham, Crockett, Bowie and Travis, are outstanding among the statuary.—A few blocks to the south, La Villita is an interesting restoration project of residential houses that were built between 1722 and 1850, the oldest ones erected by the Spaniards. La Villita contains a library, a museum, a theater, and interesting shops where the traditional weaving and pottery crafts are kept alive.—At the western side of the city's center, on the Main Plaza, San Fernando Cathedral is the oldest parish church in Texas. During the Alamo siege Santa Anna occupied the building, flying from its steeple the blood-red flag signal of "no quarter." The cathedral was restored in 1873, but its rear part is the 1738 original. On the Military Plaza the Spanish Governor's Palace is a long, low, white building of ten rooms, with the arms of the Hapsburgs carved into the

This protected path is the "Alamo Walkway."

keystone over the entrance. To the west of the city's center the large Mexican Quarter maintains San Antonio's Spanish and Mexican traditions so convincingly that one imagines oneself to be south of the Rio Grande. Among the most colorful fiestas of the Mexican section are The Blessing of the Animals on the 17th of January, the celebration of Dia de Animas; All Souls' Day, at San Fernando Cemetery, in November, and the Matachines Dances at the Guadalupe Church in December.

SPANISH BAROQUE IN THE WILDERNESS. Artistically and historically, the four missions south of the city are outstanding Concepción, San José, San Juan Capistrano, and San Francisco de la Espada. With fortress-like enclosures, chapels, convents, workrooms and quarters for the Indians they are fascinating relics of Spanish colonization in America. Thick adobe or stone walls, vaulted roofs, cloistered arches and front-wall belfries are impressive, but two of the missions can boast of truly artistic treasures. Concepción still preserves some fine ancient frescoes, painted by the monks in dyes prepared from various plants and clays, and San José, "the queen of the missions," is rich in beautiful rock-carved ornamentations in the decorative style of Spanish Baroque. The sculptor, Pedro Huizar, who worked there for five years, was a descendant of a great Spanish family of artists who helped create the Alhambra at Granada.

Gateway to the Alamo chapel, only relic of the original mission-fortress.

THE PHANTOM MOUNTAINS. Way down south where the Rio Grande, on its journey from Colorado to the Gulf of Mexico, makes a "wrong" 90-degree turn toward the northeast, instead of flowing southward, a great, untamed wilderness has been set aside as "Big Bend National Park." No railroad, airline or superhighway leads into this last frontier, but it can be reached by car quite easily. Traveling over a desert of sand and stone, one sees a row of mountains rise from the plateau, like an island, their jagged peaks cutting deep indentations into the blue sky. It is the Chisos range, and the name—meaning "phantoms"—is well chosen. For in a certain light and time of day it looks like a mirage. But the traveler finds it very real as the road winds up a canyon and the cacti and desert plants are gradually replaced by green oaks and clean-smelling pines. Cool springs trickle from rocks, and soft grass covers the ground. At a height of 5,000 feet the car rolls into a great rocky basin, and here the park headquarters are located. On the rim of the bowl, Emory Peak towers as the highest peak of the range, just under 8,000 feet tall. Casa Grande is a castle-like mass of rock, and when the morning mist rises from the valley, it looks like a medieval fortress on a mountain top. The stone wall surrounding the basin is not a complete circle, though; a V-shaped opening, called The Window, offers a breath-taking view, across Burro mesa, into Old Mexico. A horseback ride

on the South Rim presents a stretch of America that has remained untouched by civilization, a 100-mile perspective south into Mexico, and another 100-mile view north into our homeland. Three canyons cut by the Rio Grande are located within the park, the Mariscal, Boquillas and Santa Elena; all three have been negotiated, but only by the most skillful and daring navigators. Santa Elena canyon is a fifteen mile narrow chasm of wild water between sheer, towering rock walls. Then suddenly the river emerges in the open, pleasant and in broad daylight, an ideal fishing spot.

In spite of its remoteness the Big Bend country had its share of frontier history. An Indian tribe called the Basket Makers lived there in caves and had to suffer much from the raids of invading Comanches and Apaches. White man discovered the Big Bend at an early date: According to tradition colonial Spaniards found here a fabulous silver mine and worked it with Indian slaves. However, the Spanish intruders vanished from the scene, and ever since the search for the Lost Mine has stirred the imagination of treasure hunters.

THE DESERT: AN ACQUIRED TASTE. Easterners and southerners who live among lush green hills approach the desert with a prejudice; they expect it to be colorless, drab, and monotonous. But watching it with an open mind for only a few days at the right season, will change their opinion. Gradually they will come under the desert's spell. Looking at a sunset from any hill in the Big Bend desert, with the Chisos mountains, the Dead Horse Range and the Sierra del Carmen in view, they will witness a rare spectacle: As the shadows lengthen, the colors deepen. The yellow cliffs are suffused with pink light, the gray layers turn into magenta, the red bands take on a violet hue. Now the lower tiers of the range change first into purple, then into deep black while the highest peaks still flash with the bright colors of the last rays of the sun. A few more minutes, and all outlines merge into the darkness of the night.

After the late spring rains when the prickly pears and the chollas, the purple-tinged cactus and the strawberry cactus, the yuccas and the amaryllis are in bloom, the desert is a sight to behold; but to see in May the flowering of the century plants at the foot of Casa Grande is an experience to be remembered forever. For 20 to 25 years—not 100 years, as the name suggests—these agaves have grown to this climax when overnight the bright and large, yet infinitely delicate flower opens. After the magnificent feat has been accomplished, the plant begins to die. Lechuguilla belongs to the same family; the Mexican peasants extract tough fibers from it to weave a hundred household items: ropes for harnesses, and pouches, and saddle bags. Then there is the living-rock, a strange mimic cactus that looks like the rock in which it lives: gray and full of fissures.

FOUR-FOOT CLAMS AND BEWILDERED CAMELS. At the northern park entrance a rock formation

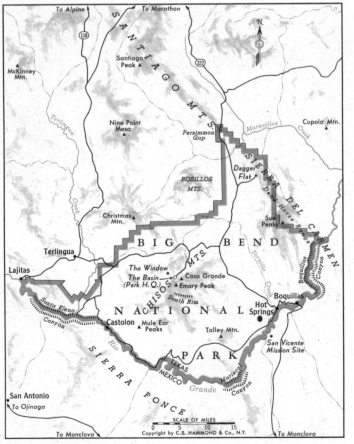

See sectional map, page 108

The wilderness mountains of the "Big Bend" offer breath-taking views into Old Mexico. In spite of its remoteness, the "Big Bend" country played a part in the frontier history of our country.

called Persimmon Gap shows that animal life has flourished here since time immemorial. Among the fossil remains are giant oyster and clam shells, one of them four feet long and almost three feet wide. Also the head of a crocodile which measured 45 feet, and the bones of dinosaurs were discovered at that spot. In historical times the fauna has not changed greatly; only the large herds of pronghorn antelopes that used to live here were either killed by hunters or wandered away when the newly introduced sheep and goats made short shrift of the fine herbs that served as the antelopes' food. Fortunately, with the founding of the National Park the "useful" animals have disappeared (John Muir called the sheep "hoofed locusts" and Freeman Tilden denounced the goats as "long-haired Japanese beetles") and the range has been happily returned to the puma and the kit fox, the flagtail and the mule deer, to the re-introduced pronghorn antelope and to all the small mammals and reptiles that inhabit the desert. In 1856 a strange cavalcade crossed the Big Bend country it consisted of a patrol of U.S. soldiers and a long file of camels. These orientals had been introduced by the army to facilitate transportation in the desert. But the Civil War ended the project, and the camels were released. It would be pleasant to report that they became a part of the American scene but they all eventually vanished.

THE HIDDEN PALACE. A huge castle pushed underground, with all its countless chambers and its three stories—that is Carlsbad Caverns in southeastern New Mexico. At 750 feet below the surface the first floor is located, at 900 feet the second, and at 1320 feet the third. How large this underground network is, nobody knows. Seven and a half miles on the first level are open to the public; over 30 miles have been explored, and how far into the Guadalupe Mountains the halls and passageways actually extend, will have to be discovered by later generations. One might wonder whether the word "palace" is not too fanciful. It is not. In fact it is rather sober and totally inadequate to describe this marvel. Nowhere on earth are there curtains and draperies as elegant and glistening as those hanging to the floor in the King's Palace and the Queen's Chamber. Some, touched by a light in back, gleam in delicate rose and pink. Others are partly raised as if expecting the sound of trumpets and the grand entrance of his majesty. The stone of the drapes looks so much like cloth that nature seems to have imitated art. As is befitting for a royal castle, there are big halls galore, like the Green Lake Room with its green pool by the passageway, the Papoose's Chamber, and the Big Room, the largest open space found underground anywhere on the globe. With a length of three quarters of a mile, a width of 600 feet, and a height that reaches 350 feet, it is 20

How large this underground network of caves is, nobody knows.

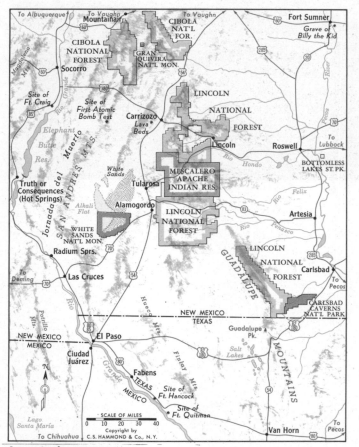

See sectional map, page 108

times larger than its nearest competitor. Its ceiling is decorated with millions of stone icicles, the stalactites, ranging in size from a pin to a belfry, and the ground is covered with a forest of stalagmites. If you tap them with your fingernail, various musical tones will emerge. If you brush lightly over a stalagmite, you will wipe off one year's growth. The natural color of the limestone formations is white, but mineral matter creates sparkling tints of tan and brown, rose and red, green and purple. A famous surprise of the Big Room is the display of the Fountain Basins, lovely clear pools as wide as 50 feet and as deep as 10 feet. "Lily pads" of stone, with limestone stems, grow in their water. That one should step from such a fairy-land into the prosaic atmosphere of an underground cafeteria, seems a sacrilege; nevertheless no luncheon guest is known to have complained about the injection of realism. The man-made improvements of the caverns are excellent. A fast elevator takes those visitors down who do not wish to climb through the natural opening, and the indirect lighting system creates effects of fantastic beauty.

THE CLOUD OF BLACK SMOKE. The story of the discovery of the caverns is equally amazing. In the twilight of a summer evening a cowboy named Jim White rode through the brush. Suddenly he spied a cloud of black smoke emerging from a mountainside and decided to investigate. As he approached, he made an unexpected discovery: Tens of thousands of bats emerged from a hole, circled upward in a spiraling cloud, and dispersed into the falling night. The spectacle lasted for three hours; then the cowboy threw burning sticks into the hole and knew that he had discovered a large cave Since Jim later became the first Chief Ranger of Carlsbad Caverns National Park, one might assume that he had visions of such a development already at this hour. But actually he knew only one fact: He had discovered a fortune. There would be bat guano in the cave in huge piles; it could be had for the asking and could be sold as fertilizer for $30 a ton. And so it was. The company he helped to found took 100,000 tons of the valuable excrements from the cave, in the following 20 years, but Jim White was also an idealist who went on exploring the caverns, fell in love with their beauty, and became their articulate propagandist. It was largely due to his efforts that his discovery became a National Monument in 1923 and a National Park in 1930. The bats are still there, some three million strong, occupying a cave which is not open to the public. During the day they sleep, hanging on delicate claws from tiny fissures in the rock, heads down; they venture forth in the evening to catch their insect dinner, and return at dawn. They are delicate animals with soft fur and silky, translucent wings, most of them belonging to the species called 'Mexican free-tailed bat." Possibly they are a remnant of the fauna

"Setting Hen Grotto" is one of the numerous chambers of the underground palace.

that flourished at a remote age of uniform, mild climate. When violent climatic changes developed, the bats took refuge in the caves where the temperature remains the same. Inside of the Carlsbad Caverns it is 56 degrees, summer or winter. During the cold season the bats hibernate, but for the rest of the year no visitor should miss the daily spectacle of the rising black cloud.

SNOWY-WHITE HILLS, AND THE SURVIVAL OF THE FITTEST. To the northwest of the Carlsbad Caverns, near the town of Alamogordo, a great basin stretches between two mountain ranges. There billowing dunes of finest texture and snowy-white color can be seen, a strange but most photogenic display that has been encompassed in the White Sands National Monument. The sand is really gypsum, alabaster ground into tiny particles which are forever pushed and moved by the wind so that the dunes and ridges are always shifting and forming new never repeated baroque outlines. Plants have a difficult time adjusting themselves to this unsteady environment. When the shifting dune rises, the plant has to grow longer to keep its crown above ground. When the sand recedes, the plant cannot contract and is left with too long a stem —a stem 40 feet tall in some cases. And the fauna has produced here a miracle of mimicry. The pocket mouse, for instance, has a black coat on the black lava beds, a red pelt in the red mountain, and white fur on the White Sands.

These shifting white dunes are of gypsum.

BEAUTY IN A SUBTLE WAY. New Mexico is the fourth-largest state in the Union. It possesses high mountains, and a dramatic mesa-and-canyon country, but much of it is semi-arid grazing land or outright desert. Long stretches might seem monotonous to the newcomer, but if he is willing to look with appreciative eyes he will discover an almost hourly change of color and light that is strangely fascinating. New Mexico's 45,000 full-blooded Indians harmonize completely with this landscape, in their appearance and their way of life, and there is beauty in such harmony. Indian and old Spanish folk art may often seem odd rather than lovely. The wooden spikes surrounding the statue of Our Lady of Guadalupe are primitive; but they are a sunburst of heavenly glory as seen through Indian eyes. Among the relics of local Spanish art there are sacred effigies of saints in full life size which, at first sight, seem almost terrifying. Yet their expressions of heart-felt anguish and sorrow reveal unusual depth and sophistication. You will have a similar experience with the Indian ritual dances; to the visitors' eyes they will appear colorful and exotic for a while, and then become monotonous. But if you stay and let the movements, the drums and the chants "sink in" without thoughts of hurry, you will feel that you are witnessing an act of art.

THE ROYAL TOWN OF THE HOLY FAITH OF SAINT FRANCIS. This city, called Santa Fe for short,

is the oldest capital city in the United States. Ten years before the *Mayflower* cast anchor in Massachusetts Bay, in 1610, Santa Fe was established, with an impressive Governor's Palace from which 60 Spanish governors ruled a strange empire. It stretched from the Mississippi to the Pacific coast, and had no real borderline at all to the north. Thousands of converts were made among the Indians, but when the latter secretly continued their old rites, and were flogged and killed because of witchcraft, the tribes rebelled and drove out the intruders. For 12 years the governor's palace served as an Indian kiva, a council house. In 1692 the Spaniards returned, and their triumphal re-entry under Vargas is to this day the most celebrated event in the town's history. Every year in June the statue of La Conquistadora is carried in a solemn procession through the streets of Santa Fe, in fulfillment of a vow made by Vargas, and the city's principal fiesta, in September, commemorates the same event; in a pageant Vargas appears again, planting before the Palace the royal banner and the Christian cross.

THE BLENDING OF SPANISH AND INDIAN WAYS. The Palace of the Governors is probably the first building the traveler wishes to inspect; it stands on the north side of the Plaza, a one-story white structure with a shady colonnade toward the street and a patio inside its rectangle. Adapting the Spanish style to the adobe construction of the Indians, it has seen many changes in its nearly three and a half centuries of existence; it was restored to its original appearance in 1909, in accordance with old plans discovered, of all places, in the British Museum. It is open to the public; interesting historic and artistic collections are on view. The Plaza, a huge, dusty parade ground in Spanish and Mexican days, was reduced in size when the Americans occupied the city in 1846. The trees, too, were planted by the Americans. Here the Santa Fe Trail ended, and when the wagon trains from Missouri arrived, entering the Plaza in a brisk trot with whips cracking, the sleepy town became alive with excitement: "Los Americanos! La caravana!" La Fonda, the inn at the southeastern corner of the Plaza, served the freighters and stage coach drivers as a terminal; it was a rambling, colorful caravanseri with stables and corrals. Unfortunately its remnants which stood until 1925, were not restored but razed to make room for a modern hotel. Of Sante Fe's churches the Cathedral of St. Francis is an imposing structure erected in 1869; the Christo Rey Church contains what is usually considered the finest piece of Spanish-American ecclesiastical art, a perfectly beautiful carved stone altar ("reredos") of 1760. San Miguel Church was built about 1636 for the Indian slaves of the Spaniards, and Guadalupe Church is a charming, tree-shaded mission-style structure with Mexican accents. Among the various museums that of Navaho Ceremonial Art is unique; it contains a complete collection of Navaho sand paintings.

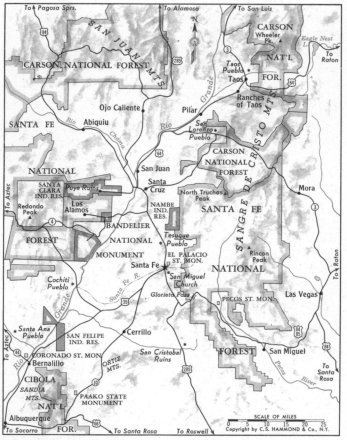

See sectional map, page 108

124

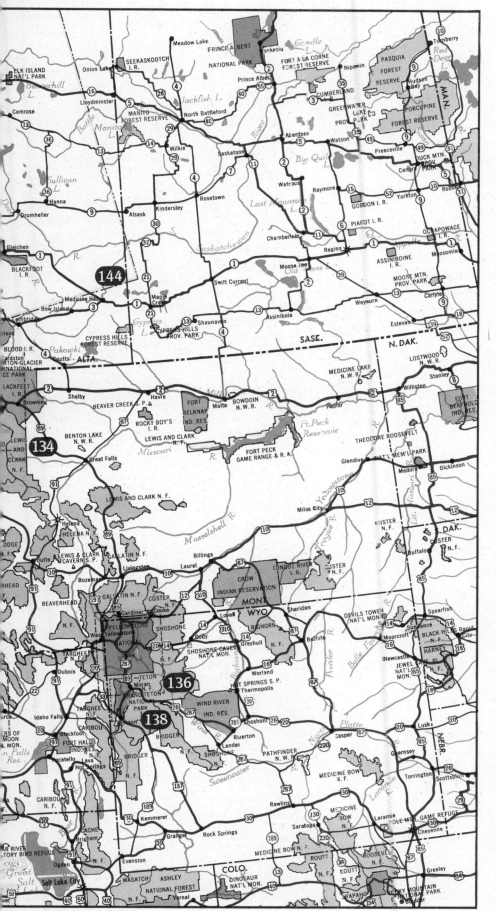

12-DAY TRIP ALONG THE AXIS OF THE NORTHERN ROCKIES. See pictures and maps on pages 130–139, also the Sightseeing Gazetteer.—Suggested stops: Jackson, Wyo., with the Grand Teton National Park—Yellowstone National Park—Helena, Mon., or Missoula, Mont., the latter via Butte and the Anaconda copper mines—Glacier National Park, Mont.—Banff, in Banff National Park, Alberta, Canada—the Lake Louise region in Banff National Park—Jasper in Jasper National Park, Alberta, Canada.—6 stops in 12 days allow for 2- or 3-day stopovers in Grand Teton, Yellowstone, Glacier, Banff and Jasper National Parks.

9-DAY TRIP THROUGH IDAHO. See pictures and map on pages 140 and 141, also the Sightseeing Gazetteer. — Suggested stops: Twin Falls, Idaho — Sun Valley — Challis, Idaho, either over rough and lonely route 93 which runs through magnificent mountain scenery and at Stanley touches the Grand Canyon of the Salmon River, or on a fairly good road southeast to Carey and then north, via Craters of the Moon Nat. Monument—Missoula, Mont.—through rich mining country to Coeur d'Alene—Lewiston, with launch excursion to Grand Canyon of the Snake River—Boise—Twin Falls. —6 stops in 9 days allow for 2-day stopovers in Sun Valley, Coeur d'Alene, Lewiston or elsewhere.

10-DAY TRIP THROUGH THE PUGET SOUND REGION OF THE PACIFIC NORTHWEST, with possible extension of 5-or-10-day cruise to southern Alaska. See pictures and maps on pages 144 to 151, also the Sightseeing Gazetteer.—Suggested overnight stops: Seattle, Wash.—Mt. Rainier Nat. Park—Olympia—Olympic National Park—Victoria, British Columbia, Canada, by car ferry from Port Angeles—Nanaimo—Vancouver, British Columbia, by car ferry; in Vancouver a 5-or-10-day steamer cruise to southern Alaska may be added—Seattle, Wash.—6 stops in 10 days allow for 2-day stopovers in Mt. Rainier or Olympic National Parks, in Victoria, Vancouver, or elsewhere.

9-DAY TRIP ALONG THE OREGON COAST AND THE SOUTHERN CASCADES. See pictures and maps on pages 152 to 158, also the Sightseeing Gazetteer.—Suggested overnight stops: Portland, Oregon—Seaside—Newport—Coos Bay—Crater Lake National Park—Bend—the Timberline Lodge area on Mt. Hood—Portland via the Scenic Columbia River Highway—6 stops in 9 days allow for 2-day stopovers in Newport, Crater Lake Nat. Park, Mt. Hood, or elsewhere.

One attraction that should not be missed on a northern East-West trip is the Grand Coulee Dam in western Washington.

MOUNTAIN SPLENDOR. Mention the words Lake Louise, Banff or the Canadian Rockies anywhere in America or in the British Empire and you will see a spark in people's eyes, as if you have spoken of something exquisite, something unique. There are very good reasons for such universal admiration. The Rocky Mountains are monumental anywhere, but besides their huge, long ridges, they produce, like the Alps, a particularly large number of jagged single peaks in Canada. For this reason they are a fruitful field for expert mountain climbers. Their geographic location in the cool north is responsible for a great deal of snow, the decorative kind that even in summertime paints the peaks a gleaming white against the sky. You will discover the loveliness of glacial lakes and glacial streams; usually they are neither clear nor deep-blue, but, rather, a cool green color of delicate jade which will strike you as new and unconventionally beautiful. In the great Canadian National Parks you will have the feeling of being at a great altitude, on the roof of the mountain mass, surrounded by sheer granite walls and snow fields. In reality you will not be higher than in the American Rocky Mountain parks in Wyoming and Colorado, but the low timberline in Canada gives the illusion of great altitude.

THE GREAT SOLITUDE. The Alps are a highly civilized mountain chain, with a history as old as that

Glacial lakes, like Bow Lake, have a clear, brilliant atmosphere of their own.

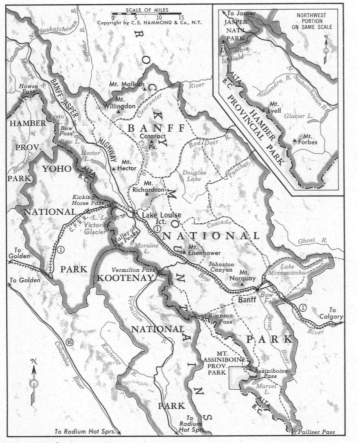

See sectional map, page 128

of Western man. Fantastic processions trekked over its passes: Hannibal with his elephants, Caesar with his legions, Napoleon and the Grande Armée. The Swiss turned their mountains into a tourist's paradise, dotting them with cable cars, ski huts and hotels. The American Rockies were opened up by mining booms and the great westward migration, events producing the "Rocky Mountain Empire" with its highways, cities, settlements and ranchlands. But the Canadian Rockies are an untouched masterpiece of nature, directly from the hands of the Creator. They have no history. Not until the end of the last century did the transcontinental railroad push across the wilderness of gneiss and granite; the few highways appeared much later. There is little silver or gold or other metals in their depths; so no noisy mining operations disturb the peace. There is little fertile soil; so few farms have sprung up in the valleys. Only a few thousand people live permanently in this huge area, and there is only one city, Banff. If you stand on top of the cliff overlooking Peyto Lake, a short stretch west of the main road, you see the emerald surface with its shoreline so delicately drawn that a celestial artist could have been at work there. Beyond the lake, on both sides of the Mistaya Valley, you see the two monumental rows of snow-and-granite peaks, reaching as far as your eye can see, with the farthest summits merging into the clouds. At that moment, you will have the strange feeling you are the only human on earth.

THE HAND OF MAN. It is a wonderfully reassuring thought that the Canadian Rockies will remain the way they are, for the Canadians have wisely turned most of their magnificent mountain ranges into a group of national parks and wildlife refuges, of which Banff and Jasper are the best-known. Both the Canadian Pacific and the Canadian National Railroads cross the district, and there are good highway connections to the east and south, as well as roads for adventurous drivers to Vancouver and the west. At two sites of breathtaking scenic beauty, the Canadian Pacific has built fine luxury hotels: the Banff Springs Hotel and the Chateau Lake Louise. From the terraces of the former you have a wide panorama of the valley of the Bow River; from the latter you look over a slope abloom with Icelandic poppies to Lake Louise, at whose water's end, framed by two dark rock walls, Victoria Glacier glistens in the sun. Besides these opulent and dignified hostelries, there are enough other smaller hotels, lodges and camps.

A MOUNTAIN ACROSS MAIN STREET. Imagine a business street cut off by a mountainous rock wall on one end, and on the other, by a bright rock garden rising from the banks of the Bow River to the stately Government House. This main thoroughfare of Banff is one of its principal charms. Other Banff attractions

Snowmobiles take passengers over the rim of the Columbia Icefield (see p. 132).

are boat excursions on the Bow River, fishing on Lake Minnewanka, golfing at Banff Springs Golf Club, where ambitious players complain about the grandiose scenery (it takes their minds off the game), and swimming in the various pools of Banff Hot Springs and Upper Hot Springs, with water temperatures ranging from 80 to 100 degrees. The fish hatchery and the buffalo paddocks are interesting and the chair-lift ride to the top of Mt. Norquay (altitude, 6,915 feet) is a must. The only road to the north divides at Mount Eisenhower (formerly Castle Mountain); the left fork leads over the Continental Divide to Kootenay National Park and Radium Hot Springs, while the main road proceeds to Lake Louise. Chateau Louise is the center for hiking or horseback excursions to the Lakes in the Clouds (Mirror and Agnes) and the Plain of the Six Glaciers. Half an hour's drive will take you to Moraine Lake in the Valley of the Ten Peaks. Along or near the highway to Jasper such bodies of water as Hector Lake, Bow Lake and Peyto Lake are jewels. All accessible streams and lakes are continually stocked with trout and offer fine fishing. The whole region is, of course, also a winter sports area, with championship downhill and slalom courses at Mount Norquay, near Banff. The latter is also the seat of the Alpine Club of Canada, and of a famous school of fine arts, associated with the University of Alberta.

Horseback riding, practically unknown in the Alps, is popular in the Rockies.

GLACIER OF THREE OCEANS. The greatest mass of ice outside of the Arctic Circle, covering 110 square miles and reaching a depth of 1800 feet, lies before your eyes at the southern entrance to Jasper, the most northerly of the group of Canadian parks in the Rockies. It is the Columbia Icefield whose huge white tongues stretch out in various directions and feed streams that grow into mighty rivers; their waters flow into the Atlantic, the Pacific and the Arctic Oceans. At your feet is the geographical center of the water system of over one quarter of North America. The glacial tongue you see from the Banff-Jasper Highway protrudes between the Snow Dome and Mt. Athabaska, two monumental peaks that frame the icefield like pillars. Snowmobiles will take you up the slope of the glacier for a stretch, and you will enjoy the delightful combination of the sharp, cold air from the ice below and the bright sun rays from above. You will also get a fascinating glance into the workings of a live glacier. From afar its surface looks smooth and stagnant; but if you ride on top of it, you discover that it is alive with thousands of little streams rushing down the slope and carving small ice ridges and gorges. You can actually hear the busy working of the water. Columbia Icefield is also an interesting example of a world-wide phenomenon that seems to indicate a gradual climatic change on earth: the recession of the glaciers. Every year

the icefield recedes, and the distance between the highway and the glacial rim becomes greater.

RESORT OF THE HIGH NORTH. The road now follows the Athabaska River which originates at the Columbia Icefield. In the early 19th century when the fur trade was flourishing, this valley was the scene of a fierce struggle between the two great rivals, the Hudson's Bay Company and the North West Company, a "cold war" which was sensibly eliminated, in 1821, by the merger of the two competitors. An important company trading post was Jasper House, which gave its name to the park. The town of Jasper is the seat of the park headquarters and an all-year resort with well-appointed tourist accommodations. Three miles away, at the shore of Lac Beauvert, the luxurious and modern Jasper Park Lodge, owned and operated by the Canadian National Railways, is located. It is a new log-cabin-type hotel with a central lodge and numerous bungalows merging naturally into a setting of snow-capped mountains and tall evergreens. At night, when its huge picture windows shine brightly in the silent wilderness, it looks like a lonely castle lit up for a royal festival.

A FAMILIAR PICTURE. Some spots on earth are so beautiful that their picture is used over and over again for various purposes, to illustrate poetry or to advertise travel or to sell camp equipment; we become familiar with those corners of the earth long before we even dream of seeing them for ourselves. Maligne Lake is such a spot; we may have noticed its picture for years, but it is incomparably more satisfying to lay our own eyes on its blue-green waters, its wooded bays, and its snow-capped peaks; its bulging white clouds travel over a blue northern sky, and in front, on the little peninsula reaching way out into the lake, the grove of tall, dark-green firs sends its slender spires straight up. Not so long ago this lake could be reached only on horseback, on a four-day pack trip. That is still a most satisfactory way of traveling there, but now the excursion can also be made in one day by riding from Jasper to Maligne Canyon and Medicine Lake by car, crossing Medicine by motor launch, and proceeding to Maligne Lake in another car. The round trip encompasses a hundred miles. Maligne, by the way, is appreciated not only by sightseers but also by alpinists and fishermen; speckled trout is the lake's specialty. —One unforgettable sight that can be reached on horseback only is the Tonquin Valley; the jagged skyline of The Ramparts towers above the lovely Amethyst Lakes. —From Jasper Park Lodge, across Lac Beauvert, you see the stately summit of Mount Edith Cavell. High up on its slope Angel Glacier consists of one compact main body in the center and two outspread "angel wings"; this dramatic spot can easily be reached on a 20-mile automobile road, rising for 2000 feet over hairpin turns with wonderful vistas. —Just off the highway to Edmonton, 38 miles from Jasper, the

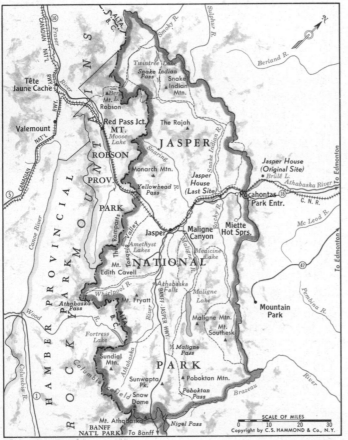

See sectional map, page 128

The jagged wall of The Ramparts rises majestically above the Amethyst Lakes, in the Tonquin Valley of Jasper National Park. This is one unforgettable beauty spot which can be reached on horseback only. The valley lies in a roadless wilderness at the western border of the park.

Miette Hot Springs have gained a reputation for their medicinal qualities. The springs pour out about 170,000 gallons of mineral water per day, at a temperature of 126° F. at the source. A modern bathing establishment offers an outdoor swimming pool in which a water temperature of 90° F. is maintained, a bathhouse, dining room, bungalows, and other facilities.

MOUNTAIN SHEEP AND MOUNTAIN LIONS. There is probably no area in the whole United States and Canada where wildlife has been maintained in its original variety to the same degree as it has been preserved in the Canadian National Parks of the Rockies. You can see moose wading through a lake or feeding in a swamp, or a bighorn sheep with its spiral horns. The grizzly bears and mountain lions hunt around the timberline, far from human habitations, and in the remotest valleys the wolf still finds a refuge.

HOW ICEBERGS ARE BORN. Two train hours to the west of Jasper, Mount Robson Provincial Park encircles the highest peak of the Canadian Rockies, with an altitude of 12,972 feet. On horseback you can ride through the Valley of a Thousand Falls to Berg Lake, on the northern flank of Mount Robson, and if you are lucky you will see a huge block of ice break off from Tumbling Glacier, splash into the lake, and sail off as an iceberg.

OLD INDIAN COUNTRY. The "Going-to-the-Sun Highway," a marvelously engineered road which crosses the park from East to West, has a name so imaginative that it seems to have originated in a public relations office on Madison Avenue. In fact the name is ascribed to a Blackfeet Indian leader named Tail-Feathers-Coming-over-the-Hill, and he created it from an old legend. For the Blackfeet had lived high up in the Canadian North, but in the 1700's moved south and settled in what is now Glacier National Park and in the adjoining plains. One of their gods, called "Sour Spirit," came to their villages and taught them the ways of the new land. After his task was finished, he hiked back to the sun god; the latter's abode was a huge mountain which, because of this journey, became "Going-to-the-Sun Mountain," and the trail leading to it is today's "Going-to-the-Sun Highway." Descendants of the Blackfeet still live in the reservation adjacent to the park, and their "Museum of the Plains Indians" in Browning is one of the finest exhibits of Indian lore, history, and art. For the name "Blackfeet" there are several explanations: one refers to a black salve which was occasionally smeared on the soles of their feet for medicinal and magic purposes; the other states that, at the first encounter of white men and the tribe, a group of the latter had marched through a burned-over prairie, and their moccasins and legs appeared black. The Blackfeet were once the scourge of the

whole region, feared and hated by the Flatheads and Kootenays, Sioux, Crows, and others. But today they are peaceful, and in the town of Browning have adapted themselves to modern western ways. They operate almost all business establishments. In the countryside they have remained more individualistic; for instance, they raise horses although there is little demand for their product. But they do so because they love horses, and love to trade horses among themselves. Out of this old Indian territory Glacier National Park arises.

THE SEA BOTTOM THAT CLIMBED TO THE MOUNTAIN TOP. The peaks of this park have as much personality as the Cascades and the Tetons; their shape and form is unmistakable; they appear to be in a lateral motion, as if they were on the march headed eastward. Sea shells and fossils of fish were found on their mountain tops, and ancient (let's say 90 million-year-old) rock layers lie above younger (let's say 30 million-year-old) strata. The phenomena that occurred here have been reconstructed by the geologists. Several shallow seas covered this land in early eras; the mud of the sea bottom hardened into stone, and gradually the rocks were lifted and became hills and mountains. Then, at one time, a huge force arose and began to push the whole mountainous mass eastward, for more than fifteen miles. In the process the rocky strata bent and broke, and the older western layers were shoved on top of the younger eastern layers; sometimes the ancient sea bottom landed on top of the pile. Then the various glacial periods descended upon the land, and huge glaciers ground and polished the mountains into the shape which they have now. Of the ancient ice fields only rather small remnants are left, but they are impressive enough to give the park its name. Sperry, Blackfoot, and Grinnell Glaciers are easily reached. The peaks of the park are not spectacularly tall —Mt. Cleveland with an altitude of 10,448 feet is the highest—but they are magnificently colored. Ribbons of red and gray, green and purple, brown and yellow sparkle and glow in the sun, and their horizontal sweep adds to the impression of lateral motion, of "mountains on the move." Of the park's 200 crystal-clear lakes McDonald is the largest and St. Mary Lake the loveliest; in their waters silent peaks mirror themselves, miniature icebergs float without motion, wildflower meadows border their shores, and tall firs and spruces frame the enchanting view. Most of these attractions, including the rocky fastness of the Continental Divide, can be enjoyed from the Going-to-the-Sun Highway; where the mountain walls leave no space for the road, a tunnel has been drilled, and the two picture windows that have been carved into the west tunnel, offer views of rarely matched mountain splendor. But those who really want to get acquainted with this third-largest of our national parks, should take to the trails; there are 1,000 miles of them, either for hiking and climbing or for horseback riding. Horses, guides, and trail-riding equipment is more amply avail-

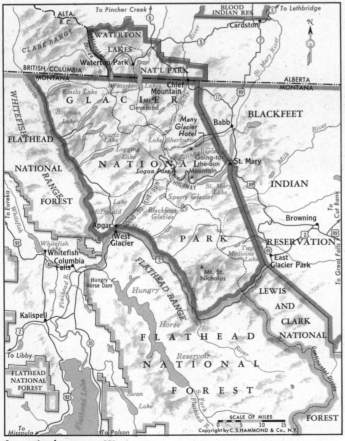

See sectional map, page 128

Swiftcurrent Falls, below Lake Sherburne, provide glacial waters and a sparkling northern setting for trout fishing. Pickere abound in Lake Sherburne and rainbow, brook and cutthroat trout are plentiful in the adjoining lakes.

able here than in other parks. The hikers and riders will travel through an abundance of wildflowers—the beargrass with its clusters of small, white lily blossoms flourishes in such profusion that it has become a symbol of the park—and will closely observe the mountain wildlife: not only the black bear and the marmot, the elk and the mule deer, but especially the bighorn sheep and the Rocky Mountain goat.

NOT GUNS BUT TREES. There is not only nature to be studied here but also politics. For the continuation of Glacier National Park on the Canadian side is Waterton Lakes National Park, and instead of fortifying the frontier with guns and fortresses, both nations decided in 1932 to unite their beautiful parks into one great area of common enjoyment and understanding, into the Waterton-Glacier International Peace Park, "forever a symbol of permanent peace and friendship." For such a gesture of good-will there is no counterpart in the game of international politics, past or present. Waterton Park —named in honor of the English naturalist Charles Waterton—has characteristics similar to those of the American park: There are the same glacier-sculptured amphitheaters with cool and clear lakes, the same red and golden yellow and purple bands in the mountain slopes, the same trout in the streams, the same hairy mountain goats on the shining peaks. Upper Waterton Lake, a deep trench between two high mountain ranges, has a charm of its own, and since the international boundary line crosses it invisibly and unnoticeably its wild beauty belongs to Canada and the United States alike.

GATEWAY TO HADES. There are three spots on our planet where you may feel very close to the mysterious hot underworld, where you can actually feel its boiling and burning chaos through the soles of your shoes. Two of these places, Iceland and New Zealand, are interesting on a lesser scale. The third one is fantastic and spectacular: Yellowstone Park.

From the sights that surround you here you can gain a deep perspective into the awe-inspiring story of the earth. An array of forbidding volcanoes once covered this area, spitting fire and belching black smoke, ashes and lava. They covered the forest with volcanic dust until the trees disappeared, and as the organic matter was replaced by minerals, the trunks became petrified; even the bark, the roots, and some leaves turned into stone. For a period the volcanoes slept, and new forests grew on top of the ancient woods. Then the craters awoke again and the trees experienced the same fate as their predecessors. Look at Amethyst Mountain in the northeastern corner of the park: A vertical rock section of 2000 feet shows 12 such successive forests. The trees under which you walk now may in time become the thirteenth.

The volcanoes are asleep, but the land is still volcanic. Rock deep in the earth still retains great heat resulting from the past volcanic action. This heat is what makes geysers possible. As water seeps down, the hot rocks turn it into steam, deep in the earth. The steam tries to escape

View from Artist Point, high above one of the great canyons of the West.

upward but is stopped by a column of cold water; the pressure increases, some water bubbles over and reduces the weight of the "stopper," and with steam rushing out the geyser erupts.

Old Faithful, which hurls a column of hot water and white steam 120 to 170 feet high into the sky approximately every 65 minutes, has become world-famous. Among the others the Giant and the Giantess throw their spouts to a height of 200 feet, but their eruptions are irregular. Beehive Geyser balances its slender column from a beehive-shaped cone, and Grand Geyser displays a huge fan of spray and steam.

PLANTS AS PAINTERS. The terraces of giant steps painted in brightly sparkling shades of pink and red, tan and brown, blue and gray are another eye-filling phenomenon; they have been created by the Mammoth Hot Springs along the northern edge of the park. The colors are the work of tiny algae which thrive in hot water. Where a spring ceases to flow, the microscopic plants die, and only the white limestone remains.

The Fountain Paint Pots are a caldron of boiling brown, pink and yellow tints that do not seem to mix properly, and the roaring explosions of Mud Volcano can be heard for a half a mile. Worth seeing are also Sulphur Mountain and Obsidian Cliff, the hill of natural volcanic glass whose chips were prized by the Indians as arrowheads.

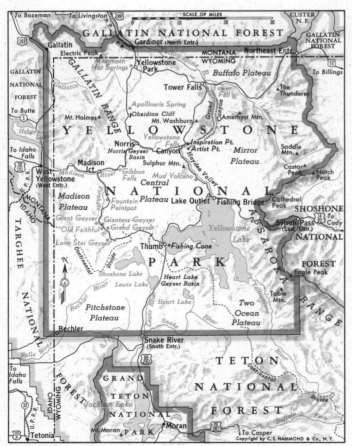

See sectional map, page 128

The World's Greatest Volcanic Outdoor Museum

CASCADES AND BEARS. If there were no volcanic wonders to be gazed at, Yellowstone Park would still be an outstanding travel goal, because its scenery is of superb beauty. Yellowstone Lake, with 100 miles of shore-line at an altitude of nearly a mile and a half above sea level, is not only the largest North-American lake at such great height but also one of the wildest or loveliest, depending on the weather and the mood of the day. The Grand Canyon of the Yellowstone River with the Great Falls—a white cloud of whirling and spraying water shooting out of nowhere and dropping 300 feet—appears from Artist Point or Inspiration Point like a symphony of yellow and white, with a pattern of mellowed red, pearly gray and jet black streaks on the rock walls which are topped with a border of evergreens.

Yellowstone Park is also one of the world's great animal preserves, a veritable outdoor zoo. Thousands of elk, moose, deer and antelope live there; bands of mountain sheep climb the rocky peaks, a herd of more than 1000 buffaloes graze in the valleys, grizzly bears roam the inaccessible slopes, and the hundreds of black bears have become as famous as the geysers. The Park Service is waging a campaign against the feeding of the bears by visitors who turn the normally self-reliant and good-natured animals into insistent and sometimes dangerous beggars. Lake and streams are stocked with various kinds of trout, notably the cut-throat and the

A typical hot pool; tiny flowers bloom in the chemically charged atmosphere.

grayling. Almost 800 species of wildflowers bloom profusely throughout the park.

TALL TALES. That so fascinating a region should have developed a folklore of its own is not surprising. Handkerchief Pool, they say, used to suck your soiled handkerchief out of sight and erupt it a minute later, clean and fresh. Early fishermen liked to ply their rods in Yellowstone Lake near Fishing Cone. They caught a trout, dropped the line on the other side into the boiling hot spring, then pulled it out and ate it, all without moving an inch. But the best tale concerns Jim Bridger, Yellowstone's Paul Bunyan. Once, while hunting, he spied a large elk and shot at it. The animal ignored Jim, so he walked on to investigate and bumped head-on into the transparent Mountain of Glass. The elk stood on the other side. Even more astonishing, the mountain acted as a huge magnifying glass; the animal he saw was actually grazing 25 miles away.

Yellowstone Park lies in northwestern Wyoming, extending slightly into Montana and Idaho. With an area of approximately 62 by 54 miles it is larger than the combined states of Delaware and Rhode Island. John Colter, of the Lewis and Clark Expedition, was probably the first white man to see this area, around 1807. Later reports by trappers were considered lies until General Washburn's Expedition of 1870 established the facts. In 1872 it was set up as the world's first National Park.

Old Faithful, the only large geyser with a regular schedule.

NATURE AND ART. If a great stage director, an outstanding artist in his field, presented a mountain range in all its glory, he would do exactly what nature has done in the case of the Grand Tetons. He would shuffle the huge granite sheets into a well balanced range, short enough so that the human eye can encompass the beginning, the towering center, and the end. He would shift the mountains so that the peaks form a giant saw against the blue sky. He would eliminate the foothills which only clutter up the scene and block the view. He would lay a string of clear, blue lakes around the range where the peaks may mirror themselves. And he would provide a huge amphitheater, in this case Jackson Hole, from where the audience can enjoy an unobstructed near or far view of the mountain spectacle. Whether we drive south from Yellowstone Park and get our first glimpse of the Grand Tetons across Jackson Lake, or whether we drive north and see the range between some gnarled old trees across Jenny Lake, it becomes quite clear that, at their most beautiful, nature and art are one.

At Moose there is a log cabin chapel which has a most unusual altar picture: A simple window with a direct view of the tallest peak of the range, the Grand Teton. This picture compares favorably with the finest altar paintings of the old masters.

THE OLD STAMPING GROUND. Whether the In-

dians and trappers enjoyed the scenic attractions of the spot, has not been recorded. But it is a fact that they returned there year after year. Jackson Hole—"hole" because it is a plain surrounded by mountains, and "Jackson Hole" in honor of a pioneer fur trader—had too severe a winter climate to be inhabited during that season, but when spring came, cavalcades of copper-skinned men and women began to move into the plain, Blackfeet and Flatheads, Crows and Shoshoni, to spend the summer hunting, fishing, trapping and fighting. John Colter, originally a member of the Lewis and Clark Expedition, was probably the first white man to see these mountains, in 1807 or 1808. In 1811 a group of fur traders bound for Astoria in Oregon passed through this region, and as the range seemed an excellent landmark on the road to the West, they called the peak "Pilot Knobs." Approximately at the same time a party of French trappers stayed there, and gave the mountains a more imaginative and longer lasting name. They fancied that the three tallest peaks resembled breasts of women, and called them "Les Trois Tetons," a name that won out and survived to this day. Between 1825 and 1845 Jackson Hole was the paradise of trappers and fur traders, and famous western characters like David Jackson and William Sublette, Jedediah Smith and Kit Carson, Jim Bridger and Joe Meek were closely connected with the region's history; of course, the "hole" had also its share of outlaws and fugitives from justice. The collapse of the fur trade in 1845—beaver hats were suddenly out of style—restored the plain to the Indians, and not until the 1880's did the first homesteaders appear, hardy pioneers who braved the terrible winters.

THE CHALLENGE. The plain of Jackson Hole is 48 miles long and 6 to 8 miles wide, at an elevation of 6 to 7 thousand feet. The Grand Tetons have a length of 40 miles and include 20 peaks over 10,000 feet tall; the Grand Teton reaches a height of 13,766 feet. There are many taller mountains in the world, but the sheer granite walls of this range are defiant and seem to have a magnetic lure for mountain climbers. American alpinists have tried their skill at the Grand Tetons for years; but now the experts come from all over the world, and find the range a most worthwhile and rewarding goal. All parties of mountain climbers must register at park headquarters, and no one is allowed to venture into the upper regions alone. An ascent of the Grand Teton will take two days, and any kind of weather may be encountered. Snow falls in every month of the year.

Less ambitious visitors will enjoy the park's system of magnificent trails, for hiking and horseback riding. The Lakes Trail circles Jenny Lake and connects all six lakes at the foot of the range. On a still day the various mirror-pictures of the peaks are perfect. To see a glacier at an elevation of 10,000 feet you may take the Teton Glacier Trail; it ends at Amphitheater Lake. To enjoy a waterfall, follow Cascade Canyon Trail; it leads to the

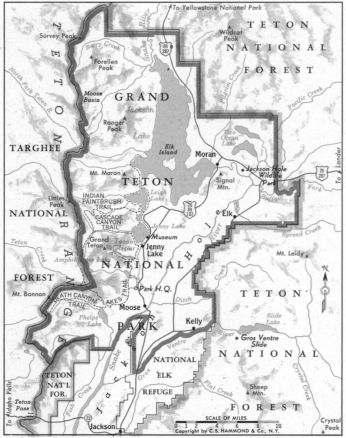

See sectional map, page 128

The huge granite "saw" of the Grand Tetons is equally intriguing to the mountain climber and to the photographer. Although not the tallest mountains in the world, the challenge of their sheer granite cliffs lures climbers from all over the world.

deepest recesses of the mountains. Death Canyon Trail passes through awesome chasms. If you love wildflowers, the Indian Paintbrush Canyon Trail will lead you through a profusion of blossoms; the Indian Paintbrush proper is the state flower of Wyoming.

Since no automobile roads lead into the mountains themselves, the trails of the park are ideal for an intimate glance at nature. Some bulky moose may be watched, especially near the Indian Paintbrush Canyon Trail, or a few mule deer. Of mountain sheep and bears, martens and coyote the visitor will only get an accidental glance, but beavers and ground squirrels may easily be observed. There is also a large elk herd in the park. The animals spend the winter in the National Elk Refuge near the town of Jackson; when the snow melts they migrate to higher pastures in the east and north; some bands wander into the Tetons. When the snows return, the elks drift back to the refuge.

WHERE ARE THE COWBOYS? Visitors who on their way to Grand Teton and Yellowstone cross Wyoming and Montana, the heart of the cattle country, often complain that they see no thundering herds or swaggering cowboys. The explanation is simple: The biggest ranches are far from highways, and during the dry summer the herds usually graze on remote hill pastures. But the rodeos are accessible, and good fun.

WITHOUT TELESCOPE AND ROCKET SHIP. It has been said that the American continent contains every conceivable type of landscape, every formation of rock, soil and water found anywhere on earth. This assertion may even be extended to the moon. No one has been there yet, but telescopic photographs accurately show the only extra-planetary landscape known to us, a distressing place of desolation, of parched deserts and barren mountains, dead volcanoes and huge lava flows spread over the surface as if to cover scars. A reasonable replica of that scene may be observed and studied in southeastern Idaho near the town of Arco, at the Craters of the Moon National Monument. There an earthly circular road takes the visitor to a moonlike area called the Great Rift, a breaking point in the crust of the earth, a well of lava which ejected the black mass slowly, or spat it sky-high in the form of lava bombs which looked like tear drops or pieces of ribbon. That violent volcanic activity occurred perhaps a thousand years ago, which is quite recent, geologically speaking, and the ground kept on smoking to our own day. The weird terraces and arches, caverns and beds, walls and flows sometimes take on graceful, billowing lines, and formations like the Blue Dragon seem iridescent when touched by the rays of the sun. Fascinating are the perfect molds of tree trunks and tree roots. The lava

had engulfed the tumbling timber, and two actions took place simultaneously: The moisture of the logs hardened the lava quickly in the shapes it had formed around the trunks and roots, and the wood inside burned out. There is one delightful difference between the landscape of the real moon and its replica in Idaho: The former is sterile, without life and vegetation. The Idaho craters look forbidding enough, but they cannot overcome the creative power of our planet, since the hot gases ceased rising through the fissures. Here and there young aspens raise their heads courageously and young pines get a firm foothold. Fair-sized red choke cherries appear in the cracks where sufficient earth has gathered and courageous shrubs make a hesitant appearance. Camping spaces are provided at the monument, as well as tourist cabins and a restaurant.

TROPICAL TAN IN GLACIAL AIR. If Idaho has its Inferno, it also has its Paradise: To the northwest of the Craters of the Moon lies Sun Valley, the famous resort in whose making nature and man combined their best abilities. Nature, of course, had been there first, providing smooth, treeless mountains of various heights, with slopes of varying steepness, with an abundance of light, powdery winter snow which turns pink and purple in the sunset, and with the delightful climate of an altitude of 6,000 feet. Man did not arrive until the middle 1930's when skiing experts, commissioned by the Union Pacific Railroad, searched the West and declared this to be the ideal winter resort. Two hotels, a number of chalets and one of the world's longest chair lifts were built, and Sun Valley has flourished ever since. There are thirty-odd ski runs, ranging from the difficult slopes of Baldy Mountain and the more regular runs of Dollar Mountain and Half Dollar Mountain to the grounds of the ski school, where beginners learn the art from a faculty of forty instructors, some of them famous aces. There is a fascinating play of contrasts: If you want to acquire a deep, tropical winter tan you may, of course, go to the tropics; but you can acquire it just as well here, by skiing in the sunshine on the high slopes, stripped to the waist, or by constructing a kind of chaise lounge of your two ski poles and the skis themselves. There you lie down, on a wind-protected slope, and let the rays of the sun work on your complexion. If you care to swim in an outdoor pool in mid-January, while the snow flakes gently drift down from the sky, you may do so here. The water is, of course, heated. Other popular winter thrills are dog-sledding over nearby trails to Trail Creek Cabin, and skijoring, the exciting Scandinavian sport in which a horse with a rider draws the skier behind.

BELLS RING ON MOUNTAIN MEADOWS. The general setting for both the Inferno and the Paradise is one of grand mountain scenery, of tall peaks and deep canyons and huge, sweet-smelling pine forests. Most of

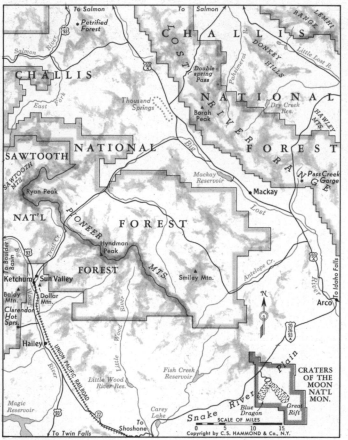

See sectional map, page 128

Sun Valley's snowy mountains turn pink and purple in the sunset. It s little wonder t s beautiful locale has become one of the country's most popular resorts for swimming and skiing.

Idaho is a wonderful, untouched wilderness, first described by Lewis and Clark, and the very name of the state reveals that spirit. In the dialect of the Eastern Shoshone Indians Idaho means "Behold-the-sur-coming-up-behind-the-mountains," a word used in the sense of "It is time to arise." There are not less than twenty-two mountain ranges, most of them untamed and untouched, and deep, narrow gorges cut into the rocky land. The slopes around the timberline are quite densely populated, though not by humans beings. Sheep live here in large numbers, and their fleecy flocks are cared for by unusual Americans. Most of the sheep herders are Basques or the descendants of Basques, and so skillful and indispensable are they at their art that urgently needed

newcomers may enter the U. S. with a minimum of red tape. On the lonely highland pastures the older Basques look like the shepherd-patriarchs of the Old Testament, even to the staff with the hook, which seems to have changed little these last 3,000 years. How do they control their wards, especially when they cannot see them in the rolling hills? The sheep instinctively separate into clans, each small flock following a leader. The latter has a bell tied around his neck and each bell has a different tone. So there is a perennial glockenspiel, and if only one note is missing in the harmony, the herder and his dog set out to investigate and retrieve the wayward flock. There is an ethereal music on those mountain pastures. It's a magic land.

TO MAKE THE DESERT BLOOM. When you slowly drive over the bridge-road along the crest of Grand Coulee Dam, the first thought to strike you will probably be the strange contrast before you; below, a huge cataract twice the height of Niagara Falls spills torrents of blue water and white, cooling foam into the valley while all around brownish, arid hills stretch their rough wasteland-ridges against the sky. The desert landscape is enlivened by tall steel towers and humming high tension wires strung in various directions. This view tells the story: Nature has provided here a great reservoir of fertile but dry soil; also a great river, the Columbia, second only to the Mississippi in volume, with a draining area of almost 260,000 square miles, delivering more fresh water to the ocean than all the other Pacific coast rivers combined. One resource nature did not provide here is oil, and of coal there is very little; but the river has a staggering potential of hydro power—42 per cent, in fact, of the whole nation's potential electric energy production. So man has taken on the role of equalizer and coordinator, and has erected, across the Columbia, the biggest concrete structure ever raised on earth, as tall as a 40-story building, the power house and pulsing heart of Washington's "inland empire," to bring into harmonious cooperation the soil, the water, and the energy, to irrigate, turn wheels, produce, create. When all the dams of the Columbia river system are built that can be built, more energy will be

The level of 151-mile-long Lake Roosevelt is controlled to avoid floods in Canada.

produced here than from all other sources in the U. S.

APPLES AND ATOMS. To furnish the magic touch for the fertile, arid soil, the Columbia Basin Project, south of the dam, uses the ancient, dried-up bed of the Grand Coulee River. Its old channel has been turned into a storage tank twenty-seven miles long, with two dams sealing off the river bed. Filled with water from the Columbia, the reservoir can irrigate more than a million acres of desert, and is slated to sustain thousands of fertile farms, to produce grain, fruits and vegetables in abundance, and to maintain and feed hundreds of thousands of cattle, sheep, hogs, turkeys, chickens. New towns will be needed, new shopping centers and newspapers. A pioneering adventure is in the making here, fortunately not a homesteading rush in the old western sense. All is done in an orderly fashion, with prices fixed by Congress on a sensible level, and expert advice and guidance for all new colonizers. The new electric current has flowed largely into two undertakings, a great aluminum industry which did not exist here before the war, and atomic energy. Quite a few of the old lumber towns like Longview and Vancouver, Wash., which used to worry about their future because of the diminishing timber supply, are operating mammoth aluminum plants now. Where the Columbia turns northward, the Hanford Plant, the Atomic Energy Commission's producer of Plutonium 239, stands in the sagebrush wasteland like the desert

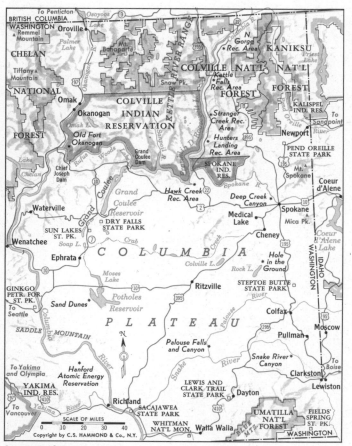

See sectional map, page 128

castle of an African legend. A good part of the energy generated at Grand Coulee Dam is needed to perform the intricate process of atomic fission.

INVITATION TO THE TAXPAYERS. Anyone who knows how great public works of this kind are heavily guarded in Europe, and considered forbidden territory for the public in general, is delighted by the friendly and open way in which such structures in America are open to public inspection; the public is actually invited. It is obvious—although only to the American mind—that the one who has paid for the plant should have the right to see it, wander through it, and learn about it. At Grand Coulee, as at most other dams, there are guided tours and interesting lectures about the intakes deep under water on the upstream side, about the biggest turbines that have ever been built, the huge generators and the delicate measuring instruments. Toward the north the dam's impounded current forms Lake Franklin D. Roosevelt, a 151-mile long, deep blue body of river water along the shores of which the government has established a chain of recreational areas. The level of the lake is controlled so that no backed-up floods spill into Canadian territory. Around the dam proper a good deal of greenery may be seen; the sprinklers turn day and night.

THE BALANCE OF NATURE. Has it been disturbed? Has the interference of man created unexpected

The old, dried-up bed of the Grand Coulee is now a 27-mile-long water storage tank.

problems? The wildlife experts are a little worried about the salmon population of the Columbia River. At Bonneville Dam fish ladders lead the mature fish on their upstream spawning migration around the dam structure, and special spillways allow the young salmon to avoid the obstacle on their way to the ocean. But no such provisions could be made at Grand Coulee Dam which has the height of a skyscraper. So thousands of salmon whose birthplace had been in the cold Canadian headwaters of the river, rammed their heads against the concrete and perished. For a considerable part of the salmon population the way home was blocked forever. So the fishery experts conceived a plan in the grand manner which may solve the problem, at least partially. They trapped masses of Chinooks headed for the Grand Coulee Dam, transferred them to hatcheries and gently removed their eggs and milt. The eggs were fertilized and placed in tributary streams below the big dam. Then the baby fish were born, and two years later set out on their journey to the Pacific, many of them tagged. Uneasily the wildlife men waited for another two years. Would the ascent of these salmon be a death journey, or would it conclude a successful resettlement project? To everybody's relief the migrants ignored Grand Coulee and returned to their foster streams; since more dams are to be built, it might be conceivable to resettle the whole salmon population in the lower Columbia Valley.

Grand Coulee Dam is the biggest concrete structure ever raised on earth.

143

A BIT OF ENGLAND SURROUNDED BY CANADA." That's how eastern Canadians sometimes call the Province of British Columbia. They are probably right as to the British Columbian capital of Victoria; that city, with its thriving flowers, its "eternal English spring," its retired colonels and its afternoon tea at the Empress Hotel, is indeed a piece of England (as a part of the Puget Sound country it is described on page 148). But Vancouver, the largest community of the province, strikes the visitor as a cosmopolitan world port. It is quite true that the stately Vancouver Hotel has a certain British dignity; that replicas of the crown jewels were objects of intense interest during coronation year; and that the best restaurants in town specialize in roast beef and Yorkshire pudding. But on the whole the atmosphere is Canadian and international, with several interesting appendices pointing to the Orient: the Chinese, Japanese and Hindu quarters. As to its origin, Vancouver was founded by the same motley crowd of gold seekers that established San Francisco. When word reached the California diggings that gold had been discovered near Lytton, 160 miles up the Fraser River, 30,000 miners sailed northward and started their upstream voyage on the Fraser. They found it a backbreaking task, encountering rapid currents between sheer canyon walls and impassable portages, and hundreds of the newcomers perished. In

Prospect Point in Vancouver's Stanley Park presents a spectacular mountain view.

the ensuing atmosphere of lawlessness and frontier brawls there was a cry for "protection" by the United States, and for "Fifty-four forty or fight." But the boom collapsed, and many of the miners stayed and turned to shipping and the lumber trade for a livelihood; they founded also a few small settlements. One of them, Gas Town at the mouth of the Fraser, became Vancouver; in about two generations it grew into a young, bright metropolitan city in a spectacularly beautiful setting, a great harbor surrounded by snow-capped mountains. —To enjoy this vast panorama you can ride by cable car to a hilltop, or in your own automobile to Mount Seymour Park, a short distance from the city over the Second Narrows Bridge. The road leading to the summit provides two view points for sightseers, one facing east, the other west, which on a clear day offer breathtaking vistas. Mount Seymour Park is a skiing resort of more than 9,000 acres, with ski tows, a ski jump, and a ski camp. In Vancouver proper, Stanley Park is a wonderful combination of forest, flower garden, and zoo, near the business center and surrounded by blue waters. It is a vantage point for watching ocean steamers cross under the British Empire's highest suspension bridge, the Lion's Gate Bridge. The Park's Theater Under the Stars is an excellent light opera stage.

THE FJORDS AND THE ISLANDS. The Inside Passage to Alaska between the continent and the hun-

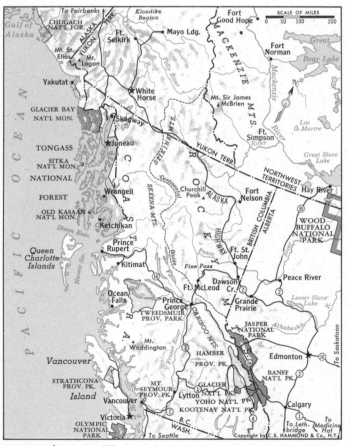

See sectional map, page 128

dreds of outlying islands has often been compared to the coast of Norway. Both have in common the mountains rising out of the water as rounded, forest-clad summits or as steep canyon walls, the glaciers and waterfalls, the inlets called fjords in Europe, and the fishing grounds which teem with herring and cod in Norway, and with salmon and halibut in British Columbia and Alaska. But the Norwegian coast is laid out almost continually with little recesses in the rocks where one or a few farmer-fishermen have their tiny settlements on a small green patch. The British Columbia-Alaska coast is grander, wilder, rockier, more forbidding, and very sparsely populated. The few coastal communities are usually perched on a mountain slope and descend to the water's rim. Ocean Falls at the head of Fisher Channel, for instance looks like an amphitheater, with a street system that includes a great many stairs and elevated planked roads on piling; the same condition prevails in other coastal communities. Ocean Falls is a spic-and-span company town, owned by Pacific Mills, a large pulp and paper producer. Prince Rupert, British Columbia's most northerly seaport and terminus of the Canadian National Railways, is not even 50 years old and has an intriguing frontier atmosphere. Ketchikan, Alaska's southernmost port, is a busy harbor teeming with fishing boats; a visit to one of its fish packing plants is very worthwhile. The huge, white halibuts, some bigger than a man, are cut

Ocean Falls, B.C., perches on the rim of fjord-like Fisher Channel.

up with a few, fast, expert strokes, then subdivided, packed and deep-frozen,—a fascinating process to watch. Some plants keep in their coldest vaults a sort of museum of curios: a strange-looking fish, an otter, a wolf,—all frozen stiff. Ketchikan's sights include two Totem Pole Parks; they preserve a world-famous Indian folk art which is no longer practiced by the natives. A five-day cruise from Vancouver to Ketchikan and back, on a steamer of the Canadian National Railways, is available every week; a longer 10-day cruise will take you farther north to Juneau, the capital of Alaska and a mining center, dramatically overshadowed by a steep granite wall, and to Skagway, the gateway to the interior of Alaska and the Yukon Territory. Although from Skagway's streets you look up to the snowy peaks, it is Alaska's flower city; its dahlias grow to a diameter of ten inches.

THE ROAD TO ALASKA. All these cities are located in the narrow coastal strip that is the southeastern corner of Alaska. To reach the Alaskan heartland proper, the Alaska Highway is available, but those who have taken it, find it a strenuous voyage, hard on the tires of the car and monotonous as far as the scenery is concerned. The best way of getting acquainted with the huge American outpost opposite Asia, is to take a steamer of the Alaska Line out of Seattle or to fly by plane. Every travel agent can supply the details of information, schedules and fares.

Lion's Gate Bridge is the highest suspension bridge in the British Empire.

ANCIENT GODS IN THE NEW WORLD. There is a legend that Jupiter, discouraged with conditions in Greece, left his holy abode, Mount Olympus by the Aegean Sea, and set out to find a heaven elsewhere. He searched for another massive, snow-capped peak that looked out on blue water, and finally found it in the northwest corner of America. There was indeed another Mount Olympus, quite similar to the one in Greece, surrounded by a rocky stronghold called the Olympic Mountains, and forming a huge promontory in the sea called the Olympic Peninsula. There the ancient god settled happily and has been at work ever since. As Jupiter Pluvius, the Rainmaker, he is drawing as much as twelve feet of rain from the skies onto the western slopes every year, while as Jupiter Serenator, the Sunshine-Producer, he dries pleasantly and sometimes too effectively the eastern slopes.

The tale has a pleasant Old-World flavor while another legend about the Olympic Mountains is of a strictly American character. It seems that Paul Bunyan's blue ox Babe got sick and was carried by its master to the Pacific shore to "take the cure" on the milk of the Western Whale. In spite of this tonic Babe's strength faded away and Paul Bunyan sadly shoveled a grave for the little blue ox. Then suddenly the patient recovered, the funeral was postponed, and the open hole remained as it was dug. In time it filled with water, but it is still there, just as the pile of

dirt and rock is still lying by the side of the pit. One is called Puget Sound, the hole filled with water, the other the Olympic Mountains, the pile of dirt and rock beside it.

FIVE SHINING RINGS. The unique beauty of this ridgeless mass of piercing peaks is perhaps best described in terms of five vastly different but equally fascinating circles. The first ring is only a three-quarter circle, and consists of the blue waters of Hood Canal, Juan de Fuca Strait and the Pacific Ocean. To sail on these wide waterways and see the snow-capped Olympics rise steeply into the sky is an impression never to be forgotten. On one side there are the towers of Seattle, Tacoma and other great and busy population centers; on the other side the Olympics tower in wild, almost untouched grandeur. Ring Number Two consists of the Olympic Loop, a 364-mile round trip through the foothills that offers such attractions as a 50-mile ride along the beautiful Hood Canal, a visit to the little city of Port Angeles with its famous salmon and crab grounds, and a view of crystal-clear Lake Crescent, which lies in the shadow of Mount Storm King, in the northern end of the park. It is the world's only lake to contain the Beardslee trout, a big species which often weighs from 10 to 15 pounds.

The next higher circle is a belt of woods which on the western slopes consists of the so-called rain forests. Exposed to the first onslaught of rain clouds drifting in from the west, these wet valleys have produced a uniquely exuberant growth, a forest scene where from a carpet of thick mosses and huge ferns, trees arise that are the giants of their species. There is a red cedar with a 20-foot-wide trunk, and a Douglas fir 17 feet wide four feet above the ground. Tilden tells of a giant log that fell to the ground many decades ago; on it, twenty-one hemlock trees took root and grew into healthy, tall specimens. There they stand now in a straight line, like a company of soldiers. Vines and mosses hang from the branches in flowing streamers as long as 20 feet, and the dim, whitish-green light and the complete stillness make the rain forest an eerie, unearthly place. This belt stretches from sea level to a height of about 5,000 feet. Beyond that the fourth ring above timberline presents the wildflower meadows which spread a blanket of avalanche lilies, tiger lilies, asters and violets, red columbines and blue lupines, bluebells and many others. And finally there is the circle of glaciers, 36 square miles of ice and snow fields which each season receives 200 to 250 inches of snow. Since the Olympics are not volcanic, there is no lava dust to spoil the clean, pure beauty of the scene. One of the largest glaciers is Blue Glacier whose ice seems to be of a clear blue color; its lower end protrudes over a steep stone wall and occasionally breaks off, crashing down into the valley with a barrage of thunder. The rain and snow statistics, by the way, should not deter any travelers from visiting the park; for the precipitation takes place mostly in wintertime, and during the sum-

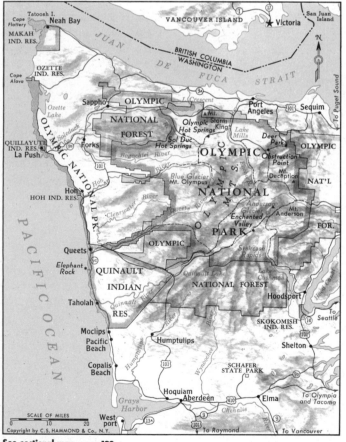

See sectional map, page 128

The Olympic Mountains are a fortress-like, rocky mass of snow-capped peaks overlooking the blue water of the sea, not unlike the original Mount Olympus which was the abode of the Greek Gods.

mer there are many weeks of fine, sunny weather, often still delightful in September and October.

MAKE WAY FOR THE ELKS. There are but a few miles of highway within the park proper. However, one road in the northeastern section climbs 6,000 feet to Deer Park where a magnificent panorama of Juan de Fuca Strait and Vancouver Island may be enjoyed. For the real nature lover there are 450 miles of trails, and the network is extended annually. Most of these trails were already in existence when the rangers arrived, and just had to be improved and connected; they were the runs of the elk, i.e., in these mountains the Roosevelt elk, so named in honor of Theodore Roosevelt. They are darker than the elk of the Rocky Mountains, and also larger, weighing up to 1,000 pounds. Their horns are shorter but heavier; they still like to use their old elk runs, and quite a few trail hikers have had the somewhat exasperating experience of hearing the approaching clop-clop-clop of a band of these big animals, of stepping aside gingerly, and seeing four or five Roosevelt elks crashing by. Black-tailed Columbian deer, black bear and the more common small animals are plentiful. In an effort to extend the range of some of the rarer species of American wildlife, a herd of mountain goats was brought in from the Canadian Rockies several years ago and is thriving.

STIRRING THE IMAGINATION. This is one of the world's great seascapes. Its dimensions are so gigantic that it cannot be encompassed in one picture by a photographic lens. But the human eye can absorb much of it on a clear day, from a plane or a boat or a high vantage point ashore. The secret of its appeal lies in a rare combination of mountains and forests, islands and bays, cities and ships, and every one of these elements stands squarely on its place, strong and solid, vigorous and permanent, a paragon of its kind. Of the three mountain masses that dominate the scene, Mt. Rainier is one of America's great peaks; so is Mt. Baker looking out over the San Juan Islands to the west, and while the Olympics across the sound only reach an altitude of 7,954 feet, they rise abruptly out of the blue water in such a broad, fortress-like mass that they are impressive indeed. The waters of Puget Sound stretch for 150 miles from Olympia, the southern terminal, to Blaine at the Canadian border, and for 200 miles through the Strait of Juan de Fuca to Cape Flattery. The sound consists of innumerable picturesque bays and inlets, including Hood Canal, a beautiful, forest-lined natural waterway half a mile broad and 80 miles long with shorelines so straight that it appears man-made. These waters teem with fish, with salmon and sea perch, and candle smelts that can be scooped up with baskets, in season; oysters and clams abound. Fishing is an old tradition here; the

Seattle's skyline and an Alaskan totem pole stand for America's northwestern life line.

original inhabitants of these shores, the Makah and Quillayute Indians, found their perpetual harvest of fish so rewarding that they never became hunters. The forests —dark firs, lighter undergrowth, and myriads of wild flowers, including wild lilacs and wild roses—cover the islands and the slopes like a velvety carpet. The deer of the woods raid orchards and the bears rob hen houses within sight of villages or even cities. Bushes and trees grow so fast that home owners forever have to cut and trim the branches to keep their picture-window views open.

SEATTLE'S HORIZONS: THE ORIENT AND ALASKA. Into this wilderness great cities have been carved. Seattle is the largest; the others—Bellingham, Everett, Tacoma and Olympia—are all growing communities and some day may merge into a continuous urban half circle, like the towns around San Francisco Bay. Visitors will find it a fascinating experience to walk through the hubbub of downtown Seattle, and between modern skyscrapers see stretches of the blue sound, or a deep-green forested slope, or the white peaks of Mt. Rainier or the snowy crest of the Olympics tower in the distance above low-lying clouds. They will be delighted to discover another big body of water beyond the hills of the city to the east, 26-mile-long Lake Washington where the University of Washington is located. Lake Washington is also the home of the many-time winner

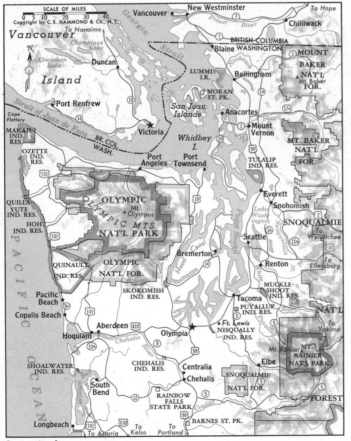

See sectional map, page 128

148

Slo-Mo-Shun speedboats and enthusiasts can sometimes see test runs on the lake. The panorama adheres to the Puget Sound pattern: There are islands and inlets, and the tree-shaded shores are connected by a famous floating bridge. To watch the big locks where the boats from the yacht basin in the lake cross over to the sound, is a popular pastime. Lovers of ships will find a stroll along the "Alaskan Way," the waterfront, with its ferry terminal and totem poles, or a ride over the sound by ferry, steamer, or sailboat most rewarding. The waters swarm with craft of every imaginable type, from Indian skiffs to the boats of the halibut fleet, from canoes to cabin cruisers, from freight scows to big, sea-going log rafts; the latter are pulled by tugs so far ahead that the uninitiated visitor's eyes will not connect raft and steamer until he spies the long cable cutting the water. Conspicuous are the freighters and tankers and passenger boats, most of them bound homeward from or outward to two specific sections of the world: the Orient to which Seattle is the closest port in the U.S., and Alaska to which the city has been the gateway ever since we bought the northern empire from the Russians. Old timers on the docks speak with familiarity of Colombo and Bengal, Yokohama and Macao, Canton or Singapore. But as to Alaska with its lumber trade and canning business, they consider it their very own domain and backyard. Today Seattle's shipping is vigorously supplemented by the airplane industry.

Leisurely sightseeing coaches drive through British-looking Victoria, B. C.

A unique floating bridge crosses Lake Washington at Seattle's back door

ENGLAND ACROSS THE BAY. One of Seattle's most popular excursions, on one of the bright Canadian "Princess" boats, is the trip to Victoria, the capital of British Columbia, across the sound on Vancouver Island. That lovely town has been called "as English as Exeter," but what primarily arrests the casual visitor's attention is the abundance of beautiful flowers. Fuchsias and verbenas, violas and heliotrope, Canterbury bells and especially roses are everywhere, in public and in private gardens, in beds, borders and flower pots, on trellises and even in iron baskets hanging from the street lamps. The huge rose gardens of the Empress Hotel and such famous plantings as Bouteham's and Pendray's are real attractions. The cause of the flowering is Victoria's wonderful climate which, according to the residents, prolongs "the perfect English spring" through nine months of the year. It's the sunniest spot on the sound. Those who like to search for British touches are advised to go to Beacon Hill Park and watch elderly Scotch gentlemen of the Lawn Bowling Club bowl "on the green" and maneuver their balls close to the "kitty," which is the one small white ball among the big black ones. Then, toward 5 o'clock they may have tea and crumpets at the Empress Hotel, watch majestic dowagers who reside there in Edwardian magnificence, sip tea from their own precious china, and listen to a trio playing Liszt's "Liebestraum." It's like the Savoy in London.

147

A **LOOK FROM THE SEA.** The crew of the British man-of-war "Discovery," which in April, 1792, sailed along Puget Sound, were probably the first white men to see the grandiose spectacle of a green forest-clad mountain range out of which huge, pure-white peaks arose skyward. The peaks appeared doubly high, since the explorers' eyes did not measure them from a plateau half way up but from sea level. It was the captain's chance. In the shining summits he immortalized, with a lavish hand, his personal friends. He thought of Peter, the admiral, and named the highest peak Mount Rainier. Mt. St. Helens had been previously christened after a diplomat-friend. As they sailed northward, Lieutenant Baker came running to point out another great white dome in the sky; the captain verified the report and promptly named the peak Mount Baker. The captain, by the way, also did well for himself; today one great city, one smaller one and one big island bear his name: Vancouver. The panorama which enthralled the early visitors is still enjoyed by thousands every day: The lofty white peaks, often towering above a layer of low clouds, do not seem to have any contact with the firm, solid earth; as shining pyramids suspended in the sky, they look like incredible and symbolic apparitions from the age of miracles.

A GLANCE FROM THE AIR: Flying over the Cascades on a clear day is an adventure of the mind never

This little lake near Mt. Rainier looks like the eye of the mountain.

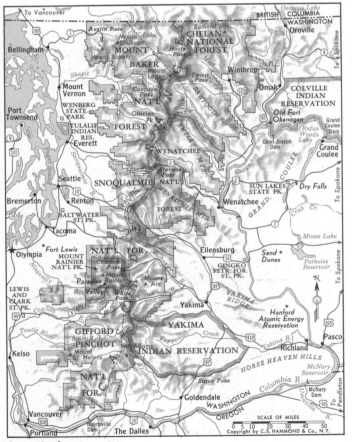

See sectional map, page 128

to be forgotten. It is also the only way to appraise the actual nature of this mountain range. You see the Southern Cascades and the southern end of the Northern Cascades as a volcanic mass, as a green carpet of rolling, wooded mountains interspersed with great, white, extinguished volcanoes. There are Mt. St. Helens, mirrored in Spirit Lake which had its last eruption in 1842; Mt. Adams towers to the east; Mt. Rainier, at 14,408 feet the tallest of the range, is uneasily dormant, still steaming a little here and there; Mt. Baker sent up clouds of black ashes in 1903. However, north of Mt. Rainier another, non-volcanic mountain mass emerges besides the volcanic section and spreads out broadly as it approaches Canada. From a breadth of about 60 miles in the south, the Cascades widen into a seemingly limitless expanse, 120 miles broad, of precipitous ridges, deep valleys, numerous glaciers. It is one of America's last true wilderness areas, almost uninhabited, to a large extent unexplored, with hundreds of mountain peaks unnamed. Its most splendid body of water is Lake Chelan, about 50 miles long at an elevation of 1079 feet; since it is 1419 feet deep, its bottom lies 340 feet below sea level.

A VIEW FROM THE ROAD. If the sea and the air present broad panoramic vistas, the highway and the trail reveal the intimate touches of the Cascades which, it has been said, violently shake mountains with one hand and tenderly raise delicate, Lilliputian mosses, ferns and wildflowers with the other. Crossing the mountains on the way to the Pacific coast, it becomes evident that the Cascades are a sharp climatic boundary. There are the high, dry plains on the eastern side, and the pine forests with little underbrush and a soft carpet of needles. There are the great irrigation works, and in the waste lands patches of orchards, shining in the spray of the sprinkler systems, which grow the apples, pears, cherries and other fruits for which Washington and Oregon have become famous. On the western slopes the great rain forests cover the valleys, with an undergrowth often jungle-like. As it is, the ranchers of the east side and the loggers on the west side would never dream of changing places. It has been mentioned that the northern part of the Northern Cascades are almost inaccessible to regular travelers, but there is an easy way to fully enjoy the Cascades: Mt. Rainier National Park.

THE WORLD'S LARGEST WREATH OF FLOWERS. No automobile road actually crosses the park, but two highways enter it and climb to appreciable heights, offering equally wonderful views. One, approaching from the west, leads to Paradise Valley, while the other, from the east, reaches the Sunrise Plateau. In the center of the park, covering almost a hundred square miles, the fourth tallest of all American mountains (excepting Alaska) raises its glistening peak, with 26 active glaciers

stretching their white tongues from the icy center downhill in all directions. Nisqually Glacier can be reached over a good trail by a short walk. For those who have the time to spare, a week's pack trip over the Wonderland Trail is a unique experience of primitive and beautiful nature. The trail completely encircles the mountain and provides shelter camps about every twelve miles. However, the two-day climb to the summit is difficult and dangerous, because of the crevassed icy flanks, the sharp ridges and the crumbling lava. It should be attempted only by well-equipped experts. One of the park's gifts every visitor can enjoy is Mount Rainier's abundant wildflowers, which thrive in the volcanic soil. In the forest zone, under the tall Douglas firs, red cedars and western hemlocks, the trillium, the anemone and the ghost-like Indian pipe are abloom. Both in the Southern and the Northern Cascades, the forest highways are sometimes framed on both sides with lush beds of bright-blue lupines. Above the timberline the gorgeous flower meadows have two peaks of blossoming. At the end of June the pasque flowers and avalanche lilies are radiant, and at the end of July, the Indian paintbrush, valerian, lupine, and many others arrive at full bloom. It was John Muir who remarked that these "parks"—meadows interspersed with lovely small groves of trees—form a great and beautiful wreath of brilliant flowers around the white peak of Mount Rainier.

The automobile road leading to Sunrise Lodge in Mt. Rainier National Park offers magnificent views of lonely, snow-capped ranges and peaks. The cool, clear, high-mountain air is exhilarating.

THE PHOTOGENIC METROPOLIS. A view of Portland in the morning, with the cone of Mt. Hood glistening in the sunlight; a photo of Portland in the evening, with night descending on the town, with myriads of electric lights aglow, and the sunset painting the great peak above as rosy as a strawberry sundae; Portland from Council Crest and Portland from Washington heights; Portland mansions buried under roses and Portland ranch homes shaded by tall evergreens. Every one has seen pictures of Portland, in magazines and photo salons, and the skeptical may wonder about the truth in back of it. However, they are advised to make the journey without hesitation; they won't be disappointed. On a clear day Mt. Hood towers above the city more majestically than the great cathedrals of Europe ever towered above their towns, and on a very clear day Mt. Rainier, 155 miles to the north, may be seen, for good measure, from many a city street or home window. The residential suburbs do lie on hills, some of them more than 1,000 feet high, and the forest is still there. Experts estimate that more evergreen trees—cedars, hemlocks, firs—grow within the limits of Portland than in any other city on earth. Roses thrive everywhere and are the regular adornment of even modest residences. There is something of the quiet, friendly spirit of New England in the air; the town was indeed founded, in 1843, by Yankees from Maine and Massachusetts. If the flipping of

Multnomah Falls plunge into a pool near the Columbia River Highway.

the coin which preceded the official naming of the settlement had turned out the other way, the city would be "Boston, Oregon" today. Portland's great hinterland is and was the fertile Willamette River valley, a beautiful, park-like Acadia where farming could be started without clearing the primeval forest and rooting out the stumps. From the succession of gold rushes—of California, of Idaho, of the Yukon—the city profited tremendously, selling its Willamette Valley grain and meat at skyrocketing prices. Industries came slowly, expanding during World War II, and the visitor who enters the city from the Cascades, will still feel that backwoods and metropolis, pioneer past and industrial future are meeting here face to face.

HEROIC LANDSCAPE. The giant Antaeus, of Greek mythology, gained rejuvenating strength whenever he touched the earth. That was the way he felt, said the second President Roosevelt, whenever he journeyed to the Columbia River valley. There is indeed an untouched, natural strength in this landscape where history came late and white man arrived only yesterday. The highway that follows the river from its mouth at Astoria to the point where the currents turn sharply to the north, is one of the continent's great scenic roads with sights full of strength and vitality. In Astoria the spiral frieze of the Astor Column tells the river's early history; here horses are used in shallow water to drag in the huge nets with

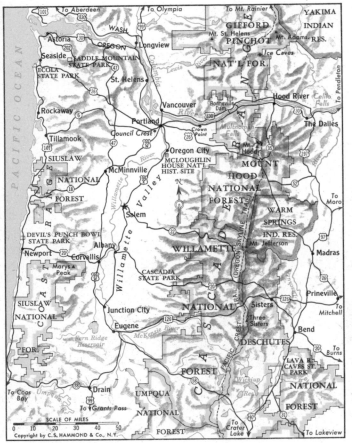

See sectional map, page 128

A Valley of Poetry, of Peace, and of Power

the salmon catches. The road to Portland takes the traveler over wooded hills and through forests and farmlands where the lush grass reaches up to the cattle's bellies. But the most spectacular stretch begins east of Portland where the green horizon is marked with the white domes of Mt. Hood and Mt. St. Helens, Mt. Adams and Mt. Rainier; Crown Point, where at the Columbia River Gorge the waters cut through the Cascade Mountains, offers a mountain-river-forest panorama never to be forgotten. Multnomah Falls, plunging its waters over the crags down to a pool near the highway, for 680 feet, may be admired from below or from a bridge perching half-way up the granite wall. Upstream the Bonneville Dam is surrounded by a pleasant park and offers interesting experiences to those who are fascinated by huge generators and turbines, and to fishermen and lovers of nature who like to watch the ingenious fish ladders which lead around the dam and enable the salmon migrating upstream to by-pass the obstacle. Proceeding with our eastward journey, we now enter the drier and sunnier climatic belt east of the Cascades. Here foliage and underbrush are less lush, but the irrigated orchards radiate freshness and life. After the town of Hood River we approach The Dalles, where the Columbia rushes through an eight-mile narrow channel. The chute begins upstream at Celilo Falls where Lewis and Clark observed, during their epochal journey, a number of Indians standing on

Portland, with Mt. Hood in the background, is one of our most photogenic cities.

At Columbia River Gorge a deep, rapid current cuts through the Cascade Mountains.

rickety, improvised scaffolds and netting or spearing salmon in the churning waters of the rapids. This very same spectacle can be observed to this day, the local fishing rights being reserved for the Indians.

THE SALMON STORY. The most fascinating inhabitant of the Columbia River (and other west coast streams) is the Chinook salmon, a creature with a strange fate: Its act of reproduction is also its act of death. Born in the crystal clear brooks and shallows that form the tributaries of the Columbia, they swim downstream at the age of two, spend two years in the ocean and then return, in a teeming upstream migration, to the very spot of their origin, spawn, and die. The principal movement takes place during the three spring months, and at the Bonneville checking station as many as 3,450 Chinooks and 2,000 steelhead trout have been counted to pass in one hour. It seems that the ladder device functions fairly satisfactorily; nevertheless the wildlife experts are worried: Of the streams of the Columbia Valley in which salmon spawned in 1883, two thirds are now blocked by irrigation dams and flumes, or are polluted by sewage from the factories. Various schemes for the salmon's rescue are being tested, for instance at Grand Coulee. In the meantime it is still possible to experience the joy that Rudyard Kipling felt when with his rod and reel he pulled salmon after salmon from a clear mountain tributary of the Columbia: "I have lived!" he wrote.

BLEAKNESS INTO BEAUTY. What do Fujiyama, Japan's sacred mountain, Krakatao off Sumatra, and the Andean Cordillera of Chile have in common with Oregon's Cascades? They are all part of the ring of huge volcanoes that circle the Pacific Ocean. At one time when their craters belched black smoke and cinders, they must have created a bleak and formidable seashore; today, when most of them have been extinct for thousands of years, their volcanic nature turns them into monuments of breath taking-beauty. They stand by themselves in massive grandeur and have an unusually regular shape. In addition, the Cascades are exposed to the first onslaught of the moist clouds drifting in from the Pacific and receive a heavy snowfall; they are clothed with the most dazzling white caps.

This range is still truly a wilderness, a last frontier, largely unsettled by man, with wide areas unsurveyed and inaccessible. A land of thundering landslides and roaring rivers, of 70-foot snow drifts and jungle-like forests on the Pacific slopes, it is nevertheless beloved by man. No range can boast of more mountain clubs; even at such tourist centers as Timberline Lodge and Crater Lake the call of the wilderness is distinctly felt.

WHITE CLOUD OF STONE. The northern column of the Southern Cascades, Mount Hood, raises its white crown of snow into a brilliant blue sky. Its height of 11,245 feet is quite modest if compared with the summits of the Rockies and the Sierras. Yet, as it stands grandly by itself, calm and aloof, rising approximately from sea level, it appears gigantic. The first settlers estimated it to be 18,000 feet high.

The "Cooper Spur" climb to its top begins at the famous old resort of Cloud Cap Inn which lies also on the 37-mile Round-the-Mountain-Trail. The 164-mile Mount Hood Circle Drive presents panoramic views that will take your breath away. There are other fine roads for motorists, but whoever wants to become intimately acquainted with these magic mountains should follow their 400-mile-long backbone, from the Columbia River to California, on the Oregon Sky Trail, a part of the 2,150-mile Pacific Crest Trail that winds along the Pacific mountain ranges from Canada to Mexico. Here the pack-train rider enjoys the silence of great Douglas Fir forests, climbs around snow-capped summits, passes torrential rivers and mirror-like lakes, marvels at meadows aflame with blossoms and forest floors soft with ferns and green mosses, small creepers and brightly painted fungi.

NATURE DESIGNS A PARK. Can the Southern Cascades offer any beauty spots that are uniquely their own, that cannot be encountered in any other American mountain range? The answer is yes. They possess wonderful parks created not by man but by nature. Circling around Mount Jefferson and the Three Sisters, these sky-meadow parks are carpeted with pink shooting stars and red Indian paintbrushes, blue lupines and graceful columbines. They are dotted with silvery pools and groves of lush alpine trees, a scene far more exquisite than a mere human landscape architect could create. The most famous of these parks—probably the nearest vision of paradise we can encounter on this earth—is Jefferson Park, a flower garden two miles square traversed by crystal-clear brooks with banks of velvety moss and with miniature lakes which mirror dark-green ponderosa pines and the straight spires of mountain hemlock. The fantastic southern backdrop to this scene, towering massively against the brilliant sky, is Mount Jefferson, suddenly rising from the floor of the valley in almost perfect architectural design; the blue-black lines of its glacial crevasses separate the shiny ice fields into a dark white pattern all its own. This Eldorado can be reached by pack-train only.

THE WORLD'S BLUEST LAKE. The question "Which is the most beautiful spot on earth?" cannot, of course, be answered with definite assurance. But there are world travelers who know our planet well and who have made their decision: It is Crater Lake whose unearthly beauty touches strangely everyone who sees it; to glance at its blue surface surrounded by colored cliffs up to 2,000 feet high, is an experience of the spirit. The blue of its water is a mystery; it is not simply a reflection of the sky, as in other lakes, for its water is

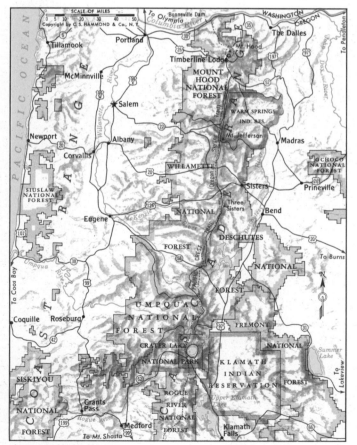

See sectional map, page 128

Mt. Hood from Lost Lake; the peak looks forbidding but has been climbed by thousands.   A sand beach on the south shore of Lost Lake affords excellent swimming and boating.
A swim in the clear, cold water which reflects the peak is an exhilerating experience

always blue, under a cloudy sky as well as on a moon-lit night. Nor is it caused by mineral contents, as a chemical analysis has proven. The most probable theory makes two factors responsible for the lake's everlasting shades of blue: the perfect clarity of the water, and its great depth of almost 2,000 feet.

Sightseers feel most strongly the weird fascination of this spot when on a boat; with a sheer, sky-high cliff towering by the shore and a water below which is so crystal clear their eyes can penetrate it deeply they have the impression of floating somewhere in space.

The lake is the product of a geological catastrophe. Once Mount Mazama stood here, a huge volcano. In an explosive eruption such masses of lava streamed out of its crater that they carried along much of the inner structure of the mountain; the upper cone remained as an empty shell and finally collapsed, creating a round lake approximately six miles across. Wizard Island with its crater has been raised by later volcanic activity, and a group of twisted lava pinnacles is called the Phantom Ship. Although without inlet or outlet, the water level remains the same, evaporation and precipitation balancing each other perfectly. The lake is stocked with rainbow trout.

To the south, 40-mile-long Klamath Lake is a paradise for bird lovers. Myriads of waterfowl can be observed there, including the giant white pelican.

The southern outpost of the Southern Cascades, the Mount Shasta and Lassen Peak region in California, is described on page 186.

THE HAYSTACK AND A STORYBOOK LIGHTHOUSE. Talapus, the coyote god of the Indians, walked along this shore, shaped the capes and the bays and determined the limit of the tide. Red warriors followed the coyote god, and the early traders found a trail along the coast. But it took many a generation to change the path into a highway; the latter was not completed until the 1930's. It starts at Astoria, the salmon port with a large Finnish population; the first stop is Seaside, Oregon's best-known ocean resort. Here the End of the Trail Monument marks the conclusion of the Lewis and Clark expedition; it commemorates not a heroic but a practical deed: Four of the men were directed to "Commence making Salt with five Kittles," and this was their "salt cairn." On the southern horizon Tillamook Lighthouse rises from a sheer, isolated rock out of the sea, its base 91 feet above the water. Winter gales isolate the keeper for weeks, and if you want to visit him, you will have to ascend in a breeches buoy. A few miles to the south Cannon Beach presents the Haystack Rock, prime example of many similar cyclopic boulders strewn here and there over the broad, white Oregon beach. Haystack is a 300-foot rock, now reached on foot over the hard sand, now completely surrounded by the swishing water of long, rolling breakers, and crowned with a densely populated metropolis of gulls, terns and cormorants shrieking and arguing.

Newport Harbor; adventurous visitors go out to sea with the commercial fleet.

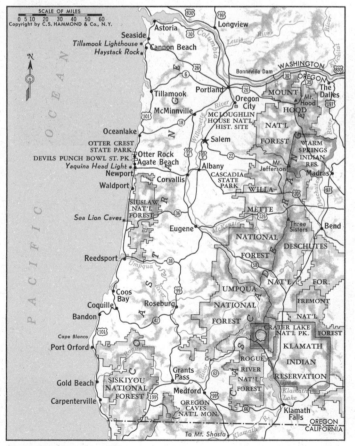

See sectional map, page 128

For Americans who only know the Atlantic, the sight is new and exciting. On the southward journey you will pass through many a small port where the forest and sea meet; in Tillamook, the smell of saltwater and of freshly cut cedar is supplemented by the aroma of cheese; it's a dairy center.

AGATES AND SILVERSIDES. The road winds up and down between sea level and the crest of high cliffs; at Otter Crest State Park the seascape, 454 feet below, is a wonderful blend of rugged promontories, dark-green forests, and the deep-blue Pacific. The shore along Otter Rock, a sea-bird rookery, and Devil's Punch Bowl, a cauldron of churning tidal waters, is rich in beach deposits of fossilized wood, jasper, and "Oregon jade" which gave its real name, agate, to Agate Beach. Agates are also popular in the souvenir shops of Newport. The resort section is located along highway 101 while the picturesque old fishing town still nestles among the hills of Yaquina Bay. To get up, on a summer morning, at 3 o'clock, have breakfast with some skippers in one of all-night coffee houses near the wharves, then sail out with the commercial fleet and come home in the afternoon with 2 or 3 silverside salmon which you caught yourself is an exhilarating experience. Or drive to nearby Yaquina Head Lighthouse, climb over the rugged cliffs, enjoy the profusion of wildflowers, watch the cormorants and gulls circling above and the starfish and sea anemones in the marine garden below, and you will feel that you have spent a few worth-while hours. There is an unusual and truly American story connected with Newport's history: In 1856 a blockhouse of the U. S. Army was to be erected at the site of an Indian cemetery consisting of hundreds of burial canoes The Indians agreed to the removal of the canoes but made it clear that they were not willing to touch them themselves. So at the turning of high tide the American soldiers set adrift the canoes each of which carried a dead warrior. The white men watched the silent flotilla glide past the tall forest from the bay into the ocean, and saw the strange craft vanish from their sight in the red sunset of the Pacific.

RED-BEAKED PIGEONS AND 12-FOOT SEA LIONS. About 39 miles south of Newport a fascinating wildlife spectacle may be observed at Sea Lion Caves, a multicolored large cavern where a herd of about 300 sea lions spends the winter and has established its rookery. The inhabitants, Stellar's Sea Lions, are the largest species of their family, averaging 12 feet in length. Originally they appeared in great numbers, but the seal hunters of the 19th century almost exterminated them, and this Oregon herd is a fascinating remnant. Stairs lead from the highway to observation posts below and make it possible to watch the harem-style family life of the huge seals which have both the tawny color

Starfish and sea anemones may be seen in the Marine Gardens near Yaquina Head Light.

and the loud roar of lions. Around the cliffs there are swarms of birds just as unusual as the mammals in the cave; outstanding are the guillemots with their bright-red beaks and the puffins with their rakish tufts. The latter look so much like small parrots that they are called "sea parrots."

CEDARS FOR BLINDS AND A HOTEL FOR SHIPWRECKED SAILORS. One of the spectacular features of highway 101 is its large number of tall, graceful bridges. They are especially in evidence at Coos Bay, the region of the Port Orford cedar (really a cypress). This straight-grained light wood is greatly in demand for special purposes, particularly for the manufacture of Venetian blinds. Bandon is a well-kept resort. To the south, Port Orford is the site of a famous Pacific coast hotel the Knapp Hotel which was erected in 1867. Among the inns of the world it has a unique distinction: Probably more stranded and shipwrecked sailors gathered here than anywhere else. The coast was dangerous, but the hotel welcomed the adventurers, and hair-raising stories were heard around its fireplace. No wonder Jack London loved it. He is said to have written here his "Valley of the Moon."—In Carpenterville the highway reaches its highest point, with an altitude of 1715 feet. The state line is near, and California already in the air. On clear days Mt. Shasta offers a majestic welcome.

The panorama from Otter Crest State Park is one of America's great seascapes.

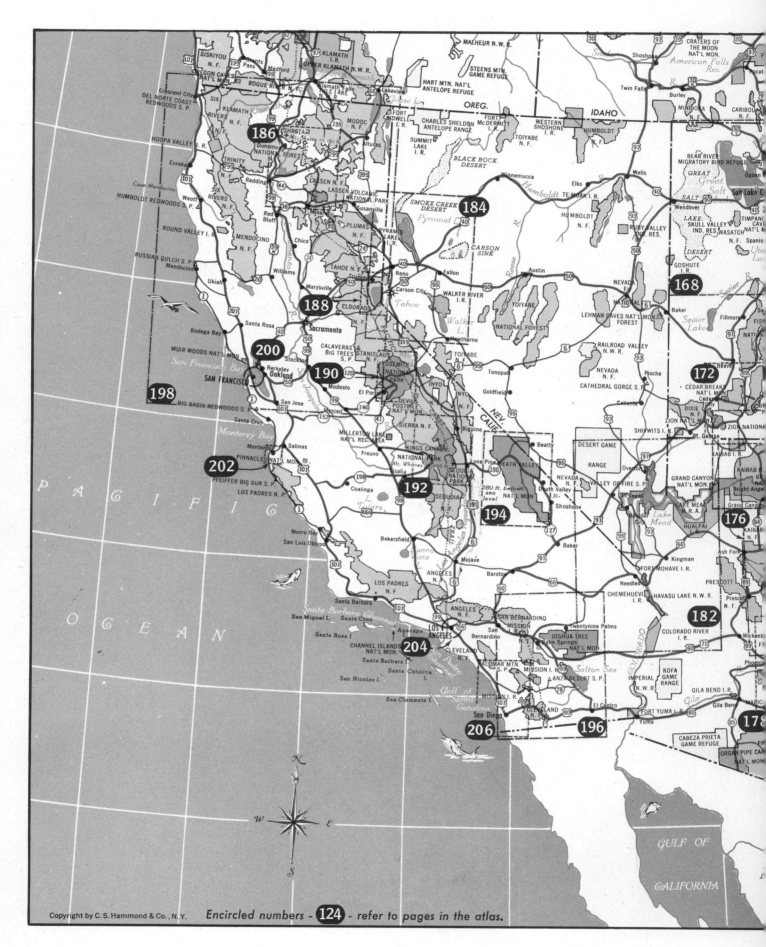

Encircled numbers - 124 - refer to pages in the atlas.

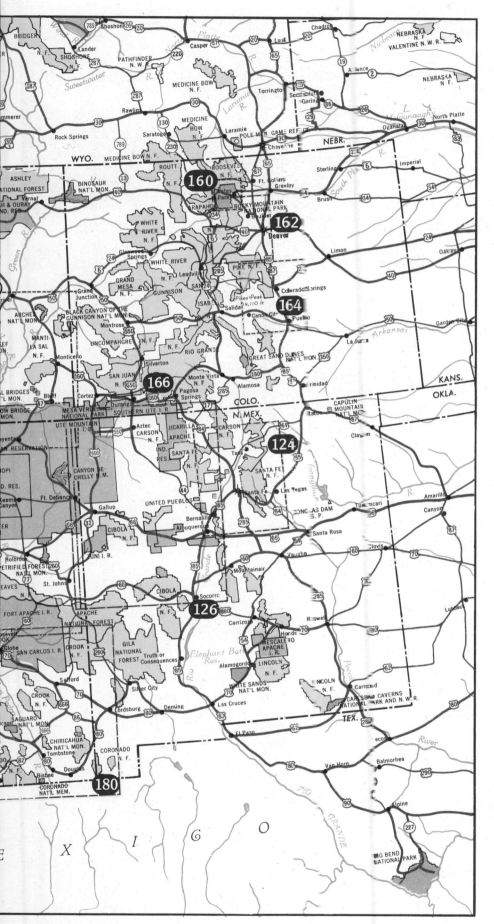

5-DAY TRIP ACROSS THE CENTRAL ROCKIES. See pictures and maps on pages 160 to 168, also the Sightseeing Gazetteer.—Suggested stops: Rocky Mountain National Park—Denver, Colorado—Colorado Springs—Montrose with Black Canyon of the Gunnison National Monument — Mesa Verde National Park, via Silverton and Durango.—4 stops in 5 days allow for a 2-day stopover in Colorado Springs, or elsewhere.

10-DAY GRAND TOUR OF THE SOUTHWEST, Tuscon to Taos. See pictures and maps on pages 174 to 182 and 124 to 128, also the Sightseeing Gazetteer.—Suggested stops: Tuscon, Ariz.—Phoenix, Ariz.—Grand Canyon, South Rim—Flagstaff, Ariz.—Gallup, New Mexico.—Albuquerque, N. Mex., via Acoma Pueblo — Santa Fe — Ranchos de Taos. — 7 stops in 10 days allow for 2-day stopovers at the Grand Canyon, Flagstaff, Santa Fe, or elsewhere.

4-DAY NATIONAL PARKS TOUR OF UTAH-ARIZONA. See pictures and maps on pages 168 to 169, and 172 to 175, also the Sightseeing Gazetteer.—Suggested stops: Salt Lake City—Bryce Canyon National Park—Cedar Breaks National Monument—Zion National Park—Grand Canyon, Arizona, North Rim.

15-DAY NATIONAL PARKS TOUR OF CALIFORNIA. See pictures and maps on pages 184 to 193 and 198 to 203, also the Sightseeing Gazetteer.—Suggested stops: San Francisco—Eureka via Redwood Highway—Shasta Dam Recreational Area — Lassen Volcanic National Park—Reno, Nevada—Virginia City, Nevada — Lake Tahoe — Yosemite National Park, California, either on easy roads via Sacramento, Stockton and Merced, or on route 395, with entrance to the park from the east over Tioga Pass; the ride over the pass is only for drivers who are not afraid of high altitudes; the scenery is magnificent —Sequoia National Park, via Fresno—Carmel and Monterey Peninsula—San Francisco. —9 stops in 15 days allow for 2- or 3-day stopovers at Lake Tahoe, Yosemite National Park, Sequoia National Park, Carmel, or elsewhere.

SOUTHERN CALIFORNIA TRIP. See pictures and maps on pages 204 to 207 and 196 to 197, also the Sightseeing Gazetteer.—Suggested stops: Santa Barbara—Los Angeles including Pasadena, Beverly Hills, and Hollywood, with excursions to Long Beach, Santa Catalina Island, Palm Springs, Arrowhead Springs, and Big Bear Lake—San Diego. On a southern East-West trip the following attractions should be included, if possible: Boulder Dam and Lake Mead, Nev. (see pp. 182, 183), Las Vegas, Nev. (also on pp. 182, 183), and the Death Valley National Monument in California (see pp. 194, 195).

THE DISTANT BLUE WALL. Over the western Great Plains a cloudbank seems to loom. As we approach it from the east, the blue vision is transformed and condensed, within an hour's drive, into a very real wall. It has a massive, forbidding, dead-end appearance, as if a huge, impenetrable fortification had been thrown up to divide the continent. The sight of it must have been disheartening to the pioneers. How were they ever to cross that barrier of solid, continuous rock? To them it was indeed a backbreaking task. To the modern traveler the entrance phase is a pleasant surprise, almost a revelation. For as we ride through the foothills, the peaks recede to the left and to the right; between them the road winds up along a raging river, through a canyon, and over a pass, and in another hour we are within one of the world's greatest masses of mountains. Many of those who want to get acquainted with "the roof of America" are headed for Rocky Mountain National Park in Colorado, about 50 miles northwest of Denver, and they have chosen an excellent starting point. From many sections of the middle states the park can be reached within a day's driving, and it plunges the visitors from the plains into medias res: In this heart of the Rockies there are 65 peaks higher than 10,000 feet; 42 higher than 12,000 feet; 15 higher than 13,000 feet; and Longs Peak, the park's highest, surpasses Switzerland's famous Matterhorn with a height of 14,255 feet. The first impression of this mountain empire

Longs Peak (14,225 ft.) is America's most frequently climbed tall mountain.

is that of closely-packed, towering density, of a massiveness that is unique. The backbone of the country, the Continental Divide, runs through the park. Mummy Range, a majestic spur of the Divide lying in the northeast corner of the park, includes some of the loftiest peaks and one of the finest glaciers.

SPECTACLE OF THE TIMBERLINE. One of the most spectacular highways on earth crosses the park and makes it possible to enjoy the high mountain country by car: The Trail Ridge Road. Where else on this or any continent can one ride above the 11,000 foot level for 11 miles, and higher than 12,000 feet for 4 miles? Crags, peaks and gorges are everywhere, but the road takes you also to many small and large mountain meadows that are carpets of wild flowers, of blue columbines and snow buttercups, paintbrushes and gentians, lilies and hundreds of other flowering plants. Another most interesting sight the Trail Ridge Road has to offer is the spectacle of the timberline. The uninitiated may imagine that the border between the forests and the rocks and meadows is a belt of peaceful and quiet transition. It is not. Here in the high Rockies one can see the perennial struggle, the field of battle between the elements and the plants. Tilden Freeman lets the trees speak: "I *will* live. I shall bend. I shall creep on hands and on knees. I shall dodge, devise, join hands, and compromise; but I *will* live." The old and young evergreens, the bushes and the naked skeletons are

See sectional map, page 158

The Roof of America

gnarled, dwarfed and staggering, bent into geometrical
half circles or twisted into absurd forms suggesting old
men or bears. One small pine—a boy could carry its trunk
on his shoulder—was found to be 258 years old and some
seedlings reached a height of three inches in 50 years. A
wonderful spot for camera enthusiasts, the timberline
especially for the imaginative ones who have a modernistic
bend. The Trail Ridge Road, by the way, is in use from
early June to late September, while the national park itself
is open all year. Also of interest to camera enthusiasts
is the abundance of wildlife in the park. This is the natural
home of the sure-footed Rocky Mountain big-horn and
these superb climbers can be observed ascending and descending precipitous slopes with amazing agility. Elk, deer
and other animals abound and beavers patiently working
on their dams may be observed along almost every drainage in the park.

APPROACH TO HEAVEN. In spite of the jumbled
massiveness of the ranges, and in spite of the struggle for
life and the snow flurries that may fall in July, these
mountains are friendly. There is a mood of good cheer
and adventure in the park; Longs Peak, for instance, is
high by any standard, and its summit cannot be reached
just by hiking; the last stretch of the trail requires sure
footwork; but actually thousands of men, women and
children have been on its top. It is the most frequently
climbed tall mountain in America. The history of the

A carpet of Indian paintbrush and other wildflowers covers the mountain meadows.

Big Thompson Canyon with its red rocks is the most picturesque approach to the park.

whole park has the tone of friendliness and enjoyment.
As early as the 1860's groups of settlers and ranchers from
the surrounding valleys used to ride with their families to
some pristine meadow between the peaks, set up tents and
enjoy the air, the view, the birds, and the fishing, for a
week or two. A famous figure of those days was Rocky
Mountain Jim, a hunter and trapper who used to trot
over the trails on a big white mule. He looked tough,
especially after a grizzly bear had scraped out one of his
eyes. But the mountains inspired him, and he wrote poetry.
Then there was the old hermit who lived in this neighborhood and had his own greeting of welcome to visitors:
"May the Lord take a liking to you." He had a distinguished neighbor: The Earl of Dunraven loved the
Rockies, and for his and his friends' pleasure established
a ranch of 6,000 acres on the east side of the park, in the
1870's. The English lord's enterprise had snobbish overtones, and the mountain settlers saw to it that it was
broken up. In 1884 a thin and eager boy arrived on the
scene, all by himself, and was strangely fascinated by the
shining mountains; Enos Mills was his name. He stayed
here most of his life, became a well-known naturalist and
writer, obsessed with one idea and one goal. He had no
money but had friends, and he never gave up the struggle.
In 1915 his vision turned into reality: His beloved peaks
became the property of the nation, to be preserved forever.
In that year Rocky Mountain National Park was born.

"**1** MILE—300."" This is the magic formula that makes Denver a popular goal for vacation travelers and a wonderful city to live in all year 'round, for the community lies on a plateau one mile high—the exact marker can be seen on the steps of the capitol—and enjoys 300 sunny days per annum. The climate is fine, and those occasional notices in the eastern press about unseasonal snowstorms in Denver are misleading. Denver is by no means an arctic waste during the winter; in fact, some winter days are pleasant enough to enjoy a picnic. The favorable weather is supplemented by an abundant water supply that taps mountain lakes and streams fed by the winter's accumulation of snow. The supply system even reaches out beyond the Continental Divide and syphons water from the Pacific draining area over the ridge to the Atlantic side.

AN AMPHITHEATER HEWN INTO THE ROCKS. Beyond the city limits proper, Denver's Mountain Park System is the special pride of its citizens. It lies southwest of nearby Golden, can be reached in an hour's drive and covers about 25,000 acres of canyons and mountains, trout streams and lakes, picnic grounds and shelter houses, barbecue pits and softball diamonds. It also includes a good part of the Front Range, some of America's most spectacular scenery. Probably the most famous single feature of the park system is the Red Rocks Theater that has been carved into the red

Denver's City and County Building is part of the neo-classic Civic Center.

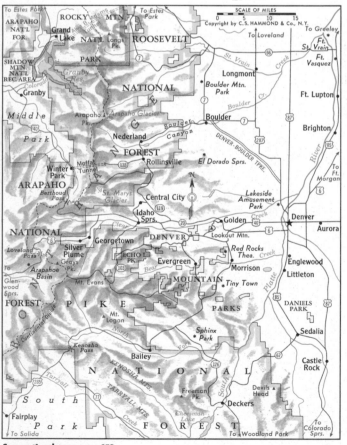

See sectional map, page 158

sandstone. There the Denver Symphony Orchestra plays under the stars on summer nights, or folk dance festivals are held, or an opera is performed. The acoustics are said to be so excellent that the slight thud of a pencil dropped on the stage is heard in the last rows. Also within the park system are a highway to the top of Mt. Evans (altitude 14,260 feet) on whose summit a physical research laboratory studies the nature of cosmic rays, and Lookout Mountain, where Buffalo Bill is buried. Visitors toss coins over the iron railing around his grave for good luck.

THE QUEENLY WAYS OF TODAY. One has to see Denver from an airplane on a clear day, the neat gridiron of streets surrounded by the rolling prairies, with the backdrop of tall mountains, to understand the various flattering by-names the city has acquired over the years: "Queen City of the Plains," or "Capitol of the Rocky Mountain Empire." If, in the birdseye view, bright splashes of sunlight play simultaneously on the tall buildings and the snow-capped ridges of the Front Range, there is indeed something monumental about that panorama. In the city proper, the boulevards, the state capitol and the neo-Greek Civic Center with the impressive City and County Building, the mall and the esplanades are laid out broadly in the same manner and spirit. Denver has even been called "the American Capital of the West," for it houses more federal agencies and offices than any other city outside of Washington. Best known among the bureaus is perhaps the Denver Mint, our biggest gold depository after Fort Knox. As can be expected, Denver's museums stress the Western theme; there are collections of American Indian culture in the Denver Art Museum (which is housed in the City and County Building) and the State Museum; the Denver Public Library owns eight priceless albums of early photographs of the West (1870) by W. H Jackson the greatest Western photographer of his day.

THE YOUTHFUL PRANKS OF YESTERDAY.
Culturally and economically, the Denver of our time is considered progressive but quite conservative; its gaudy past as a mining and cattle town lives on only in numerous tales of the days when the Windsor Hotel served banquets at $100 a plate, and the swashbuckling owners of the Denver Post viciously attacked rival editors and non-advertising merchants. Many a tale centers around H.A.W. ("Silver Dollar") Tabor, a mining tycoon who built the Tabor Grand Opera House on 16th Street. When at the opening in 1881 he spied a picture of Shakespeare in the lobby, he asked angrily, "What has Shakespeare ever done for Colorado?" Promptly the Bard was removed, and replaced by Mr. Tabor's portrait. In Denver's earliest days, the Elephant Corral was a frontier log hotel, so-called because of its size. In its notorious gambling saloon killings were so fre-

When the aspen trees turn yellow in the fall, the Rockies are magnificent.

The Red Rocks Theater, carved into red sandstone, has excellent acoustics.

quent that the hotel featured free funerals, with all expenses charged to the house; the hotel undertaker owned his private cemetery where he buried his customers but saved the coffins. He was said to have used the same coffin 30 times, the last time for his own burial. The Corral burned down in 1863.

CENTRAL CITY: REVIVAL OF THE GAY 90's.
Denverites have still another means of reviving the lustier past. Every summer for several weeks they take over the picturesque little mining town of Central City, which once was called "the richest square mile on earth." It enjoyed nation-wide fame when Horace Greeley wrote glowingly of its fabulous diggings in his New York *Tribune;* with his own hands he had panned gold from a placer mine, unaware of the fact that speculators had shot gold dust into the mine just for that purpose. Later on, Central City became a ghost town, but in the 1930's the University of Denver inherited the Central City Opera House, and with the help of civic groups an annual Festival of Opera and Drama was instituted. The incomparable scenery—the town dangles precariously from a mountainside—the Broadway stars, Metropolitan Opera singers, the old Opera House itself with its gaudy Victorian style and audiences often wearing costumes of the same period, the Glory Hole night club and the Teller House combine to make the festival a huge success.

PIKES PEAK COUNTRY. "Pikes Peak or Bust" was the lettering that could be seen on the canvas cover of many a westbound Conestoga wagon, in 1859. The occasion was a gold rush in Colorado. The matter came to national attention again several months later when hundreds of the same wagons, worse for wear, recrossed the plains in an easterly direction; this time an additional inscription proclaimed "Busted, by God." Pikes Peak, the disappointing goal of the gold-seekers, became so well known that the whole region was named for it; with 14,110 feet it was not the highest mountain, but its prominent, lonely position had made it a landmark to the Indians a hundred miles around, and it may have been the northernmost point seen by the Spanish explorers. The first white man to describe it was Lieutenant Zebulon Pike, in 1806, and as a result, the name Pikes Peak was adopted. Pike, who predicted that the wild Great Peak, as he called it, could never be scaled, would be surprised to discover that today not only a cogwheel railroad leads to its summit, but also an automobile road, and that thousands of Americans enjoy the view from its top.

INGREDIENTS OF A SUCCESSFUL RESORT. It was inevitable that in the shadow of Pikes Peak, at the approach to the Ute Pass, a city should spring up, and Colorado Springs had the good luck of being planned and built, from the very beginning, as a resort town.

The Royal Gorge. with the world's highest suspension bridge.

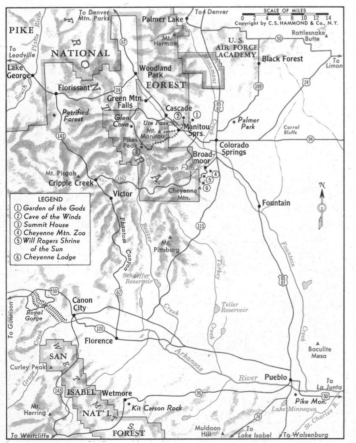

See sectional map, page 158

Well-to-do families with freshly accumulated mining fortunes looked for a place to erect their residential mansions, and found the spot ideal. The climate pleased them, and the scenery—the forested foothills, the rugged canyons, the backdrop of Pikes Peak—had the romantic wilderness-beauty of the West. So broad streets were laid out, planted with trees and lined with ditches in which clear, cool mountain water bubbled along. Soot-and-smoke-producing factories were kept out. At a time when the word "vacation" had a somewhat frivolous ring, while "taking the cure" was considered a respectable activity, the health springs at the neighboring village of Manitou were refurbished, and Colorado Springs now attracted health seekers from all America. As the climate was considered a boon for TB patients, several sanatoria were established; the customers liked the resort but were outraged when the town's new playhouse opened with a performance of "Camille." Gradually all the scenic beauty spots became accessible, and they are still outstanding attractions. Beyond the river, west of the city, the Garden of the Gods is a municipal park strewn with grotesque rock masses of fantastic shapes (Siamese Twins, Buffalo, Punch and Judy, Balanced Rock). In the late afternoon when the rays of the setting sun suffuse the sandstone columns and figures with a glowing red set off by an azure sky, this spot is a heaven for color-photo enthusiasts. A little beyond, the resort village of Manitou Springs is the starting point for the inclined railway to Mount Manitou (9,453 ft.) and of the Diesel-powered cogwheel railroad to Pikes Peak. On a clear day the vista reaches out over Colorado Springs and the Black Forest to the wheat fields of Kansas, 200 miles away. The Summit House, which can also be reached by car, on a spectacular highway, is built on a mass of boulders held together by ice. From Manitou Springs, Williams Canyon with the Cave of the Winds is easily accessible. Modern Colorado Springs is clean, green, bright and attractive, given to golf and polo tournaments, rodeos and flower festivals.

INGREDIENTS OF A FABULOUS HOTEL. One of the sights of Colorado Springs merits a special chapter: the Broadmoor Hotel, located south of the city in a suburb of the same name. Its setting is in the grand manner: The white, red-roofed group of buildings lies in a cluster of green trees by a blue lake, against the bold contours of Cheyenne Mountain which turns purple in the afternoon sun. Besides, the hotel cultivates a truly western atmosphere, not only with its collection of guns and frontier relics, and its rodeo grandstand, but also by keeping alive the tradition of its flamboyant founder, Spencer Penrose. When out of Harvard, the young, gay extrovert "Spec" went West and plunged into all sorts of mining ventures, with varying luck. Once, when broke, he cabled his brother in Pennsylvania for

The Garden of the Gods contains fantastic sandstone rock formations.

a new grubstake. One hundred fifty dollars arrived promptly but with the warning that the money was to be used as the railroad fare to Philadelphia, to mark the end of Spec's frontier filibustering. Spec did not answer, but appeared in person, several months later, and handed his brother a check for $75,000. He had invested the railroad money in the Colorado mining boom, he remarked casually, and this was the dividend.

THE GORGE WITH THE STEEPEST RAILWAY AND THE HIGHEST BRIDGE. To the southwest of Colorado Springs near Canon City, the Royal Gorge, also called the Grand Canyon of the Arkansas River, is one of Colorado's most popular sightseeing spots. The narrow canyon, the sheer red granite walls with picturesque bands of rock strata and the rushing river below are accented by several touches of civilization: The bands of the tracks of the Denver & Rio Grande Western Railroad glisten on the canyon floor beside the river, and occasionally a diesel-powered train thunders into the gorge and comes to a hesitant halt, so that the passengers may enjoy the unusual view. From the rim to the bottom of the canyon sightseers may ride on an inclined railroad, said to be the steepest in the world, or they may drive their car or walk over the Royal Gorge Suspension Bridge said to be the highest in the world. Its 880-foot main span connects the rim of the chasm 1,053 feet above the river.

Pikes Peak is the impressive backdrop of Colorado Springs.

VISION AND REALITY. To round up stray cattle in the lonely canyons of Mesa Verde, in southern Colorado, was a trying job, on that December day of 1888. Weary and cold, the two cowboys found a sheltered resting place and began to build a fire. Then they looked across to the canyon wall, and their eyes suddenly opened wide: They saw a city of walls, houses, balconies and towers rising from a heap of ruins, all built on the ledge of a giant cave, whose upper cliffs overhung the town like a canopy. Excitedly the two men climbed into the ruins and found bones, pieces of fine pottery and other relics, but no life. What had happened to the builders of the towers? Had a war or a siege forced them to surrender? Had an epidemic wiped them out?

Word of the sensational discovery spread, and curious settlers and travelers visited the site, helping themselves to souvenirs and doing a great deal of damage. However, in this process many more ruins of cliff dwellings were discovered. America at large hardly took notice, until a famous Swedish archeologist, Baron Nordenskiöld, visited the cliff dwellings and pronounced them "so magnificent that they surpass anything of the kind known in the United States." That brought action, and in 1906 the Mesa Verde National Park was organized. Systematic excavation began, and those separate communities were restored—each in a huge cave of its own—

Cliff Palace, built 200 feet above the canyon floor, contains 200 rooms.

which today are known as Spruce Tree House, Cliff Palace, Far View House and Balcony House. Sun Temple, a strange structure which apparently served as the religious sanctuary of the region, stands on top of the canyon's rim. Altogether more than thirty ruins were dug out of the debris of centuries, and exploration is still proceeding.

A PREHISTORIC APARTMENT HOUSE. Guided by rangers, tourists may visit one or several of these ghost towns in the rock. Some are easily accessible (the Spruce Tree House, for instance), while visitors to Balcony House have to climb a thirty-foot ladder fastened to the canyon wall high above the valley, and have to squeeze through one or two small, connecting tunnels. Best-known, perhaps, is Cliff Palace, built 200 feet above the canyon floor in a cave 100 feet deep and about 300 feet long. Two hundred bedrooms and storage rooms, usually square in shape, were built of stone four stories high, each provided with a hole for a ladder. Daytime activities including the preparation of food were carried on in the courts or the pleasant, loggia-like open space by the rim. Besides, there were the "kivas," 23 of them in Cliff Palace alone. These round underground chambers, about twelve feet across and provided with a "sipapu," a small hole that was thought to connect with the underworld, served as ceremonial and religious club rooms for the men.

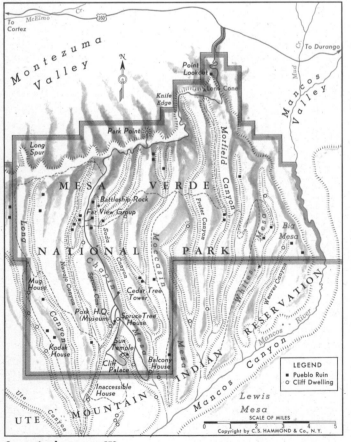

See sectional map, page 158

Castles of a Vanished Civilization

THE TREE CALENDAR. Today we know the story of the cliff dwellers quite well; this reconstruction of pre-Columbian history became possible by an epochal invention of Dr. A. E. Douglass, famous scientist of the University of Arizona. He set up a tree calendar based on the fact that trees grow one ring every year and the nature of the ring varies according to the weather conditions in each particular year. A cross cut of a freshly felled tree from the Mesa region offered valuable information for perhaps the last 200 years. A cut from a log used in the construction of a 500-year-old neighboring pueblo was compared with the cut of the tree; the innermost rings of the tree matched, in their characteristics, with the outer rings of the log. That pushed the calendar back another few centuries. Now a cut from a log in the cliff dwellings was matched, in the same fashion, with the cut from the pueblo. In that ingenious way the tree calendar could be reconstructed for more than 1900 years, to the year 11 of our Christian era. Among other things it showed clearly why the cliff dwellers had left their homes. The mystery was solved.

THE GREAT SPIRIT WAS ANGRY. It did not rain. For years it did not rain. The corn and cotton beans withered; the wild berries shrank. Neither the sorcery of the medicine men nor the dances of the warriors placated the gods. The disastrous drought

Sun Temple, on the canyon's rim, apparently was the religious sanctuary.

began in 1276 and lasted for 24 years. It was more than the cliff dwellers could bear; clan after clan left, and gradually the great houses were deserted. No one came back. The emigrants probably wandered in a southerly direction and were absorbed by their blood brothers, the Hopi Indians and the other tribes of the region.

The question of from where the cliff dwellers came is equally interesting: Shortly after the birth of Christ they began to inhabit the Mesa as farming Indians, living in natural caves. Around the year 400 they had learned to make pottery, use the bow and arrow and build themselves one-family pit houses, consisting of shallow excavations with roofs of poles and adobe. Around 700 their civilization had become more ceremonious and close-knit, and pueblos were erected as community houses. This new prosperity attracted savage raiders, and soon after the year 1000 the first castles in the canyon walls were erected. They served their purpose for more than 250 years.

PANORAMA OF A CIVILIZATION. To this day, ruins of all those stages in their civilization can be observed within the Mesa Verde National Park—the pit houses, pueblos and cliff castles. Besides, the excellent museum at park headquarters connects the threads and fills in the gaps, so that the visitor sees, in a fascinating perspective, the rise and fall of a valiant people.

The "apartment houses" were deserted because of a 24-year drought.

167

STRONGHOLD OF THE CENTER. After a night's drive through the desert the morning begins to engulf us with the glowing light and the blistering heat of the white salt flats and the barren hills. But suddenly we are in Salt Lake City, and in a bowl surrounded by stark-naked mountains there lies a metropolis, presided over by a great capitol perching halfway up on a rocky "bench." Lovely trees line the street, clear mountain water rushes through all the gutters and thousands of ever revolving sprinklers rain sparkling drops on lawns and flower beds. Here we understand the Oriental poets: "To arrive at a lush oasis, after a trek through the Sahara, is a delight." It will take but a few hours to sense the very special atmosphere of this city; just as it is a physical stronghold circled by mountains, it is also a stronghold of the spirit, independent of and set apart from the civilizations of the Atlantic Seaboard and the Pacific Coast. Everywhere we encounter its four symbols: the sea gulls (these graceful birds which saved the Mormons' first crop, threatened with destruction by crickets, by devouring the crickets, and so helping the young settlement survive); the bee hive (the symbol of systematic and energetic activity, the power which made the desert habitable and prosperous); Deseret (a word denoting the state of the Mormons) and Zion (the biblical kingdom of heaven). There is little smoking and drinking to be

The Temple with its 6 spires has become the symbol of the Mormon Church.

observed, and almost nothing which could be called "night life." This quiet state is particularly striking if we arrive from Utah's neighbor, Nevada, with its clicking roulette tables and revival of the Old West spirit. However, Salt Lake City is by no means drab; there is a great deal of singing and laughing, of dating and dancing, and it claims to possess the loveliest girls of the mid-continent.

"THIS IS THE PLACE." Visitors approach the world capital of Mormonism with a mixture of awe and curiosity. Usually they have a few vague notions about Brigham Young and polygamy. Although only 60 per cent of the town's inhabitants are Mormons, they set the pace, and they see to it that visiting travelers are set straight on the principal issues. Temple Square is Salt Lake City's great attraction, and throngs from all states of the Union move leisurely between the impressive buildings and the bright flower beds. We join a tour and discover that our guide is an insurance executive, who frequently donates his time to this service. Such devotion to the church, we learn, is the rule. From him we hear about the history of Mormonism, the organization of the church, its admirable self-help program, and its huge industrial enterprises making Mormonism a way of life. We see the Temple with its six spires and its "Earth Stones," "Moon Stones" and "Sun Stones," and learn about the ceremonial and genealogical work

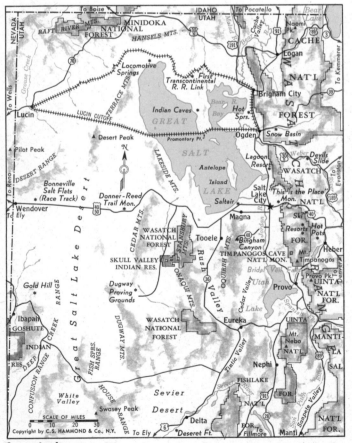

See sectional map, page 158

carried on there. The building itself, however, is closed to non-Mormons. On the other hand, the Tabernacle is not only open to our inspection but we are welcome to hear a free organ concert; this oval auditorium, looking on the outside like a huge turtle, offers seats for 5,000. Its organ is a mammoth instrument of nearly 7,000 pipes, ranging in size from five-eighths of an inch to 32 feet. Its construction was started in 1866 with the use of native timber and glue boiled from buffalo hides. There are many other interesting historical buildings on and near the square. Also, a ride to the capitol is worth while; from its steps the view of a bright modern city between high, barren desert peaks is fascinating. A circular drive over the foothills will lead to an imposing group of statues with a strange name: "This Is the Place" Monument. It commemorates the 24th of July, 1847, when Brigham Young's wagon emerged from the canyon at this spot; the leader looked into the giant desert bowl and decided to establish there his heaven on earth.

BUOYANT WATERS. The Great Salt Lake, located about 14 miles west of Salt Lake City, is known throughout the world; although it is the largest American lake west of the Mississippi, measuring approximately 75 by 50 miles, it is not its size that made it famous, but its salt content. The water of this unique inland sea contains about 6½ billion tons of salt, representing a salinity 6 to 8 times that of the ocean. There are various resorts along highway 40 where the visitor may discover for himself the lake's buoyancy: He will float with his body partly above water; he will crouch in a sitting position, with his shoulders well above the surface; he will learn that it is nevertheless not easy to swim in such a strong brine. Otherwise, he may find the big lake somewhat disappointing and desolate, although at certain seasons there is a real magnificence about its green water that the tourist certainly will enjoy. The so-called Lucin Cut-Off is an interesting railroad trestle which runs across the lake for 30 miles.

PICKLED BUFFALO MEAT. The Great Salt Lake was discovered in 1324 by Jim Bridger, the merry Paul Bunyan of America's center. Floating down Bear River on a "bull boat," he arrived at the lake and proceeded to take a drink of water. Instantly he spat it out and announced: "Hell, we are on the shore of the Pacific." This error was corrected a year later. At times Bridger returned, and among his various reports, the one on the winter of 1830 is noteworthy. It snowed for seventy days, until the whole region was blanketed with a white 70-foot layer. All the wildlife perished, and in spring the shore was strewn with the frozen carcasses of dead buffaloes. He rolled them all into the brine of the lake, providing pickled buffalo meat for himself and the Ute Indians for years.

The Mormon Tabernacle, open to the general public, offers famous free organ concerts. The monument on the left side honors the sea gulls which saved the crops of the early Mormon settlement from a cricket plague.

ARCHES ARE NOT BRIDGES. The old saying that Utah is 98 per cent scenery and 2 per cent farmland seems confirmed along the lonely desert highway which, as No. 160, turns south at Crescent Junction, becomes No. 47 at Monticello and proceeds toward the state line of Arizona. The trip might be called an "accrued" adventure; beginning comfortably enough, it gradually leads into grandiose and lonely Indian lands where only the venturesome travel. The first stop is for lovers of arches, i.e., of stone formations created in cliffs by wind and weather erosion. There are eighty-eight of them in Arches National Monument, east of the road. The largest is Landscape Arch, with a length of 291 feet, believed to be the longest natural stone arch in the world. To the north a jumble of huge red slabs, not yet fully explored, is called Devil's Garden. Delicate Arch (the cowboys call it "Schoolmarm's Pants") has a splendid setting, with the Colorado River Gorge and the snow-capped La Sal Mountains in the background. From highway 160 to the right, a rough, one-lane road leads to Dead Horse Point. There you will come upon a vista never to be forgotten: tier upon tier of towering cliffs, overlooking what is perhaps the most wonderful view in the state.

MAMMOTHS AND URANIUM. The towns along the road—Moab, Monticello, Blanding—are typical Mormon settlements, green oases in the desert, compactly

The skyscraper rocks of Monument Valley rise a thousand feet.

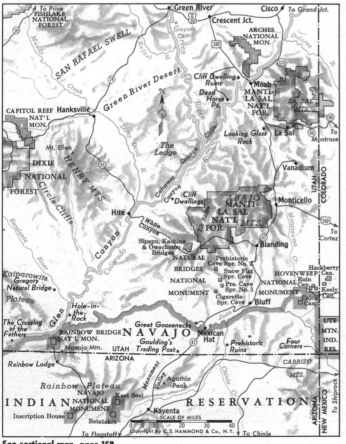

See sectional map, page 158

built, with a clean and pleasant atmosphere. If you look down a Moab street, and on the red hill beyond the Lombard poplars a cavalcade of cowboys appears, you may think the horses a little too fancy and the riders too swaggering. Your suspicions will be justified, for this is a "location" town and many a Hollywood western had its origin in these valleys. The story-tradition is genuine, some of the best novels of Zane Grey are placed in this very setting. The romantic past is complemented by a realistic present. The blasting in the mountains, the trucks rumbling by and the roads being built spell the source of the boom: uranium. The painted cliffs, by the way, do not only contain the atomic metal but also fascinating prehistoric pictographs. One, near Moab, shows the drawing of a mammoth that puzzles the scientists. The big animals died out 30,000 years ago, while man appeared here only about 15,000 years ago. Could some remnants of the mammoth tribe have survived until the arrival of the first human beings?

BRIDGES ARE NOT ARCHES. They are carved by water and span a river, either one that is flowing now or used to be there eons ago. Three such natural bridges of immense proportions, as well as several villages of prehistoric cliff dwellers can be studied at Natural Bridges National Monument, located west of Blanding. Owachomo Bridge, which can be reached by car, is the smallest and considered the oldest of the three. It spans the 200-foot Armstrong Canyon at a height of 108 feet. According to the ranger "it is customary to hike" the 9-mile triangle trail that leads to Kachina Bridge (named for the symbols of the Kachina dance of the Hopis carved into the rock), a deep-red massive span of 186 feet, 205 feet above ground. Finally the trail will take you to Sipapu Bridge, which is magnificent in its symmetrical proportions. "Sipapu" is the Hopis gateway to the underworld.

THE GREAT AND LONELY LAND. Proceeding southward, on highway 47, the road becomes rough. Past the small town of Bluff, it leads to the "Great Goosenecks," which have been called "the convolutions of the San Juan River," 1500 feet below your observation point. From now on a jeep or a horse are a better means of transportation than a car, but the land that is surrounding you is an American sanctuary: Monument Valley. Out of the forbidding red plain the huge skyscraper castles rise into the sky for a thousand feet, in a lonely expanse whose horizons are serrated by the distant ranges of Arizona, New Mexico and Colorado. An Indian boy on horseback or a hiking old Navajo may be the only human beings you meet between the "Emperor" and the "Stagecoach," or the "Bear and Rabbit" and "Brigham's Tomb." When the sun is setting and, in a violet haze, the towering sentinels merge into the

Snow in the desert seems incongruous, but is a reality in wintertime.

darkness, you are witnessing one of this continent's great spectacles. At Goulding's Trading Post near the Arizona border, you may see Navajos trading rugs and silver jewelry for groceries, and you may join a pack trip to Rainbow Bridge National Monument.

RAINBOW'S END. You can also travel there by car, over a "road" through the Navajo Reservation of Arizona to Rainbow Lodge, but according to late reports, the sand traps still cause spinning wheels and the bottomless holes still exist. Nevertheless, quite a few adventurous travelers brave the desert and reach the least accessible of America's great sightseeing spots, the Rainbow Bridge. This natural bridge is the largest on earth; with a span of 278 feet and a height of 309 feet, the National Capitol could be placed under it and not nearly fill the space. The bridge is beautiful as well, with its salmon-pink rock, symmetric lines and curved surface above. These qualities suggested the same phenomenon to all who saw it; the Paiutes, the Navajos and the whites gave it the same name in three languages: the Rainbow.

From Goulding's Trading Post to the east you can take a trail to Four Corners, the only spot in America where four states meet: Utah, Colorado, Arizona and New Mexico. The cowboys claim that on occasion the geographical point of contact is a wonderful refuge; by walking in a small circle you can elude any sheriff.

Besides this double arch, 87 single arches are in Arches National Monument.

GENTLE PEOPLE AND ECCENTRIC CLIFFS. The first white settlers in southwestern Utah were Mormons, hardy and gentle pioneers. When Brother Joseph Black one day discovered the wonderful kaleidoscope of colors flashing around the canyon of the Virgin River, he was overwhelmed. "Little Zion," he called it reverently. When, ninety miles to the east, Brother Ebenezer Bryce came upon a valley of marvelous statuary in all tints of the rainbow, he exclaimed: "What a place to hunt for a stray cow!" As for Black's discovery, Brigham Young inspected it, thought its name a little sacrilegious and declared it to be "Not Zion." His word was law, and the name of the chasm became "Not Zion Canyon." The Indians had called it "Arrow Quiver," and the maps of the U.S. Army had marked the spot as Mukuntuweap. When it became a national monument in 1909 and a national park ten years later, Brother Black's suggestion prevailed. It's Zion Canyon now. The realism of Brother Bryce also carried the day: We have not only Bryce Canyon and Bryce Canyon National Park, but one of the most beautiful bright peaks on the rim is Bryce Point.

MIRAGE OF AN ORIENTAL CITY. The road leading to Bryce Canyon National Park gives no indication of the spectacle to come. Visitors park their cars and walk up to the rim. There they suddenly see a valley

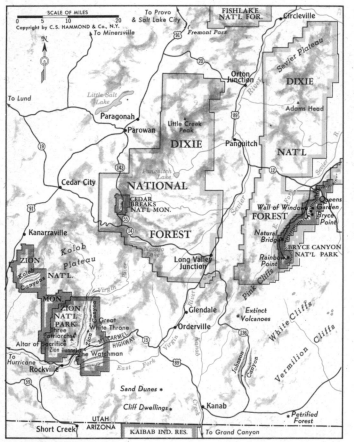

See sectional map, page 158

of such flaming beauty and radiance that the impact almost touches them physically. Every one, of course, has a different, individual reaction, but to this visitor it seemed as if a vague vision of a silent, mysterious city of columns, turrets and spires, far away in the jungles of the East Indies, had become reality and stood before him; only that reality was brighter and more fantastic than the dream. Factually speaking, the valley is not really a canyon, but a basin carved into the soft sandstone by rain and snow, three miles long and two miles broad, at an altitude of 8,000 feet. The thousands of strange formations glow in all colors of the spectrum, from white, yellow, orange and pink to tan and purple, but the basic, predominant color is red. The names given to the various columns and towers may sound a little trite, but they do express the infinite' variety in the shapes of the rocks: Queen Victoria and the Pope in Queens Garden, the Wall of Windows, the Pipe Organ and Bluebeard's Castle. A trip to the canyon floor is most worthwhile, for to look up between the tall, fragrant pine trees is an entirely new experience. From here the canyon seems to take on different but not less beautiful forms, shapes and colors.

TUNNEL WITH WINDOWS. To the west, in Zion Canyon National Park, the small Virgin River has performed an incredible feat: Into the porous Navajo sandstone, it has ground a 15-mile chasm 2,000 to 3,000 feet deep, with walls in some places as straight as if cut by a knife. The canyon is half a mile wide at its broadest point and less than twenty feet at its narrowest. Here the water may suddenly rise to twenty-five feet in the case of a downpour, grinding the gorge to new depths. One of the most striking features of the rocks is their "color scheme": A thick layer of bright-red stone is topped by a narrower layer of white rock, with a thin second layer of red added in places. There are wonderful mountain peaks in the park, most of them adhering to "the scheme," like the red Watchman and the forbidding Three Patriarchs. One cliff shows red stone formations in its white layer; implying a similarity to blood stains, it was given the rather morbid name of Altar of Sacrifice. Most famous and most photographed of the Zion mountains is the Great White Throne, whose solid mass rises to an altitude of 6,744. Green are the pines at its base; red at first, then buff and lastly white is the rock above. Green again is the forest that grows on its plateau-top, and deep blue is the sky behind and around. Another marvel of the park is the Mount Carmel Highway, beginning at the lower end of Zion Canyon. In three miles it climbs 800 feet, and in six skillfully engineered switchbacks rises to the mile-long Zion Tunnel, built into the side of the canyon wall. Like several famous tunnels in Switzerland, it has "windows," i.e., six openings or galleries providing breathtaking views. When the tunnel was built, the engineers feared that the debris thrown into the canyon would choke the

A canyon floor view, like this photograph of Bryce Canyon, is often as fascinating as a rim view. To look up between the tall fragrant pine trees to the top of the canyon walls is an entirely new experience.

river, but the little stream took the rubble in its stride, and in three months had carried away and neatly removed the last vestiges of it.

ZION CANYON BY DAY AND NIGHT. If Zion National Park is a stunning kodachrome spectacle when the sun shines, it is an enchanted land on a clear, calm, silent night when the wind has stopped and the fragrance of earth and of pines is in the air. When the moon rises and touches the cliffs and the summits, the grandiose color display reappears in subdued, ghostlike tints. But you can distinguish clearly and admiringly the reds and pinks and yellows. No wonder human beings were always attracted to this canyon

A MOUNTAIN-TOP WHEEL. North of Zion and west of Bryce National Park lies a bowl filled with eroded ridges that radiate from the center like spokes of a wheel. It is Cedar Breaks National Monument. As far as colors are concerned, it is perhaps the high point of the "color land" of Utah and Arizona, with white and rose, coral and orange, rich brown and lavender tints whose brilliance is not surpassed anywhere. An especially pleasant feature is its alpine foliage, at its height from mid-July to mid-August. Since Cedar Breaks towers two miles above sea level, its coolness is a wonderful contrast to the seething summer heat of the desert. The ground is moist, the fir and spruce forests smell sweetly.

PERPETUAL COLORAMA. A huge gorge filled with mile-high mountain ranges, bathed in all the colors of the spectrum in an ever changing kaleidoscope—that is Grand Canyon, Arizona's wondrous chasm. Nobody will ever see the same spectacle of tints and hues twice, just as nobody will see the same sunrise or sunset, spring or fall. Nobody has attempted to describe it. Few have tried to paint it. The first one to do so, Thomas Moran, probably came nearest to a true interpretation of this drama in stone. His painting hangs in Washington's Capitol. The tool which nature employed in creating the canyon, is an extraordinary river, the Colorado. At times its current reaches a speed of 20 miles per hour. Every day it carries through the gorge nearly a million tons of silt, sand, loose gravel, rocks and boulders; therefore, it appears colored, and its name Colorado is most appropriate. Such a river has tremendous "digging power." Hundreds of millions of years ago these mountains were rolling hills, and as they gradually rose, the stream had to grind on fiercely just to stay where it was; during the following eons of growth and decay, building and eroding, the external rock formations changed so many times that today the Colorado does not flow down a slope but, strangely, cuts across one. The river did not work alone; it had helpers, from rains and storms and frost to the plants whose roots loosened the rocks.

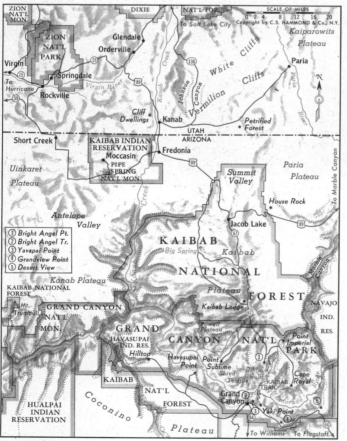

See sectional map, page 158

A JOURNEY INTO TIME. The sudden impact of seeing the Grand Canyon—and there is no gradual way of coming upon it—is one of cosmic awareness. We know that our planet was created in time measures that are beyond human comprehension; here we have before us a cross-cut of the process: The canyon walls expose layer after layer, era after era, distinguishing each stretch of untold millions of years by another color, from brown and red to yellow and green. Some layers are so old that they do not show any fossil life. Others yield petrified remnants of living creatures, ranging in size from huge dinosaurs to tiny sea worms. The near-eternity lying between the beginning of this canyon and the day of our visit is before our eyes, and we feel that the great forces around us are still at work. We do not stand here at the end of a chapter but in the middle of one.

CONQUISTADORES, PILGRIMS AND A MID-WESTERNER. Even in the tiny span of white man's history in America, the canyon is an interesting landmark. Those Americans who think that our country got its start at Plymouth Rock, while beyond the Appalachians the "new" America begins, may note with surprise that thirteen white men, Lopez de Cardenas and twelve companions, stood at the rim of the Grand Canyon almost three generations before the landing of the Pilgrims. It is true the Spaniards did not want to erect here, in 1540, a new kingdom of Heaven, but they did not give up this land, either. Others followed, like Padre Garces and Padre Escalante, and traders and soldiers. In time the Spaniards here became Mexicans, and since 1848 they have been Americans, with a tradition as American as any and quite a bit longer than that of any other white group. But the man who explored the river within today's boundaries of the National Park was Major J. W. Powell, a professor of geology at the University of Illinois who was doing field work in the neighborhood with a group of students. Although he had lost his right arm in a battle of the Civil War, the project fascinated him, and two years later his expedition started out from Green River City, Wyoming, on the 24th of May, 1869. Four boats and nine men, among them the painter Moran, took part. The trip took three months and four days, and none of the survivors ever forgot it. There was no turning back between the precipitous cliffs, and it seems a miracle today that in the river's mad plunges, rapids and cataracts only one boat got smashed. The clothes of the explorers were always wet and their food supplies became soaked and rotted. Sometimes the boats had to be lowered one past another, the last man on the upper cliff jumping into the water below, where he was hauled into the boat. On the 29th of August the party arrived at the Grand Wash, tired but happy. "Our joy is almost ecstasy," Major Powell wrote.

CONCENTRATED GEOGRAPHY. Grand Canyon

Grand Canyon, created by the extraordinary Colorado River, has been called "a drama in stone" and "a journey into time." The various strata of the canyon wall reflect era after era in the millions of years of its development.

National Park consists of two distinct sections: the South Rim, accessible by car or train all year, and the North Rim, which can only be reached by car during the summer season from June to September. The distance between the two rims is 12 miles by airplane, 21 miles by trail, and more than 200 miles by automobile road. To look into the canyon is like thumbing through a book. To descend to the bottom of the gorge is like reading the book chapter by chapter. It is not only a journey into geological time but also an excursion into plant geography. At the canyon floor the vegetation is Mexican; you then pass through four floral zones and when you arrive at the North Rim, where the great evergreen forests begin, you may study some of the plants of Canada. The descent is usually done on muleback, over Bright Angel Trail or Kaibab Trail to Kaibab Bridge, a cobweb of steel over the rampaging river. While the geologists enjoyed a heyday, and the anthropologists discovered 700 sites of prehistoric Indian dwellings, and the botanists studied species of southern cactus and northern blue spruce separated only by canyon walls, the zoologists pondered a challenging mystery: The 300-acre top of Shiva Temple might have contained living beings shut off, for thousands of years, from normal changes of evolution by the mountain's inaccessible, vertical sides. So a group of mountaineer-scientists ventured to the summit in 1937. But they did not discover any sensational forms of life.

COOL MOUNTAIN TOWN. The fact that you can go skiing in Arizona on the 4th of July illustrates the great variety of scenery and climate which this canyon-mesa-desert state has to offer. The cool area lies in the north-center around Flagstaff, on the high Coconino Plateau. To the north the dark-green Elden Mountain towers above the city, and beyond that the San Francisco Peaks rise into the clear-blue sky. Humphrey's Peak is the tallest, with an altitude of 12,655 feet. The Hopi name for the range is "High Place of the Snows," and the snow-filled ravines and slopes offer fine skiing from December to May; in a few isolated places the snow lasts even until July. Thirteen miles from Flagstaff, the Arizona Snow Bowl boasts of ski tows, practice slopes, ski trails through beautiful pine forests, a ski lodge and various tournaments. Sometimes schools in southern Arizona organize class excursions to Flagstaff so the children may discover what snow is. Among the wildlife of this forest-covered plateau, large herds of pronghorn antelopes survive in the open pine lands. Flagstaff itself is a busy town where Hopi and Navajo women sell silver jewelry and blankets, ceramics and baskets, where dudes from neighboring ranches strut across the street in clothes and boots more Western than those of the cowboys, where Indian ponies clop-clop on the pavement and buckboards and wagons bring Indian shoppers from the nearby reservations. The town's most

The Walnut Canyon Cliff Dwellings were inhabited between 900 and 1100 A.D.

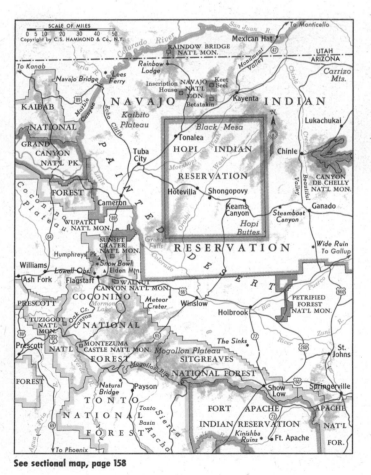

See sectional map, page 158

exciting days are on July 3rd, 4th, and 5th, when the annual Nahohi is held; this is a "powwow" of 20 tribal nations from 7 states, including a gay all-Indian parade and rodeo, ceremonial dances, chants and an exhibit of Indian folk art in the Museum of Northern Arizona.

THE FAMOUS SIGHTS AROUND FLAGSTAFF. The many points of interest in the neighborhood of Flagstaff will be listed here in clockwise fashion, beginning in the north. The map indicates the roads on which they can be reached. In *Wupatki National Monument,* one Hopi house of the 12th century has been restored. The Wupatki Ruins are interesting because they cling around natural walls of red sandstone and seem to grow out of the soil. *Sunset Crater National Monument* contains a pit 400 feet deep and 1300 feet in diameter; its sloping sides are bright yellow near the rim and gradually change to orange, red and black—a display of colors which suggested the name "Sunset Crater."

In *Walnut Canyon National Monument,* remains of some 300 cliff dwellings can be seen in the walls of the gorge; in the "apartments," which are believed to have been occupied between 900 and 1100 A.D., primitive hoes and other crude instruments have been found. *Meteor Crater* is a huge pit in the flat desert, about a mile in diameter and nearly 600 feet deep. Near the rim is the American Meteorite Museum which collects and studies meteorites, the only objects on earth to have come from outer space. A ride through *Oak Creek Canyon* is a wonderful adventure. The road twists along the rushing creek at the bottom of the canyon, through miles of dark-green pines and light-green maples and oaks, sycamores and aspens, and between red stone walls rising 2000 feet above the stream. *Montezuma Castle National Monument* is a 500-acre tract around what is probably the best preserved cliff dwelling in the U. S. There is a large cave in a vertical rock wall, 145 feet above the ground, and into that cave the grayish pink adobe castle has been built. To associate the castle with Montezuma was a mistake of the early white visitors, but the name survived and is used today. *Tuzigoot National Monument* is a restored ancient pueblo that differs from the usual type of construction; it is erected of stone, with mud used as mortar. Occupied by several hundred persons around the year 1200 A.D., its community had reached an unusually high degree of culture. Many of the excavated objects are now displayed in the Tuzigoot Museum; they include fine mosaics of shells and turquoise, storage ollas 27 inches high and tools of stone and bone that are remarkably symmetrical. *Prescott* is a welcome oasis for the traveler who has just crossed the desert and now deeply inhales the scent of the pine forests, feeling the coolness of the mile-high plateau. Mountain ranges surround the city, and Indians, prospectors, cowboys and sheepherders give the

The Navajos raise sheep on desert pastures, an almost impossible task.

Northeast of Flagstaff the large, arid Navajo Reservation begins.

town a Western flavor, which is enhanced by historic Pioneer Square, a group of houses dating back to Prescott's pioneer days. The local Frontier Days Rodeo, held every summer since 1888, is the oldest U.S. rodeo.

PAINTED SANDS AND SAND PAINTINGS. North of the Little Colorado River and clearly seen from Wupatki National Monument, the Painted Desert stretches its dunes and escarpments for 300 miles. There is no other desert like it, for its hills, mesas and terraces glow in warm colors of yellow, red, magenta and mauve. The highly colored shales, sandstones and marls often create, in the air above, a pink or purple haze, and changing tints of amethyst and lilac, scarlet and russet seem to dance along the mesas. In the slanting light of the early morning, when the shadows are deep, the terraced walls glow in blood-red and distant mountain ranges rise in near and clear profiles, the Painted Desert is at its most spectacular. (For additional information about the Painted Desert see the note on the Petrified Forest National Monument under Arizona in the Sightseeing Gazetteer which begins on page 209.) From time immemorial the Indians have used these colored sands to make their brilliant sand paintings, an art that has been especially developed by the Navajos. Executed by long-trained experts, these circular paintings are "painted" on the flat ground in various decorative patterns as a ritual of religious significance.

ARISING FROM THE ASHES. Among the first pioneers who settled at Arizona's Salt River was an English globetrotter who called himself "Lord Darrel." He was an alcoholic but also a scholar of sorts, and when he noticed that the new community was rising from the ruins of old houses and irrigation ditches abandoned eons ago, he remembered the Greek legend of how the phoenix bird, after being consumed by fire, arose brilliantly from its own ashes. He saw the parallel, and ever since the community has been called Phoenix, an imaginative and meaningful name. To-day's modern city, shaded by trees and studded with parks, rises dramatically from the barren desert. If you look through the broad, level streets, you see stark lonely mountains closing the horizon: the Four Peaks, Superstition, Camelback. The state capitol, of neo-classic design, has its east entrance appropriately flanked by two pedestals of petrified wood; its cactus garden, with innumerable varieties, is also in keeping with the locale. The Arizona Museum and the Heard Museum preserve relics of the country's ancient Indian cultures and mementoes of Arizona's pioneer days, and La Ciudad is the excavation of a pueblo-like adobe structure which was inhabited 1,500 years ago. The City of Phoenix has two claims to importance: It is the center of Arizona's "saddle-and-suntan industry" and it is a great agricultural market. Both achievements are based

The Arizona Biltmore is a luxurious desert resort.

on the dry, sunny climate which blesses Phoenix with 230 entirely clear days every year; this figure, the people point out, compares with 180 in Los Angeles and 100 in Miami. The winter climate, with a sunny 70 degrees by day and pleasantly cool nights, is exhilarating. The summers are hot, but all-year residents comfort themselves with the thought that Phoenix is thoroughly air-conditioned. During the winter season there is entertainment galore; in February the town goes "western" during the World's Championship Rodeo, in March it turns "Spanish" for the gay Fiesta del Sol and in April Old Arizona is reenacted in the Pioneer Reunion. The most original annual affair is the Lost Dutchman's Search, also called Superstition Mountain Trek, held every spring. On that day several thousand citizens assault Superstition's slopes and crags with picks and shovels, to rediscover America's most famous lost mine.

THE LURE OF THE DESERT. The winter vacation industry is located in the desert near Phoenix. That might seem strange since we associate few pleasant thoughts with the desert. Many people don't like it when they see it, but the desert has a way of casting a spell on you, especially in the morning when the mountains rise sharply into the sky and the wind carries a wonderful, fresh scent of herbs, or at night when the columns of the saguaro cactus throw long shadows and darkness and silence fall on the land. Most doubting

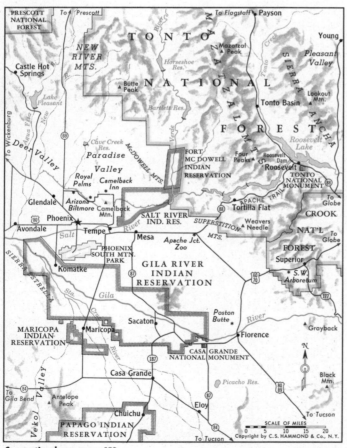

See sectional map, page 158

178

Thomases gradually change their minds and become very fond of the desert and its moods. Vacationists stay either on a guest ranch, which is a luxury hotel with a spectacular view, like the Arizona Biltmore, the Camelback Inn or the Royal Palms, or on a dude ranch, where horseback riding is the outstanding feature. A popular entertainment is the chuck-wagon dinner held somewhere out in the desert at a picturesque spot where you watch the sun go down in a blaze, hear a coyote howling far away, smell the wood smoke of the camp fire and eat a hearty steak dinner while the stars begin to glisten close over your head. The feeling of health and exuberance, the comfortable, bright clothes, the camp fire tales, the gay music, the square dances and the good-looking cowboys add up to a worth-while vacation with a western twang. Not the least attraction is the potential danger of the desert; no stranger on horseback may venture into it alone, for if he is thrown, the horse will find its way home, but the rider may be lost.

LETTUCE FOR ALL AMERICA. The other aspect of the Phoenix area is more utilitarian but also interesting. After driving for miles through barren cactus-and-mesa country, you suddenly find yourself in the middle of green fields sprouting in neat rows of carrots, cabbages, cantaloupes, broccoli, alfalfa or cotton. The reason for this fertility is, of course, irrigation. Nowhere is the magic of water more spectacular than in the po-

San Xavier del Bac (see page 180) was both a mission and a great ranch.

tentially fertile soil of the desert, and Phoenix is the center and market for a rich farming oasis of 560,000 acres. The cotton grown there is of an excellent long-staple variety; alfalfa can be harvested six or seven times in a favorable year and during certain weeks, lettuce grows nowhere in the U. S. but in this oasis, so it is quite probable that most Americans have tasted the Phoenix variety. Oleander bushes bloom, orange groves thrive and date palms grow into tall shade trees.

THE ROAD TO ROOSEVELT DAM. Behind this astounding fertility, an intricate network of ditches and dams, valves and reservoirs harnesses and distributes the available water supply. The beginning of the project was the small-scale revival of the simple irrigation methods of the prehistoric Indians. When a flash flood destroyed most of the fields in 1891, a modern scientific system was inaugurated on a grand scale. About 75 miles northeast of Phoenix, Roosevelt Dam was started in 1906 and completed in 1911, the first of our great reclamation projects and the father of all western dams. The site was so inaccessible that a 60-mile road had to be cut through the steep mountains; 40 miles were actually hewn into the solid rock. This highway is now the spectacular Apache Trail, State Highway 88. Over hairpin curves and along deep chasms, past gorges and caves it winds its way to a long chain of quiet, man-made lakes, where flowers and trees bloom profusely.

The columns of the saguaro cactus grow to a height of 50 feet.

THE OLD PUEBLO." That's what the people call Tucson, pronounced Too-sahn, the major city in southern Arizona. Originally it was a Spanish town, and in the Mexican section, the so-called Barrio Libre, there are still many flat-roofed adobe houses, built around patios, with flower beds and blossoming trees set into the hard-tramped and clean-swept adobe floors. But on the whole, Tucson is a modern city which does not accent too emphatically its Indian-Spanish past; rather, it reflects the American West. It fits well into the broad desert valley, surrounded by hills and jagged peaks towering in the distance in blue and purple tints. To the cowboys and cattle men it is a market place, and also the big town which offers the right kind of entertainment. The annual Fiesta de los Vaqueros is considered a climax in the rodeo circuit. To several thousand college students it is the seat of the progressive State University which has attracted national attention in many ways; through its Steward Observatory, its research in tree rings as an invaluable aid to archaeology and its fostering of modern art, it contributes definitely to the cultural atmosphere of the city. And for a host of visitors Tucson's climate makes it an ideal vacation and health resort.

INDIANS PAINT THE LIFE OF CHRIST. Located about seven miles south of Tucson, the Mission San Xavier Del Bac (see illustration on p. 179) is a priceless

work of art, a white, asymmetrical building with Spanish-baroque and Moorish overtones like a castle in Spain. Founded in 1700 by the Jesuit Padre Kino, both as a church and headquarters of a big ranch to be worked by the Indians, it had a stormy history. Plagued by Indian revolts and the dissolution of the Jesuit Order, the mission was taken over by the Franciscans. Almost immediately it was attacked and plundered by the Apaches, but the Franciscan brothers rebuilt it in its present form in the 1760's. On the outside, the central panel of the front is particularly striking; in contrast to the plain white side panels, it shows in soft red tints the carved shell-and-arabesque decorations of the baroque period. Of the two identical belfries one is crowned with a dome, but not the other—a shrewd economy move on the part of the padres, for no tax was due to the Crown of Spain on an "unfinished building." The interior is richly decorated with wood carvings and paintings of an unusual character, executed by Indians. A series of panels depicts the life story of Christ, and while they may lack subtlety, they have the vividness of primitive art, which today has many admirers.

A CACTUS FOREST. Seventeen miles to the east of Tucson, Saguaro National Monument is a 63,000-acre tract preserving the finest specimens of America's giant cactus, the saguaro. This fascinating plant reaches an age of nearly two hundred years and a height of fifty feet. In very dry areas it consists of a single fluted column; in more favorable spots it develops side branches up to twenty feet long. The limbs grow in a perpendicular fashion like the arms of a candelabrum, in a striking design that seems highly modern. It is a corrugated marvel of water preservation; in the event of rain it expands its spiny accordion pleats into a reservoir, and shrinks them during a drought. The saguaro forest is a magic place to visit in early May, when the creamy-white waxy blossoms are scattered over the columns. By the end of June the red fruit appears, a favorite food of the Papago Indians.

THE WILDEST WEST. "Welcome to Tombstone and Boothill Graveyard. Buried here are the remains of–." At this point you will read a number of names followed by such remarks as "Killed in Earp-Clanton Battle, Sept. 26, 1881," or "Hanged legally for the Bisbee Massacre, March 8, 1884," or "Murdered March 8, 1882." In a corner of the graveyard one marker is unusual. It says: "M.E. Kellogg—1882. Died natural death." These mementos can be seen in the town of tombstone, southeast of Tucson. It is one of America's ghost towns that has been revived so visitors may get a first-hand impression of the lusty chapter of American history that took place in the Wild West. For such studies, Tombstone certainly is a vantage point. After having been a prospectors' disappointment at first, a "tombstone" of their hopes, some rich silver strikes were made later on, and mines like the Lucky Cuss, the Goodenough and

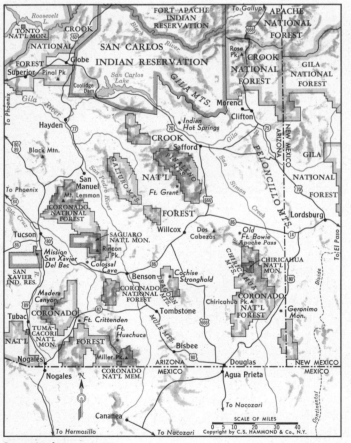

See sectional map, page 158

Dude ranch vacations in the Southwest offer the exhilarating winter air of the desert, good horses, real cowboys, chuck-wagon dinners, square dances, and good fellowship. Many dudes own elaborate outfits including a saddle, and return year after year. Numerous among the guests are girls from the East.

the Tough Nut poured out their riches. The town was organized at a relatively late date, in 1879, a fact which had rather sinister consequences, for by that time many veins in California and other mining areas had run out, and prospectors and gamblers were looking for new fields of action. The Australian gold diggings had come to an end, and hundreds of treasure hunters were returning to the States. Finally, the older mining communities had organized vigilante committees to uphold a semblance of law and order and rid the towns of their worst characters. Most of these gentry assembled in Tombstone. Add to this calamitous situation the fact that the fierce Apaches, under Chief Victorio, main-

tained their headquarters in the neighboring Dragoon Mountains, and you can imagine the life and atmosphere that prevailed in Tombstone during its roaring decade. Among relics of that time, the Bird Cage Theater is the best known. In its day it was operated twenty-four hours a day, seven days a week, as a variety theater, bar, saloon, gambling establishment and dance hall, swarming with adventurers, trigger men and girl-entertainers. The name was derived from its bird-cage-like boxes in the theater auditorium; those on one side were often occupied by one of two feuding factions, those on the other side by the rival. The result was bedlam. Today the Bird Cage is a museum and also a restaurant.

THE HIGHEST STAKES. There are, no doubt, people who travel to Las Vegas because of its dry, sunny winter climate, but the vast majority visit the famous resort in southern Nevada because of the special brand of gambling offered there. Not that its black jack or roulette games are different from those played at Reno or Monte Carlo, but Las Vegas has evolved a kind of vacation establishment that seems to have a special appeal to a great many people: a hotel, restaurant, nightclub and gambling casino. The last department brings in the great and steady profits; consequently, the other sections can offer de luxe accommodations with valet service and swimming pool, wonderful meals by outstanding chefs and nightclub entertainment by the brightest stars of Hollywood and Broadway at a cost surprisingly reasonable. Even the motels operate as luxurious sleeping-eating-gambling units. This method elevated Las Vegas to a kind of "cinema dream" in about ten years. Highway 91, just out of town, is known as "the strip"; there an ever-growing number of luxury hotels draw crowds from all the states. Originally a winter resort, Las Vegas operates now on an all-year basis, with thorough air conditioning counteracting the heat of the summer. Many gambling casinos are open twenty-four hours a day, and the swanky Desert Inn is said to allow higher stakes than are permitted anywhere else in the world. Chips of various denomina-

The Colorado is one of the most useful and spectacular rivers on earth.

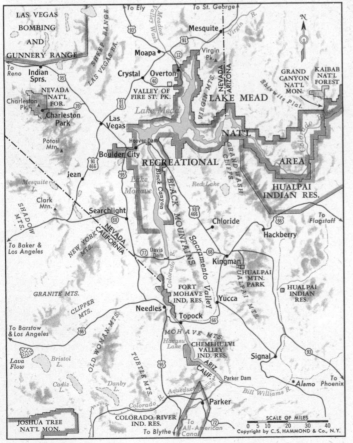

See sectional map, page 158

tions are used like money in town, and tales of lucky windfalls create an air of excitement. There is, for instance, the story of a world record, as reported by Lucius Beebe. It happened at the Desert Inn, where one day an unidentified young man placed a single dollar in play. Twenty-eight straight passes followed. Had he left his winnings to be doubled with each roll, he would have wound up with 268 million dollars. As it was, he won 750 dollars, but the house paid out $150,000 in side bets, and did so gladly because of the publicity. The fact that Los Angeles is only 300 miles distant often attracts members of the motion picture colony to Las Vegas—another addition to the town's glamour. Las Vegas proper is a friendly, tree-shaded town which celebrates its Western past every spring, with a parade-rodeo-street-dance festival called Heldorado. The whole population turns out dressed and bearded in Western pioneer style. As a community, Las Vegas is both old and new. The gushing springs which mark the site were known as good watering places even in Spanish days, but settlers, ranchers and prospectors came and went, and the modern town was not founded until 1905, as a project sponsored by railroad interests. It has prospered ever since.

THE HIGHEST DAM. One of the luxury resorts of Las Vegas refers to itself, in a circular, as "the Old West in New Splendor." This label might be much more appropriately attached to the airplane view one can enjoy about thirty miles southeast of Las Vegas. In a mountain region so bleak and forbidding that before twenty years ago only a few adventurous prospectors had set foot in it, there is now a huge, deep-blue lake created by the bright concrete structure of the Hoover Dam. Seeing this giant producer of electricity, irrigation and recreation in its wilderness setting, you cannot help feeling proud; it will strike you as a great American monument. Built in the early 1930's, the task was of Cyclopean proportions. At first the Colorado River had to be diverted, and for that purpose four tunnels were blasted through Black Canyon. Then the grooves into which the dam was to fit were chiseled into the canyon walls. For the flood waters from the spillway, ninety-one tunnels were bored. All these operations involved the removal of millions of tons of solid rock. Then the dam began to rise, and the artificial lake, created by the backed-up waters of the Colorado, flooded and submerged a thousand-year-old pueblo along the Virgin River. Completed, the barrier rose to a height of 727 feet, the greatest dam in the world. Nobody who rides by car over its crest can appreciate the size of the enterprise. The powerhouses at the base may seem like toy buildings, yet they are huge plants sending torrents of electric current to California, Nevada and Arizona. The turbine houses and other departments are open for inspection, and visitors will find them not only functional—but also decorated in good taste, in a mod-

Lake Mead, a man-made reservoir 115 miles long, is a colorful water-sports playground.

ern style adapted to the Indian patterns of the Southwest. Most of the irrigation water is carried through the All-American Canal to the deserts of southern California.

A MAN-MADE SEA. The waters of the Colorado River are muddy, but after they have deposited their silt at the bottom of Lake Mead, they take on a deep, indigo-blue, which contrasts strikingly with the red, green and yellow streaks in the rocky cliffs and steep ranges lining the shores. For 115 miles the lake winds its way into the Colorado near the Grand Canyon, forming picturesque arms and bays, inlets and capes, promontories and islands. Hemenway Wash, five miles from Boulder City, is the chief water-sports center, where swimming, boating and water-skiing flourish. But sailing is most popular in this spectacular rock-and-water setting, and the lake's fleet of yachts and sailing vessels of all types is always increasing.

THE VALLEY OF THE FLAME. To the west of Lake Mead, the Valley of Fire State Park is traversed by a road leading from Crystal, on highway 91, to the east; in a fabulous crescendo of colors and eerie stone formations, it reaches its climax in a narrow pass called the Valley of the Flame, high above the northern arm of Lake Mead. There rock colors of incredible intensity, petroglyphs of a people long vanished and the remains of petrified trees combine to create an impression of unearthly splendor.

Hoover Dam, world's tallest, gives electricity, irrigation, recreation.

STATE OF CHANCE. The minute you cross the state line into Nevada you realize that "gaming" (the word "gambling" is frowned upon here, as not quite appropriate) has become a big industry in this state. You knew, of course, about Reno and Las Vegas, but the neon signs begin at the border, and there is hardly an eating place without roulette tables and slot machines. If you are a puritan, you hurry on without stopping, but most visitors don't mind investigating personally what the casinos are up to, although they would be horrified at the thought of legalized gambling at home. The Nevadans' viewpoint is this: Their state is largely a desert; outside of mining there is practically no industry; there is little land fertile enough for agriculture. At the same time a far-flung network of highways has to be maintained, and an adequate school system. The money has to come from some source. And legalized and continuously supervised gaming is better than underground gambling. At any rate, it is strictly a Nevada affair.

"THE BIGGEST LITTLE CITY IN THE WORLD." Although this slogan is not very meaningful, it has penetrated into the consciousness of America, and everybody knows that Reno is meant. Your first visit there will be a curious and intriguing experience. You will like the tree-lined Truckee River and the bright appearance of the city. You will watch the young women downtown and wonder whether they are all divorcees.

Rhyolite (see map on page 194) is Nevada's most impressive ghost town.

You will walk through the clubs, marvel at the democratic atmosphere, and smile at the signs and inscriptions: "Be careful with your money." "All this is very solid and respectable." "This club is operated by a family of Vermont farm boys." "Come and see our historical collection of the Old West, in back of the black jack tables, it's very educational." And if you watch an elderly lady with a lapful of silver dollars operating three clattering slot machines simultaneously, with a face as serious and concentrated as if she were working at an assembly line, —that appears both comical and pathetic. Whatever you may think, Reno is a genuine corner of America, and worth seeing.

"THE BUCKET OF BLOOD SALOON." Not far from Reno there is one of America's great historic shrines; it is neither a battlefield nor the birthplace of a hero, but it is the area where the Old West "happened" in its gaudiest and most fantastic form: Virginia City. In 1859 a certain ore which the prospectors disregarded and called "black stuff" was assayed and yielded over $3000 worth in gold and almost $5000 worth in silver per ton. The Comstock Lode had been discovered, the greatest strike ever made anywhere on earth. Two mines, the Consolidated Virginia and the Consolidated California, rose in value from $100,000 to 159 million dollars within four years. Fortunes made in Virginia City built great west coast cities, constructed continental railroads,

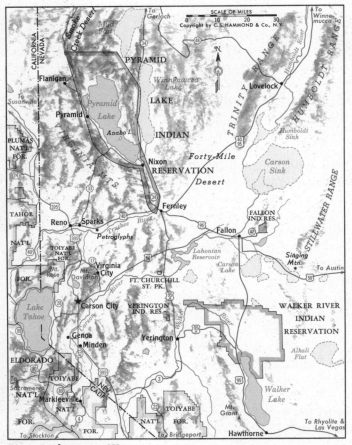

See sectional map, page 158

184

financed the first cable across the Atlantic, and reduced the debt of the War Between the States. A city with such a past must be fascinating, and it is. Part of it is a ghost town which always creates an eerie interest in outsiders; part of it has a pleasant Victorian residential atmosphere; part of it is a revival of the old Western spirit, and it certainly is fun to visit the Bucket of Blood Saloon which has done business on C Street since 1876, and the Crystal Bar with its ancient chandeliers in red and green, dressed up with prisms in splendid tiers. There is Piper's Opera House where a voluble audience acclaimed the most famous actors and actresses of its day, and the "Territorial Enterprise," the newspaper office where Mark Twain once worked, and where now Lucius Beebe, colorful connoisseur of food, wine, and old Western lore, carries on the torch. Besides the flamboyant history, there is the spectacular scenery. The city lies on the eastern slope of Mt. Davidson, with a choice seat in the "theater-in-the-round" that is formed by high, rocky mountains. Two thousand feet below the Carson River winds its way between green pastures and tall cottonwood trees; farther on you see the white dunes of the Forty-Mile Desert; and the snow-capped blue mountain chain that massively closes the horizon in the crystal-clear air is the Humboldt Range, 150 miles away.

"THE BREATH OF THE ERRING WOMAN."
There are other see-worthy sights in the western section

Reno's casino district has a perpetual fiesta atmosphere.

Virginia City's Crystal Bar, famous for its fancy old chandeliers.

of Nevada. Carson City, for instance, the smallest state capital in America is a lush oasis in the desert, a fertile, well-watered spot, a lovely park above which the white dome of the capitol arises. Mt. Rose is a wintersport center; its "Reno Ski Bowl" offers slopes of various steepness and a modern chairlift. But the most unusual sight, and one of breath-taking beauty at sunset or in full moonlight, is Pyramid Lake, a large body of water 30 miles long and up to 10 miles wide. Deep blue, surrounded by sharp-edged hills, studded with islands of tufa that jut steeply from the surface, it offers a view that cannot be duplicated, notably when the rays of the setting sun paint rocks and islands red, orange, and purple. Anaho Island is, in season, a white, seething mass: Pelicans cover it, the greatest rookery in the West and, fortunately, a national bird refuge. When the cui-ui-fish run, the mouth of the Truckee River swarms with fishing pelicans, and the awkward and weird-looking birds fit well into the eerie landscape. Beyond Anaho Island a pyramid rises 475 feet above the water, and the Paiute Indians have a colorful legend about the huge boulder at whose foot steam rises from several hot springs. Once upon a time there was a handsome girl who, however, fell into erring ways. So the great spirit clapped a giant basket over her, and she turned into rock. But she still breathes. Just look: Her breath is clearly visible. Another tufa formation is the Squaw and her Basket.

SWEAT SHOP OF THE GODS." To look up from the broad Sacramento Valley toward the Cascades, and see one of the peaks belch a huge cloud of coal-black smoke five miles into the air, the cloud finally taking on the ominous shape of a mushroom, would be considered surprising indeed. Yet that happened not so long ago, in May, 1914, when Lassen Peak erupted. That this region had shown signs of mild volcanism was known before. In 1843 Fremont reported volcanic activity in Mt. Baker and Mt. St. Helen. Even the name the Indians had given the harmless-looking peak, long before it became Lassen Peak, contained a warning; they called it "Sweat Shop of the Gods." But when the first eruption occurred, on Decoration Day in 1914, without previous rumbling or quaking, the awakened volcano made world news. Within two weeks the crater expanded from 25 to 1500 feet; the intermittent explosions, the hissing steam and the volcanic dust came up to expectations, and it rained ashes as far away as Nevada. A year later, in May, 1915, a fiery mass of glowing lava spilled over the rim of the crater, became a huge black tongue as it crawled over the snow and melted the icy ground. Consequently a torrent of mud swept down the valley of Lost Creek and into Hat Creek, across the divide. The slimy flood carried along rocks and logs, uprooted trees and boulders weighing up to 20 tons and filled a lonely ranch house, fortunately without loss of life. One

Shasta Dam is the second largest in the world.

See sectional map, p. 158

boulder was reported to have sizzled in the water all day; it took a week to change from hot to warm. Three days later a few additional mud flows occurred, accompanied by a new phenomenon.

MOWING DOWN THE TREES IN ROWS. A terrific blast of steam and hot gasses mixed with dust and ashes blew from the crater into the valley and mowed down the big forest in neat, uniform rows, all the tree tops pointing away from the crater, like a grain field cut with a scythe. It also appeared as if some woodworking machinery had been applied; all the tree trunks had their bark sandblasted on the upper side, and the stumps seemed nicely finished and polished. Strangely, no fires occurred. After this spectacular outbreak the periodic eruptions diminished in force, and in February, 1921, all grew quiet again.

HONORING A BLACKSMITH. Whether any one in Denmark knows that one of America's famous peaks is named in honor of a Danish blacksmith seems doubtful. Yet it is so. Peter Lassen, who was born in the little kingdom in 1800, came to this country as a young man, worked in smithies in the East but soon drifted into Mexican California and established a ranch in the shadows of a great peak. In 1849 he was not tempted by the gold rush, but stayed at his home and acted as guide to the many wagon trains bound for the Sacramento

Two Northern Californians, One Half Wild, the Other Fully Tamed

Valley. His mountain became a landmark, and his grateful clients, the riders of the covered wagons, called it Lassen Peak. Today the area is Lassen Volcanic National Park. Visitors find the climb to the white-cloaked summit quite easy and the 150-mile view rewarding. There are other dormant volcanoes in the park, among them the smaller Cinder Cone, which had its last eruption in 1850–51. In its crater, not difficult to reach, a ribbon of painted volcanic sand contrasts sharply with the dark lava. Other signs of volcanic activity are the bubbling hot springs of Boiling Springs Lake; a sulphuric basin of mud pots, warm springs and steam vents called Bumpass Hell (Bumpass was a farm hand who, in 1865, broke through the thin crust, scalded his leg, and named the place) and the Chaos Crags and Chaos Jumbles. The Crags were once hard lava plugs standing upright; then terrific explosions and avalanches tore them down and spread them in a wild and indescribable disorder over a two-mile stretch of ground. Lassen Peak Highway passes through the helter-skelter of the Chaos Jumbles. The various volcanic eruptions caused lava flows and avalanches, which in turn blocked several creeks and thus created a number of beautiful mountain lakes. In some cases whole groves of trees were submerged, and in Snag Lake you still can see, through the crystal-clear water, the remains of trees standing on the bottom. Lake Helen is a beauty spot, and on its shore two tantalizing signs attract attention. One says: "Dozens of rainbow trout will come for crumbs tossed in this lake." The other announces: "Closed to fishing."

COULD THIS VOLCANO SUDDENLY ERUPT WHILE I AM HERE? This question is often heard by the park rangers, and the only answer they can give to the slightly worried visitors is a shrug of the shoulders. Nobody knows, but tourists are advised to return with cameras cocked, in 1980. No eruption is guaranteed, but geologists believe this volcano operates on a 65-year cycle and the last outbreak occurred in 1915.

A VOLCANO COOPERATES. Thirty miles northwest of Lassen Peak, the huge and splendid Mount Shasta looks over the rich, checkered farmlands of the Sacramento Valley, its five glaciers furnishing a glamorous ermine cloak for its summit. Mount Shasta, too, is a dormant volcano, and to this day, a number of steam vents and fumaroles around its peak emit hot gases. But so sure are the scientists of its continued good behavior, this scene of ancient eruptions has been turned into one of man's huge technical projects. Shasta Dam has been built there, with its height of 602 feet and its width of 3500 feet at its crest the second largest in the world. Thus the once fiery volcano and the once violent Sacramento River combine forces to create electric power, irrigate desert lands and control floods.

In spite of its quiet beauty, Mt. Lassen might erupt again in the future, according to some scientists. The volcano, now extinct, seems to follow a seventy-six-year cycle of eruption.

"**D**AZZLING, BRILLIANTLY SO.**"** Lake Tahoe is the essence and paragon of an American mountain lake. It has an old Indian name of pleasant sound. It lies in the crisp mountain air at an altitude of 6,225 feet. It is large—more than 22 miles long and about 12 miles wide. It is very deep, and contains so much water that it could flood the whole state of Texas to seven or eight inches, according to California estimates. Mark Twain glowingly expressed the most startling aspect of the lake: "Down through these great depths the water was not merely transparent but dazzling, brilliantly so; we could see trout by the thousands winging about in the emptiness under us." It is this combination of clarity and depth that accounts for the water's deep colors. The lake is surrounded by mountains towering some 4000 feet above it, the tallest summits being Monument Peak, Freel Peak and Job's Sister. In the morning the ranges are "brilliantly photographed upon its still surface," as Mark Twain saw them. In the evening, when low clouds hover over the lake shore, the mountains rise into the clear sky above the clouds like a mirage. Evergreen forests with a carpet of heather, Indian paintbrush, primroses and other wildflowers descend to the banks; it was there we picked up the handsome 15-inch sugar-pine cones which, together with holly branches, now adorn our house door at Christmastime. There is no crowding, despite the many sandy beaches,

Emerald Bay is a jewel of rare brilliance.

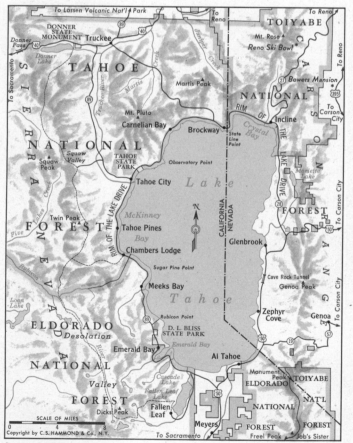

See sectional map, page 158

summer resorts, state parks, public camping grounds, and estates of millionaires like Henry J. Kaiser. The scenery can be enjoyed from excursion boats or from the road circling the lake, and sportsmen will find the trout fishing good. Tahoe City is the largest community, Meeks Bay has a fine bathing beach and on the Nevada side, visitors may try their luck at roulette in simple gambling halls or luxurious casinos.

SKIING IN THE MID-TWENTIETH CENTURY. According to the sports chroniclers, the first skiing and ski racing in America took place in the mountains around Lake Tahoe, about a hundred years ago. To pass the time while they were snowbound, Scandinavian miners cut down spruce trees, fashioned the trunks into 12-foot skis and revived the art of skiing which had been popular in northern Europe for generations. After this auspicious start, however, skiing resorts sprang up elsewhere, in less rugged terrain, and only lately the Lake Tahoe region came into its own again. It did so on a grand scale, and some now consider it the greatest concentration of skiing resorts in the world. This late second start had a considerable advantage, because all experience gained elsewhere was taken into account when creating the new center. According to the experts, skiing never became popular in America until the chairlift was invented; Europeans would trudge up the mountains in order to slide down, but not Americans. Lazy? No, just traditionally opposed to an inefficient waste of time. So the Sierra Nevada side of the lake is a chairlift country now, and the biggest one, at the Squaw Valley resort, is a marvel. Its trim seats, with room for two persons, climb to such a height that they almost seem to proceed into the blue horizon. Swinging out high above the snow-covered forests, valleys and gorges, the ride is an unparalleled thrill. The lift is also the most efficient one on earth, carrying a maximum of 800 skiers to the top, per hour, although 600 is the more usual number. In summertime the speed of the lift is reduced to allow more minutes for sight-seeing, and no traveler in that neighborhood should miss the ride.

AN AMERICAN CAVALCADE. The Lake Tahoe country is also an historic shrine. It has no connection with wars or revolutions, but with that particularly American brand of stirring history that concerns the settling of a great continent. Two monuments recall the westward trek that passed by here: the Pony Express Monument at Meyers, near the southern tip of Lake Tahoe, on Highway 50, and the Donner State Monument, to the northwest of the lake, on Highway 40. The latter commemorates the stark tragedy of the Donner party, which was snow-bound at that spot during the winter of 1846. Of eighty-one members in the party, only forty-five survived the nightmare of hunger and cold; in the despair of starvation, the living ate the corpses of their dead

Skiing flourishes near Lake Tahoe. This chairlift is in the Reno Snow Bowl.

companions. On the other hand, the bronze relief south of the lake honors a cheerful American enterprise, the Pony Express of 1860 that carried letters, at $5.00 a piece, from St. Joseph to Sacramento in eight days. Eighty pony riders were "in the saddle all the time, night and day, stretching a long, scattering procession from Missouri to California, forty flying eastward and forty toward the west, and among them making four hundred gallant horses earn a stirring livelihood." Each messenger "rode a splendid horse, kept him at his utmost speed for ten miles, and then, as he came crashing to the station where stood two men holding fast a fresh impatient steed, the transfer of rider and mail bag was made in the twinkling of an eye, and away flew the eager pair." (Mark Twain) Highway 50, now the southeastern part of the lake's circle drive, saw a great deal of thrilling history besides the pony riders. In the early 1850's it was an almost unmarked, barely passable immigrant trail. In 1858 the first wagon rolled over an "improved" roadbed. Then the Comstock Silver Lode was discovered, and the boom hit the road. Huge crude wagons, loaded with eight tons of ore, rattled along, drawn by teams of ten mules. Hay for the animals cost six cents a pound, and the franchise holders who maintained the road and the bridges charged whatever the traffic would bear. The toll for a six-horse team and wagon, for the whole length of the course, was $36.

Donner Lake and the Donner Pass Bridge

FABULOUS CAREER. Of all the great scenic spots in this country none won recognition, protection, admiration and international fame as quickly and enthusiastically as the Yosemite Valley. It seems that the only visitor who expressed a critical opinion was one of the valley's discoverers: Major James Savage. "It's a h... of a place," he is reported to have said.

There was a reason. Savage owned a trading post on the western flank of California's Sierra Nevada, 15 miles away. There he exchanged trinkets for the "yellow sand" the Indians of the neighboring five tribes brought him, and to improve his customer relations, he married five squaws, one from each tribe. In spite of this precaution, there were raids on his property, so he organized the Mariposa Battalion which proceeded, under his leadership, toward the valley of the Yosemite Indians. On the 25th of March, 1851, the men saw the great valley with their own eyes. Savage suspected a redskin hidden behind every boulder, and expressed his feelings as quoted above, but the young physician of the expedition, L. H. Bunnell, recognized the extraordinary beauty of the spot and began to sing its praises. Soon parties which included writers and artists found their way to Yosemite, and when the arduous horse trail was widened into a primitive wagon road, travelers came by the hundreds. A quickly constructed railroad (now

El Capitan, probably the largest rock on earth, could hold four Gibraltars.

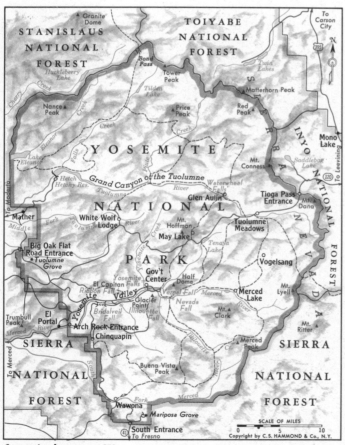

See sectional map, page 158

defunct) brought thousands and the modern highways now open the park to millions. As early as 1861 Abraham Lincoln signed an Act of Congress giving the region to the State of California as a reservation.

"YOU ARE YOURSELF A SEQUOIA." Yosemite's most famous promoter was John Muir, who, although a well educated naturalist, spent years in the wilderness of the high Sierras as a shepherd. He has been called the "Thoreau of the West," and in his harmony with nature and disdain for material comforts, he was a Thoreau. But quite unlike Thoreau, he was also an articulate and effective missionary and prophet, and in countless articles spread the exciting news throughout the country. He invited the Concord philosopher, Ralph Waldo Emerson. "You are yourself a Sequoia," he wrote. "Stop and get acquainted with your brethren." The famous man came but was not as vociferous in his praise as Muir had hoped. He spoke little, "yet it was a great pleasure to be near him, warming in the light of his face." Another celebrity did not hesitate to express his views. Horace Greeley inspected the valley, and far away in the East, his New York *Tribune* praised Yosemite as "the marvel of the continent."

"ELEVEN NIAGARAS." The heart of the National Park is the seven-mile-long Yosemite Valley, a grassy, parklike floor walled-in by towering cliffs, domes and pinnacles. Its most celebrated spot is the rock over which the Yosemite Falls tumble their white torrents in spring or their graceful, swaying ribbons in the drier summer months. The Upper Falls leap 1,430 feet, which equals nine Niagaras, to which the Lower Falls, with 320 feet, add two more Niagaras. With the intervening cascades, the total leap covers almost half a mile. Among the other "falling waters" the Ribbon Falls have a sheer drop of ten Niagaras, with 1,612 feet, and Nevada, Vernal and Illilouette Falls, as well as Bridalveil, have their own beauty, ranging from the graceful to the spectacular.

V INTO U. The process by which nature created this abundance of falls is interesting. In an early geological era, when volcanic upheavals crushed the crust of the earth and raised the peaks that are today the Sierra Nevada, an antediluvian river cut the first V-shaped groove into the rock. Three times in the following twenty million years, glaciers invaded the valley and slowly transformed the narrow V into an ever broader and deeper U, employing as grinding tools masses of loose rocks and boulders embedded in the moving ice. But while the main stream deepened to a lower and lower floor, the side streams could not keep pace; they too ground their grooves, but not as speedily and forcefully, and upon meeting the main valley had to throw their waters over the cliff. They still do, pre-

The missing half of Half Dome (center) was ground away by ancient glaciers.

senting America's most unique collection of cascades.

"FOUR GIBRALTARS." Among the peaks of the valley a few have achieved great fame, like Half Dome (best seen from Sentinel Bridge), in the very center of the valley's activities. The missing half was ground out as neatly by ancient glaciers as if turned by a machine tool. Another majestic mountain is El Capitan, on the all-year road, a few miles from the western entrance. It is probably the greatest single rock on earth, quite capable of accommodating four Rocks of Gibraltar. Glacier Point, high on top of the canyon rim but easily reached by automobile, offers a breath-taking panorama. In the northern part of the park is Hetch Hetchy, which used to be a canyon almost as beautiful as Yosemite Valley, now a reservoir for San Francisco.

While the valley proper is crowded with visitors, lovers of lonely nature can find, within the park limits, many untouched square miles of high country, of—to use the words of John Muir—"smooth, silky lawns—the noblest forests, the highest granite domes, the deepest ice-carved canyons—. On these high slopes wildflower gardens grow in the sun—at their feet lie new-born lakes, blue and green. They are sometimes dotted with drifting icebergs like tiny Arctic Oceans, shining, sparkling, calm as stars." The park's three Sequoia groves are wonderful sights but, of course, do not compare with the Big Trees in Sequoia National Forest.

The height of Yosemite Falls equals eleven Niagaras.

PAUL BUNYAN TALES? When Americans in the East heard of trees nearly 300 feet tall, 30 feet wide and 3,000 years old, they would not believe it. These trees, the tales went on, were sometimes hollowed by lightning and fell to the ground; in one such hollow shell a man by the name of Tharp had set up housekeeping, in 1858, in a living room 58 feet long and 8 feet high, and in another fallen tree a U. S. Cavalry patrol was stabling 32 horses. Had a California-style Baron Münchhausen been revived? When as late as 1875, a Big Tree trunk was sent to the Centennial Exposition in Philadelphia—because of its bulk it had to be shipped in sections—it was ridiculed as an easily detected hoax.

THE DICTUM OF THE SCIENTISTS. To be sure, the scientists knew of the existence of the Big Trees since the 1830's, but with academic reticence did not broadcast their knowledge. A London botanist inspected some sample branches and named the new genus Wellingtonia, in honor of the British hero. Outraged, an American botanist renamed it Washingtonia. Finally the Austrian botanist Endlicher created today's name Sequoia, in honor of the Cherokee Indian chief, and a French scientist made the final distinction between the coast redwood—Sequoia sempervirens—and the Big Tree of the Sierra Nevada, Sequoia gigantea. Gradually the public began to accept the facts, particularly when the popular John Muir wrote his glowing accounts of these unique American trees. The

Many sequoias are over 3,000 years old, among the oldest living things on our planet.

details that became known astonished the world. Tree-ring counts of felled trees indicated that many were about 3,000 years old, and among the still standing giants some might have reached their 4,000th year. The tree blooms during the winter, when the ground is covered with ten or perhaps twenty feet of snow. The seeds are tiny, about one fourth of an inch long, set in small cones. The roots spread as far as 150 feet. The wood does not seem to rot, and may be used after the log has been lying on the ground for centuries. The bark is practically fireproof.

THE STUBBORN LUMBERJACKS. Of course, the timber interests also heard of the Big Trees in the Sierra Nevada and soon began to move in on them. The struggle was terrific. The first felled trunks splintered into a million bits, so elaborate beds had to be built to cushion the fall, and scaffolds 20 feet high as working platforms for the hewers and sawyers. To bring down a single tree took two weeks. Most of the lumber was wasted, and what finally reached the Pacific ports cost as much as the lumber shipped from Maine around Cape Horn. For about ten years the battle lasted, then the trees won out and man gave up. But to this day it is well worth while seeing the main scene of destruction, Converse Basin; it is located in Sequoia National Forest, north of the General Grant Grove, and can be reached easily. Here giant stumps 20 or 30 feet high dot the ground, and logs and branches are strewn around pell-mell. But some old trees are left stand-

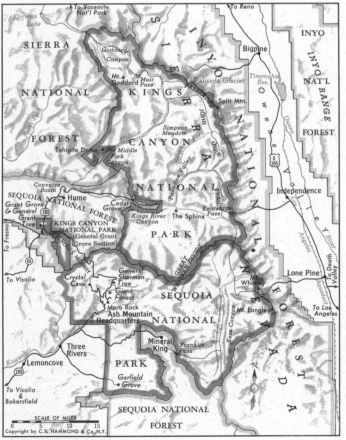

See sectional map, page 158

192

ing, and the life cycle continues. Quite a few young sequoias raise their crowns above the undergrowth; they will be a fine grove two thousand years from now.

THE CRUSADING JOURNALISTS. The Save-the-Big-Trees movement was largely the work of western nature lovers; the journalists took up the cause, and Col. George W. Stewart, editor of the weekly paper of Visalia, California, campaigned so vigorously that in 1890 Sequoia National Park was created. The small General Grant Grove Section, located to the north, became a preserve even earlier; it was extended into Kings Canyon National Park in 1940. In the Sequoia Park the number of Big Trees is estimated at nearly a million, the most impressive group being the Giant Forest, and the most famous sequoia the General Sherman, the biggest and possibly the oldest living thing. Like a 27-story tower it is 272 feet high, 36 feet wide at the bottom and 17 feet wide at a height of 120 feet. The General Grant in Kings Canyon National Park is equally impressive, with a width of 40 feet at the base, and a height of 267 feet.

AMERICA'S TITANIC LANDSCAPE. Besides the sequoias, the two great parks of the Sierra Nevada offer to the visitor many of America's most sweeping views, a landscape of true grandeur that includes 75 peaks more than 11,000 feet tall, and 7 that exceed 14,000 feet in height. Among them is Mt. Whitney, the giant of them

Mt. Whitney, the highest point, looks into Death Valley, the lowest point in the U. S.

all, whose towering peak, 14,495 feet in the sky, looks eastward into the desert of Death Valley, 280 feet below sea level. The wonder of it all is that not only experienced alpinists may reach that highest spot in the United States, but almost anybody may do so, on horseback or on foot. The trail leads right to the peak. In the sister park, Kings Canyon is a mountain scene of giant proportions, without the cascades of a Yosemite but on a grander scale.

Those visitors who come by car will receive an impressive sampling of all this beauty. But the great adventure of the Sierra Nevada is the foot-or-burro trip from Sequoia to Yosemite National Park, on the John Muir Trail which winds its way along the ridge of the great range, crossing five sky-high mountain passes; the trail rarely drops below and frequently rises above 8,500 feet.

INYO COUNTRY: FORGOTTEN CALIFORNIA. Between Kings Canyon and Sequoia National Parks and the Nevada state line there lies a wild and beautiful stretch of America: the land of the Inyo Range. To the south, in the Owens Valley, where water is diverted to Los Angeles, some activity can be observed, but the rest of Inyo Country consists of mountains in lonely grandeur, tree-lined lakes, and a few gold-rush ghost towns abandoned and in ruins. Outside of the north-south Highway 395 there are few roads, no hotels, no resorts, almost no people. Outdoor enthusiasts with a distaste for the tame and accessible should explore and enjoy these forgotten highlands.

Base of the General Sherman tree is 36 feet wide; tree is as tall as a 27-story tower.

GROUND AFIRE. That is the translation of the word Tomesha, the Indian name for this valley which for 140 miles stretches its parched floor between the barren ranges of east-central California. Its two famous distinctions are rather on the unattractive side: It is one of the hottest spots on earth (the thermometer reaches up to 137°), and it contains the lowest point in America, with an altitude—if that seems the right word—of 280 feet below sea level. Therefore the question is in order why such a scene of desolation was made a National Monument, in 1933, and why it is listed here as an American Travel attraction. The answer is simple: During the summer months Death Valley is indeed unbearable. But during the winter it is one of the most fascinating spots on this planet. Then it has a delightful climate, and it presents an ever-changing symphony of the spectrum: shiny white salt beds and jet-black volcanic masses, gray clays and red granites, yellow dunes and various sandstones which appear green and blue, pink and red. Yet this drama of color is not at all like that of the Grand Canyon; for Death Valley is not the product of erosion, and instead of the delicate and the lacy, the pattern here is bold, strong, and barbaric. It hardly ever rains—the annual precipitation is less than 1½ inches—and in the dry, incredibly clear air distances seem to melt. The high ranges which surpass 11,000 feet to the west are, to our eyes, within a stone's throw.

"Death Valley Scotty" allegedly built this castle from proceeds of a second gold mine.

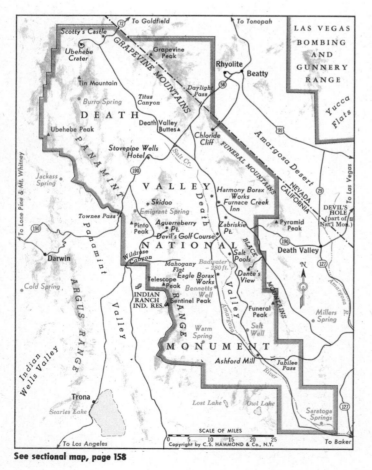

See sectional map, page 158

FUNERAL MOUNTAINS AND SARATOGA SPRINGS. The place names of this valley are as original as the whole region is unique. Skidoo and Mahogany Flat, Chloride Cliff and Telescope Peak speak for themselves. The western mountains are the Panamint Range, and to the east the names of the Grapevine Mountains and the Funeral Mountains express a grim good humor. On the southern end of the valley a swampy, desolate marsh with a few pools is named after a fashionable spa of the East: Saratoga Springs. Two well-known hotels are Furnace Creek Inn and Stovepipe Wells; the latter is built around some ancient water holes which saved many human lives; as the flying sands tended to obscure the spot, it was marked with a stovepipe. One famous lookout is Dante's View; it has an altitude of 5,700 feet and is named after the great poet's Purgatorio. If that implies a glance into the deepest depths and to the highest heights it is well chosen; for from here both the lowest and the highest points on our continent can be seen, the Badwater salt pools just below our feet, and Mt. Whitney far away in the High Sierra. However, an exceptionally clear day is the prerequisite for such an experience.

THE LIVING DESERT. The name of the valley implies the absence of all life; that however, is an erroneous impression. Every few years Death Valley is in bloom, and desert holly and creosote bush, paper-bag bush and cigarette plant, brittlebush and several others blossom profusely and ripen their seeds speedily. To survive, these plants possess a special tenacity, and their seeds remain dormant but creative for long periods. For their cycle does not last one year but five to ten, depending on the rainfall. Animal life is actually abundant, although it functions mostly at night. Flocks of Nelson bighorn sheep live in the mountains, as well as bushy-tailed antelopes. There are kit foxes and desert coyotes, and a great variety of colorful lizards, from horned toads to chuckwallas. Rattlesnakes are rarely encountered. In Saratoga Springs and Salt Creek the Tiny Death Valley Fish survive from the days when the whole region consisted of a lake; these "desert sardines" belong to an order which occurs both in salt and in fresh water. Finally another unusual member of the local fauna should be mentioned because it was not placed there by nature but by man: Small herds of wild burros roam the hills and canyons. They cannot claim the noble ancestry of the wild mustangs whose original progenitors were Arabian steeds escaped from the Spaniards. The first wild burros were runaways, too, but merely from the grueling routine of a prospector's helper.

"A SINGLE-BLANKET JACKASS PROSPECTOR."

To white man Death Valley remained terra incognita until 1849. Indians had occasionally ventured into the

The picturesque "20-mule teams" of the 1890's are revived for the filming of movies.

desolate area but had hardly ever lived there. Then, during gold rush days, an impatient wagon train of immigrants, called the Bennett-Arcane Party, broke away from the Salt Lake—Los Angeles trail, in search of a short cut, got lost in the canyons and wastes of Death Valley, and suffered incredible hardships, particularly thirst. When their panic had turned into apathy and resignation, a pioneer named Manly came and led them to San Fernando, and it was he who gave the region its present name. During the following decades prospectors combed the area, and some gold, silver and copper deposits were discovered. Many a searcher and wanderer died there, like Shorty Harris who on his gravestone called himself "A Single-Blanket Jackass Prospector." Between 1882 and 1927 borax was mined intermittently and carried out on 20-ton trailer-wagons drawn by 20 mules. The coachman had to be an artist to handle the 125 foot check line. One old-timer who prospered was Death Valley Scotty who built himself a two-million-dollar castle at the northern end of the valley near Ubehebe Crater. For years he was rumored to retire, periodically, to his secret gold mine in the desert, to replenish his cash funds. In fact the establishment was maintained by Scotty's millionaire-partner who enjoyed the hoax. The castle is worth seeing and also offers accommodations for guests. In its unlikely surroundings it is, as Freeman Tilden puts it, "as unobtrusive as a symphony conductor's bandaged thumb."

At the bottom of the valley, Badwater's "altitude" is 280 feet below sea level.

STRANGE SCULPTURE ON A MOUNTAIN-SIDE. Once upon a time the Cahuilla Indians migrated westward, guided by a fiery arrow of the Great Spirit. Many a mile they wandered, until the arrow affixed itself in a mountain and pointed to boiling springs and a fertile valley below. Here the Indians settled. The Great Spirit's arrowhead can still be seen, chiseled into the slope of quartz and granite, overgrown with whitish weeds and covering a sheet of seven and a half acres. The Indians healed their sick in the mineral waters, still a main attraction of the modern spa of Arrowhead Springs that arose from the Cahuilla settlement. There are steam caves, where you may enjoy a ten-minute sweltering session at 160 degrees, or you may take a mineral mud bath at 100 degrees (a popular tonic for body and soul) or swim in the hotel pool, fed by hot and cold mineral springs. The village has a European atmosphere, with its turreted and gabled buildings, Tyrolean leather shorts and dirndl dresses, Bavarian vocalizing and genuine Swiss yodeling, although a resort with so genuine an American past hardly needs a European model. The San Bernardino Mountains are the "stand-in" for the Alps. The resort is pleasant and informal, with an accent on health and youth. Los Angeles is only 70 miles away to the west and sends enough Hollywood people to provide a touch of glamour, but it is the younger set who enlivens the streets, rather than

Famous hotels are the Palm Springs Biltmore (above), the Desert Inn, the Racquet Club.

long-established stars and studio magnates. Perhaps this accounts for the gay and informal atmosphere.

DATE-PALM OASIS. Not far away, in a southeasterly direction and about 100 miles from Los Angeles, another Indian spa has achieved spectacular national prominence. In fact, Palm Springs has become the winter mecca of America's rich and up-to-date. As long as only Indians and a few health-seekers used its hot springs, it remained an insignificant little hamlet, but in the 1930's the movie colony discovered the wonderful assets of the place, created the bright mood of the resort, attracted various industrial and financial leaders and turned the sleepy village into a unique resort of modern, multicolored ranch houses, luxury hotels, smart shops on Palm Canyon Drive, terraces and swimming pools. Of the latter there are hundreds, more per-capita than anywhere else in the world. As a winter vacation spot Palm Springs is perfect; the very thought of spending some January weeks on an oasis in the desert appeals to the imagination, and the dry climate (about 80° at noon, with cool nights) promotes a state of physical well-being. The San Jacinto range, with its sculptured ridges rising more than 10,000 feet into a glassy-blue sky, is not only a decorative background to the fashionable desert town, but also provides plenty of water, usually a rarity in the arid valleys. It is going to furnish something even more unusual in the future: skiing. A tramway to the crest of

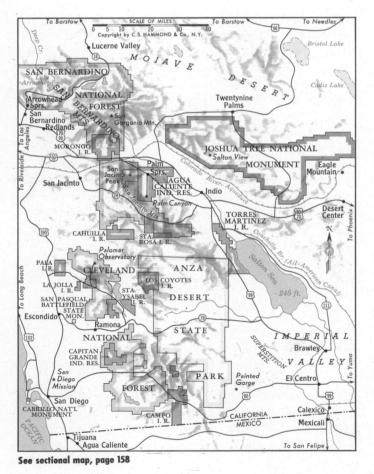

See sectional map, page 158

196

San Jacinto is projected, and the snowy slopes are already there. In the meantime, rodeos, fashion shows and parties keep the visitors occupied and the week-end fiesta called Desert Circus is a starstudded event. Dude ranches provide horseback rides into the mountains and chuckwagon picnics in the spirit of the Old West. Famous hotels in Palm Springs are the Biltmore, the Desert Inn and the Racquet Club.

HALF CELEBRITIES, HALF INDIANS. There is another fascinating touch in Palm Springs: It is one place where the original Americans have not been crowded out. Half the town still belongs to the Indians. The town map is a checkerboard, and every other block is the property of the Cahuilla Indians of the Agua Caliente Reservation. Since the Indians cannot sell their real estate and are legally only allowed to lease it for periods of not more than five years—stipulations enacted to protect the Indians from exploitation—they cannot take full advantage of the city's real estate boom. Nevertheless, they receive a tidy annual sum from rentals. They also operate the resort's mud baths. The latter were once quite famous but no longer play an important part in Palm Springs; their sulphuric smell is not appreciated by many. The Indians don't care. Unchanging in a rapidly changing community, they are the fixed pole in the new resort life.

The Joshua tree is a landmark of the Mojave Desert.

THE BIBLICAL TREES. East of both Arrowhead Springs and Palm Springs, the Mojave Desert stretches to far horizons. In the part adjacent to the San Bernardino Mountains the Joshua Tree National Monument has been created; its 560,000 acres protect from extinction and help to a healthy survival the spectacular Joshua tree, a landmark of southeastern California becoming rare elsewhere. This plant, which reaches a height of 38 feet, belongs to the lily family. When in bloom, a grove of Joshua trees is a sight to behold: At the end of their angular branches magnificent clusters of creamy white blossoms glisten in the sun. The biblical name is said to have originated with the Mormons, who considered them roadsigns on their westward trek. To the pious explorers the outstretched branches of these trees obviously pointed to the Promised Land, the Kingdom of Zion.

INLAND SEA WITH A TURBULENT PAST. The Salton Sea is an unusual lake south of the San Bernardino chain. Lying 245 feet below sea level, it is too salty for most fish, but mullet may be caught in some quantity; mullet-spearing is a local sport. Geysers and hot springs surround the lake. In 1905, when the Colorado River inundated the Imperial Valley in a catastrophic flood, the Salton Sea filled up to a length of fifty miles. At present it is receding, however, and some day it may entirely disappear.

Chuck-wagon breakfast in the San Jacinto Mountains is in the Old-West spirit.

THE LONG, DARK-GREEN BELT. There are "celebrities" among the highways of America: the Trail Ridge Road in Colorado, the Grand Canyon Rim Road, the Blue Ridge Parkway, the Skyline Drive in Virginia and others. All of them glorify the mountains. But there is one famous road devoted to a forest. It is the Redwood Highway, U.S. 101, which runs along the redwood belt, a strip of land extending from southwestern Oregon to the Santa Lucia Mountains in California. The redwood belt is 450 miles long but only 1 to 40 miles broad. The tree Sequoia sempervirens flourishes no other place in the world. The moist and foggy climate of the coast is its natural habitat. It is a species quite different from the Sequoia gigantea of the high Sierras.

THE UNFORTUNATE FIFTY YEARS. For many millennia the redwood forest stood on the coast between the hills and the ocean, in quiet, gigantic majesty. The trees lived on and on; the floor was fertile with the rotting needles of 50,000 years, but because of the semi-darkness little underbrush developed, and only delicate small mosses, ferns and similar miniature plants formed a green carpet. This period of peace was suddenly interrupted by fifty years of destruction and chaos. During the late nineteenth century the coast was developed. Wood was needed. Great fortunes could be made. The forest could be had for the asking (men were willing to

The "Chandelier" has been fashioned into a gateway for automobiles.

See sectional map, page 158

stake a homestead claim, get the land from the U. S. government for next to nothing and sell it for a few dollars to a speculator) and the timber was worth millions. So trees tumbled to earth after growing for a thousand years, and one of the most wasteful logging operations started. Only a part of the timber was taken out, but it was considered an unproductive waste of time to fight the numerous forest fires. The operators simply let the flames rage and moved to another part of the woods. Finally, in 1917, a group of leading Americans decided that the reckless destruction had to be stopped, and the Save-the-Redwoods League was founded. The California legislature, the *Saturday Evening Post,* the National Geographic Society and other organizations joined the campaign, and about 18 million dollars were spent in buying and preserving the most beautiful groves. Today even the lumber industry is cooperating. When driving south from Eureka, it is well worth while to stop at the Pacific Lumber Company in Scotia; their modern mill utilizes the timber as well as the bark.

NOT THE BIGGEST, BUT THE TALLEST. While there are scattered groves to the north and the south, the redwood empire proper lies in Humboldt County, and between the Avenue of the Giants, south of Scotia, and Richardson Grove at the Mendocino County line, the finest groves can be enjoyed at leisure. South of Dyerville the world's tallest tree may be seen, with the path leading to it clearly marked by arrows. Its height is 364 feet, with a circumference of 47 feet at the base. In a way this giant sets the pattern: The coastal redwoods are taller than—but not as big as—the sequoias of the sierras, nor are they as ancient. None of them is believed to be more than 2,000 years old. The general impression of these redwood groves is also very different. The sequoias of the mountains tend to stand farther apart, which lets in more light, and when the rays of the sun strike the compact armor of red bark and the green of gnarled branches, each single tree is a great work of art in itself. In contrast, the coastal redwoods keep close company, and it is this unity which turns their groves into cathedrals. The light is as subdued as in a Gothic church; the floor as soft as a carpet. At sunset the evening damp curls here and there like smoke from incense vessels. Even the bird calls are distant and hushed. There is a great and unique experience to be enjoyed, if possible on a Saturday or Sunday. On the other days the parade of lumber trucks—some of them carrying a single giant log—is a bit disturbing. All along the highway dishes, bowls and vases of redwood burls may be bought, and no matter what you may think of souvenirs, you will find many pieces among them that are beautiful and unique products of a truly American local art.

The coastal redwoods are not the largest but the tallest trees on this planet.

The two drivers (beside cab of truck) are dwarfed by the huge logs.

RUSSIAN RIVER AND ITALIAN WINE. Proceeding southward toward San Francisco, the groves occur more rarely; one, the Muir Woods National Monument, lies almost at the entrance of the Golden Gate. In Sonoma County we are on historic ground: This part of California was once a Russian colony. Russian soldiers camped here, Russian administrators traveled here, and their Aleut slaves were sent out in their kayaks to hunt the precious sea otter. There is another contact with world history: Fort Ross, the Russian stronghold restored now as a state park, was founded in 1812, the year Napoleon entered Moscow, and it was equipped with French cannon Napoleon left behind on his retreat. In 1841, when practically all the sea otters had been destroyed, the Russians gave up their California outpost, but the Russian River and the Russian Gulch still remind us of that strange interlude in our history. In this same neighborhood a more peaceful enterprise draws our attention: The countryside is dotted with lush vineyards and old stone wineries. Particularly well-known is the Italian-Swiss Colony at Asti, where a modern winery may be inspected. Here you will learn of a happy marriage of redwood and wine: The redwoods furnish ideal material for the storage casks. Don't forget to include a visit to the tasting room, and name your preference. You can have all the wine you want, just for the asking.

FABULOUS GEOGRAPHY. The world's most beautiful cities, like Rio de Janeiro or San Francisco, are built on hills by the sea, with rockbound, bay-studded harbors and small islands set into the surrounding waters like jewels. In Rio the hills are really mountains, while San Francisco's "peaks" stay well below the 1,000 foot altitude. But the Golden Gate city is washed by choppy waters on three sides, and the bracing smell of the sea is everywhere. Its panorama may be enjoyed from such famous lookout points as the Coit Tower on Telegraph Hill, Twin Peaks in the center of town or the cocktail lounge of the Mark Hopkins Hotel, nineteen stories above Nob Hill. In addition, there are any number of streets where you look ahead casually and, way down in the distance, see a dark island resting in the sunny water of the bay or a steamer from the South Seas slowly approaching the wharf, or distinguish the silhouettes of the Golden Gate Bridge and the 4½-mile-long Oakland Bridge and realize how their man-made beauty harmonizes perfectly with their nature-made surroundings. Part of the local geography is the weather and that, too, is unique. With the absence of heat waves and cold waves, it has been described as a perpetual, invigorating fall climate. To be sure, there is a good deal of rain, and the thick, regular fog is not popular, either. But the more frequent, local type of fog has picturesque qualities of its own and is an important in-

At Fisherman's Wharf fresh-caught fish are sent from boats to restaurants.

gredient of the San Francisco atmosphere; in low-hanging drifts it roams around the bay and between the hills, its serpentine motions covering and uncovering section after section. One end of the Golden Gate Bridge may stand out in super-clarity, the other may be hidden completely in a white blanket.

CENTER OF THE WORLD. Not only is San Francisco's locality fascinating but also its global geography. While its civilization remains thoroughly American, there are touches of the Orient everywhere. Its Chinatown is the largest Chinese settlement outside of Asia, and Americans of Far-Eastern extraction are found among the people on every street. Wonderful Oriental food may be eaten here, and Oriental spices and teas may be purchased. In New York the museums and the houses of the rich are filled with pieces of European art. In San Francisco masterpieces of Oriental art abound in fine homes, museums, and stores; treasures in jade and china, tapestries and sculptures of the East may be bought here as easily as in Hong Kong. Every American should know both New York and San Francisco. Such a double acquaintance will give him a proud center-of-the-world feeling: Our country is a young giant, who with one arm touches the old civilization of the Occident, with the other that of the Orient.

FLOWER STANDS AND CABLE CARS. The best

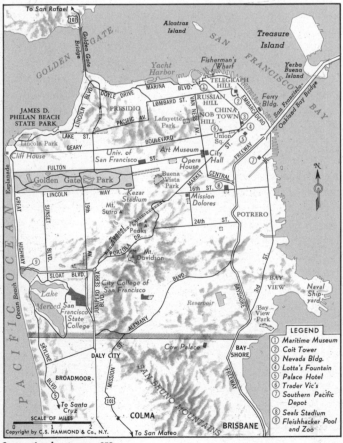

See sectional map, page 158

LEGEND
① Maritime Museum
② Coit Tower
③ Nevada Bldg.
④ Lotta's Fountain
⑤ Palace Hotel
⑥ Trader Vic's
⑦ Southern Pacific Depot
⑧ Seals Stadium
⑨ Fleishhacker Pool and Zoo

sights are free in San Francisco. You may enjoy the spectacle of the city's hills and bays, with the ever-changing lighting effects of towering cloud formations, bright sunshine and meandering fog banks, from the previously mentioned vantage points. You may park your car in the huge underground garage under Union Square and stroll through the shopping center where super-elegant stores, smartly dressed women and incredibly bright flower stands will catch your eye. In Chinatown you will have the feeling that you are not merely witnessing a show staged for tourists but are in a genuine Chinese settlement; on a sightseeing tour—a Chinese-American graduate student may be your guide—you will learn a great deal not only about Chinese-American life but also about China's religious cults. Two blocks to the west Nob Hill arises, once crowned with the million-dollar mansions of various bonanza kings. The palaces have been largely replaced by hotels and apartment houses, but a certain aristocratic air still prevails. Some of the hills may be climbed by small, half-open cable cars, an 80-year-old institution close to the hearts of all San Franciscans who refuse to have them scrapped for more modern means of transportation. If you are interested in history, don't miss the Mission Dolores where, in the midst of a howling wilderness, the first mass was sung five days before the Declaration of Independence. The present building was started in 1782; the Indian work-

While dining at Cliff House, you may watch the sea lions frolicking on the rocks.

To San Franciscans the old-fashioned cable cars are an institution.

men did not use a single nail but tied the beams of the arched roof with leather thongs. Another more-worldly landmark is the Palace Hotel, which used to cater to the very wealthy and famous and is still one of the world's fabulous dining spots. You may enjoy luncheon at the Cliff House while watching the sea lions frolic among the rocks near the shore, or have a seafood meal at the Fisherman's Wharf and observe the brightly painted fishing boats ride into port and unload their glistening cargoes. At Trader Vic's you'll eat Oriental food that is heavenly. San Francisco's museums are fascinating, among them the Maritime Museum on the waterfront, where you may interrupt your study of Pacific shipping history with a swim from a sandy beach below. Famous is the Wild West Museum of the Wells Fargo Bank in the Nevada Building, whose most honored exhibit is, quite appropriately, a shiny red stagecoach which crossed the Sierra Nevada. There are many more attractions, like Golden Gate Park, the Opera House where the United Nations was born and Lotta's Fountain, given to the city by a charming actress of the gold-dust era. You will enjoy not only the sights but also the atmosphere: Out of a violent and vibrant past of gold rush, earthquake and phenomenal growth, a spirit of true friendliness has emerged. No "cold theological eye" here, says George West, no "lifted eyebrow," no "cautious hand withheld."

POINT OF THE SEA WOLVES. Flat, dark-green umbrellas on top of gnarled, contorted trunks — that is the way the Monterey cypresses grow, the only ones of their species; nowhere else on earth do they exist but here. Singly or in small groves they rise from precarious slopes or hidden fissures in the cliffs that jut out into the sea. The rocks beneath the trees appear ghastly gray in a fog bank, bright yellow in the sun of noon, and glowing orange-red at sunset. The most spectacular of these cliffs, because of the sea lions playing among the rocks, was named Punta de los Lobos Marinos, Point of the Sea Wolves. Unfortunately, the name was anglicized into a rather meaningless "Point Lobos." Robert Louis Stevenson roamed these cliffs, and according to some scholars Point Lobos became the Spyglass Hill of Treasure Island. "The finest meeting of land and water in existence,"—that was the verdict of the great cosmopolitan poet. Perhaps he sensed an affinity to the Orient; to many modern visitors the lacy, wind-swept landscape looks Japanese.

PADRES AND ARTISTS IN CARMEL. In 1602 three Carmelite priests visited the southern corner of the peninsula and were impressed by a hill which reminded them of Mt. Carmel in Palestine. The Lord's mills turned slowly in Old Spain, but in 1771 the Carmel Mission was established there, with the same eye for scenic beauty and inspiring views that guided the build-

The cypresses that grow here are a species found nowhere else in the world.

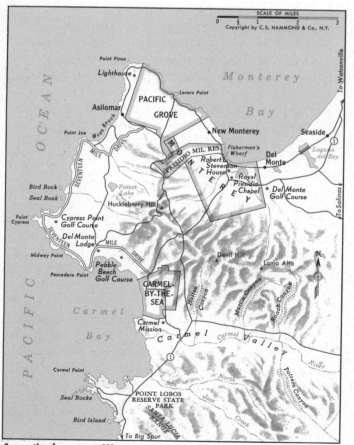

See sectional map, page 158

ing of missions and monasteries in Europe and Latin America. Today the rambling establishment is restored, and the visitor from the East who cherishes the plain, small, white New England churches at home, will enjoy a fascinating new experience: In the colorful halls, with their lovely objects of art and the leather-bound volumes of a library established in the virgin wilderness, he will feel something of the magnificent Hispanic empire of the mind.—Akin to the padres, in their appreciation of scenic beauty, are the artists who appeared at this lovely spot after the turn of the century and founded the now famous Carmel-by-the-Sea. The initiated complain that the true artist-residents (among them are famous names) have been joined by so many "dilettantes, charlatans and idlers" that the village has been turned into a "Walt-Disney-type Montmartre." Whether that is true seems debatable. To this visitor, at least, Carmel-by-the-Sea is a splendid resort, with dark-green pines on roads and walks, a main street that leads to a broad, white, sloping beach, with clusters of brilliant blossoms everywhere, with art stores that display the finest creations from France or Sweden or the South Seas, with art galleries and an open-air-theater, an annual Bach festival and a Shakespeare festival.

THE ENCHANTED FOREST. It has been called "the Monaco of America," and "the last stronghold of feudalism" in the western hemisphere,—this real estate venture of the Del Monte Properties Company, just north of Carmel. Three thousand carefully selected "citizens" live among the grandeur of the forest ridges, the primeval groves, the costly homes and the famous golf courses whose setting is so breathtaking that some golfers complain about it. They don't play their best golf there; the natural beauty distracts them.—Mere sightseers have to pay 50 cents per car for the privilege of entering this sanctuary. But its main road, the 17-Mile Drive along the peninsula's shore, offers sights worth many times that modest toll. There is Del Monte Lodge with its Pebble Beach golf course where every January Bing Crosby's National Pro-Amateur Golf Championship game is played; Midway Point with its lone cypress is the world's most painted and photographed tree-rock-ocean ensemble; on the huge granite mass of Seal Rock hundreds of sea lions sun themselves, play and cavort unmindful of the nearby human visitors; here it becomes clear why the German language calls these animals "See-Hunde," for sometimes their barking fills the air as if a thousand hounds were let loose. Bird Rock, a stony island near the shore, swarms with a seething mass of sea gulls and pelicans, cormorants and other birds. Finally we reach the northern toll gate and arrive in Pacific Grove, a prim, neat, tavernless city that had been founded as a Methodist retreat. It retains its spiritual independence of both the festive life of the

The Robert Louis Stevenson House in Monterey is an old Spanish adobe structure.

artists in Carmel and the "grand living" of the rich.

MONTEREY AND TORTILLA FLAT. At the northern end of the peninsula history is again in evidence. Monterey was the capital of Spanish California before the United States had been founded, and with its interesting old adobe houses of Spanish days—the Royal Presidio Chapel, the Casa Abrego, the Old Whaling Station, the Old Custom House, and others—it has sometimes been called "the Western Williamsburg." The Robert Louis Stevenson House, originally built by a Mexican customs official, contains in its thick-walled rooms with high ceilings many interesting mementoes of the author's stay in Monterey in 1879. One rectangular adobe building houses the first American theater in California. The state museum illustrates the way of life of the Spanish days: A primitive burro cart with solid wheels of wood is exhibited beside a belle's evening dress that had been imported from Paris to Monterey for $1,000.—The town's liveliest spot is the Fishermen's Wharf where Japanese abalone divers and Italian skippers mingle with Mexican and Chinese cannery workers and tourists from many states; the wharf's seafood restaurants are widely known. Fishing—sardines, albacore, and abalone are the principal crop—and canning are the city's major industries, and the Monterey of the workers is the setting of two of John Steinbeck's famous novels: "Tortilla Flat" and "Cannery Row."

Midway Point is America's most painted and photographed seascape.

NO PAST, ALL FUTURE. If you step into your car at Los Angeles Harbor and drive northward until you reach the Los Angeles city limit sign at Olive View, your speedometer will register 57 miles. You have just crossed the largest city in area in the United States. If you travel through Los Angeles County, which is the metropolitan area as a whole, you'll find it half as big as the State of Vermont. Sprawling over a pleasant plain between the mountains and the sea, practically all of it is new, and an air of expansion and progress hovers over the city and its suburbs which form a confused melee of administrative units and subdivisions, typical for the ways of uninhibited growth. Hardly anything is left of the old Spanish days; not even the "Plaza" is today where it had been laid out in 1781, and the Plaza Church, the Avila Adobe (a private museum) and one or two other adobe houses are the only remnants of the "pueblo." Olvera Street looks like Old Mexico, but it was built in the 1930's. The town's most valuable Spanish heritage is its name, and although the words Los Angeles have been cut quite arbitrarily out of a resounding El Pueblo de Nuestra Señora la Reina de los Angeles de Porciúncula, the modern name has still a pleasant Spanish-exotic flavor, is easily recognized as meaning "the angels," and therefore suggests a paradaisical place.

MAKE-UP AND MAKE-BELIEVE. There are two schools of thought about Los Angeles, and the visitor will find it fascinating to explore their teachings. One school—its strongest rampart is found in San Francisco—maintains that Los Angeles is an impossible monstrosity, an improvised catch-all. "If you tilt the country sideways," Frank Lloyd Wright is quoted to have said, "Los Angeles is the place where everything loose will fall." It has been called the capital of bad taste, of quacks and faddists, of weird cults and strange sects, a "nightmare in technicolor" where the Hollywood gossip columns are the most important news of the day, where promoters flourish and intellectuals despair, a perpetual convention, a giant circus and the Coney Island of the Pacific Coast. There is and always was a tendency toward makeshift. "Even the trees and plants did not belong there," said Frank Fenton. "They came, like the people, from far places, some familiar, some exotic, all wanderers of one sort or another—" The other school, while admitting a grain of truth in all these statements, points out that the end is not yet, and that Los Angeles may eventually emerge as America's most truly American metropolis. For it was not settled, in its modern version, by Europeans who brought along their Old-World heritage, but mostly by Midwesterners of the second generation who had not yet time to develop a cultural heritage of their own. Consequently their judgment in matters of art and style, philosophy and taste proved often deficient, but they did not bring along any prejudices either; they created an unmatched open field for experimentation.

FRESH WATER, SEA WATER. The hundreds of thousands of solid citizens who are neither quacks nor faddists, point with pride to their city's fantastic material achievements. From the viewpoint of physical geography Los Angeles was built at an extremely unfavorable location: It had no natural harbor, and it had no water resources in the form of fair-sized rivers or lakes. So, at a spot which Richard Henry Dana in "Two Years Before the Mast" had described as perfectly desolate, its citizens proceeded to build the world's largest artificial harbor, capable of holding our whole Pacific fleet. And to provide a sufficient water supply, the entire flow of the Owens River was diverted from the Sierra Nevada Mountains over 240 miles to the city. In addition, the Colorado River was tapped in the 1930's, and today a gigantic agglomeration of dams and pipelines furnishes streams and torrents of water for a million households, for sprinkler systems and swimming pools, and for irrigation canals that have transformed 300,000 arid acres into bright orange groves and lush vegetable gardens. Another civic project of similar magnitude is the new system of freeways, of modern automobile highways which, however, do not yet solve the traffic problem of a city which owns more automobiles per capita than any other place in the world.

ROSE BOWL AND BLUE BOY. Besides the purely

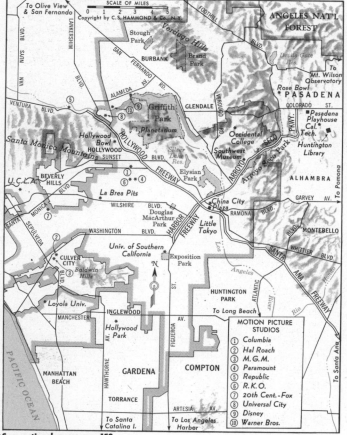

See sectional map, page 158

Douglas MacArthur Park is a focal point in America's largest (in area) fastest-growing metropolis, Los Angeles, the much insulted, sprawling, bizarre and beautiful city.

material, Los Angeles and its suburbs have exerted a wide influence with their flair for entertainment. Hollywood has left its imprint on America and on the world, and at least some of its motion pictures have been masterpieces. Pasadena's Tournament of Roses and the annual Rose Bowl game on the first of January have become an American tradition. Pasadena Playhouse and Hollywood Bowl are widely known to lovers of drama and music, and the Huntington Library with its first-rate collections of arts and letters—van Dyke's "Blue Boy" is a center of attraction—lures both casual visitors and research scholars from many parts of the country. On the natural rather than the cultural side it must be stated that the young people of Los Angeles are good to look at: Year-round sunshine and unlimited quantities of orange juice and fresh fruit salad have indeed produced a healthy and handsome race, including thousands of lovely girls and the world's best tennis players. The setting in which this pleasant sector of humanity is living has been described by Cecil Roberts "The twenty-mile-long valley stretching from Los Angeles through Hollywood and Beverly Hills, with its bordering foothills and mountains, seemed to me as beautiful a scene as the earth could show—"

THE ROMANTIC RUINS. San Juan Capistrano, San Luis Rey, San Diego de Alcalá—these names along the coast road from Los Angeles to the south are reminders of the Spanish mission days, when trails were laid out, orange groves planted, medicinal herbs cultivated, libraries collected and Christian tenets preached before the United States was born. San Juan Capistrano is particularly interesting: It was the most beautiful of all California missions with seven domes and an arched roof, a tall belfry visible for ten miles and stone carvings by a Mexican sculptor. The superstitious said it was too elaborate for a house of God; at any rate an earthquake destroyed most of it only six years after it had been completed. In the 1860's the church was being rebuilt with adobe bricks when torrential rains descended and reduced the work to a puddle of mud. More attempts at reconstruction were made, but the buildings were demolished again by the earthquake of 1918. At that point man gave up the struggle, and the ruins remain. It is an uncanny place at night. The old bells were said to ring by themselves, at times, without any pull of the bell ropes, and on a still night you can hear them now. At the Mission San Lui Rey the most interesting remains are the white belfry and the murals on the interior columns and beams.

THE SKY ATLAS. A bit inland, to the east, the most famous observatory on earth awaits you on Palomar

Torrey Pines Mesa is a beauty spot on a bluff by the sea, north of La Jolla.

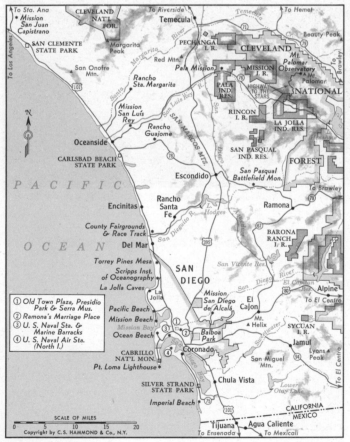

① Old Town Plaza, Presidio Park & Serra Mus.
② Ramona's Marriage Place
③ U. S. Naval Sta. & Marine Barracks
④ U. S. Naval Air Sta. (North I.)

SCALE OF MILES
0   5   10   15   20
Copyright by C. S. Hammond & Co., N.Y.

See sectional map, page 158

Mountain, at an altitude of 6,126 feet. Visitors are sometimes disappointed; for in the grandiose mountain setting, the Palomar Observatory looks small. But once inside the dome, they realize that they are standing in a huge, twelve-story cavern. The 200-inch telescope, with its 16-ton mirror, is not an oversized spyglass but a camera. Photographing a distant star with this huge apparatus has been compared to "aiming a rifle at a rolling penny twenty miles away." One interesting project is being carried out with the 48-inch telescope camera called "Big Schmidt." It is a sky atlas of some 1700 photographs presenting "maps" of three quarters of the heavens to the world's students of astronomy.

SPANISH LABEL, AMERICAN CONTENTS. The nomenclature of Southern California is so predominantly Spanish that some visitors are surprised to discover how completely American the country is. To be sure, San Diego possesses some mementos of its Spanish past. There is, for example, the Cabrillo National Monument, north of the lighthouse, which honors the Portuguese navigator in the service of Spain; in 1542 he discovered the harbor, stayed for a week and took possession of the land for the Spanish Crown. He was familiar with Montalvo's then popular romance which indicated that "on the right hand of the Indies there is an island called California, very near to the terrestrial Paradise." Cabrillo believed that he had arrived at that paradisaical land, and ever since, the name of his discovery has been California. To call a province or a state after a piece of fiction seems unorthodox, yet the later development of California amply justified the conquistadores' fling of imagination. The Old Town Plaza, the center of the original city, is still lined with a few adobe houses of old Spanish flavor, among them Ramona's Marriage Place (*Casa de Estudillo*). The house is open to the public and exhibits relics of the days of Spanish California; it is known as the house where Ramona—of the novel and the song—was married. The San Diego Mission, six miles up the valley of the San Diego River, is a restoration of the ancient buildings, the first mission on the coast and the starting point of the chain established by Padre Serra. Several structures in Balboa Park, the city's 1400-acre recreation center, also are in the style of the Spanish Renaissance, for instance, the California Building, the Museum of Natural History and the Fine Arts Gallery, which prides itself on owning some famous Spanish masters including El Greco, Murillo, Goya and Zuloaga. But behind the Spanish traditions there is American life and thought, just as the city as a whole bears the stamp of modern America.

DRAMATIC PORT. San Diego harbor, twenty square miles of water sheltered by islands and promontories and studded with picturesque bays and inlets, is the city's primary sightseeing attraction. As the great Pacific

In San Diego, the harbor and the city have grown in harmony.

Naval Base of the U.S., it offers to the cruise-boat tourist a most impressive panorama of our naval power. Displayed in a twelve-mile curve are airplane carriers towering high above the water, rocket-launching craft stared at with awe, landing ships and troop carriers; submarines, destroyers and destroyer escorts are measured by whole flotillas. The cruise boats wind through this huge maritime exposition, and ride past the "billion-dollar, mothball fleet" maintained as a reserve, its guns preserved under glistening half-spheres of aluminum. The shores are lined with naval installations and training centers which turn out sailors, fliers, leathernecks and the "frogmen" of the underwater-demolition squads. San Diego is also a great fishing port for tuna and albacore; its modern tuna clippers venture out as far as Panama, the Galapagos Islands, South America.

THE SHORT THERMOMETER. The people of San Diego are proud of their climate; in their city, they say, only short thermometers are needed—a scale of thirteen degrees is enough. The average summer temperature is 68°, the average winter temperature 55°. The climate and the numerous industrial opportunities attract a constant stream of newcomers to San Diego, one of the country's fastest growing cities. Also its beaches are attractive, particularly La Jolla, which combines fabulous scenery with lovely homes, bright gardens, smart shops and cultural interests.

*MENT-OPERATED SIGHTSEEING
EAS*

government and preserved for public use
ty (as in the case of Yosemite and Rocky
ecause of its scientific or historic interest (as
Iesa Verde National Parks). Fishing is per-

a smaller scale.

deral government for permanent timber pro-
nd public recreation. Fishing and hunting
ns. The National Forests cover about 179

State Park:

A recreational area maintained by the state. It may be a small lookout point
with a few picnic tables, or a large forest, or a wildlife refuge.

Provincial Park:

The Canadian counterpart to the state park in the U.S.

Wild Area:

An area of 5,000 to 100,000 acres, within a National Forest, which is maintained in its primitive condition. While kept roadless, it is not without trails,
and it is open to pack trips on horseback or to canoe trips.

Wilderness Area:

Same as Wild Area, but larger than 100,000 acres.

National Wildlife Refuge:

A refuge set up for the protection of migratory birds along the principal
migration routes, or for the preservation of now rare native animals like the
buffalo. There are about 300 of such refuges.

ALABAMA

For information, write to Division of Records and Reports, State of Alabama, Montgomery 5, Ala.

NORTHERN ALABAMA *The Muscle Shoals Area* near Florence contains several TVA dams (Wilson and Wheeler) and lakes created by the Tennessee River. Lakes Wilson and Pickwick are popular for fishing, boating, camping.

CENTRAL ALABAMA *Birmingham*, the "Pittsburgh of the South," is a center of the steel industry based on nearby iron, coal and limestone deposits. From Red Mountain the statue of Vulcan, Roman god of the forge, overlooks the city; it is the largest iron statue on earth, mounted on a 20-foot tower with an excellent view. 48 parks; "Dogwood Trail Caravan" in April. *Tuscaloosa* on the Black Warrior River is the seat of the University of Alabama. *Montgomery*, the state capital, is a city of traditional southern dignity. It was the first capital of the Confederacy; on the grounds of the capitol "the First White House of the Confederacy," where Jefferson Davis lived, is preserved as an historic shrine and museum. *Tuskegee Institute*, two miles from Tuskegee, is the country's most-famous school for Negroes. The names of two outstanding Negro leaders are linked with it: Booker T. Washington, its founder, and George Washington Carver, the great scientist whose researches helped to bring revolutionary changes in southern farming.

SOUTHERN ALABAMA *Mobile*, with its "Azalea Trail," and the Bellingrath Gardens, are described on page 78.

NATIONAL FORESTS IN ALABAMA *William B. Bankhead Nat. F.*, U.S. 31, 43 (limestone gorges and Clear Creek Falls); *Conecuh Nat. F.*, U.S. 29 (large, clear ponds, good fishing); *Talladega Nat. F.*, U.S. 78, 231, 82 (skyway scenic drive to Mt. Cheaha, 2407 ft., highest point in Ala.).

STATE PARKS For details, write to Division of State Parks, Dept. of Conservation, Montgomery 4, Ala.

ARIZONA

For information, write to Division of Publications and Travel, Arizona State Highway Dept., Phoenix, Ariz. "Arizona Highways" is an excellent travel magazine published by the state.

NORTHERN ARIZONA *Monument Valley* lies in the northeastern corner of the state, partly in Utah; it is not easy to reach but has magnificent scenery; described on page 170. *Canyon de Chelly National Monument* in Navajo Reservation, north of Petrified Forest; an impressive canyon with cliff dwellers' ruins. Navajos keep peach orchards and cultivate small farms on its bottom lands. Included are Monument Canyon with Spider Rocks and Canyon del Muerto, an unusual gorge with deeply undercut walls. *Navajo Reservation*, with a size of more than three times that of Massachusetts, is the largest Indian Reservation in America. The soil is mostly desert land, but the reservation contains some of the continent's most fascinating scenery, from the Painted Desert to part of the Grand Canyon. Navajo National Monument includes several elaborate cliff dwellings. *Pipe Spring National Monument*, northwest of the Grand Canyon, is an historic Mormon Fort. *Grand Canyon of the Colorado*, known throughout the world as America's greatest nature spectacle, is described on page 174.

CENTRAL ARIZONA *Petrified Forest National Monument* twenty miles east of Holbrook. Some people are disappointed because they expect the petrified trunks to stand erect as in a forest, while the logs actually lie on the ground. Most of the trees did not grow there but were probably washed to the spot by floods. The giant logs are strikingly colored and up to 250 feet long.

They lie in six separate "forests" and are the greatest display of petrified wood on earth. *Painted Desert*. A desert region whose eroded shales and limestones are spectacularly colored. The Painted Desert Lodge can be reached from the Petrified Forest N.M. See also page 176. *Flagstaff and the San Francisco Peaks*. Flagstaff, almost 7000 feet high on the Coconino plateau, and the three San Francisco peaks, a popular region for skiing and all winter sports, are described on page 176. On that same page data are given for the numerous sightseeing spots of that area: *Wupatki Nat.M.* (a red sandstone pueblo), *Sunset Crater Nat.M.* (a crater with brightly colored walls), *Walnut Canyon Nat.M.* (cliff dwellings in low caves), *Meteor Crater* (the scene of a huge prehistoric catastrophe), *Oak Creek Canyon* (a pleasant combination of green woods and red canyon walls), *Montezuma Castle Nat.M.* (a five-story cliff dwelling of prehistoric Indians), *Tuzigoot Nat.M.* (ruins of a prehistoric pueblo). *Prescott*, "the mile-high city," is described on page 176. *Castle Hot Springs*, near U.S. 89, 60 miles northwest of Phoenix, has a daily flow of 400,000 gallons; its pools of mineral water of various temperatures serve the sanatorium and popular resort. *Phoenix*, the state capital and winter resort, and the *Apache Trail* with the *Roosevelt Dam* are described on page 178. *Tonto Nat.M.*, south of the Roosevelt Dam, preserves two cliff dwellings of the twelfth century which in their day were nearly impregnable. Near the city of Globe, the *Southwestern Arboretum* (a lovely outdoor museum of the plants and flowers native to the Southwest) is located. The latter, in the Pinal Mountains, includes *Signal Peak* (7,875 feet) which offers splendid 100-mile views in every direction. *Coolidge Dam*, the first multiple-dome dam, and the man-made San Carlos Lake in the heart of the old Apache country are 26 miles southeast of Globe, on U.S. 70. West of the Coolidge Dam, the *Casa Grande Nat.M.* is an impressive adobe tower built some 600 years ago by Indian farmers.

SOUTHERN ARIZONA *Tucson*, the famous desert resort and seat of the University of Arizona, is described on page 180. The Tucson Mountain Park is a 28,000 acre recreational area with many trails and good roads. The *Mission San Xavier del Bac*, built in the style of Spanish baroque, and the *Saguaro National Monument*, a forest of cactus plants up to 50 feet tall, are described on page 180. South of Tucson the *Tumacacori Nat.M.* preserves the ruins of a mission believed to be founded by Padre Kino in 1696. At the Mexican border, *Nogales* is a lively and colorful frontier town and market; of interest to tourists is its unique underground café, operated in a cave that used to be a mine and was later employed as prison for Geronimo, the Apache chief. On the international border south of St. Highway 85, the *Organ Pipe Cactus Nat.M.* lies in an uninhabited area; 20-foot cactus columns without branches stand straight up like organ pipes; their lovely white flowers, with a tinge of lavender, bloom in May. In the Kofa Mountains 60 miles northeast of Yuma, *Palm Canyon* is an island of Arizona's only native palm trees; they grow on the sides of the narrow red-granite canyon. *Yuma*, on the California line, is the center of a highly prosperous, irrigated valley surrounded by jagged mountains; the All-American Canal, carrying irrigation water from the Colorado to California, can be seen from the Colorado bridge. To the east of Tucson, *Tombstone*, with its Boothill Cemetery, is an amusing museum town of the old Wild West; it is described on page 180. In the southeastern corner of the state, the region of *Bisbee* and *Douglas* is a rich mining country. The open-pit copper mines look like titanic amphitheaters. Bisbee is built on such a steep mountain slope that there is no mail delivery in town: no mailman can be expected to trudge up and down that many stairs. Near the New Mexico state line, the *Chiricahua National Monument* is a wilderness of weirdly-shaped rocks.

NATIONAL PARK IN ARIZONA *The Grand Canyon Nat.Park* is described on page 174.

NATIONAL FORESTS IN ARIZONA *Apache Nat.F.*, U.S. 60, 260, 666 (scenic Coronado Trail; Blue Range and Mt. Baldy Wilderness Areas). *Coconino Nat.F.*, U.S. 66, 89, 89A. (Mormon Lake, largest natural lake in Arizona, popular summer resort near Flagstaff; 1000 miles of scenic drives through timber; Sycamore Canyon Wild Area). *Coronado Nat.F.*, U.S. 80, 89; State 84 ("cactus to pines and swimming to skiing" in an hour's time, 40 miles apart; Chiricahua Wild Area). *Crook Nat.F.*, U.S. 60, 70, 666; State 77, 88 (nearby Coolidge Dam, several wilderness areas, vegetation: semidesert to alpine). *Kaibab Nat.F.*, U.S. 66, 89; State 64, 67 (Grand Canyon National Game Preserve with Kaibab Forest deer herd and buffalo herd; only habitat of Kaibab squirrel; interesting Supai Indian Village in nearby Havasu Canyon). *Prescott Nat.F.*, U.S. 89, 89A (rugged high mountain country; several wild areas; former "billion-dollar copper camp" at Jerome). *Sitgreaves Nat.F.*, U.S. 60, State 77, 173 (scenic drive along Mogollon Rim; pueblo ruins and large herd of elk). *Tonto Nat.F.*, U.S. 60, 70, 80, 89 (unusually varied and colorful topography of famous Tonto Basin, from semidesert to ponderosa pine forests; Roosevelt Dam; several wilderness areas).

STATE PARKS For details, write to Arizona Game and Fish Commission, Arizona State Building, Phoenix, Ariz.

ARKANSAS

For information, write to Publicity and Information Commission, 162 State Capitol, Little Rock, Ark.

NORTHERN ARKANSAS *The Ozark Mountains,* known for their original folkways, their huge springs, their float trips, their picturesque hills and limestone caverns, are described on page 110. *Fayetteville,* the largest city in the Ozarks, is the seat of the University of Arkansas. *Eureka Springs,* near the Missouri state line, is an Ozark spa with 63 mineral springs within its city limits; it is picturesquely built on a steep hillside, and is a center for the display and sale of native crafts (wood carvings, pottery, quilts, hooked rugs). See also page 110. *Bella Vista,* on the edge of the Ozarks, is a popular resort with a spring from which two million gallons gush out every day; the town's Wonderland Cavern, a night club in an underground cave, is a tourist attraction. In north-central Arkansas, the *Norfolk and Bull Shoals Dams* are two of the larger dams in the nation. *Mammoth Spring,* east of Norfork Dam, is a fabulous spring with a flow of 840,000 gallons a minute. *Fort Smith,* on the Oklahoma state line, is the gateway to the Ozark Mountains in the north and the Ouachita Mountains in the south. The Old Fort of 1818 still stands and is now a museum. The annual Arkansas-Oklahoma Rodeo is an outstanding event.

CENTRAL ARKANSAS *The Ouachita Mountains* are a pine-covered highland popular with fishermen and campers. Wild flowers abound in the scenic Petit Jean State Park near Morrilton. *Little Rock,* the state capital, is famous for its three capitols. The restored Territorial Capitol is a frontier cabin of hand-hewn oak logs. The "Old State House" is rated as the most beautiful building in Arkansas; it is a war memorial now and the present state capitol, with its guilded dome and walls of Arkansas white marble and granite, is a splendid successor to its modest forerunners. The rice center of *Stuttgart,* southeast of Little Rock, is well-known for its duck hunting. *Hot Springs,* both the national park with its 47 mineral springs and the luxurious resort city which welcomes northerners in wintertime and southerners in summertime, are described on page 110. To the southwest of Hot Springs, the only diamond mine in the U.S. is located near Murfreesboro.

NATIONAL PARK IN ARKANSAS *Hot Springs National Park,* see above and page 110.

NATIONAL FORESTS IN ARKANSAS *Ouachita Nat. F.*, U.S. 70, 71, 270 (Crystal Cave, Little Missouri Falls; this is historic ground explored by De Soto, La Salle, De Tonti). *Ozark Nat.F.*, U.S. 64, 71, State 22, 7. See above under Ozark Mountains, and on page 110. (Mt. Magazine, second highest point in Arkansas, is surrounded by a great recreational area with three lakes).

STATE PARKS 7 state parks. For details, write to Division of Forestry and Parks, Arkansas Resources and Development Commission, Box 1940, Little Rock, Ark.

CALIFORNIA

For information, write to California State Chamber of Commerce, 350 Bush Street, San Francisco 4, Cal.

NORTHERN CALIFORNIA *Tule Lake Nat'l Wildlife Refuge,* just below the Oregon state line, is a large preserve for wild fowl, particularly ducks and geese; in certain parts of the refuge, hunting is allowed during open season. To the south, *Lava Beds National Monument* is a forested area of lava beds and cinder cones; some of the lava caves have patches of ice throughout the year. Thousands of ancient Indian stone drawings can be seen on Petroglyph Point. *Castle Crags State Park,* south of Dunsmuir on highway 99, features a row of giant domes, crags and spires, up to 6,000 feet high, which line the Sacramento River for a mile. *Mt. Shasta, Shasta Dam, and Shasta Lake* form a great recreational area with fascinating scenery. It includes the snow-capped Mt. Shasta, which is an extinct volcano over 14,000 feet high; the second-largest irrigation-and-power dam on earth and a huge man-made lake. See also page 186. *Old Shasta* is a ghost town preserved as an historical monument, 5 miles west of Redding; it is an interesting relic of gold-rush days when a hundred thousand dollars worth of gold dust was produced there every week. To the southwest of Shasta, *Lassen Volcanic National Park* preserves the most recently active volcanic mountain in the U.S.; it is described on page 186. To the south, highway 24 runs through the scenic *Feather River Canyon* for 50 miles, sometimes proceeding on the canyon floor and sometimes ascending along the walls and bridging the canyon above the foaming river; the Feather River country is a famous hunting area. On the northern coast of California, *Eureka* is a fishing and lumber port, and a center for the display and sale of fine, locally manufactured gifts of redwood and myrtle wood. The nearby *Redwood Highway* (U.S. 101) crosses numerous groves and state parks of the world's tallest trees; it is described on page 198. Farther down the coast, *Russian Gulch State Park* is a redwood preserve offering surf fishing from its promontories; it is part of the rugged Mendocino Coast. *Clear Lake,* picturesquely surrounded by wooded hills and dotted with islands, is the center of a recreational area which includes other, smaller lakes. *Fort Ross State Hist. Monument* marks the southernmost point of Russian penetration in America; Russian fur hunters built the stockaded settlement in 1812; by 1841 they had practically exterminated the sea otters of the coast and sold the site to Sutter of Sacramento. The Greek Orthodox Russian Church has been restored. A number of interesting spots are found in the neighborhood of *Santa Rosa:* The experimental *Gardens of Luther Burbank,* the genius of flower and plant culture and propagation; the *Home of Jack*

London, in the Sonoma valley, now a dude ranch, and the *Sonoma Mission,* the last and most northerly of the chain of Missions—in front of it the Bear Flag of the Republic of California was raised in 1846. The whole district around *Mt. Helene* and *Napa* is one of America's leading wine producers; see also page 198. *Muir Woods National Monument* is a redwood sanctuary in the shadows of San Francisco, honoring John Muir, the great naturalist; some redwoods there have a diameter of 17 feet. *San Francisco,* the Pacific metropolis, is described on page 200. Mt. Diablo is a lonely peak 3,849 feet high, which stands by itself in the plain east of Oakland. It is surrounded by *Mount Diablo State Park,* a forested recreation area with an automobile road leading to the summit.

CENTRAL WESTERN CALIFORNIA   East of San José, the *Lick Observatory* of the Univ. of California is located on top of Mt. Hamilton; the view from the summit is magnificent, and the observatory is open to visitors on Saturday nights. On the coast north of Santa Cruz, the *Big Basin Redwoods State Park* includes some truly gigantic trees 300 feet tall; the park is a popular resort. *Santa Cruz* is a seaside resort with a casino and municipal pier. On Highway 101 the *San Juan Bautista Mission,* the largest of the chain, is partly preserved and partly restored; nearby, several other interesting adobe buildings from Spanish days are open to the public. *Monterey and Carmel-by-the-Sea,* connected by a shoreline of breathtaking beauty, are described on page 202. To the southeast of Monterey, the *Pinnacles National Monument* is spectacular. On a solid mountain backbone, tall, dark-red rock spires tower against the blue sky. The various canyon caves are said to have been the hiding places of early-day bandits.

CENTRAL EASTERN CALIFORNIA   *Donner State Monument,* honoring the pioneers who died there in the winter of 1846-47, is located at Donner Pass, northwest of Lake Tahoe; it is described on page 188. *Lake Tahoe,* considered one of the world's most beautiful bodies of water, is also described on page 188. *Sacramento,* the capital of California, is a center for mementos of the gold-rush days of 1849. Gold was discovered nearby on the land of John Sutter, and Sutter's Fort has been restored as a museum filled with pioneer relics. Sacramento was also the terminus of the Pony Express, and in the Pony Express Museum visitors may inspect the saddle bags and spurs, the prairie schooners and ore wagons of the early 1860's. Southeast of Sacramento, *Calaveras Big Trees State Park* is the northernmost important stand of sequoias, the bigger but shorter brothers of the coastal redwoods. It is also a popular skiing and tobogganing resort. Mark Twain's hilarious story of "The Jumping Frog of Calaveras County" made the name of the county and of the park famous. In the same county, the *Columbia Historic State Park* preserves and restores twelve blocks of the ghost town of Columbia as it looked during the gold rush. This is the Mother Lode Country, once a typical Wild West area. Sonora was a Mexican settlement, and Chileans discovered the Big Bonanza but soon saw control of the mine slipping into the hands of Yankees; the Chinese camp was the scene of a fierce tong war, the first in California. *Yosemite National Park,* with America's highest and loveliest waterfalls, is described on page 190. East of Yosemite Park, *Devils Postpile National Monument* is a basaltic lava flow in form of a column. *Fresno* is a bright, clean city with tree-lined streets, interesting as the center of the Upper San Joaquin Valley, which on fertile, irrigated soil produces an abundance of wonderful fruits: peaches, apricots, figs and many others. A popular recreation spot for the people of Fresno is lovely *Huntington Lake,* to the east in the Sierra Nevada. *Kings Canyon and Sequoia National Parks,* guardians of America's Big Trees and of the highest mountain in the U.S., are de-

scribed on page 192. The lonely but beautiful *Inyo-Mono Country,* between the Sierra Nevada and Death Valley, is mentioned on page 192. *Death Valley National Monument,* lowest point on the continent, is described on page 194.

SOUTHERN CALIFORNIA   *San Miguel Mission,* close to Highway 101, contains interesting original designs and paintings by Indian artists. *San Luis Obispo* has a fine mission now restored; it was the first one to use tile roofs to foil the Indians who liked to set fire to the thatched roofs. There are also many beautiful beaches with good surf bathing. *Pismo Beach* is noted for the rare and delicious Pismo clams. *Santa Barbara* is a lively, popular seaside resort; its mission, whose altar light has never been extinguished since 1786, is considered by many the most beautiful of the California chain. *Los Angeles,* the young giant city which embraces such famous sections as *Pasadena* and *Hollywood* is described on page 204. *Long Beach* is one of the leading seaside resorts of the West Coast. It has a wonderful bathing beach, and its protected outer waters are popular with fishermen. The mile-long amusement area ("the Pike") and the "Rainbow Pier," which in its half-circle embraces a 32-acre lagoon for water carnivals, caters to youthful tastes. North of Long Beach are other well-known resorts: *Redondo Beach, Venice, Santa Monica, Malibu Beach. Santa Catalina Island,* with its submarine gardens and glass bottom boats, its Bird Park and Skyline Drive, is also a popular resort.   *San Juan Capistrano Mission,* the home of the faithful swallows; *San Luis Rey Mission* with its Indian paintings; *Palomar Observatory,* where the stars are studied with the greatest lens ever made, and *San Diego,* proud harbor of our Pacific fleet, are described on page 206. *El Centro,* near the Mexican border, looks like a Latin tropical city; palm trees and patios, flower beds and overhanging second stories give it a romantic accent. It is the center of the irrigated desert of the Imperial Valley, abundant producer of lettuce, melons, dates, grapefruit. In the desert country of southeastern California, the *Anza Desert State Park* protects colorful plant life and interesting wildlife; the *Salton Sea* and the *Joshua Tree National Monument* are described on page 196, together with the mountain resort of *Arrowhead Springs* and the fashionable desert resort of *Palm Springs. Big Bear Lake* is a popular watersports resort at an elevation of 7000 feet, east of *Lake Arrowhead;* both lakes are connected by the spectacular "Rim of the World Drive."

NATIONAL PARKS IN CALIFORNIA   *Lassen Volcanic National Park,* see page 186. *Yosemite Nat. Park,* see page 190. *Kings Canyon and Sequoia National Parks,* see page 192.

NATIONAL FORESTS IN CALIFORNIA   *Angeles Nat.F.,* U.S. 6, 66, 99 (rugged mountains adjoining metropolitan area of Los Angeles; Devil Canyon and Bear Canyon Wilderness Area). *Cleveland Nat.F.,* U.S. 101, 395, 80, State 78, 94 (in San Diego area between desert and sea; Agua Tibia Wilderness Area). *Eldorado Nat.F.,* U.S. 50 (rugged mountains; hundreds of lakes, including south end of Lake Tahoe). *Inyo Nat.F.,* U.S. 6, 395 (High Sierra Wilderness Area; contains many peaks higher than 14,000 feet, including Mt. Whitney). *Klamath Nat.F.,* U.S. 99 (Klamath River, famous for steelhead trout and salmon; several wilderness areas). *Lassen Nat.F.,* U.S. 395, State 36, 89 (southern end of Cascade Wonderland; old immigrant trails; several wilderness areas). *Los Padres Nat.F.,* U.S. 101, 99, 399, State 1, 166, 150 (home of the rare and protected California condor; primitive forest, several wild areas). *Mendocino Nat.F.,* U.S. 99 W. (Middle Eel-Yolla Bolly Wilderness Area; Columbian black-tailed deer). *Modoc Nat.F.,* U.S. 299, 395, State 139 (Glass Mountain lava flows; winter range of interstate deer herd). *Plumas Nat.F.,* State 89, 24 (Feather River County, Feather

Falls, historic gold mining areas). *San Bernardino Nat.F.,* U.S. 66, 99; State 18, 74 (includes Bear and Arrowhead Lakes). *Sequoia Nat.F.,* State 65, 178, 190 (High Sierra Wilderness Area with 200 peaks over 11,000 feet; Mineral King Recreation Area). *Shasta Nat.F.,* U.S. 99, 97, 299 (includes Mt. Shasta and five living glaciers). *Sierra Nat.F.,* U.S. 99, State 41, 168 (many lakes and several wilderness areas; Devils Postpile Nat.M. and part of John Muir Trail). *Six Rivers Nat.F.,* U.S. 101, 199, 299 (giant redwood and fir forests). *Stanislaus Nat.F.,* State 4, 108, 120 (rugged mountain country near San Francisco; Emigrant Basin Wild Area). *Tahoe Nat.F.,* U.S. 40, State 20, 49, 89 (includes shoreline of Lake Tahoe; Donner Pass; Mother Lode Country, scene of California gold rush). *Trinity Nat.F.,* U.S. 299, State 36 (virgin timber; several wilderness areas).

STATE PARKS   83 state parks, and state beaches and historic monuments. For details, write to Division of Beaches and Parks, Department of Natural Resources, 1211 16th Street, Sacramento 14, Cal.

COLORADO

For information, write to State of Colorado Advertising and Publicity Dept., Capitol Building, Denver, Colo.

CENTRAL COLORADO   *Rocky Mountain National Park,* with its breath-taking mountain scenery, is described on page 160. *Estes Park* is a lively resort at the eastern entrance of Rocky Mountain National Park. On the southwestern edge of the park, *Grand Lake* is a popular center for trout fishing, sailing (an annual yacht regatta is held there), trail riding and hunting; this glacial lake is the largest natural body of water in the state. *Boulder,* to the southeast of the park, is the seat of the *University of Colorado. Denver,* the state capital, with its fabulous system of city parks and the famous Red Rocks Theater, is described on page 162. *Central City,* west of Denver, is a revived ghost town with an amusing late-nineteenth century atmosphere; it is described on page 162. *Leadville,* southwest of Denver, has two superlatives to its credit; at an altitude of 10,188 ft. it has the highest location of any city in the U.S., and nearby is the largest molybdenum mine in the world. The great resort of *Colorado Springs,* with its numerous attractions such as *Pikes Peak, the Garden of the Gods, Broadmoor* and *the Will Rogers Shrine of the Sun,* is described on page 164. *Cripple Creek,* southwest of Colorado Springs, is another ghost town that has been revived for modern visitors, with exhibits of old-time relics, old-style dramatic performances, and similar attractions. *The Royal Gorge,* southwest of Colorado Springs near Canon City, is a spectacular canyon with modern touches; it is described on page 164.

WESTERN COLORADO   *Dinosaur Nat. Monument,* straddling the Colorado-Utah state line, is listed under Utah. *Colorado National Monument,* not far from the Utah state line near Highway 50, is a mountainous country of pine forests traversed by deep, winding canyons and studded with towering monoliths of odd shapes ("the Devil's Kitchen," "the Coke Ovens"). Petrified forests, fossils of dinosaurs, Indian picture writing and a refuge for buffaloes are additional attractions. Two splendid roads lead to the monument: from Fruita, the Rim Rock Road and from Grand Junction, the Serpents Trail Road. *Grand Mesa,* east of Grand Junction, is the world's largest flat-topped mountain (altitude 10,500 feet). It has a recreation area with sparkling, snow-fed lakes, and from Land's End on the western rim the unexcelled panorama covers hundreds of miles. South of Grand Mesa, the *Black Canyon of the Gunnison Nat. Monument* includes the most spectacular ten miles of the Gunnison

River Canyon. The granite walls, most of them black, drop to a depth of 2,000 feet.

SOUTHERN COLORADO   *Yucca House National Monument,* located near the four-state meeting point of Colorado, Utah, Arizona and New Mexico, preserves the remnants of an Indian village which was thriving in prehistoric times. *Mesa Verde National Park,* principal exponent of America's ancient civilization of cliff dwellers and one of the country's most fascinating sightseeing spots, is described on page 166. *The Durango-Silverton-Ouray Valley* is a wonderful sightseeing and vacationing area for those who do not mind being away from the crowded tourist routes; the mountain scenery is grand, and the roads have some thrilling stretches, particularly the so-called Million-Dollar Highway, which runs midway on a canyon wall, south of Ouray. Everywhere there are relics of the old mining days (odd photos, little engines, cabooses like play houses, abandoned mines, ghost towns and semi-ghost towns); quite a few links with the past are very much alive, i.e., the small railroad from Durango to Silverton; the hotels that keep up the old traditions, like those in Silverton and Ouray, and the mines that have been operating since the 1870's. Near Ouray the Camp Bird Mine, whose six-mile gold vein produced the fortune of the Walsh-McLean family of Hope Diamond fame, may be visited, upon application at the office. In Ouray the "Scenic Jeep Tours" are thrilling. *Great Sand Dunes National Monument,* north of Alamosa, embraces a sea of shifting sand dunes; they are the country's largest, reaching a height of 1,000 feet, and produce beautiful effects of color, light and shade at sunrise and sunset. The Sangre de Cristo Mountains loom to the east.

NATIONAL PARKS IN COLORADO   *Rocky Mountain Nat. Park,* see page 160. *Mesa Verde Nat. Park,* see page 166.

NATIONAL FORESTS IN COLORADO   *Arapaho Nat.F.,* U.S. 6, 34, 40 (gold and silver mining; ghost towns). *Grand Mesa Nat.F.,* U.S. 6, 24, 50 (Grand Mesa Plateau, see above). *Gunnison Nat. F.,* U.S. 50 (27 peaks higher than 12,000 ft; ghost towns; several wilderness areas). *Pike Nat.F.,* U.S. 24, 85, 285 (includes Pikes Peak, historic gold camps of Cripple Creek and Alma, scenic Rampart Range Road, Platte and Arkansas River watersheds). *Rio Grande Nat.F.,* U.S. 160, 285 (rugged mountain country; active mining camps; several wilderness areas). *Roosevelt Nat.F.,* U.S. 287 (Continental Divide, with three glaciers and many alpine lakes; Rawah Wild Area). *Routt Nat.F.,* U.S. 40 (Continental Divide with perpetual snow and ice; Big Creek Lakes Recreation Area). *San Isabel Nat.F.,* U.S. 24, 50, 285 (highest average elevation of any U.S. national forest; twelve peaks higher than 14,000 feet; more than forty timberline lakes; Lake Isabel Recreation Area). *San Juan Nat.F.,* U.S. 160, 550 (alpine lakes, cataracts; historic mines; several wilderness areas). *Uncompahgre Nat.F.,* U.S. 50, 550 (many peaks higher than 13,000 feet; gold mines; Ouray Scenic Area). *White River Nat.F.,* U.S. 6, 24 (Glenwood Canyon; Hanging Lake; caves and mineral hot springs; zinc and silver mines; several wilderness areas).

CONNECTICUT

For information, write to State of Connecticut Development Commission, State Office Building, Hartford, Conn. Connecticut does not offer any spectacular sights but has a lovely atmosphere of its own created by old trees, velvety village greens, fine homes and beaches. It is also noted for its good roads; the Merritt Parkway is the traffic artery between New England and New York.

THE COAST OF CONNECTICUT   Near the industrial city of Bridgeport, *Seaside Park* has a beautiful beach of several miles; the P.T. Barnum Museum of Circus Life and Mr. Barnum's old home are nearby. To the east in Stratford, the *Judson House* of 1723 is noted for its fine antique furniture and fireplaces. In *New Haven* the *Yale University Campus* is interesting. Open to the public are the Peabody Museum of Natural History, the Botanical Garden, and the Gallery of Fine Arts. East Haven boasts of a Trolley Museum. In the town of Guilford the *Whitfield House* which was one of the first stone houses built in America, is now a museum. In Madison, fine houses of the eighteenth and nineteenth centuries line the village green; one of them, the *Nathaniel Allis House*, is a museum. Nearby, *Hammonasset Beach State Park* is the largest public beach in Connecticut. *Rocky Neck State Park* in East Lyme is a popular resort. *New London,* the largest seaport in the state, is the seat of the *U.S. Coast Guard Academy*, and a submarine base. *Mystic* with its restored old seaport and Marine Museum is a fascinating tourist goal. Among its outdoor exhibits of historic craft are the wooden whaling ship Charles W. Morgan and the square rigger Joseph Conrad. Some thirty museum buildings show ship models, intricate ivory carvings and figureheads of old sailing ships. Among Mystic's old houses, the Denison Homestead of 1717 is remarkable: It was occupied by eleven generations of the Denison family; today it is a museum of New England home life. *Stonington,* near the Rhode Island state line, has many old homes of former sea captains. In the Peleg Brown House of 1798 log books and other mementos of seafaring days may be seen.

THE INTERIOR OF CONNECTICUT   *The Danbury Fair,* held the first week of October, is one of the major fairs in the East. In *Litchfield,* the historic Tapping Reeve Law School with its early law books is a landmark in the development of law education in America. *Old Newgate Prison* near East Granby is open to the public. It was a rather barbaric Revolutionary jail, and before that a copper mine. *Hartford,* the state capitol, is also the "insurance capital" of America; some of the world's largest insurance companies have their headquarters in Hartford's skyscraper buildings. Guided tours to the dome of the state capitol offer an interesting panorama. Noted among the city's historic houses are those of Harriet Beecher Stowe and Mark Twain. The Gun Museum (Colt) is of interest to marksmen. Between Hartford and the Massachusetts state line the large tobacco fields covered with thin white cloth are an unusual sight; outside wrappers for cigars are raised there scientifically. In *Farmington,* the Whitman salt box house of 1660 is now a colonial museum. In nearby Wethersfield the *Webb House* of 1752 was the meeting place of Washington and Rochambeau. In Southington the *Powers Auto Museum* is of interest. Middletown is the seat of *Wesleyan University.* Near *East Haddam* are the Gillette Castle State Park and the Devil's Hopyard State Park, also the Nathan Hale School House. The birthplace of the revolutionary patriot is in South Coventry.

STATE PARKS   53 state parks, 26 state forests and numerous wayside picnic areas. For details, write to State Park and Forest Commission, P.O. Drawer 1558, Hartford, Conn.

DELAWARE

For information, write to the Delaware State Development Department, Legislative Hall, Dover, Del.

NORTHERN DELAWARE   *In Claymont,* near the Pennsylvania state line, the old Swedish Blockhouse still stands; this remnant of the Swedish settlement of 1654 is open to the public. *Wilmington,* the capital of the Du Pont industrial empire, has a number of sightseeing attractions of historical interest. A state park preserves the site of Fort Christina at "the Rocks" where

the Swedes landed in 1638, the first permanent white settlement on the Delaware River. A fine modern monument created by the famous Swedish-American sculptor Carl Milles and a gift of the Swedish people marks the spot of the landing. Nearby, Old Swedes Church of 1698 is Wilmington's oldest public building and one of the oldest Protestant churches in America; the lovely stone building was erected by masons from Philadelphia; for the glass work a glazier was imported from Holland. The Du Pont Winterthur Museum, and Brandywine Park with its lovely gardens along the river are worth visiting. *Longwood Gardens,* the baronial estate of the Du Ponts, just beyond the Pennsylvania state line, is fabulous for its flowers, plantings, fountains and conservatories. Newark is the seat of the *University of Delaware. New Castle* is a charming outdoor museum of colonial days, on the west bank of the broad Delaware. The "green" is shaded by stately trees and faced by the Dutch House dating from the 1650's, the court house and the Amstel House, now a museum. On the third Sunday in May, "A Day in Old New Castle" is celebrated every year, with all colonial buildings open to visitors. At *Odessa* the David Wilson Mansion of 1769 has interesting exhibits, including an early library. *Dover,* the tree-shaded capital, has a lovely colonial atmosphere. The State House is the country's second oldest state capitol still in use.

SOUTHERN DELAWARE   *Lewes* is a busy port for fishing and pleasure craft. The Dutch landed there in 1631 and established the Zwaanendael colony, destroyed by Indians less than a year later. The event is commemorated by Zwaanendael House, a museum built like the town hall of Hoorn, Holland, in an adapted Renaissance style. *Rehoboth Beach* and *Bethany Beach* are popular fishing and bathing resorts. *Trap Pond* near Laurel is a recreation area.

STATE PARKS   In reference to various state-owned recreational and historic areas, write to State Park Commission, 225 State Street, Dover, Del.

FLORIDA

For information, write to Florida State Advertising Commission, Tallahassee, Fla.

NORTHERN FLORIDA   *Jacksonville* is the gateway to Florida and its financial and commercial metropolis. The nearby Oriental Gardens have beautiful displays of tropical flowers throughout the year; forty miles of pleasant beaches attract tourists and vacationists. The St. Johns River, which looks like a series of lakes, is a famous fishing ground, particularly in its upper reaches. *St. Augustine,* the oldest city in the U.S. and an ancient Spanish stronghold, is described on page 68, together with the *Marine Studios,* a unique aquarium and outdoor museum of oceanic life. *White Springs,* an old southern spa on the Suwannee River, with its memorial of Stephen Foster who made the river famous, is described on page 66. *Tallahassee,* the capital of Florida and seat of Florida State University, is surrounded by fine old plantations antedating the Civil War. The Killearn Gardens State Park near Tallahassee is worth visiting, and the Wakulla Springs are a remarkably clear body of water. In *Pensacola* the ruins of the Spanish Fort San Carlos of 1698 look out on a fine, natural harbor; the town is perhaps best-known for its air base, the country's largest. Across the bay, on Santa Rosa Island, *Pensacola Beach* is a lively Gulf-Coast resort.

CENTRAL FLORIDA   In *Gainesville,* the University of Florida is located; interesting plantations of Chinese tung trees are in the neighborhood. Near the residential town of *Ocala,* Florida's *Silver Springs* is one of the state's major sightseeing attractions, with its 150 natural springs and its glassbottom boats; it is described on page 72. Another tourist spot near Ocala is Ross Allen's Reptile Institute. Almost as impressive as Silver Springs is the resort of *Rainbow Springs,* near Dunnellon. The daily flow of crystal-clear water is 547 million gallons, and unusual types of underwater plant and animal life may be seen there. On the east coast of Central Florida, *Daytona Beach* is a year-round resort; on its beach a continuous 17-mile stretch of sand is so hard-packed that at low tide automobile driving is popular there. Speed records have been set on that beach by Sir Malcolm Campbell and other racing experts. *Sanlando Springs,* south of Sanford, is another of Central Florida's big, gushing springs. *Orlando,* a beautiful garden city and a cultural center, is described on page 72. On the central west coast of the state, *Homosassa* offers "Nature's Giant Fish Bowl" and, to the south, the bubbling Weekiwachee Springs. The major towns and resorts of Florida's west coast are described on page 70: *Tarpon Springs,* the Sponge Capital of the World; *Tampa,* both an industrial and resort city; *St. Petersburg,* of the "three-score-and-ten" club and the "green benches"; and *Sarasota* with its Jungle Gardens, the Ringling Museums, and the circus winter quarters. The St. Petersburg region and the Sarasota region are now connected by the "Sunshine Skyway," a long, majestic bridge across Tampa Bay. Of modern design and sweeping lines, the white of its concrete pillars and rails contrasting with the blue of the bay, the skyway is a work of art in grand style, pleasantly practical to cross and beautiful to behold. *Lakeland,* with fourteen lakes within its city limits, is a center of the citrus industry and mentioned on page 72. Two of Florida's main attractions, the *Cypress Gardens* near Winter Haven and the *Bok Tower* near Lake Wales, are described on page 72. East of Lake Wales, on the east coast, the *McKee Jungle Gardens* near Vero Beach are well-known.

SOUTHERN FLORIDA *Lake Okeechobee,* a near-circle with a diameter of 31 miles, is the largest fresh-water body not only in Florida but also in any single state of the Union. On its southwestern shore the town of *Clewiston* is both a resort and an interesting market center of the cane-sugar and winter-vegetable area around Lake Okeechobee. On the southwest coast, the lively resort town of *Fort Myers* is America's "City of Palms." This appellation is well deserved, for seventy different varieties grow in its gardens, parks and streets. Its First Street offers an imposing view: It is the country's longest avenue of royal palms. Thomas Edison used to spend his winters in Fort Myers, and conducted there a number of experiments. Florida's Gold Coast, on the eastern shore, is described on page 74: *Palm Beach,* the society resort; *Fort Lauderdale,* an Eden for all water sports; *Miami* and *Miami Beach; Coral Gables,* with the modern campus of the University of Miami; the Overseas Highway; the picturesque *Keys* and *Key West.* Additional attractions near Miami are the Parrot and Monkey Jungles and the Musa Isle Seminole Indian Village, offer a tourist version of native Indian life. The fascinating *Everglades National Park,* which preserves the only subtropical plant and animal jungle life in the U.S., occupies the southern tip of Florida. It is described on page 76. *Fort Jefferson National Monument,* the abandoned fortress on Garden Key of the Dry Tortugas, can be explored only by a seagoing boat.

NATIONAL PARK IN FLORIDA   Everglades National Park, see page 76.

NATIONAL FORESTS IN FLORIDA   *Apalachicola Nat.F.,* near Tallahassee; U.S. 90, 319 (Southern Forest; Old Fort Gadsden). *Osceola Nat.F.,* near Lake City; U.S. 41, 90. (Flat country studded with many ponds and cypress swamps; state game breeding ground). *Ocala Nat.F.,* U.S. 17, 41 (Forest of scrub pine and subtropical palms; includes Juniper Springs with daily flow of 8 million gallons; national game refuge).

STATE PARKS   15 state parks, 2 recreational areas, 12 state monuments. For details, write to Florida Park Service, P.O. Box 1200, Tallahassee, Fla.

GEORGIA

For information, write to Georgia Dept. of Commerce, 100 State Capitol, Atlanta, Ga.

NORTHERN GEORGIA   *Augusta,* the important cotton center, is also a mecca for golf enthusiasts, particularly since President Eisenhower showed a preference for Augusta golf vacations. *Athens* is the seat of the *University of Georgia,* the oldest chartered state university in the United States. *Atlanta,* the capital of Georgia, is a rather young city which developed rapidly as a railroad center. It was burned to the ground by General Sherman on his march to the sea but recovered quickly. Today its interests are not only industrial and political but also educational: It is the seat of Emory University, Georgia Institute of Technology, Oglethorpe University and Atlanta University. Among the local attractions, a huge 50-foot-high painting is widely known; it is a realistic representation of the "Battle of Atlanta," in the Cyclorama Building of Grant Park. Created by a group of German artists in 1886, it commemorates the bloody 22nd of July, 1864. One of America's beloved folklore figures originated in Atlanta: Uncle Remus. The home of his creator, Joel Chandler Harris, has been restored and is a museum now. Sixteen miles to the east of Atlanta, *Stone Mountain* is a huge exposed granite dome, said to be the largest in North America. A Confederate Memorial was to be carved into the mountain, to honor the three southern heroes Davis, Jackson and Lee; work at the memorial was started but so far has remained unfinished. In *Rome,* near the Alabama state line, the *Berry Schools* are an unusual and interesting project. Founded by the late Martha Berry, their method combines learning and working; twenty industries are operated by the students. The *Chickamauga Battlefield* in the northwest corner of the state commemorates, in the form of monuments and through a museum, the battle that took place there in 1863. *Mt. Oglethorpe* (3,290 ft.) is the southern terminus of the Appalachian Trail which begins at Mt. Katahdin in Maine. To the south of the mountain, the famous Georgia marble quarries at *Tate* are fascinating; both the quarries and the plants which cut and polish the marble may be visited in guided tours.

THE COAST OF GEORGIA   Savannah and the "Golden Isles" are described on page 64; the latter include the lovely resorts of *Sea Island Beach, St. Simons Island,* and *Jekyll Island State Park.* Guarding the entrance of the port of Savannah, Fort Pulaski is a well-preserved fortress, which was shelled in the Civil War. It is a national monument now. *Brunswick* is Georgia's central market for shrimp and crabs. It is connected with St. Simons Island by a causeway.

CENTRAL GEORGIA   Near Macon the *Ocmulgee National Monument* preserves the remains of four successive Indian cultures; among the relics are ceremonial mounds and a council chamber. Nearby is the Piedmont National Wildlife Refuge. To the west, *Warm Springs* (operated by the Warm Springs Foundation) has become nationally known both for its beneficial treatment of victims of polio and for the personal interest President Franklin D. Roosevelt took in the development of the health resort. Franklin D. Roosevelt State Park, at Warm Springs, is traversed by a scenic highway (State 190) which runs along the ridge of Pine Mountain. *Columbus,* an industrial city, lies just north of Fort Benning, the largest infantry post in the country.

SOUTHERN GEORGIA   The fascinating, jungle-like wilderness of that huge swamp, the *Okefenokee National Wilalife Refuge,* is described on page 66. The *Georgia Veterans' Memorial State Park* is situated near Cordele. To the south, near the Florida state line, *Thomasville* is a winter resort famous for its roses. Its annual Rose Show in late April is magnificent. Many fine old antebellum estates surround the town.

NATIONAL FOREST IN GEORGIA   *Chattahoochee Nat.F.,* near Gainesville in the north of the state, U.S. 19, 23, 27, 41, 76 (includes Brasstown Bald, with an altitude of 4,768 feet the highest point in Georgia; Blue Ridge Mountains; Tallulah Gorge; Appalachian Trail).

STATE PARKS   22 parks. For details, write to Dept. of State Parks, 418 State Capitol, Atlanta 3, Ga.

IDAHO

For information, write to State Board of Publicity, 443 Yates Building, Boise, Idaho.

NORTHERN IDAHO   In the Idaho Panhandle, *Lake Pend Oreille,* the largest in the state, is a glistening mountain lake, its eastern shore lined with cliffs of the Cabinet Range. Snow-capped peaks loom in the far distance. The scenery has grandeur, and the lake is an ideal fishing spot. Many fishermen set out from the Pend Oreille Yacht Club, at the southern end of the lake, to catch landlocked salmon of the blueback variety, or cutthroat, steelhead and Kootenay rainbow trout. Some anglers return with astonishing catches, with steelheads, migrants from the Columbia River, weighing up to 30 pounds, and Kootenay rainbows of 32 pounds. Fishing is good as late as November, and at that time may be combined with deer hunting and black-bear hunting. Hunters stalking game in the nearby mountains will encounter groves of huge cedars almost as tall as the redwoods of the northern California coast. *Lake Coeur d'Alene,* south of Lake Pend Oreille (what an array of imaginative French names!) is one of America's fresh-water gems, with a sparkling blue surface and cone-shaped evergreen trees dotting the hilly shores. Heyburn State Park, at the southern end, accommodates campers and fishermen. A Fourth of July carnival is an annual feature. The pleasant city of Coeur d'Alene is located at the northern end of the lake. Travelers interested in mining will find Kellogg, east of Coeur d'Alene, a center of extensive silver, zinc and lead mining operations; some of the plants are open to visitors. The Sunshine Mine is the largest silver producer in the United States. Leading south from Coeur d'Alene toward Lewiston, near the Washington state line, highway 95 descends 2000 feet from the Palouse highlands in 95 spirals, with ten miles of magnificent views.

CENTRAL IDAHO   *Grand Canyon of the Snake River,* part of the Idaho-Oregon state line, is the deepest gorge on the North American continent; south of Hat Point it reaches a depth of 7900 feet. At the spot called Hell's Canyon, the canyon walls approach each other to less than 100 feet. The perpendicular cliffs of multicolored rocks combine with the turbulent river rushing through the gorge to create spectacular scenery; Kinney and Horse Mountain lookouts offer great panoramas, but on land the canyon is still quite difficult to reach. It is simpler to take a boat trip from Lewiston through part of the canyon. A tributary of the Snake River, the *Salmon River,* winds its way through the gorges and canyons of Central Idaho; for a stretch it can be observed from highway 95, and some adventurous boatmen brave the river's white water on a downstream trip.

But as far as is known, nobody has dared to undertake the upstream voyage. Near the river's source, the awesome *Salmon River Gorge* can be viewed, in a setting of wild mountains and forests, at Challis, from highway 93. To the south, between Challis and Clayton, the *Malm Gulch Petrified Forest* includes petrified logs of sequoia and redwood trees. *Sun Valley,* the modern all-year luxury resort, and the weird *Craters of the Moon National Monument* are described on page 140. Between these two sightseeing spots, the *Sawtooth National Forest,* with headquarters in Hailey, offers pack trips into majestic mountain country; fishing and big-game hunting are popular. *Boise,* the state capital, was founded as a gold rush camp in 1862; 24 miles to the east, Arrowrock Dam is one of the highest irrigation dams on earth.

SOUTHERN IDAHO   *Bear Lake* straddles the Idaho-Utah state line and is a popular water-sports and fishing resort in both states; 25 miles long, it has numerous delightful beaches of white sand. *Lava Hot Springs* is a health resort southeast of Pocatello. Mineral springs gush water of 140° F. into an outdoor swimming pool and three hot-water natatoria. *Pocatello* is noted for its Rodeo and Indian Ceremonial held every year in the second week of July. To the west, *American Falls Dam* is a huge hydro-power and irrigation project on the Snake River. *Fort Hall* is the central point of the Fort Hall Indian Reservation. Late in July the small town attracts many visitors when the Indians perform their annual Sun Dance and other ceremonials. In the city of *Twin Falls,* the Jerome Bridge over the Snake River offers magnificent views; 476 feet above the river's surface, it is one of the highest cantilever bridges on earth. To the west one can see the Blue Lakes, lovely bodies of water of deep azure color. Irrigation projects have considerably reduced the scenic splendor of Twin Falls and Shoshone Falls, except early in the year when the spring floods rush over the horseshoe of the Shoshone Falls, plunging into an abyss 212 feet deep.

NATIONAL FORESTS IN IDAHO   *Boise Nat.F.,* U.S. 20, 30, 95, State 15, 16, 17, 21, 52 (active mining region with placer, hydraulic and shaft mining; ghost towns of gold rush days; splendid stands of virgin ponderosa pine). *Caribou Nat.F.,* near Pocatello, U.S. 91, 191, 30N (high plateau divided by narrow ranges with towering peaks; the world's largest known phosphate deposit, containing about one third of the world's supply, is located in the forest; natural soda springs; lovely waterfalls). *Challis Nat.F.,* U.S. 20, 93, 93A (includes Mt. Borah, with an altitude of 12,655 feet, the highest peak in Idaho; majestic Sawtooth Primitive Area; several wilderness areas; headwaters of the Salmon River). *Clearwater Nat.F.,* State 9, 11 (the Lolo Trail Road of the Lewis and Clark Route; large stands of virgin white pine; the spring log drive on Clearwater and North Fork is spectacular). *Coeur d'Alene Nat.F.,* U.S. 10, 95 (rich mining area producing zinc, lead, silver). *Kaniksu Nat.F.,* U.S. 2, 95, Washington State 6 (includes Lake Pend Oreille which is circled by a 107-mile Loop Drive; rugged Selkirk Mountain Range; Roosevelt Ancient Grove of Cedars). *Minidoka Nat.F.,* U.S. 30 (an area of fantastic rocks formed by wind and water erosion is called "Silent City of Rocks"; alpine lakes and panoramic views of Snake River Valley). *Nezperce Nat.F.,* U.S. 95, State 9, 13, 14 (includes Hell's Canyon of the Snake River, Seven Devils Range between Salmon and Snake Rivers; Red River Hot Springs; historic Elk City). *Payette Nat.F.,* U.S. 95, State 15 (Grand Canyon of the Snake River; Payette Lakes Vacation Land). *St.Joe Nat.F.,* U.S. 10 (Rugged Bitterroot Range of Idaho-Montana divide; stands of virgin white pine). *Salmon Nat.F.,* U.S. 93, State 28 (Lewis and Clark Trail; Salmon River Canyon; Big Horn Crags). *Sawtooth Nat.F.,* U.S. 93 (Sawtooth Wilderness Area; many glacial lakes). *Targhee*

Nat.F., U.S. 26, 91, 191, State 31, 32, 33 (Grand Canyon of the Snake River; numerous lakes, streams, waterfalls).

STATE PARKS 3 state parks, 2 state forests, 2 recreational areas. For details, write to Dept. of Public Works, State Capitol, Boise, Idaho.

ILLINOIS

For information, write to Division of Department Reports, State House, Springfield, Ill.

EASTERN ILLINOIS *Chicago,* America's inland metropolis, is described on page 96. Chicago's tree-shaded lake-shore suburb of *Evanston* is the seat of Northwestern University. Near Utica, *Starved Rock State Park* contains interesting rock formations, scenic hills, bluffs and gorges. From the Illinois River the steep walls of Starved Rock arise for 130 feet; the unusual name of the rock commemorates a tragic incident: A band of Illinois Indians sought refuge on the isolated summit from a larger group of Iroquois; during the siege the Illinois refused to surrender but rather starved to death. The park was also the site of a French frontier fort erected in 1682. *Urbana* is the seat of the *University of Illinois.* Nine miles east of Lawrenceville, where the Lincoln Memorial Bridge crosses the Wabash at the Indiana-Illinois state line, the *Lincoln Trail Monument* pictures the Lincoln family as they entered Illinois, at this point, in March, 1830.

WESTERN ILLINOIS In *Galena,* near the Mississippi River, the Ulysses S. Grant Home is a state memorial now. After the Civil War General Grant lived in the pleasant red brick building which had been erected in 1857. South of Galena, the *Mississippi Palisades State Park* offers picnic and camping facilities near rocky bluffs with such names as Twin Sisters and Indian Head. Bob Upton's Cave is another attraction. *Black Hawk State Park* near Moline marks the site of the Indian village of the Sac and Fox tribes where Chief Black Hawk was born. The highest point in the park is known as Black Hawk's Watchtower. The modern museum, adjacent to the inn, houses the famous Hauberg Indian Collection. Near Peoria the *Fort Creve Coeur State Memorial* is the site of a fort built by La Salle in 1680. *New Salem State Park* with Lincoln Village, an excellent restoration of young Lincoln's environment, and *Springfield,* the state capital, with Lincoln's home and tomb, are described on page 100. Southwest of Springfield, *Pere Marquette State Park* indicates with a simple cross the spot where Father Marquette, Louis Joliet and five companions began their canoe journey up the Illinois River. This largest state park includes hilltop lookouts with broad views of the Illinois River Valley; there are also Indian mounds and relics. In the southern corner of the state, *Giant City State Park* is located ten miles south of Carbondale; there huge blocks of stone with vertical walls give the effect of a city skyline. One formation is called the "Natural Amphitheater". *Cairo* at the southern tip of Illinois and Cairo in Egypt have two points in common: the fertile soil and the life-giving river. In the case of Egypt it is the Nile, in Illinois the Mississippi with its tributary, the Ohio.

NATIONAL FOREST IN ILLINOIS *Shawnee Nat.F.,* in the southern part of the state, U.S. 45, 51, State 1, 3, 34, 127, 144, 145, 146, 151. (Prehistoric stone forts and Indian mounds.)

STATE PARKS 16 parks, 3 state forests, natural and vacation areas, 33 state memorials, numerous wayside picnic areas. For details, write to Division of Parks and Memorials, 604 Armory Building, Springfield, Ill.

INDIANA

For information, write to Division of State Publicity, Dept. of Commerce and Public Relations, Indianapolis, Ind.

NORTHERN INDIANA The industrial city of *South Bend* is the seat of the *University of Notre Dame.* On the campus, the Sacred Heart Church, a fine Gothic structure, and the Main Building with its golden dome, are landmarks. *Michigan City,* just below the Michigan state line, is a lively lake resort. Its special attractions are the International Friendship Gardens and the Indiana Dunes State Park. The white, sweeping sand dunes are equally beautiful in the glistening summer sun and when whipped by fall and winter winds. Visitors interested in industrial operations will find *Gary* interesting. Many of the big steel works and manufacturing plants conduct guided tours for visitors. There is a certain picturesque grandeur in the towering blast furnaces, the tall smokestacks, the huge docks, the great ships. In the commercial center of *Fort Wayne* the body of a beloved American folklore figure is buried—Johnny Appleseed, who spent a lifetime planting Christian faith and apple seeds throughout Pennsylvania, Ohio, Indiana. As the frontier moved westward, so did his apple orchards. His grave is in Archer Cemetery. On highway 9, *Rome City* is noted for its Wildflower Woods. This lovely garden of 20,000 wildflower varieties, started by the authoress Gene Stratton Porter, is open to the public.

CENTRAL INDIANA *Indianapolis,* the state capital, is internationally known for its annual 500-mile auto races held on Memorial Day. The great Motor Speedway has a two-and-a-half mile track. Visitors from all over the world stream to Indianapolis to witness the event. Scotch-American tourists visiting Indianapolis will be interested in the Scottish rite Cathedral with its huge organ. Another attraction is the old home of James Whitcomb Riley, Indiana's beloved poet. It is preserved the way it looked during Riley's lifetime, and is open to the public. A charming way of honoring the Hoosier poet was found in the Children's Hospital of the Indiana Medical Center: Walls and windows are alive with scenes from his poetic tales, to the delight of the small patients. Riley's birthplace is in *Greenfield,* on highway 40, east of Indianapolis, a log cabin—since then the kitchen of the Riley Homestead, a Victorian home built in 1850—it is now a museum. James Whitcomb Riley Memorial Park surrounds the original Old Swimmin' Hole of Riley's poem.

SOUTHERN INDIANA *Bloomington* is the seat of the modern campus of the University of Indiana. *Vincennes,* Indiana's territorial capital and the oldest city in the state, lies on the green, fertile banks of the Wabash. It has a colorful history; in 1732 it was founded by and named for the Canadian nobleman Sieur de Vincennes who, four years later, was burned at the stake by the Chickasaw Indians. The French lost the fort to the British, and the British to the Americans; in 1779 George Rogers Clark conquered it with an "army" of 350 Virginians, lost it and took it again. His victory is commemorated by the *George Rogers Clark Memorial,* a Greek-Doric temple on the site of the old fort. When Indiana became a territory, in 1800, Vincennes was chosen as its capital; the *Old Territorial Legislative Hall* where the first general assembly met and where the state law code was written, is a small frame building impressive because of its friendly simplicity. The country-made furniture, the bare floors, the candles, and the quill pens reflect unpretentious pioneer days. Of interest is also the *Old Cathedral* with the "Liberty Bell of the Northwest" and the Cathedral Library. The Lincoln Memorial Bridge and the Lincoln Trail Monument are listed in the Illinois section. *French Lick,* with its three mineral springs, is a famous vacation and health resort

45 miles east of Vincennes. Southeast of French Lick, the *Wyandotte Cave* is an immense limestone cavern; guided tours take visitors on longer or shorter sightseeing excursions. *Santa Claus*, near the Kentucky state line, is a busy place at Christmastime, when thousands of letters are re-mailed from there with the Santa Claus postal stamp. A monument to Santa, a toy village and a candy castle appeal to the younger set. Immediately west of Santa Claus is the *Nancy Hanks Lincoln Memorial* which includes the grave of Lincoln's mother and the site of the Lincoln family's log cabin when Abe was a young child. *New Harmony* on the Wabash was the scene of one of the numerous nineteenth century experiments in Christian community living which condemned private property. The Rappites, a sect founded by George Rapp, prospered there with farming and small industries. Today New Harmony attracts many visitors when the trees are in bloom in June: The Golden Rain Tree Festival is held every year at that time.

NATIONAL FOREST IN INDIANA *Hoosier Nat.F.,* in southern Indiana near Bedford, U.S. 50, 150 (includes the Pioneer Mothers Memorial Forest of fine specimens of black walnut trees and the old trail from Western Plains to French Lick, cut across the country and leveled out by migrating buffaloes).

STATE PARKS 18 state parks, 12 state memorials, 15 state forests, numerous wayside picnic areas. For details, write to Division of State Parks, Lands, and Waters, 405 State Library Building, Indianapolis 9, Ind.

IOWA

For information, write to Iowa Development Commission, 708 Central National Building, Des Moines 9, Iowa.

EASTERN IOWA *McGregor,* on the Mississippi River north of Dubuque, is the center of a scenic area: From the bluffs there is a broad view of the big river, and the Mississippi forms a number of so-called bayous where beds of the famous lotus flowers are thriving. In the luxuriantly verdant *Pikes Peak* region such attractions as the Bridal Veil Falls, the Sand Cave and the Painted Rocks are popular. Nearby to the northwest, the town of *Decorah* has scenic surroundings that are delightful; there are bluffs and hills, large springs in the valleys and even some "ice" caves perpetually refrigerated by nature. Of historical interest are nearby Old Fort Atkinson, and the Historical Museum of the Norwegian-American Society, which keeps the colorful traditions of the homeland alive in the New World. Near *Cedar Rapids* the limestone cliffs along the Cedar River are striking, in Palisades-Kepler State Park. The nearby seven Amana villages are an interesting social experiment. They were founded, in the nineteenth century, as Christian communities with communal workshops, including kitchens, bakeshops and mills, and still preserve many old-world customs. In *Iowa City* the *State University of Iowa* is located. On Homecoming Day in the fall, when thousands of alumni return to their alma mater, it becomes apparent that Iowa is the Corn State; even the lampposts are decorated with ears of corn. The Fine Arts Building on the campus exhibits an interesting collection of paintings by American artists, and preserves the studio of Grant Wood, great recorder of the Midwestern scene, from the days when he was associated with the university. The Sac and Fox Indians of the Reservation near *Tama* are adept in beadwork and basketwork and sell their handicrafts to tourists. To the north, in Nashua, the small church may be visited which inspired a nationally known song: "The Little Brown Church in the Vale."

CENTRAL IOWA *Ames* is the seat of Iowa State College and of an experiment station of the U.S. Dept. of Agriculture. *Des Moines* is not only the capital of Iowa but considers itself also the farm capital of the nation. One of its institutions has become so famous that it has been glorified in song hits and on the screen: the Iowa State Fair. While the fair conjures, in most minds, visions of a giant midway, of auto races and square dances, it is, more properly, a serious competition of the nation's top corn raisers, steer breeders, home bakers and other farming experts. Des Moines is also a great publishing center of newspapers and national magazines, and the seat of Drake University.

WESTERN IOWA The northwest of the state is a much frequented Midwestern resort area. *Spirit Lake,* the state's largest glacial lake, and the Okoboji Lakes offer swimming, fishing and boating. In *Sioux City,* musical and other programs are presented in Grand View Park's natural amphitheater. *Council Bluffs,* across the river from Omaha, is picturesquely located on the high bluffs above the Missouri. As the name implies, the Indians held their councils there and traded with the French trappers and traders. The city's early history is remembered in the Lewis and Clark Monument. Council Bluffs is also one of the country's centers for the growing of roses and other flowers.

STATE PARKS 17 state parks, 48 reserves, 13 state monuments, 10 state forest areas, 6 wayside picnic areas. For details, write to Division of Lands and Waters, Iowa State Conservation Commission, 914 Grand Avenue, Des Moines 8, Iowa.

KANSAS

There may be no spectacular scenery in the conventional sense in the State of Kansas, but a golden-ripe wheatfield that reaches to the horizon and a huge meadow sparkling with sun flowers are sights to behold. Tall white grain elevators tower against the blue sky as "the cathedrals of the plains," and there is no more intriguing work to be watched than the operation of a harvester combine. For information, write to Kansas Industrial Development Commission, Topeka, Kansas.

EASTERN KANSAS *Kansas City* (not to be confused with the Missouri city of the same name) is a major center of stockyards and meat-packing plants; some of the latter are open to visitors. The old Wyandot Indian burial ground is surrounded by the tall business buildings of the downtown district. *Leavenworth,* originally founded to protect the Santa Fe traders from marauding Indians, is now one of the country's largest Army posts; the latter, Fort Leavenworth, includes the Command and General Staff School. A federal penitentiary is also located there. Tree-shaded *Topeka* is the capital of Kansas; the state capitol is noted for Curry's murals of the dramatic John Brown story. The Reinisch Garden and Gage Park with the Old Settlers' Memorial Cabin are interesting. Between Topeka and Kansas City, *Lawrence* is the seat of the *University of Kansas* which owns valuable collections of Indian arts and crafts, notably in silver and glass (Spooner-Thayer Museum of Art) and of Greek and Roman arts and crafts (Wilcox Museum). Also the federal government's largest Indian school, the Haskell Institute, is located in Lawrence. To the south, *Osawatomie* was once John Brown's Kansas headquarters; the log cabin of the abolitionist leader is preserved in a park and his bronze statue honors his idealistic struggle. *Fort Riley* is a military reservation with an Army Command School and an Officers Candidate School. The restored first territorial capitol of Kansas stands within the reservation. The historic fame of *Abilene* is twofold: In the middle of the nineteenth century it was the teeming terminal of the Chisholm Trail of longhorn and cowboy fame; today it is best-known for President Eisenhower's boyhood home. A museum preserves various mementos of the President's youthful days. West of Abilene, the *Salina-Minneapolis region* is noted for "Rock City," a group of huge, weirdly shaped rock formations, and a large Indian burial pit with a museum of Indian relics. To the south, *Wichita* is the largest city in Kansas; it is the seat of Friends University.

WESTERN KANSAS In *Dodge City,* Boot Hill and the Beeson Museum with its frontier-day mementos keep alive the 1880's when the city was the Cowboy Capital of the West.

STATE PARKS 21 state parks, 1 state forest, 2 state game preserves, 70 wayside picnic areas. For details, write to Forestry, Fish and Game Commission, Pratt, Kansas.

KENTUCKY

For information, write to Division of Publicity, Commonwealth of Kentucky, Frankfort, Ky.

CENTRAL KENTUCKY *Natural Bridge State Park* is located to the southeast of Lexington. *Lexington and the Bluegrass Country,* the world's foremost area for the breeding of fine race horses, are described on page 104. The Keeneland race course near Lexington is visited by thousands of tourists even when no races are in progress. *Harrodsburg* has the distinction of being the first permanent settlement west of the Alleghenies; Daniel Boone was one of its founders. Accordingly, the *Pioneer Memorial State Park* has been established there, with a reproduction of the historic Fort Harrod, an exhibit of early pioneer life. Pioneer Cemetery, Mansion Museum, and a Lincoln shrine are additional attractions. The area of the *Kentucky River palisades* is a popular excursion goal in Central Kentucky. *Frankfort,* the capital of the state, lies on both sides of the Kentucky River. Some of the finest bourbon whiskies are distilled in and around Frankfort. *Louisville,* on the Ohio state line, is celebrated for its hospitality and for its races at nearby Churchill Downs. Climax of the season is Derby Week in May. See also page 104. Several distilleries in Louisville are open to the public. *Fort Knox* is a military base, although in the mind of the average American its association is of a huge hoard of gold. The larger part of the world's gold is indeed stored there as the U.S. gold reserve. *Bardstown* where "My Old Kentucky Home" was written, and the *Lincoln Birthplace Memorial* are described on page 105.

SOUTHERN KENTUCKY *Cumberland Gap,* in the southeastern corner of the state, is the historic gateway to the West, through the wooded Cumberland Mountains. A toll road leads to the summit of Pinnacle Mountain, which offers a spectacular view. *Cumberland Falls State Park,* noted for a strange "moonbow" over the falls, is described on page 105. Between Mammoth Cave and Cumberland Falls, the large man-made *Lake Cumberland* is impounded by *Wolf Creek Dam. Mammoth Cave National Park,* one of the great sightseeing attractions of the South, is described on page 104. The *Jefferson Davis birthplace* at Fairview is marked by an obelisk 351 feet tall; an elevator takes visitors to the top.

WESTERN KENTUCKY Near *Henderson* on the Ohio River, nature lovers are attracted by Audubon Memorial State Park and Museum, and turf enthusiasts by the race course at Dade Park. Near Cadiz, the *Kentucky Woodland Wildlife Refuge* is a large preserve of deer and wild turkey. *Kentucky Dam,* across the Tennessee River, is one of the largest on earth and an important link in the TVA system. To top the superlatives, *Kentucky Lake* is at present the world's largest man-made body of water; its southern half is in Tennessee. This is a wonderful

recreation area, with three Kentucky park areas and numerous private developments bordering the lake. All water sports flourish, and bass and crappie fishing are said to be especially fine. *Paducah* is the site of an immense atomic installation; to the southwest, near Wickliffe, the *Ancient "Buried City"* is an interesting relic.

NATIONAL PARK IN KENTUCKY *Mammoth Cave National Park,* see page 104.

NATIONAL FOREST IN KENTUCKY *Cumberland Nat.F.,* U.S. 25, 27, 60 (western rim of Cumberland Plateau; Sandstone cliffs; Red River gorge; natural rock arches; limestone caves; mineral springs) .

STATE PARKS 15 state parks, 6 historic sites, 1 recreational area. For details, write to Department of Conservation, New State Office Building, Frankfort, Ky.

LOUISIANA

For information, write to Louisiana Tourist Bureau, Dept. of Commerce and Industry, Baton Rouge, La.

NORTHERN LOUISIANA *Shreveport* is named after the famous Captain Shreve who rammed and broke loose the centuries-old log jam on the Red River and opened the river for navigation; the town calls itself Queen City of a three-state area, embracing parts of Louisiana, Arkansas and Texas. From all three states visitors are attracted to Shreveport in late April when it celebrates, for one gay week, a "Holiday in Dixie." In its surroundings, the countryside of unspoiled nature has touches of modern technology: In the region of Caddo Lake oil-well derricks tower between the live oaks.

CENTRAL LOUISIANA *Alexandria,* "the Heart of Louisiana," is headquarters for the famous Kisatchie National Forest, a picturesque region of bayous and lakes, cypresses and live oaks draped with Spanish moss. The forest contains a stand of virgin pine, extensive plantations of longleaf, loblolly and slash pines and one of the world's largest pine nurseries. *Natchitoches* is the oldest town in Louisiana, founded about 1714 as a trading post. It retains fine old colonial homes, many of French and Spanish architecture, and a French atmosphere still prevails.

SOUTHERN LOUISIANA *New Orleans,* the French-American metropolis near the mouth of the Mississippi River, is described on page 82. *Lake Pontchartrain,* reached from New Orleans on a palm-lined highway, is a very large, almost circular body of water with many miles of sandy beaches; it is an ideal spot for swimming and sailing. Fontainebleau State Park is located at the lake's northern rim. The location of *Baton Rouge,* the capital of Louisiana, is 200 miles from the sea, yet the city is a port for ocean-going vessels, with extensive modern docks flanked by huge industrial plants. It is an interesting town with a colorful history. A red staff (*baton rouge*) on a bluff above the Mississippi River is said to have indicated the demarcation line between the territories of neighboring Indian tribes, and after the white settlement had been founded, a succession of nine different flags flying over the town reflected turbulent politics. The city's outstanding structure is the skyscraper of the state capitol, one of the most impressive legislative buildings in the country. Standing on a bluff above the river, it is seen from everywhere, and in turn its lookout platform, some 30 stories above ground, offers a grand panorama of the city, the winding river, the broad plains. Baton Rouge is also the heart of the southern magnolia country and the capitol is surrounded by some perfectly beautiful specimens with dark-green, lustrous foliage and large, velvety white flowers blossoming from April to June; these magnolias are not bushes but trees, up to 80 feet tall and perhaps a century old. At the southern edge of the city, the campus of the Louisiana State University is located. The *Bayou Country,* in scenery, population, customs, language and folklore unique in the United States, is described on page 8; its principal points are *St. Martinville* with *Longfellow-Evangeline Memorial Park,* and *New Iberia* with *Avery Island.* The town of *Lafayette* has its own 15-mile "Azalea Trail," marked for visitors every year in the middle of March. The trail is a spectacle of blazing colors, similar to the Azalea Trail of Mobile, Alabama. *Lake Charles,* surrounded by oil fields and rice plantations, is both a modern deep-sea port and a recreational area. The Sabine National Wildlife Refuge, a haven for millions of migrating water fowl, is nearby.

NATIONAL FOREST IN LOUISIANA *Kisatchie Nat.F.,* U.S. 71, 165, 167, 84, State 19, 21 (See above under Alexandria).

STATE PARKS 8 state parks. For details, write to State Parks Commission, 218 Balter Building, New Orleans 12, La.

MAINE

For information, write to Maine Development Commission, Augusta, Me., or Maine Publicity Bureau, Gateway Circle, Portland 4, Me.

THE COAST OF MAINE A general view of the Maine Coast is presented on page 24. At the southern end of the coast, the resort of *York Town,* has restored its one-room schoolhouse of 1745; this interesting educational relic is open to the public. *Old Orchard Beach,* one of America's oldest seaside resorts, has 9 miles of sandy bathing beaches; its amusement park caters to youthful visitors. *Portland* with its island-studded bay is described on page 24. Among its fine old homes is the Wadsworth-Longfellow House where the poet spent his boyhood; it contains numerous mementos. In the midst of green forests and farms, the *Desert of Maine* is a 300-acre area of sand dunes near Freeport. The dunes are spreading and gradually bury surrounding trees. *Brunswick* is a pleasant college town with the Bowdoin campus, and the center of various resorts. From the high bridge over the Kennebec River, the well-known shipyards of *Bath* can be seen in full activity; they perpetuate an old Maine industry that flourished all along the coast in sailing ship days. The tree-shaded resort town of *Wiscasset* is noted for its frequently photographed old sailing ships laid up in its port and, unfortunately, rotting away. Nearby Fort Edgecomb is an octagonal blockhouse erected in the early nineteenth century, with a lovely view of blue inlets, rocky islands, wooded peninsulas. *Boothbay Harbor,* a well-known, popular summer resort, is the seat of several art schools. Twenty miles out in the ocean, *Monhegan Island* is reached by a steamer voyage from Boothbay Harbor. The trip to the small island— it is 2½ miles long and one mile wide—is well worth while. Burnt Head and Cathedral Woods are the Visitors' favorite spots. *Rockland* is a great lobster port; its Farnsworth Art Museum houses a fine collection of paintings of the Maine scene. *Camden* can be called an ideal summer resort; with the sea and a busy, landlocked harbor at its feet and lovely hills with wide maritime views at its back; with old shade trees, fine homes, all sorts of cultural interests and an annual lobster festival it is one of Maine's prime attractions. Captain Swift's "Windjammer Cruises" are conducted from there, on old coastal schooners converted for the purpose. In *Searsport,* the Penobscot Marine Museum keeps alive the days when Maine was a maritime power. Nearby Fort Knox still looks grim with its granite walls and heavy cannon. The fashionable *Bar Harbor* and *Acadia National Park* with Cadillac Mountain are described on page 24. The fishing town of *Eastport* is very appropriately named, for it is the easternmost city of the United States. The coastal tides of Maine are powerful there, rising and falling as much as 24 feet. In nearby Quoddy Village an attempt was made to harness the tides for the generation of electricity, but the project was abandoned.

WESTERN MAINE *The Rangeley Lakes* are a connected chain of sparkling blue waters lined with scented pine forests and surrounded by sweeping hills. The best way of getting acquainted with the area is a 50-mile canoe trip from Rangeley Village to Upton; it takes a week of paddling over lakes and streams. To the southwest are the foothills of New Hampshire's White Mountains. As almost everywhere in the interior of Maine, landlocked salmon and trout are most highly prized by fishermen. *Sebago Lake,* large in itself, is connected with Long Lake and thus forms a 42-mile waterway. To the west, the outline of the White Mountains looms in the blue distance. This is another vacation area for water-sports enthusiasts and fishermen.

CENTRAL MAINE *Augusta* on the Kennebec River is the state capital. Fort Western, built in 1754 as a stronghold against the Indians, is an historical museum now. North of Augusta, the *Belgrade Lakes* are a favorite playground. Within their area are Winslow with Fort Halifax, a blockhouse of hand-hewn timbers, and Waterville with Colby College. To the north, *Skowhegan* on the rushing upper Kennebec is a tourist town; the nearby resort of Lakewood is famous for its summer theater. *Bangor,* once the world's leading lumber port with a "Barbary Coast" of its own, is a quiet commercial center today. With its many old-established businesses catering to logging camps and outfitting sport camps, it has a northern frontier atmosphere of its own; north of Bangor, in the town of Orono the University of Maine is located. Close-by is *Old Town,* seat of a nationally-known canoe factory; it is open to visitors. Many of the skilled craftsmen are Indians from the reservation on the island in the Penobscot River. They perpetuate an art which white man learned from their forefathers.

NORTHERN MAINE The *Northwoods of Maine,* with *Moosehead Lake* and *Mt. Kineo,* are described on page 22, as well as *Baxter State Park* and *Mt. Katahdin,* the highest peak in Maine. The latter is the starting point of the *Appalachian Trail* which follows the principal eastern and southern ranges and ends on Mt. Oglethorpe in Georgia. The Maine potato country in Aroostook County, around Presque Isle and Fort Kent, is not particularly scenic, but its rolling hills and huge potato fields, when in bloom, have a quiet charm of their own. Every summer some twenty communities unite in celebrating a Potato Blossom Festival, with a parade, a queen, a barrel-rolling and a potato-peeling contest.

NATIONAL PARK IN MAINE *Acadia National Park,* see page 24.

STATE PARKS 14 state parks and historic memorials. For details, write to State Park Commission, State House, Augusta, Me.

MARYLAND

The most outstanding geographical factor in the life of Maryland is the Chesapeake Bay which provides the state with 3000 miles of waterfront and 2500 square miles of inland water. Consequently, Maryland's opportunities for swimming, fishing, boating and yachting are excellent. For information, write to Dept. of Information, P.O.B. 706, State Office Building, Annapolis, Md.

EASTERN SHORE OF MARYLAND *Wye Oak* at Wye Mills is a white oak, the state tree of Maryland, and one of the largest in America, but it grows in the smallest state park. The tree is believed to be over 400 years old, has a circumference of more than 21 feet, a spread of 165 feet and a height of 95 feet. *Ocean City,* on a sandy reef on the Atlantic side, is a popular bathing resort and a center of deep-sea fishing; in some years 500 marlin were caught there. *Princess Anne* is one of the state's earliest settlements, with several churches dating back to the 1700's, avenues of big trees and old and dignified homes. Here and there along the shore line of Chesapeake Bay, mountainous piles of oyster shells can be seen, reflecting one of the region's major industries. The center of oyster-fishing and crabbing is the city of *Crisfield,* self-styled "Seafood Capital of the U.S." Its lively dock area, built on "the residue of 70 years of oyster shucking," has a salty sea flavor.

CENTRAL MARYLAND *Havre de Grace,* by the Susquehanna River Bridge, is a widely known racing resort. To the northwest, *Conowingo Dam* forms a 14-mile long lake, with good perch and bass fishing. Near Towson, north of Baltimore, at the *Hampton National Historic Site,* the 18th-century Hampton House is open to visitors. *Baltimore,* one of America's top-ranking ports, has been called "a blend of northern industry and southern charm." A fascinating story lies behind the present-day metropolis: Founded as a tobacco depot in 1729, it launched the U.S. Frigate *Constellation,* became the birthplace of the Star-Spangled Banner, erected the first Catholic Cathedral in the U.S., built hundreds of clipper ships so skillfully that the expression "a Baltimore clipper" stood for excellence and received the world's first telegraph message. It became the seat of Johns Hopkins University, the first American university to offer work on a graduate level, and of the John Hopkins Hospital and Medical School world-famous institutions ever since. During the twentieth century it collected a great many industries, particularly in steel and aircraft, but still retains an air of graciousness. It has an impressive skyline and narrow cobblestone alleys on the waterfront, fine mansions and rows upon rows of identical red brick houses with marble steps in front. The star-shaped Fort McHenry, whose flag inspired the writing of the Star-Spangled Banner," is a national monument; the flag, by the way, was of outsized proportions, made by Mary Pickersgill in the Flag House, now an historic museum. Other sightseeing attractions are, besides the previously mentioned John Hopkins University, the Washington Monument, the Walters Art Gallery, the Baltimore Museum of Art, the Shot Tower, and the Pimlico Race Track. *Frederick,* to the west of Baltimore, possesses several historic shrines: the Barbara Fritchie Home, now a museum; the grave of Francis Scott Key and nearby to the north, historic Catoctin Furnace. South of Frederick, the water gardens ("Lily Ponds" at Lilypons) are beautiful when their aquatic plants are in bloom. Northwest of Frederick, near Boonsboro with its Crystal Grottoes, and near Sharpsburg, there is a great historic area; on the *Antietam Battlefield* the bloodiest single-day battle of the Civil War was fought. Washington Monument State Park is nearby to the north. *The Great Falls of the Potomac* are a spectacular cataract about 15 miles above Washington, D.C. A scenic park surrounds the 200-foot gorge with the 35-foot waterfall. In this same area the old Cheasapeake and Ohio Canal is restored for canoeing and fishing. Among the world's farm experts, *Beltsville* is well-known as the seat of the national Agricultural Research Center where every American farm product is studied, reshaped if advisable and improved, from full-breasted turkeys fit for small apartment ovens to wheat that lives on in 60 degrees below zero. In the neighboring town of *College Park* the campus of the University of Maryland is located. *Annapolis,* during the eighteenth century a gay and gracious residential town of rich tobacco planters, still has a colonial atmosphere, but it is primarily a political and educational center. The State House, built in 1772, is the oldest American capitol still in use. The campus of the U.S. Naval Academy is impressive, and fairly breathes America's great naval traditions, remembering in plaques, relics and names John Paul Jones and Macdonough, Perry and Dewey, Dahlgren and Mahan. St. John's College is an outstanding, small liberal arts college which grew out of the King William's School, the first free school in Maryland. Of the city's lovely colonial homes, the Hammond-Harwood House is open to the public. Just north of Annapolis, the *Chesapeake Bay Bridge* is a fabulous structure of beautiful modern design; with an all-over length of more than 7 miles, it is the longest over-water steel bridge on earth. To the south, in *St. Marys City,* a replica of the original first state house may be seen; Maryland was founded there.

WESTERN MARYLAND North of *Cumberland,* a famous pioneer route to the west (now highway 40) passes through the Cumberland Gorge, with walls up to a thousand feet high. In the western "handle" of the state, the area around *Oakland* is Maryland's mountain playground. The attractions include the large man-made Deep Creek Lake, Swallow Falls State Forest, Herrington Manor Recreation Area, the New Germany Recreation Area and the Pleasant Valley Recreation Area.

STATE PARKS 8 state parks, 8 state forests, 7 recreation areas. For details, write to Dept. of State Forests and Parks, State Office Building, Annapolis, Md.

MASSACHUSETTS

For information write to Massachusetts Development and Industrial Commission, 20 Somerset Street, Boston 8, Mass.

EASTERN MASSACHUSETTS Historic *Boston* is described on page 30. In *Quincy,* a southern suburb of Boston, the mansion of the Adams family is an historic shrine, and in the southwestern suburb of *Dedham,* the Fairbanks House of 1636 is the oldest frame house in America; family heirlooms of eight generations are on display. *Concord,* of Thoreau and Emerson fame; *Salem* with the House of Seven Gables; *Marblehead* with rock-lined harbor and *Gloucester* of "Captains Courageous" are described on page 30. *Rockport* on Cape Ann is an artists' colony; the red lobster barn on the wharf is probably the most frequently painted motif in the U.S. To the northwest in *Amesbury* the homestead of John Greenleaf Whittier, the Quaker poet, may be inspected; some of his manuscripts are on display. Between Boston and Plymouth, in the town of Duxbury, the John Alden House of 1653 is preserved by his descendents as a museum. *Plymouth* and Plymouth Rock are described on page 32; the Harlow Old Fort House is an exhibit of Pilgrim crafts in a 17-century home. At *Bourne,* at the foot of Cape Cod, a replica of the Aptucxet Trading Post, first building on the Cape, is open to visitors. *Cape Cod* and the art-and-fishing village of *Provincetown* are described on page 32. In *New Bedford,* the Whaling Museum exhibits a half-size model of the whaling bark Lagoda. South of Cape Cod, the triangular island of *Martha's Vineyard* is a scenic summer resort of high cliffs and landlocked ports, old towns and lovely flowers. *Nantucket* is probably America's most famous North Atlantic island: It is an early 19th century whaling community frozen in its tracks and presented, in its original charm, to 20th century visitors. When the bottom fell out of the old-style whaling business, because of the discovery of petroleum, the isolated island could not attract other industries; "progress" passed by and Nantucket stayed as it was, to the delight of present-day vacationists who enjoy the cobblestone streets, the rambler roses, the horse-drawn coaches, and the mansions of rich whaling captains long dead. The Pacific Bank and the Pacific Club remind all visitors of the world-circling operations directed from the island, once upon a time. The white beaches, the moors, the cranberry bogs and the Scotch heather add to Nantucket's allure.

CENTRAL MASSACHUSETTS   In *Sudbury*, west of Boston, the *Wayside Inn* of 1686 is still operated as an inn; Longfellow immortalized it in his "Tales of a Wayside Inn." In *North Oxford*, southwest of Worcester, the birthplace of Clara Barton, founder of the Red Cross, is open to visitors. Nearby the *Old Sturbridge Village* is a replica and living museum of a New England country town in the early 19th century. Life of that day is reenacted in some thirty shops, mills, and homes, a church and a general store. The tavern serves the Yankee foods of the 1800's. At *Princeton*, north of Worcester, a Museum of Antique Autos is interesting. To the east, in *Harvard*, the four *Wayside Museums* are reminders of New England's history; one is "Fruitlands," the farm establishment of the New Eden colony of A. Bronson Alcott; the goal was community living without exploiting man or animal. The second museum is the Shaker House, with relics of an unusual religious settlement. A portrait gallery and an Indian Museum are the third and fourth components of the group.

WESTERN MASSACHUSETTS   The *Berkshire Hills* are a charming combination of peaceful, green scenery and a strong cultural tradition that is maintained to this day. The mountains are not high—the two tallest peaks, Mt. Williams and Mt. Greylock, attain a height of about 3000 feet—but they are steep and varied, covered with dense woods and traversed by rushing brooks. Towns with calm village greens, large estates, and friendly resorts make these hills both a residential and a recreational area, in and around Great Barrington, Stockbridge, Lee, Lenox, Pittsfield, and Williamstown, where Williams College is located and where the Mohawk Trail begins. Skiing is popular in wintertime. The literary traditions of the Berkshires are fabulous. Hawthorne lived at Tanglewood, and Melville wrote "Moby Dick" near Pittsfield. Thoreau climbed Mt. Greylock, and Oliver Wendell Holmes enjoyed the cool summers in the hills. Today, many creative writers and artists live in the Berkshires, and of the area's cultural institutions the annual Berkshire Music Festival is to America what the Salzburg Music Festival is to Europe. On the Tanglewood Estate near Lenox a rare blend of excellent symphonic music and wonderful scenery—a green valley, a blue lake, and a horizon of distant ridges—may be enjoyed. Such famous conductors as the late Serge Koussevitzky and the present leader of the Boston Symphony Orchestra, Charles Muench, are in charge of the musical activities which include a summer school for professional musicians. Nearby, the Berkshire Playhouse at Stockbridge and the Jacob's Pillow Dance Festival at Lee are celebrated institutions. *The Pioneer Valley* is the broad valley of the Connecticut River between the Berkshire Hills and the large Quabbin Reservoir. Beginning in the north, the village of *Northfield* is the headquarters of AYH, the American Youth Hostel Movement. *Amherst* is the seat of Amherst College and of the University of Massachusetts. In *Northampton* Wiggins Tavern and the Smith College campus are sightseeing attractions. Near the industrial city of Springfield (also a great arsenal of weapons), the village of *Storrowtown* is a colonial restoration.

STATE PARKS   10 state parks, 28 state forests, 2 reservations. For details, write to Division of Parks and Recreation, Department of Conservation, 15 Ashburton Place, Boston 18, Massachusetts.

MICHIGAN

11,000 lakes and the longest shore line of any state in the country make Michigan a popular goal of swimmers, canoeists, sailors, fresh-water fishermen and visitors who enjoy the forest-and-lake scenery. For information, write to Michigan Tourist Council, 114 South Walnut Street, Lansing 1, Mich.

UPPER PENINSULA   The small but beautiful and historically interesting *Mackinac Island*, the *Sault Ste. Marie* with the *Soo Locks* and the *Soo Canal* which handles more traffic than any other canal on earth and the *Tahquemenon Falls* in the northern wilderness are described on page 92. *Marquette* is the center of the Upper Peninsula's recreation area where lakes and streams offer good fishing for a variety of species, from wall-eyed pike to trout and perch; hunting is varied, too, and includes bear and deer, prairie chicken, grouse and pheasant. Marquette's Presque Isle Park is a scenic spot on a small peninsula north of the town. Southwest of Marquette, *Iron Mountain* is a popular winter-sports center; for tobogganists it offers two slides, and for skiers various ski jumps, ski tows and the Roosevelt Mountain Ski Slide, said to be the highest on earth. Sportsmen appreciate also the *Keweenaw Peninsula*, and in Copper Harbor tourists can make a boat connection to Isle Royale National Park. To the west, *Porcupine Mountains State Park* accomodates tourists and fishermen on the shore of Lake Superior. *Isle Royale National Park* in Lake Superior is described on page 90.

LOWER PENINSULA NORTH   *Petoskey*, on Little Traverse Bay, is a popular resort which celebrates its summer season with the Hiawatha Indian Pageant and climaxes its winter events with a gay ten-day Winter Carnival in February, with speed skating and ice-boating included in the rounds of cold-weather sports. The calm and sparkling waters of Grand Traverse Bay make *Traverse City* a great Midwestern recreation center. Nature provides a pollen-free temperate climate and broad lake surfaces for deep-sea trout trolling and water-skiing, swimming and canoeing. Man-made attractions are concentrated in Clinch Park; this waterfront park includes a small zoo, an aquarium, an Indian Museum and a yacht basin. The Leelanau Peninsula, separating Grand Traverse Bay from Lake Michigan, is a delightful scenic spot, and the circular shore-line drive a highly recommended excursion. The region has another pleasant distinction: It is one of America's principal cherry-growing districts; the National Cherry Festival is a three-day fiesta held every July. See also page 93. The country's best-known music camp is located at *Interlochen*, southwest of Traverse City. Music students from all states of the Union attend its summer sessions, and the symphonic concerts presented in the "concert bowl" in sylvan surroundings and led by prominent conductors are the outstanding musical events of the region. On the Lake Huron side, the 200-mile shore drive from the top of the Lower Peninsula to Bay City runs through a forest-and-lake country noted for good hunting and fishing, particularly in the wilderness region of the *Au Sable River*.

LOWER PENINSULA, SOUTH   Travelers interested in interior decoration will find a visit to the Furniture Museum in *Grand Rapids* a rewarding experience; it contains fine pieces of period furniture from all over the world. Wooden shoes, flowing skirts, lace caps and millions of tulips in full bloom, blazing in red and yellow, orange and lavender, are the marks of the annual Tulip Festival at *Holland*, beginning on the Saturday nearest May 15th. Festivities start with the scrubbing of Eighth Street by Dutch-costumed townspeople, 90 per cent of whom are of Dutch descent. The cleaning-up preliminaries are followed by parades, concerts and exhibits; wooden-shoe dances are presented as a special treat. In May, the numerous tulip farms of Holland,

Michigan, rival those of Holland, Europe. West of Holland, the shore of Lake Michigan is studded with white sand dunes and bathing beaches. *Lansing,* Michigan's capital, is also the seat of Michigan State College. *Detroit,* the world's automobile capital; *Dearborn,* with the River Rouge Ford Plant, and the cultural center of *Cranbrook* are described on page 98. *Ann Arbor,* west of Detroit, is the seat of the *University of Michigan,* one of America's great centers of learning.

NATIONAL PARK IN MICHIGAN *Isle Royale National Park,* see page 90.

NATIONAL FORESTS IN MICHIGAN *Huron Nat.F.,* center of the Lower Peninsula, U.S. 23, 27 (easily accessible woodlands; includes Lumbermen's Monument) . *Manistee Nat.F.,* near Cadillac, adjoining Huron Nat.F. toward the coast, U.S. 10, 31, 131 (popular hunting, fishing and skiing area) . *Hiawatha and Marquette Nat. Forests,* Upper Peninsula, U.S. 2, 41, State 28, 94, 123 (touch Lakes Huron, Michigan and Superior; nearby Mackinac Island and the Pictured Rocks on Lake Superior) . *Ottawa Nat.F.,* in the western corner of Upper Peninsula, U.S. 2, 45, State 28, 35, 64 (lakes, falls, forests; state fish hatchery) .

STATE PARKS 54 state parks, 13 recreational areas, 22 state forests, numerous wayside picnic areas. For details, write to Parks and Recreation Division, Dept. of Conservation, 400 Bauch Building, Lansing, Mich.

MINNESOTA

The sparkling blue of 10,000 lakes and the deep green of immense evergreen and hardwood forests are the features of Minnesota's vacation and wilderness areas. For information, write to Dept. of Tourist Information, Room 114, State Capitol, St. Paul 1, Minn.

NORTHERN MINNESOTA *Brainerd* on the Mississippi River is the starting point for a tour of the Lake Country. Its annual Paul Bunyan Carnival is a colorful pageant celebrating the exploits of the lumberjack giant who left 10,000 footprints (the lakes) in Minnesota. To the north, *Bemidji,* on a lake of the same name, is another fishing and hunting center. The statue carved in wood of the Indian Chief Bemidji of the Chippewas stands in Library Park, while the huge concrete images of Paul Bunyan and his blue ox tower over the lake shore. The climax of the summer season is the Paul Bunyan Water Carnival, an event for which the men of the town grow Bunyanesque beards. Southwest of Bemidji, *Lake Itasca* used to be considered the source of the Mississippi. Together with 156 other lakes, it is included in Minnesota's largest state park, nearly 32,000 acres of woods which shelter herds of deer and other wildlife. The wilderness of the *Arrowhead Region, Superior National Forest* and the *North Shore Drive* along Lake Superior from Duluth to Port Arthur in Canada are described on page 90. Just below the international boundary, six miles off the North Shore Drive, the village of *Grand Portage* has been restored with stockade and old landmarks, just as it looked when it was the first white settlement in Minnesota. The *Gunflint Trail* offers a famous wilderness excursion from Grand Marais to Lake Saganaga. See also page 90. To the northwest of Duluth, the frontier town of *Hibbing* is the center of that interesting area where most of America's iron ore is dug from huge, reddish-brown, open-pit iron mines in the Mesabi, Vermilion and Cuyuna ranges. Those pits are the biggest man-made holes on earth. In 1919 the whole town of Hibbing was moved a mile because the old location interfered with mining operations. The Mesabi mineral wealth, as well as grain from the prairies, is funnelled to the twin harbors of *Duluth-Superior,* where the varied dock operations are fascinating to watch: the automatic collaboration of ore trains, ore piers and ore steamers; the grain elevators and their loading devices and the perpetual going and coming of the ore ships and grain ships, all with the same long silhouette and a flag of smoke from the funnel astern. Duluth is also the gateway to the Arrowhead Region and Superior National Forest. Among the city's attractions are the Aerial Lift Bridge which is raised in toto when a steamship passes below, Minnesota Point with its recreation area, the Skyline Parkway and the Enger observation tower. There are also 74 parks in the city.

SOUTHERN MINNESOTA "Midway between the Equator and the North Pole," Minnesota's great twin cities are both friendly neighbors and rivals. Minneapolis is more modern, vigorous and progressive, St. Paul more traditional, dignified and gracious. In *Minneapolis* the visitor will enjoy the "Grand Rounds," a fine boulevard around the city and a link between numerous lakes and parks. The town's residential districts, permeated with blue waters, trees and flowers, are ideal for open-air living. In the city proper the outstanding sights are the Mississippi with the Falls of St. Anthony, the Minnehaha Falls of Hiawatha fame, the campus of the University of Minnesota, the Walker Art Center and the Minneapolis Institute of Arts. During the summer the Aquatennial, a ten-day water festival, is a popular diversion, and during the winter the concerts of the Minneapolis Symphony Orchestra are outstanding musical events. *St Paul,* the state capital, is built on "Seven Hills" and enjoys a great many lakes and parks. On River Boulevard one can drive to historic Fort Snelling, on the picturesque high bluffs along the Mississippi. The State Capitol and the botanical conservatory in Como Park are St. Paul landmarks. Ever since 1886 St. Paul has celebrated a nine-day winter carnival with a unique feature. Every year a 4500-ton, medieval ice palace is built in Como Park. Floodlighted and topped with fireworks, it is a spectacle indeed. North of Minneapolis-St. Paul the St. Croix River rushes through a rocky gorge 200 feet deep. The walls of the *Dalles of the St. Croix* arise vertically from the river like the sides of a canyon. *Red Wing* on the Mississippi is the seat of a great clay and pottery industry. From there to La Crescent, highway 61 follows the Mississippi River and offers delightful vistas into the "*Hiawatha Valley.*" *Rochester* is the seat of the Mayo Clinic, a world center of medical treatment and research. South of Harmony, in the southeastern corner of the state, the *Niagara Cave* is unusual. About 200 feet below the ground, it contains two rivers, a lake and a 60-foot waterfall. In the southwestern corner of Minnesota, the *Pipestone National Monument* preserves the red pipestone quarries from which the Indians obtained the material for their peace pipes. Stone formations of the area include the Three Maidens, the Indian Head and the Great Stone Face.

NATIONAL FORESTS IN MINNESOTA *Chippewa Nat.F.,* U.S. 2, 71, 371 (includes the headwaters of the Mississippi River and stands of virgin red pine; present home of the Chippewa Indians) . *Superior Nat.F.,* U.S. 53, 61 (millions of acres of virgin forest; historic water route to the Northwest; 5000 lakes, many with sandy beaches and picturesque islands; several Roadless Areas; see also page 90) .

STATE PARKS 30 state parks, 6 memorial parks, 15 state wayside picnic areas, 13 state forests, numerous roadside areas. For details, write to Division of State Parks, State Office Building, St. Paul 1, Minn.

MISSISSIPPI

For information, write to Travel Dept., Mississippi Agricultural and Industrial Board, Jackson, Miss.

NORTHERN MISSISSIPPI *Sardis Dam,* a three-mile-long earth dam, creates a lake of 110 square miles where watersports facilities are available. In *Oxford,* east of Sardis, the University of Mississippi is located. The home of William Faulkner famous Nobel Prize winner and novelist, is also in that small southern community.

CENTRAL MISSISSIPPI East of *Laurel,* the industrial and oil center of the state, a popular recreational area has been created around Boguehomo Lake, near the De Soto National Forest. In *Jackson,* the state capital, both the old and the new capitols are of interest; the former is Mississippi's most distinguished historic building. The classical Governor's Mansion at the city's busiest corner, has been headquarters for both Grant and Sherman. Trenches of the city's fortifications in the Civil War can still be inspected. *Vicksburg* with the National Military Park and the U.S. Waterways Experiment Station and *Natchez,* where the greatest concentration of beautiful ante-bellum plantation homes in the South can be found, are described on page 86.

SOUTHERN MISSISSIPPI The *Mississippi Gulf Coast* with its lovely resorts along the Old Spanish Trail, from *Bay St. Louis* to famous *Biloxi* and historic *Pascagoula,* is described on page 80.

NATIONAL FORESTS IN MISSISSIPPI *Bienville Nat.F.,* near Jackson, U.S. 80, State 35 (pine and hardwood forest, with a stand of virgin loblolly pine). *Delta Nat.F.,* between Jackson and the Mississippi, U.S. 61 (large areas of virgin bottom-land hardwoods). *De Soto Nat.F.,* between Laurel and Gulfport, U.S. 11, 90 (site of the field trials of the South Mississippi Gun and Dog Club). *Holly Springs Nat.F.,* near the Tennessee state line, U.S. 72, 78 (this area contains some of the biggest erosion gullies known; erosion control projects are carried on). *Homochitto Nat.F.,* in the southwestern corner of the state, U.S. 61, 84 (one of the finest natural timber growing sites in the U.S.; picturesque eroded loess country near Natchez).

STATE PARKS 10 state parks. For details, write to Mississippi Board of Park Supervisors, Box 649, Jackson, Miss.

MISSOURI

For information, write to Missouri Division of Resources and Development, Jefferson Building, Jefferson City, Missouri.

EASTERN MISSOURI *Hannibal,* with Mark Twain's Boyhood Home, is described on page 100. Mark Twain was born in the village of *Florida,* southwest of Hannibal; his birthplace stands in a state park. *St. Louis,* the "Dowager Queen of the Mississippi," is described on page 102. Lindbergh's epochal flight across the Atlantic, in the "Spirit of St. Louis," was projected largely in St. Louis and the Lindbergh trophies are exhibited in the Jefferson Memorial in Forest Park. One interesting St. Louis project is carried on by the Jefferson National Expansion Memorial which develops a wide section of the river front as an exhibit of and memorial to the westward growth of the United States. Appropriately, the original copy of the Louisiana Purchase is preserved in the Museum.

CENTRAL MISSOURI *Columbia* is the home of the University of Missouri and the center and market of a district famous for raising Missouri mules. A few miles to the west, the town of *Boonville* is the seat of Kemper Military Academy, once attended by Will Rogers; this is the oldest military school west of the Mississippi. To the south, approximately in the center of the state, *Jefferson City* is delightfully located on a high bluff

above the Missouri, a splendid setting for the state capital. The impressive capitol of Carthage marble is decorated with murals by Thomas Hart Benton, the great painter of Midwestern and Southern farm scenes. The 130-mile-long *Lake of the Ozarks,* the largest of Missouri's five man-made lakes, is described on page 110.

WESTERN MISSOURI *St. Joseph* on the Missouri River was the starting point of the Pony Express in 1860. Mementos of that exciting enterprise may be inspected at the Pony Express Stables. The Jesse James House and several other old homes are open to the public. King Hill, an ancient Indian battlefield, is an observation point now. *Excelsior Springs* boasts of ten mineral springs; it is a noted health resort. *Kansas City* used to be a boisterous outfitting town for wagon trains rolling west. It is still a traffic center, with twelve trunkline railroads keeping up a steady flow of goods, farm products, cattle, horses and mules. Visitors will like the city's landscaped boulevard system which extends for 100 miles. Of interest are also the Liberty Memorial with its perpetual flame, the beautiful William Rockhill Nelson Gallery of Art and the Museum of Fine Arts. At the northeastern rim of Kansas City, *Independence* has historic significance as the starting point of the Santa Fe and Oregon Trails. Today it is known as the hometown of former President Harry S. Truman. The *Ozark Mountains* area with Lake Taneycomo, the so-called "Shepherd-of-the-Hills Country," is described on page 110. Also the *Big Spring Country* on the eastern edge of the Ozarks is presented there. See also below, under Clark National Forest.

NATIONAL FORESTS IN MISSOURI *Clark Nat.F.,* U.S. 60, 67 State 8, 19, 21 (Big Spring Country, fast-flowing, crystal-clear streams; oak and pine forests, magnificent during spring bloom of redbud and dogwood and during brilliant fall coloring). *Mark Twain Nat.F.,* U.S. 63, 66 (in Ozark Mountains; numerous coves, rock cairns and springs).

STATE PARKS 23 state parks, 9 state forests and wildlife refuges, numerous wayside picnic areas. For details, write to State Park Board, Monroe Building, Jefferson City, Mo.

MONTANA

For information write to Travel and Advertising Department, State Highway Commission, Helena, Montana.

NORTHERN MONTANA *Fort Peck Dam* is a huge, earth-filled structure about 250 feet high, with a broad highway across its crest. It dams up a man-made lake extending for 189 miles. While its main purposes are irrigation and the improvement of navigation on the Upper Missouri River, it has also created a great recreational area for campers, fishermen and sailors. The Fort Peck Game Range protects mountain sheep and pronghorn antelope, elk, white-tailed deer, and mule deer, waterfowl and upland birds. A great number of fossils which were discovered during the construction of the dam are on display in the Fort Peck Theater. The town of Fort Peck is an old fur-trading post. *Great Falls,* Montana's largest city, was the home of the great cowboy artist Charles M. Russell who had his studio in a log cabin; much of his work is preserved in the odd Cigar Store Museum and in the Charles M. Russell Memorial Museum. Four and a half miles northeast of Great Falls, on the south bank of the Missouri River, the *Giant Springs* discharge 388 million gallons of water every day. The park surrounding the springs and the pool is a popular picnic spot. According to a legend of the local Indians, the Giant Springs flow from a beautiful lake in the sky, the abode of the sun god whose tepee stands on the sky lake's shore. The *Blackfeet Indian Reservation* and the excellent *Museum of the Plains Indians* in the interesting Indian town of *Browning* are described on page 134. *Glacier National Park,* one of America's most magnificent scenic spots, and the *Going-to-the-Sun Highway* are described on page 134. South of Glacier National Park, on the western shore of the large Flathead Lake, the Flathead Indians have their reservation with communal grazing grounds. Their tepees can usually be seen from Highway 93. South of the lake, the *National Bison Range* maintains America's second largest herd of buffaloes; the animals are scattered, in small groups, over the 18,000-acre refuge.

WESTERN MONTANA *Missoula* is the home of the University of Montana. *Helena,* the state capital, developed from the Last Chance Gulch mining camp, and gold was dug where Helena's main street is located now. Some of the old placer diggings in the neighborhood are still worked successfully, on occasion. Also silver and lead have been mined there. Historically speaking, this is Lewis and Clark country; everywhere there are plaques and reminders referring to the advance of the explorers, and a mural in the capitol, by Charles M. Russell, glorifies their great adventure; the boat which they used on the Missouri River is an interesting relic. The capitol, by the way, stands on the summit of a hill and offers a broad panorama of a great valley and distant mountain ranges. Helena is not on but near the Missouri, and a boat cruise on the river, to the *"Gate of the Mountains,"* is a worth-while excursion. *Butte* has been called "the richest hill on earth," and "the world's greatest mining city." Such claims may sound exaggerated but are well founded. The city has nearly 300 miles of streets on its surface, and 2000 miles of tunnels underground. The borings reach a depth of 3700 feet. Although the town was founded in the gold rush of 1864, and changed to silver mining when the big silver deposits of Silver Bow Creek were discovered in 1874 (at the foot of the hill on which Butte stands), it was the copper discovery of 1880 that established Butte's fame. One third of the copper output of the United States, and one sixth of the world's production is taken from the mines of Butte. Besides the quantity, the quality of Butte copper is said to be outstanding and of better than average tensile strength. The copper ore is shipped to Anaconda, 26 miles to the west, where the Washoe smelter and various manufacturing plants turn the ore into metal and the metal into copper wire and other copper products. Even the smokestack of the Washoe smelter is a superlative: With a height of 585 feet it is the tallest on earth. The Leonard Mine in Butte is open to visitors who are also welcome at the excellent Geological Museum. The latter is a department of the Montana School of Mines which attracts to Butte students from every state of the Union and many foreign countries; the school, a branch of the University of Montana, is noted for its library and its research laboratories. The climate of the region is pleasant, and the sun shines almost 300 days during the year. Among the scenic attractions are the Continental Divide at *Pipestone Pass,* south of Butte, and the *Lewis and Clark Cavern State Park* to the east. This is a large limestone cave of multicolored and weird stalagmite and stalagtite formations; guided tours are available. To the west, near the Idaho state line, the *Big Hole Battlefield National Monument* commemorates the fierce fight that took place there on August 9, 1877, during the retreat of Chief Joseph of the Nez Percé Indians. South of Butte, *Virginia City* has been recreated, in Williamsburg fashion, the way it looked when it was the second capital of the territory. This, of course, is Virginia City, Montana, not to be confused with Virginia City, Nevada, which has also been revived from its ghost-town slumber. Both Virginia Cities merrily recreate, for twentieth-century visitors, the spirit of western frontier days.

SOUTHERN MONTANA The *Red Lodge Highway* is a magnifi-

cent 60-mile mountain road from Red Lodge to Yellowstone National Park. Splendid vistas of the Beartooth Mountain country unfold on all sides, with lookout points provided at frequent intervals. A zoo near Red Lodge exhibits the animals and birds typical of Montana, and in the neighborhood of Cooke the *Grasshopper Glacier* is a natural curiosity. Fourteen miles from town, on a mountain trail at the northeastern rim of Yellowstone National Park, a large icefield a mile and a half long is permeated with layers of millions of frozen grasshoppers imbedded in the glacier. *Billings* is the center of a great ranching area; large crowds of tourists are attracted by the annual Midland Empire Fair and Rodeo held in August. One of the local sights, about ten miles from the city near the boundary of the Crow Indian Reservation, is the *Pictograph Cave.* Visitors may see there the picture writings of human beings of an unknown race; excavations and restorations are under the direction of the University of Montana. Three interesting sightseeing spots may be visited south of *Hardin.* One is the *Crow Indian Agency,* about 13 miles south of Hardin on Highway 87. In summertime the driver along that road has the illusion of early trapper days, for the broad lands are studded with groups of tepees. The Sun Dance in July is a great ritual and late in August the Crow Indian Fair is a colorful spectacle of fancy horseback riding and ceremonial dancing, racing and arrow throwing. The Crows are outstanding artists in beadwork and beadwork articles are, of course, for sale. A few miles to the south, on the same highway, the *Custer Battlefield National Monument* honors General Custer and his 300 officers and men who on June 25, 1876, were wiped out by the Sioux and Cheyenne. "Custer's Last Stand" was the climax of the Indian wars which were bitter and bloody in Montana. Marble stones mark the graves of the heroes buried on the field of the Battle of Little Bighorn. To the southwest of Hardin, *Big Horn Canyon* is a scenic marvel. From Horseshoe Bend Lookout, one glances down into the winding canyon of the Bighorn River which has twice the depth of Yellowstone Canyon. The view is breath-taking: From the groves and pastures of the canyon floor, the brightly colored stone walls rise vertically to the top; their sides show dark gashes of immense caverns, and their rims are decorated with strikingly formed rocks.

NATIONAL PARKS IN MONTANA *Glacier National Park,* see page 134. *Yellowstone National Park,* see page 136.

NATIONAL FORESTS IN MONTANA *Beaverhead Nat.F.,* U.S. 91, State 1, 41, 34, 36, 43 (includes Big Hole Battlefield Nat. Monument, Anaconda-Pintler Wilderness Area, alpine lakes). *Bitterroot Nat.F.,* U.S. 93 (Selway-Bitterroot Wilderness Area is the largest in the U.S.; ancient Indian hieroglyphics, St. Mary's Mission, Fort Owen). *Cabinet Nat.F.,* along the Clark Fork River Valley near the Idaho state line, U.S. 10, 10A, State 28 (mountain grandeur, rugged ranges, alpine lakes and mountain streams; contains also farm lands). *Custer Nat.F.,* U.S. 10, 12 (includes spectacular Red Lodge Highway; snow-clad Granite Peak, almost 13,000 feet, the highest point in Montana; 900-ft. Woodbine Falls; rich fossil beds; Indian hieroglyphics and burial grounds). *Deerlodge Nat.F.,* near Butte, U.S. 10S, 10A, 91, State 38 (Tobacco Root Mountains, many alpine lakes). *Flathead Nat.F.,* east of Flathead Lake, U.S. 2, 93, State 35 (spectacular formations like massive Chinese Wall and jagged Mission Mountains, glaciers and glacial lakes; several wilderness areas). *Gallatin Nat.F.,* northwest of Yellowstone Park, U.S. 191, 10, 89 (Great Gallatin Valley; snow-clad peaks of Crazy Mountains, with 11 large waterfalls, 200 lakes, several wilderness areas). *Helena Nat.F.,* U.S. 10N, 91 (Continental Divide; Gate of the Mountains at the Missouri River; the original blockhouse of old Fort Logan; ghost towns; wilderness areas). *Kootenai*

Nat.F., in northwest corner of state, U.S. 2, State 37 (Cabinet Mountains Wilderness Area). *Lewis and Clark Nat.F.*, south of Great Falls, U.S. 87, 89, State 6 (scenic limestone canyons and rolling mountains with many natural open parks). *Lolo Nat.F.*, near Missoula, U.S. 10, 93, State 20 (Lewis and Clark Trail, several wilderness areas).

STATE PARKS 10 state parks and monuments, 4 waysides. For details write to Montana State Park Commission, Box 308, Bozeman, Montana.

NEBRASKA

For information, write to Division of Nebraska Resources, State Capitol, Lincoln 9, Nebraska.

EASTERN NEBRASKA Halfway between New York and Los Angeles, *Omaha* is America's crossroads city. Wagon trains set out from Omaha in the days of the Mormon Trail and the Oregon Trail, and today ten trunk-line railroads handle the city's market traffic of grain by the trainloads and hogs, sheep and cattle by the millions. Originally a freighters' stop on a terrace above the Missouri, it now extends far into a pleasant countryside of rolling hills. Carter Lake and Levi Carter Park are delightful recreational spots; the Joslyn Memorial is a beautiful art gallery of pink Georgian marble and houses fine collections of paintings and folk arts; the Union Pacific Museum commemorates the first transcontinental railroad whose westward advance started from Omaha; the Mormon Cemetery is a grim reminder of pioneer life: It contains the graves of almost 600 Mormons who, during the fierce winter of 1846–47, perished on their westward trek. The city has a large and active Czech community whose Sokol Auditorium is the scene of an annual "Bohemian Grape Festival." Eleven miles west of Omaha, a nationally famous social project is carried on: *Father Flanagan's Boy's Town* for homeless boys. An incorporated village of 1200 acres, it has a city commission, and a chapel, post office and auditorium, farm and trade schools—and most of these activities are operated by the boys themselves. In *Lincoln*, the state capital one of the few modern capitol buildings in the United States, raises its 400-foot tower proudly into the blue sky of the prairies it is visible for miles. The great white shaft is capped by a dome of gold tile, and on top of the half-sphere there stands a 27-foot bronze statue, the symbol of the plains: the Sower. The Nebraska State Historical Society's Museum, in the west wing of the Capitol Building includes collections of Indian relics ancient guns and pioneer musical instruments. The capitol by the way, houses the only one-house legislature in the United States. On the campus of the University of Nebraska the Nebraska State Museum offers to naturalists "the Hall of Elephants" and a large exhibit of fossils, and to art lovers, an excellent gallery of American art, including many modern paintings. South of Omaha on the Missouri River *Nebraska City* is the home of the Arbor Day founder, J. Sterling Morton. His arboretum in Arbor Lodge State Park is open to the public. To the south of Lincoln, near Beatrice, the *Homestead National Monument* encloses the first land claim of 160 acres under the historic General Homestead Act of 1862, occupied by a Union soldier named Daniel Freeman. Some of the original buildings of the earliest homesteaders have been restored. *White Horse Ranch*, near Naper on state highway 12, is a popular attraction. A herd of fine white horses is trained daily in the White Horse Bowl. Pretty girl riders add glamour to the sports spectacle.

WESTERN NEBRASKA At Valentine, near the South Dakota state line, the *Fort Niobrara National Wildlife Refuge* preserves a large herd of American bison; besides, it is populated with a lively cross section of Nebraska wildlife, from elk and coyote to bobcat and pronghorn antelope. In the northwest corner of the state, *Chadron State Park* is a wooded area of high bluffs, striking rock formations and deep canyons. *Scotts Bluff National Monument*, near the Wyoming state line, is a huge tableland of sandstone, a towering pioneer landmark above the Oregon Trail. An automobile road leads to the top of the table, from where a sweeping panorama of the North Platte Valley may be enjoyed. A museum depicts the trail history, the westward migration and the days of the buffalo hunters. Ten miles to the south, the *Wildcat Hills State Game Reserve* maintains another buffalo herd. *Kingsley Dam* on the North Platte River is a huge earth-filled structure forming Lake McConaughy, with a capacity of two million acre-feet, the biggest body of water in the state. Facilities for fishing and water sports are available.

NATIONAL FOREST IN NEBRASKA *Nebraska Nat.F.*, in north Nebraska, U.S. 20 (nesting grounds of great blue heron, grouse, prairie chicken; largest herd of mule deer in Nebraska).

STATE PARKS 7 state parks, 52 recreational areas, 9 wayside picnic areas. For details, write to Game, Forestation and Parks Commission, Lincoln 9, Nebraska.

NEVADA

For information, write to Dept. of Highways, Carson City, Nevada.

EASTERN NEVADA Those who would like to see a typical cattle town teeming with ranchers and cowhands, with mooing herds in the stockyards, with bars crowded and roulette wheels spinning, should visit *Elko* during the fall roundups and at the time of the county fair. *Lehman Caves National Monument*, near the Utah state line, is an underground cavern with rock formations in striking shapes. Illumination brings out the white, gray and various other colors of the columns and walls. In a state park 11 miles south of Pioche, *Cathedral Gorge* is a bastion of colored rock arches and spires. At sunset, when shadows and coloring are most dramatic, a few sections resemble indeed some medieval cathedral with double towers. *Lake Mead* with the *Hoover Dam* and the spectacular *Valley of Fire* are described on page 182. At Overton, at the northern end of Lake Mead, a museum exhibits the Indian tools and artefacts which were found and excavated at Lost City, a thousand-year old pueblo now at the bottom of Lake Mead. *Las Vegas*, the fashionable all-year resort, is described on page 182.

WESTERN NEVADA The magnificent *Pyramid Lake*, the university-and-casino town of *Reno*, the lively Old West re-creation of *Virginia City*, and *Carson City*, America's smallest state capital, are described on page 184. *Lake Tahoe* which is shared by California and Nevada, and the "Reno Snow Bowl" at Mount Rose are described on page 188.

NATIONAL FORESTS IN NEVADA *Humboldt Nat.F.*, near Elko, U.S. 93, 40 (includes areas of a thriving livestock industry around Northfork and Mountain City; Owyhee River Canyon; Wildhorse Reservoir). *Nevada Nat.F.*, U.S. 6, 50, 93, 95, State 39 (includes Lehman Caves National Monument and Mt. Wheeler, with 13,061 feet the highest peak wholly in Nevada; the Charleston Division is outstanding for two reasons: It is covered with huge pine trees, and it enjoys a delightfully cool climate in the midst of a hot desert). *Toiyabe Nat.F.*, center of the state to California line, U.S. 395, 50, 40, 6, 95, State 8A, 31, 3, 22 (Sierra Nevada, Toiyabe and Santa Rosa Ranges; alpine lakes; Hoover Wilderness Area).

STATE PARKS 4 state parks, 5 wayside picnic areas. For Details, write to Nevada State Park Commission, Heroes Memorial Building, Carson City, Nevada.

NEW HAMPSHIRE
For information write to Information Division, State Planning and Development Commission, Concord, N.H.

NORTHERN NEW HAMPSHIRE In the northern corner of New Hampshire, near the Canadian border, the *Connecticut Lakes* region is a famous hunting and fishing wilderness. In the early 1800's this area was disputed territory; for a while the local backwoodsmen rejected both Canadian and United States sovereignty and operated an independent storybook republic. At *Dixville Notch,* the Balsams is a popular modern resort in a vast mountain-and-forest country.

THE WHITE MOUNTAINS America's first mountain resort area, with *Mt. Washington, the Old Man of the Mountains, the Flume,* and other famous sightseeing spots, is described on p. 26. All of these points are within the White Mountain National Forest. At the rim of the forest, north of the pulp and timber town of Berlin, the *Berlin Ski Jump* is said to be the world's highest. South of Lancaster, *Mt. Prospect State Park* offers a fine view from a lookout tower. Bethlehem is a lively resort; a toll road leads to the top and observation platform of Mt. Agassiz, named for the famous Swiss-American naturalist. At the southern rim of the national forest, *Wonalancet* is the home of the Chinook Sledge Dog Kennels where powerful huskies from the Arctic are trained, and at the eastern rim *North Conway* is a great ski center with a comfortable hill-climbing installation called skimobile.

CENTRAL NEW HAMPSHIRE This is the region of the great blue lakes of which *Lake Winnipesaukee* is the largest; it is described on p. 26. To the northeast of Winnipesaukee, *Lake Ossipee* and the *Mystery Pond* are tourist spots; the latter provides rides with glass-bottom boats for underwater views. The picturesque *Squam Lake* and *Newfound Lake* are popular water-sports centers. North of Newfound Lake the *Polar Caves near Plymouth* are an interesting maze of caverns and tunnels. *Hanover* is a lovely New England college town, tree-shaded, dignified and friendly, and *Dartmouth College* is the intellectual center of the region. The impressively modern Orozco murals are an unexpected sight in the traditional building of the Baker Library. The Dartmouth Winter Carnival, held each February, is one of the country's best-known winter festivals of its kind; its snow-and-ice-sculpturing contest often creates wonderful, lifelike statues of a humorous tenor; sports features like a torchlight figure-skating show and the Eastern Intercollegiate Speed-skating Championship race are high lights of the carnival. South of Hanover, near Plainfield, the *St. Gaudens Memorial* preserves the studio, the burial place, and a number of works of the famous sculptor. To the southwest of Lake Winnipesaukee, near the town of Franklin, the *Daniel Webster Memorial* exhibits, in the modest birthplace of the New England statesman, mementoes of his life and furnishings of his period. West of Franklin, *Lake Sunapee* is a recreational area, with a chair lift to Mt. Sunapee. Three miles north of Lake Sunapee, the Collins Old Clock Museum has a collection of more than 200 old and rare clocks, among them mechanical clocks whose figures act out historical scenes.

SOUTHWESTERN NEW HAMPSHIRE At Acworth, the odd *Button Museum* contains thousands of buttons of every conceivable type. In Hillsboro, the *Franklin Pierce Homestead* shows interior decorations of the times of the 14th President of the U.S.; the mansion's scenic wallpaper is a conversation piece. *Peterborough* is a cultural center. The MacDowell Music Colony, named for the composer Edward MacDowell who is buried there, provides to those accepted as members an opportunity for creative composing and writing, in lovely, peaceful, sylvan surroundings. The Goyette Museum is an especially fine collection of early Americana. Three miles to the east, *Miller State Park* offers a panorama of the hills of New Hampshire, Vermont, and Massachusetts, from the top of Pack Monadnock Mountain. *Mt. Monadnock* proper lies to the west of Peterborough, in a state park; from the peak of this isolated 3,166-ft. high mountain all six New England states are said to be visible on a clear day. To the south, near Rindge, the *Cathedral of Pines* is a beautiful evergreen sanctuary.

SOUTHEASTERN NEW HAMPSHIRE Concord's state capitol is built of fine-grained granite from neighboring quarries. One of the country's largest printing establishments is Concord's Rumford Press where visitors on guided tours may see the printing of magazines like the *Reader's Digest.* In the 19th century, a local manufacturing specialty of the city became world-famous: the Concord Coach. It sold for a dollar a pound, and was so excellent that most western and many foreign stage lines used it. Old models of these sturdy and elegant coaches are exhibited in New Hampshire at various tourist centers. To the south, *Manchester* is the state's largest city, at the Amoskeag Falls of the Merrimack River. The Currier Gallery of Art is interesting. To the west of Manchester, the summit of Uncanoonuc Mountain can be reached by a railway. To the south, at Hudson, an *Animal Farm* is open to visitors; wild animals are raised and trained there for zoos and circuses. *Durham,* to the northeast, is the seat of the University of New Hampshire. South of Durham, *Exeter* is another educational center, the home of Phillips Exeter Academy. *Portsmouth,* New Hampshire's only seaport, had its great days early in the 19th century when its seaborne trade brought wealth to its merchants and shipowners, when John Paul Jones' "Ranger" was built there, and Captain Jones himself had a fine mansion constructed in town. The Jones home is now the headquarters of the Historical Society. Among the other fine buildings—some of them open to the public—are the Moffat-Ladd Home with its splendid staircase and the St. John's Church which owns such relics as an organ built in England in 1710, an ancient bell recast by Paul Revere and one of the four "Vinegar Bibles." The town's narrow streets preserve a colonial atmosphere.

NATIONAL FOREST IN NEW HAMPSHIRE *White Mountain National Forest,* U.S. 2, 3, 302 (includes most of the White Mountains, with Mt. Washington, the Presidential Range, Tuckerman Ravine, Glen Ellis Falls, Lakes of the Clouds).

STATE PARKS 24 state parks, 2 reservations, 1 state forest. For details write to Forestry and Recreation Department, Concord, N.H.

NEW JERSEY
New Jersey is called the Garden State, an appellation which is quite correct; it is also called the Mosquito State (a name which is no longer justified, as the mosquito-control agencies have all but eliminated the insect plague) but it should certainly be called the Highway State, because its excellently marked highway net is second to none. It is the cross-roads between the North and the South, New York and Philadelphia; Highway 1, the Pulaski Skyway, the N.J. Turnpike and the Garden State Parkway manage the heaviest traffic in the world. The visitor

who approaches New York by car from the New Jersey side and rides over the broad highway ribbons which twist and loop above, below and alongside each other, will somehow feel that he is motoring in the metropolis of the future. For information, write to State Promotion Section, Dept. of Conservation and Economic Development, Trenton 7, N.J.

NORTHERN NEW JERSEY   *High Point State Park,* in the northernmost corner of New Jersey, offers a broad view of the wooded Delaware Valley; with an altitude of 1803 feet, this park is the highest point in New Jersey. The adjoining Stokes State Forest is a popular camping area. To the south at *Hamburg,* the Gingerbread Castle, with its fairy-tale paraphernalia, appeals to all children. East of Hamburg, *Greenwood Lake,* which lies half in New York state, is a major recreational area 7 miles long and surrounded by rocks as high as 700 feet; it is a picturesque and popular vacation spot, as are all the lakes of northern New Jersey, particularly *Lakes Mohawk and Hopatcong.* East of Greenwood Lake, Ringwood Manor State Park preserves a fine old manor house whose wealth was derived from an iron furnace operating nearby. Still farther to the east, *Saddle River* presents the Tricker Water Gardens, with their aquatic plants and tropical fish, and the Grassyfork Fisheries, both open to the public. In *Paterson,* the first successful submarine is displayed in Westside Park; it was built by J.P. Holland, pioneer designer of our earliest submarine models. The New Jersey Section of *Palisades Interstate Park* includes the picturesque rock wall of the Palisades that rises straight up from the bank of the Hudson River, north of George Washington Bridge. A panoramic highway runs along the crest. On the heights of Weehawken occurred the historic duel between Aaron Burr and Alexander Hamilton. In the suburban area of Newark, *West Orange* is the seat of the Edison Museum, displaying the original models of many of Edison's inventions, as well as his desk and library. Eagle Rock is a famous lookout point over the metropolitan area toward the New York skyline. *Newark* is a modern, energetic industrial center, the largest city in New Jersey and part of a huge urban area including Jersey City, Hoboken and a dozen additional communities ranging from lovely hill-and-garden suburbs in the Oranges to manufacturing-and-residential sections near the Hudson. It is also an important communication center, a sea port and a large airport serving both Newark and New York. Toward the west we are in historic territory, with innumerable mementos of the American Revolution. In *Springfield,* in the center of town, is the fine old white church near which the battle of Springfield was fought. When the Revolutionary troops lacked gun wadding, Pastor James Caldwell did not hesitate to haul out the hymn books and use them for this patriotic purpose. In *Morristown National Historical Park,* the Ford Mansion, George Washington's headquarters during the winters of 1777 and 1779, is a museum now. Also the Continental Campgrounds at Jockey Hollow, with reconstructed Fort Nonsense and the Wick House, may be inspected. In the hills to the west the ruins of the ancient blast furnace at *Oxford* are interesting. The iron works furnished cannon balls both for the Revolutionary and the Civil Wars. At the Pennsylvania state line, the famous *Delaware Water Gap* is an impressive highlight of the beautiful Delaware Valley. The highway passes through the gorge on the Pennsylvania side.

CENTRAL NEW JERSEY   In *Elizabeth* a historic building of interest is Boxwood Manor, the mansion of Elias Boudinot, first President of the Continental Congress; the plain wooden house stands on East Jersey Street beside tall, modern office buildings. In Menlo Park, Edison operated his first large experimental laboratory, and there the electric lamp was invented. As a

memorial of this epochal event, the 134-foot *Edison Tower* is crowned with a huge, glowing replica of the original incandescent lamp bulb. New Brunswick and Princeton circumscribe the state's foremost area of education and research. *New Brunswick* is the seat of *Rutgers University,* colonial college, land grant college and state university in one; on its main campus, Queen's Building of 1810 is an historic landmark. The university's agricultural experiment station is one of the leaders in the field and its Institute of Microbiology is the world center for research in antibiotics. The Squibb Institute of Medical Research also is located in New Brunswick. *Princeton,* a lovely, tree-shaded town with fine old mansions in large gardens, is the home of *Princeton University,* famous for its research in physics and other fields, and pleasant to visit because of its splendid campus; its Nassau Hall of 1756 played an important role during the Revolutionary War: It served as the home of the first state legislature and of the Continental Congress, as a hospital and even as a battlefield when a decisive struggle came to an end within its walls. Also the Rockefeller Institute of Medical Research, the Institute of Advanced Studies, where international celebrities like Einstein are at work, and the Westminster Choir College have their homes in Princeton. Outside of Princeton, the Walker-Gordon Farm at *Plainsboro* opens its Rotolactor Building to the public; the automatic milking of cows on a sort of merry-go-round attracts crowds of spectators. The world's largest cooperative egg, poultry and livestock auctions may be witnessed in *Flemington,* farm center of central New Jersey; the town is also the seat of pottery and cut-glass works. Although the famous painting of "Washington Crossing the Delaware" was created on the Rhine, and although it shows the Stars and Stripes which did not exist at the time of the crossing, it has publicized effectively one of the most daring deeds of the Revolutionary War; the spot where the crossing occurred is now the pleasant *Washington's Crossing State Park.* *Trenton,* the state capital, is proud of several outstanding historic relics. The Trent House, a splendid Georgian colonial mansion built by William Trent in 1719, is open to visitors. The Old Barracks, an architectural gem erected in 1758 for colonial troops during the French-Indian War, housed British, Hessian and American soldiers; it is now a museum, whose collections include one of Continental currency. To the east near *Freehold,* the Old Tennent Church of 1751 and the Molly Pitcher Well mark the field of the Battle of Monmouth, of 1778. Along the coast, *Atlantic Highlands* offers a splendid marine view over Sandy Hook and Raritan Bay. *Asbury Park* and the other resorts of the coastal area are described on page 42.

SOUTHERN NEW JERSEY   *Burlington,* surrounded by large peach orchards, is the hometown of James Fenimore ("Leatherstocking") Cooper and Captain James ("Don't Give Up the Ship!") Lawrence. The Cooper birthplace is a museum of antique costumes, period pieces of furniture and manuscripts. The Lawrence home contains mementos of the naval hero of the War of 1812. In *Camden,* across the Delaware from Philadelphia, the Walt Whitman House at 330 Mickle Street is now a museum; the poet spent there the last eight years of his life, from 1884 to 1892; his grave is nearby. To the southwest, the Salem Oak at *Salem* is a magnificent, centuries-old tree under which the Quakers used to barter with the Indians. South of Salem, the *Hancock House* at Hancock's Bridge is a masterpiece of colonial brick masonry; it was the scene of the "patriot massacre" and is open to visitors. The Jersey shore, including *Atlantic City, Barnegat Lighthouse, Island Beach and Cape May* is described on page 42. At *Beach Haven,* on the same island on which Barnegat Lighthouse is located, the three-masted schooner Lucy Evelyn is now a marine museum.

STATE PARKS 20 state parks, 17 historic sites, 9 state forests. For details, write to Bureau of Forestry, Parks and Historic Sites, State House Annex, Trenton 7, N.J.

NEW MEXICO

For information, write to New Mexico State Tourist Bureau, State Capitol, Santa Fe, New Mexico.

NORTHEASTERN NEW MEXICO At *Capulin Mountain National Monument* a road leads to the summit of a recently extinct volcano rising 1500 feet above the surrounding plain.

NORTH CENTRAL NEW MEXICO The picturesque pueblo towns of *Taos* and Ranchos de Taos and the state capital, *Santa Fe,* are described on page 124. Twenty miles west of Santa Fe the *Bandelier National Monument* preserves ancient Pajaritan cliff dwellings, including a ceremonial cave. *San Ildefonso* is noted for its beautiful pottery with a texture and design all its own. Some Ildefonso Indians have become artists of repute. In the Cerrillos region, also near Santa Fe, the *Gem Turquoise Mines* are interesting; in the course of centuries they have been operated by such divergent interests as prehistoric Indians and the Tiffany people; guided tours are available. The pueblo nearest to Santa Fe is *Tesuque,* of the Rio Grande Pueblo Indians; the latter are adept in pottery making and painting in water colors. In the neighborhood of Santa Fe are also the *Puye Ruins* of a prehistoric Tewa Pueblo, and the ruins of the *Pecos Pueblo* of the 14th century, in the Pecos State Monument; on the same site are the ruins of a seventeenth-century mission church. A seven-foot-long, plumed serpent can be seen carved into the cliff of the *Tshirege Ruins* in Pajarito Canyon, twenty miles to the northwest of Santa Fe. The numerous cliff dwellings and ruins are reputed to have been the last ones to be abandoned. The carved serpent, by the way, is one of the finest examples of Indian art. To the east of Santa Fe, in the town of *Las Vegas,* New Mexico, relics of the Santa Fe Trail can still be inspected: deep ruts of the wagon tracks, and the ruins of Fort Union, which held such outlaws as Billy the Kid and the savage Indian chief Geronimo. *Albuquerque* with the University of New Mexico, and *Acoma Pueblo* near the Enchanted Mesa are described on page 126.

NORTHWESTERN NEW MEXICO *Aztec Ruins National Monument* was an "apartment house" of 500 rooms, with a great *kiva,* in the 12th century. *Chaco Canyon National Monument* preserves eighteen pueblo ruins, among them the Pueblo Bonito of 800 rooms. *Gallup* and its Indian festival are described on page 126. Forty-two miles south of Gallup, *Zuni Pueblo,* with its red sandstone houses and ancient mission church, is the home of the Zuni Indians, noted makers of turquoise jewelry. Nearby *El Morro National Monument* is a natural sandstone tower on which travelers of three and a half centuries have carved their names and sometimes their adventures, beginning with the Spanish explorers. This is the famous *Inscription Rock;* the earliest legible inscription is of the year 1605.

SOUTHERN NEW MEXICO The huge *Elephant Butte Dam* has transformed some 180,000 acres of desert into fertile farm lands producing long-staple cotton, sugar beets and vegetables; boating and fishing (bass, catfish, crappie) are popular on the reservoir. *Truth or Consequences* was formerly Hot Springs, a health resort offering mineralized mud baths. *Ruidoso* is a popular resort in the Sacramento Mountains, and at *Cloudcroft* golf may be played at an altitude of 9000 feet. *White Sands National Monument,* with its gypsum dunes, is described on page 122. *Roswell,* to the east, is the home of the New Mexico

Military Institute; every October the Eastern New Mexico State Fair and Roswell Rodeo attract thousands of visitors. Thirteen miles to the southeast, *Bottomless Lakes State Park* embraces a chain of lovely lakes surrounded by bluffs of delicate colors; the lakes were formed by cave-ins and are as deep as 600 feet. The famous *Carlsbad Caverns National Park* is described on page 122.

NATIONAL PARK IN NEW MEXICO *Carlsbad Caverns National Park,* see page 122.

NATIONAL FORESTS IN NEW MEXICO *Apache Nat.F.,* U.S. 60, 260, 666 (scenic Coronado Trail; Blue Range and Mt. Baldy Wilderness Areas). *Carson Nat.F.,* U.S. 64, State 3, 75, 38 (includes the home and burial place of Kit Carson, the Taos Indian Pueblo, Sangre de Cristo Mountains with 13,151 ft. Wheeler Peak, lakes and hot springs). *Gibola Nat.F.,* near Albuquerque, U.S. 85, 66 (Mt. Taylor and Sandia Crest, accessible by automobile road; ancient "sky city" of Acoma; antelope herds). *Gila Nat.F.* in southwestern New Mexico, U.S. 260, State 180, 61, 78, 25, 59 (five mountain ranges; several wilderness areas; Gila Cliff Dwellings National Monument). *Lincoln Nat.F.,* adjoining Carlsbad Caverns National Park and White Sands Nat. Monument, U.S. 54, 70, 380, State 83 (includes 12,000-ft. high White Mountain and extensive ponderosa pine and fir stands). *Santa Fe Nat.F.,* U.S. 285, 85, 64 (Sangre de Cristo Range; several wilderness areas; Indian villages; ruins of ancient pueblos and Spanish missions; cliff dwellings).

STATE PARKS 5 state parks, 10 state monuments, 16 wayside picnic areas. For details, write to State Park Commission, Santa Fe, New Mexico.

NEW YORK

For information, write to Travel Bureau, Dept. of Commerce, 112 State Street, Albany 7, N.Y.

EASTERN NEW YORK The skyline of New York City rivals the Grand Canyon as the foremost American sight, best-known to the world at large. A description of *New York City* is found on page 34. As an educational center, New York is the seat of some of the world's largest and best institutions of higher learning: *Columbia University, New York University,* the Catholic *Fordham University,* the urban *City Colleges* and the *New School for Social Research.* Those interested in an outline of all the sights of the big city, including the schedule for steamer trips to the Statue of Liberty, may write to the New York Convention and Visitors Bureau, 500 Park Avenue, New York 22, N.Y. Of the various beaches of the metropolitan area, *Coney Island* is a world-famous super-amusement park, a great attraction for the younger set and quite interesting to their parents. *Jones Beach* to the east on Long Island, handles tens of thousands of visitors, yet it is one of the cleanest and most pleasant Atlantic resorts; its 2400 acres consist of three miles of white beaches, facilities for all sorts of sports, a mile-long boardwalk, bath houses, restaurants and the Marine Stadium at Zach's Bay, where operettas in extravaganza style delight 10,000 spectators every summer night. One of the most fashionable resorts on Long Island is *Southampton,* 110 miles from New York City; elegant summer residences and expensive shops predominate, but the resort is also an historic town with interesting old houses, some of them dating back to the seventeenth century. *Montauk Point* is the picturesque eastern end of Long Island, a popular surf fishing, deep-sea fishing and sailing area. In the beautiful *Hudson Valley,* the following sights are described on page 36: on the eastern bank *Tarrytown* with Washington Irving's "Sunnyside"; *North Tarrytown* with the Phillipse Castle; *Pough-*

keepsie with Vassar College; *Hyde Park* and the Franklin D. Roosevelt Library; *Staatsburg* with the Mills Memorial; *Kinderhook* with the Van Buren homestead and *Rensselaer* with Fort Crailo, erected in 1642, believed to be the birthplace of "Yankee Doodle" (a British officer watched American militiamen riding by; their appearance struck him as humorous, and he wrote down the words of the famous song). On the west bank, *Bear Mountain State Park,* the Storm King Highway and *West Point* are listed on page 36. West of West Point, *Goshen* has a famous track for trotting races; it is the seat of "the Hall of Fame of the Trotter." *Newburgh* is picturesquely located on bluffs above the broad Hudson. During the Revolutionary War it was Washington's headquarters for 16 months; in the Hasbrouck House, where the General stayed, his famous letter opposing monarchy for the U.S. was written. Hasbrouck House is a museum now. Opposite Newburgh, on the other side of the river, the summit of Mt. Beacon may be scaled with an electric incline railway. North of Newburgh, the *Catskill Mountains,* one of the most popular resort areas near New York City, are described on page 36. Near Catskill, the Catskill Game Farm raises various animals for zoological gardens, from donkeys and ostriches to llamas and bisons; it is open to the public. Other attractions in the Catskill area are the *Belleayre* ski center, with a 3000-foot chair lift, and *Mt. Utsayantha,* near Stamford, with a height of 3213 feet and a toll road leading to the summit. In *Albany,* the state capitol and the pre-revolutionary Philip Schuyler mansion are interesting; the observation tower of the state office building offers a fine panorama of the city. *Saratoga Springs* is one of America's oldest resorts. Its famous race track, established in 1865, was the first one in the U.S.; its spa and its mineral waters enjoy a wide reputation; east of the town are Saratoga Lake and Saratoga National Historical Park, where the turning point of the Revolution occurred: There American troops won their victory over Burgoyne in 1777. To the west of the city, the Petrified Sea Gardens show a "garden" of plants which grew there when the sea covered the valley eons ago. To the west, a number of smaller communities have points of interest of their own. *Gloversville* is America' glove manufacturing center; plant tours can be arranged. In *Johnstown,* the colonial mansion of the Mohawk Valley leader Sir William Johnson, is a museum now. In *Amsterdam,* Guy Park Manor was also built by Sir William, in 1766; its period furnishings are interesting. Near Amsterdam, the Auriesville Shrine is on the site of St. Isaac Jogues' martyrdom in 1646; in the Coliseum (seating 10,000 people) daily services are held during the summer. The *Howe Caverns* near Cobleskill, 200 feet underground, are a popular tourist attraction. *Cooperstown* on Otsego Lake (of Leatherstocking fame) is the home of the Fenimore House, with folkart displays and historical exhibits; the Baseball Hall of Fame and the Farmers' Museum, which contains early farm implements. At Dolgeville, the *Beaversprite Sanctuary* is a colony of tame beavers; they can be seen "working" in the late afternoon.

NORTHEASTERN NEW YORK   At *Glen Falls* on the Hudson River, *Cooper's Cave* has been made famous by James Fenimore Cooper's *Last of the Mohicans.* *Lake George* is a long-established recreational area and one of the loveliest spots in the state: 32 miles long, it is surrounded by wooded mountains and dotted with green islands and white sailboats; also, all winter sports flourish in the area. At Pottersville, the *Natural Stone Bridge* arches 62 feet above the river in a 180-foot span. The restored *Fort Ticonderoga,* with its heavy masonry walls, dark dungeons and big cannon, is a fascinating contrast to the little wooden palisade forts of the frontier; the view over *Lake Champlain* is superb. In the *Crown Point Reservation,* also at Lake Cham-

plain, the ruins of two forts are mementos of the French-Indian Wars. To the north the *Ausable Chasm* near Keeseville is the spectacular canyon of the Ausable River; see also page 38. Also a description of the *Thousand Islands* of the St. Lawrence River can be found on page 38. To the southeast, near Carthage, the *Natural Bridge Caverns,* 1000 feet underground, may be inspected by boat; the "natural bridge" spans the Indian River. *Syracuse,* a thriving industrial center, is the seat of *Syracuse University* and of the French Fort which dates back to the very first attempt to settle central New York. The *Finger Lakes, Ithaca* with *Cornell University* and *Watkins Glen* are described on page 40. Near Waterloo, the *Scythe Tree* is an oddity; a Balm of Gilead tree has grown around the scythes which the farm boys hung on the tree branches when they left home for the Civil War and World War I. South of the Finger Lakes, *Corning* is a world-famous glass center; glass factory and glass museum are open to visitors. To the southwest of the Finger Lakes, the *Hammondsport-Naples-Urbana* region is one of America's leading wine and champagne producers. *Rochester* is a world center for the manufacture of photographic and optical goods; the Eastman Kodak plants may be seen on guided tours and the Photo Museum, at the George Eastman House, has interesting exhibits. On the cultural side, the city is the seat of the University of Rochester, the famous Eastman School of Music, the Rochester Symphony Orchestra and the beautiful Lilac Gardens.

WESTERN NEW YORK   50 miles southwest of Rochester, *Letchworth State Park* is a popular 13,000-acre recreational area. Farther south, at the Pennsylvania state line, *Rock City* offers a broad view of the surrounding country from huge rock formations. To the west, *Panama Rocks* is an erupted ocean floor, with gorges and crevices. *Chautauqua,* on the lake with the same name, is the seat of the Chautauqua Institution and its program of adult education. Once a nation-wide organization, it is now restricted to the summer resort of Chautauqua proper. *Buffalo,* New York's second-largest city, has a fascinating waterfront on Lake Erie, with huge grain elevators, wharves and ships; the Peace Bridge to Canada and the Albright Art Gallery are other attractions; the city is also the seat of the University of Buffalo. The nearby *Niagara Falls* and Fort Niagara are described on page 40.

STATE PARKS   64 state parks, 5 state reservations, 2 state forest preserves and numerous historic sites. For details, write to Division of Parks, 509 Arcade Building, Albany 7, N.Y.

NORTH CAROLINA

For information write to State Travel Bureau, Dept. of Conservation and Development, Raleigh, N.C.

THE COAST OF NORTH CAROLINA   The *Kill Devil Hill National Memorial,* honoring the Wright Brothers, the *Fort Raleigh National Historic Site* on Roanoke Island and the *Cape Hatteras National Seashore Recreation Area* are described on page 56. *Edenton* on Albemarle Sound, site of the Edenton Tea Party, is a fine old town with colonial homes and public buildings. In *New Bern,* at the mouth of the Neuse River, Tryon Palace is the early colonial capitol, being restored now. In *Wilmington,* North Carolina's largest port, tourist attractions are the Cornwallis House, believed to have been built in the 1770's, and Greenfield Park. South of the city, Airlie gardens and Orton Plantation gardens are famous for their beautiful azaleas, camellias and ancient oaks. The innumerable sounds and inlets of the coast offer fine fishing. Freshwater lakes also are available; *Lake Mattamuskeet,* near Pamlico Sound, is the largest, with a water surface of approximately 100 square miles.

PIEDMONT NORTH CAROLINA In the southern tier of the state, *Charlotte* is the seat of the Mint Museum, an exhibit of arts, crafts and historic relics in a former mint building. To the east, *Gaddy's Goose Refuge* in Ansonville is a safe haven for thousands of wildfowl where visitors are welcome; the season lasts from October to spring. Farther to the east, *Pinehurst* and *Southern Pines* are famous mid-South resorts with magnificent golf courses and all facilities for equestrian sports; steeplechases and horse shows are annual events. In *Fayetteville*, the Old Slave Market is a beautiful building with tower and arcades, housing a Civil War museum and library. In the northern tier of the Piedmont plateau, *Winston-Salem* is said to be the world's greatest tobacco manufacturing center, since Camels and other cigarettes are made there. Both the factories and the tobacco auctions are interesting. Old Salem preserves a number of colonial buildings of the Moravian community of 1766, including the Home Moravian Church and God's Acre (the graveyard), Bethabara Moravian Church, Moravian Brothers' House, the Salem Tavern, and the Wachovia Historical Society Museum. North of the city, *Pilot Mountain* offers a broad panorama, with a toll road leading to the summit of the solitary pinnacle; *Hanging Rock State Park* is a recreational area. East of Winston-Salem, *Greensboro* is the site of *Guilford Courthouse National Military Park,* with monuments and a museum honoring the Revolutionary battle. Nearby *Sedgefield* is a popular resort. To the east, *Chapel Hill* is the seat of the *University of North Carolina;* of special interest on the campus are the Coker Arboretum and the Morehead Planetarium. *Durham,* the town where Chesterfields and other cigarettes are manufactured, is the seat of *Duke University.* On the beautiful campus the chapel's campanile with a 50-bell carillon is a landmark; the Sarah Duke Gardens are lovely. *Raleigh,* the state capital, has a number of attractions: the state capitol built of local granite; the Hall of History, where exhibits illustrate the history of North Carolina, and the tiny frame building where the seventeenth President of the United States, Andrew Johnson, was born. On the State Fairgrounds is the *State Fair Arena,* one of America's most striking modern structures. Raleigh is also the seat of North Carolina State College, home of a nuclear reactor and a center of nuclear research.

WESTERN NORTH CAROLINA The spectacular *Blue Ridge Parkway* is described on page 58. At *Mt. Airy,* near the Virginia state line, the open-faced granite quarry is one of the largest on earth; visitors are welcome. *Blowing Rock,* to the south on the Parkway, offers a wide mountain view. The unusual name is derived from the strange air currents in the flume formed by the walls of the mountain, causing a piece of paper or a feather thrown into the gorge to be blown back by the wind. In the resort town of Blowing Rock the Moses Cone Memorial Park and the Parkway Craft Center are of interest. In nearby *Boone,* the Daniel Boone Amphitheater presents the open-air drama "Horn in the West" in a natural setting of hills and trees. To the southwest, the noted resort of *Linville* offers a number of tourist attractions: Linville Caverns, just east of the Parkway; Linville Falls and Gorge and Grandfather Mountain, which has an abrupt rise of 5,964 feet but may be scaled on an automobile toll road. Another mountain peak reached by a side road from the Blue Ridge Parkway is *Mt. Mitchell,* at an elevation of 6,684 ft. the highest summit east of the Mississippi. North of Asheville, the *Craggy Gardens* contain the largest stand of purple rhododendron found on earth; some bushes are twelve feet tall. The resort town of *Asheville,* with the Biltmore Estate, is described on page 58. The boyhood home of the famous novelist Thomas Wolfe also is in Asheville. East of Asheville, *Lake Lure* with Hickory Nut Gorge and *Chimney Rock* is a tourist attraction; the latter is a 300-ft. boulder, with an elevator to take visitors to the top. South of Asheville, a number of resorts are popular with winter guests from the Deep South: Waynesville, Hendersonville, Saluda, Tryon (famous for fine hand weaving), Brevard (home of the Transylvania Music Festival) and Highlands. Near Highlands are the Bridal Veil Falls; a visitor can drive his automobile right under the rushing waterfall. Between Highlands and Cashiers a toll road leads to the summit of Whiteside Mountain (4,930 ft.). The *Great Smoky Mountains National Park,* the *Cherokee Reservation* and the mountainside theater where the outdoor drama "Unto These Hills" is enacted during the summer are described on page 60. *Fontana Dam,* the world's fourth highest and a part of the TVA system, creates a 30-mile long reservoir with good fishing facilities. Fontana Village is a nearby resort. *Hot Springs,* north of the Great Smoky Mountains National Park, has been a popular spa ever since Indian days.

NATIONAL PARK IN NORTH CAROLINA *Great Smoky Mountains National Park,* see page 60.

NATIONAL FORESTS IN NORTH CAROLINA Croatan Nat.F., U.S. 17, 70 (three miles from Atlantic Ocean, includes historic New Bern; Civil War breastworks; five large lakes; stands of pine and swamp hardwoods). *Nantahala Nat.F.,* U.S. 19, 64, 129, 23 (includes Fontana Dam; Joyce Kilmer Memorial Forest with magnificent virgin hemlocks; 60 miles of Appalachian Trail; waterfalls; azaleas, rhododendrons). *Pisgah Nat.F.,* U.S. 19, 23, 25, 64, 70, 221, 276, 321 and Blue Ridge Parkway (Mt. Mitchell, Mt. Pisgah, Looking Glass Mountain; Craggy Gardens; Roan Mountain; several Game Management Areas with annual big game hunts).

STATE PARKS 10 state parks, 3 recreational areas. For details, write to Division of State Parks, Box 2719, Raleigh, North Carolina.

NORTH DAKOTA

For information write to Greater North Dakota Association, 311 Broadway, Fargo, N.D.

NORTHERN NORTH DAKOTA The *Turtle Mountains* are gently rolling hills embracing lovely small lakes, near Dunseith. To commemorate more than a hundred years of peace between Canada and the United States, the *International Peace Garden* has been established astride the international border; its central feature is a cairn of stones and boulders from both countries. At the Turtle Mountain Indian Reservation, the Sun Dance of the Chippewas is an attraction every year in June. To the west of the Peace Garden several wildlife refuges have been established; the largest is the *Souris National Migratory Bird Refuge.*

EASTERN NORTH DAKOTA *Devils Lake* is the remnant of a glacial sea that has been steadily shrinking; half a century ago, the town of Devils Lake was a thriving steamboat landing; now its location is five miles inland. Nevertheless, the lake is still the largest in North Dakota. Adjoining the lake, *Sully's Hill National Game Preserve* is a refuge for deer, elk, and bison. The whole area is popular with campers and picnickers. West of Mayville, one mile south of highway 7, the original prairie homestead of the *Thorval Stavens Farm* is now an interesting pioneer museum. *Fargo,* on the Minnesota state line, is the farm supply center of the prosperous Red River Valley. Its many parks, the campus of the North Dakota Agricultural College and the grounds of the State Fair are attractive. Nearby,

Ft. Abercrombie was restored with palisades and blockhouses.

CENTRAL NORTH DAKOTA At *Beulah,* a tour into a large lignite coal mine, on an underground train and in a miner's outfit, is an interesting experience. *Bismarck's* landmark is the 18-story state capitol which rises as a bright and functional column from the plains. On the capitol grounds the statue of Sacajawea, the "bird woman" of the Shoshone Indians who guided Lewis and Clark to the West, looks toward the setting sun. Other mementoes of the past are the Chimney Butte ranch house of Theodore Roosevelt, built of cottonwood logs, which was taken from the Badlands to Bismarck, and the Liberty Memorial Building with a fine historical collection of Dakotiana. At nearby Mandan, *Fort Lincoln State Park* is established on the site from which General Custer set out to his "last stand" at the Little Big Horn; the old fort has been reproduced with its blockhouses and stockades; also several Indian earth lodges have been reconstructed. To the south, straddling the North and South Dakota state line at Fort Yates, the *Standing Rock Indian Reservation* of several thousand Sioux Indians has been so called because of a sacred gray stone which is shaped like a sitting woman. To the Sioux, this "standing rock" is a holy symbol which they always took along on their tribal migrations. Another Indian sanctuary at Fort Yates is the grave of Sitting Bull.

WESTERN NORTH DAKOTA The *Badlands of North Dakota,* which have no connection with those of South Dakota, consist of fantastically shaped buttes of various colors, with tops that are level with the big plateau. The Little Missouri winds its way through canyons and land cuts. The Badlands can best be seen in *Theodore Roosevelt National Memorial Park* which also includes a Petrified Forest and parts of the old Roosevelt Ranch. The park consists of three units, the north unit near Watford City and the two units around *Medora.* The latter city was a thriving cattle center when Teddy Roosevelt operated his Elkhorn Ranch near there in the 1880's. The Rough Riders Hotel still stands on Main Street; the name may have suggested the "Rough Riders" slogan for Teddy Roosevelt's cavalry outfit in the Spanish American War. Also in Medora is the De Mores Historic Site, the 28-room chateau of a French pioneer who became a ranching-and-meat-packing millionaire. South of Medora at *Amidon,* perpetually burning coal mines are a weird sight. To the northeast of the Roosevelt Memorial park, the *Verendrye National Monument* commemorates the explorations of Verendrye in North Dakota.

STATE PARKS 4 state parks, 6 recreational areas, 16 state historic sites. For details write to State Historical Society of North Dakota, Bismarck, N.D.

OHIO

For information, write to Development and Publicity Commission, 21 W. Broad Street, Columbus 15, Ohio.

EASTERN OHIO For an all-round view of *Cleveland,* the observation platform of the 52-story Terminal Tower is recommended. Visitors will be impressed with the colorful harbor and lakefront; the nine beautiful parks with 14 miles of waterfront that can be reached by a parkway circling the metropolis and the Public Square and Mall with the Cleveland Museum of Art, the Municipal Stadium and Severance Hall. The Cleveland Symphony Orchestra and Western Reserve University are outstanding institutions. American groups of foreign birth or background have been especially active in Cleveland in keeping alive their colorful Old-World costumes, dances and songs; in one instance, thirty such groups have united in creating the international Cultural Gardens, each group contributing the loveliest and most typical flowers of their homeland. Southwest of Cleveland, *Oberlin* is the seat of Oberlin College, the world's first coeducational academic institution. South of Cleveland, *Akron* is the country's rubber capital; it uses about forty per cent of all the raw rubber produced on earth, with automobile tires its principal product. The International Soap Box Derby, well-known to every boy ten or twelve years of age, is held in Akron in August. South of Akron, near New Philadelphia, *Schoenbrunn Village* has been authentically restored as it looked in 1772 when it was a Moravian mission colony, the first town in Ohio; it was abandoned in 1777. *Marietta* on the Ohio River was the first permanent white settlement in the state. It is the home of Marietta College and the Campus Martius Museum with historic relics of Indian and pioneer days.

CENTRAL OHIO On a peninsula between Lake Erie and Sandusky Bay, *Marblehead* and the neighboring archipelago of Lake Erie islands are a popular recreational area; all water sports flourish. Two famous landmarks dominate the scene: the lighthouse of Marblehead and Perry's Victory Nat'l Monument on South Bass Island at Put-in-Bay. *Columbus,* the state capital, is also the seat of *Ohio State University,* one of America's leading institutions of higher learning. The Ohio State Museum, located on the campus, contains a unique relic of the state's history: the Coonskin Library, first collection of books in Ohio. To the southeast of Columbus, near the town of Logan, the *Hocking Parks* are a chain of state parks in a region that is ideal for hiking, camping and picnicking; streams and waterfalls, spectacular rocks and caves, gorges and boulders dot the pleasant forest land. Cantwell Cliffs and Ash Cave State Parks are best-known in the series. *Mound City Group National Monument,* south of Columbus near Chillicothe, preserves some fascinating remnants of a prehistoric civilization once flourishing there. Surrounded by a three-foot embankment are twenty-three mounds containing human skeletons and altars; the mounds were built by an unknown race which made utensils of wood, stone and pottery, learned to weave fabrics and used freshwater pearls as ornaments. The most amazing of these prehistoric relics is the 1,300-foot-long *Serpent Mound,* southwest of Chillicothe; the structure of this weird effigy, whose original purpose or meaning is not known, is especially impressive if seen from the air.

WESTERN OHIO *Toledo* has a famous art museum; besides paintings and sculptures, the museum maintains a collection of ancient and modern glass said to be the most extensive and outstanding in the world. At the Indiana state line, *Fort Recovery* has been reconstructed as it was built by General Anthony Wayne in 1793; an interesting pioneer museum is on the site of the fort. *Dayton* is a symbol of the birth and growth of American aviation. It was the home town of the Wright brothers, and the small plane that made history on December 17, 1903, was designed and built in Dayton. Ever since then the city has been an aviation center, and today its Wright Field is the foremost experimental base of our Air Force; numerous improvements in modern aviation have been developed there. Dayton Art Institute displays some unusual specialties like an old Florentine Art Studio, and Dayton's Carillon Park with Deeds Carillon and various historic relics is a showplace. East of Dayton, *Yellow Springs* is the home of Antioch College, leader of a progressive system of education in which theoretical study alternates with practical work. A general panorama of *Cincinnati* can best be enjoyed from the top of the 574-foot-high Carew Tower; it is the city's tallest building. Also the Navigation Monument in Eden Park offers a broad view. Among Cincinnati's outstanding cultural institutions are the Taft House, the Museum of Art, the University of Cincinnati and the Cincinnati Symphony Orchestra.

NATIONAL FOREST IN OHIO *Wayne Nat.F.,* U.S. 21, 23, 33, 35, 50, 52 (hardwood forests, especially beautiful in fall coloring; old charcoal and iron furnaces; nearby points of interest are Marietta, Gallipolis and a barren island in the Ohio River named Blennerhasset's Island, where a wonderful story of intrigue and treason took place with Aaron Burr as the principal actor).

STATE PARKS 33 state parks, 1 recreational area, 19 state forests, 52 state memorials. For details, write to Division of Parks, Ohio Departments Building, Columbus 15, Ohio.

OKLAHOMA

For information write to Oklahoma Planning and Resources Broad, 533 State Capitol, Oklahoma City 5, Oklahoma.

NORTHERN OKLAHOMA *Pensacola Dam* near Vinita and Pryor forms Lake o' the Cherokees and thus creates a great playground for fishermen and sailors; like many man-made reservoirs, Lake o' the Cherokees has a "contour line" of numerous little bays and harbors where people from northern Oklahoma keep boats for vacations and weekends. The *Woolaroc Art Museum* stands in a game preserve, 14 miles south of Bartlesville; buffaloes and longhorns are kept in the preserve, also big-game animals from other continents; the museum collection displays Indian art objects, trophies and costumes, mostly of the Osage Tribe. In the Oklahoma Panhandle, *Hallock Park* is a recreational area of mesas, canyons and 120 springs, with good swimming in an artificial lake; fascinating are the Indian pictographs of the park: They are six feet high, are painted in brilliant blue on sand-colored rock and extend for a whole mile. Near Freedom, 110 miles northwest of Enid, the *Alabaster Caverns* may be visited on guided tours; electric lights bring out the unique and often fantastic shapes and colors of the rocks. As in the Carlsbad Caverns, huge numbers of bats live in the caves, swarm out at twilight and return before sunrise. A 150-foot-high natural bridge is a special attraction near the caverns. *Tulsa,* the "oil capital of the world," and the *Will Rogers Memorial* at Claremore are described on p. 112. Sixty miles southeast of Muskogee, the three ancient *Spiro Indian Mounds* antedate the era of the white man. The origin of these archaeological relics is not certain; possibly Aztecs built them.

SOUTHERN OKLAHOMA *Oklahoma City* with the state capitol is described on page 112. Twenty miles to the south, *Norman* is the seat of the *University of Oklahoma* and its widely known university press. Northwest of Lawton, the *Wichita Mountains Wildlife Refuge* is not only an interesting game preserve of buffalo, antelope and elk herds (see p. 113), but also a public playground with 90 small and 15 large lakes, all of them man-made and stocked with various species of fish. From the summit of Mt. Scott which can be reached by car, a wide panorama of hills, blue waters, boulders and rock formations may be enjoyed. The annual fall round-up of the big-game animals for vaccination, transfer to another preserve, or slaughter is a thrilling spectacle; cowboys on fast horses are in charge of the corralling. The Wichita Mountains Easter Pageant, staged by the citizens of Lawton in the Wildlife Refuge, is a famous annual event which draws large numbers of spectators. Near Sulphur, *Platt National Park* is a preserve of thirty-one large and many small springs, in a picturesque setting of streams and wildflowers, woods and far views of the Arbuckle Mountains. It is described on page 113. West of the park, at Davis, the *Turner Falls* are a lovely landmark. South and east of Ardmore, a great vacation

and water-sports area has been created. Within a 20,000-acre park, *Lake Murray* is a rendezvous for fishermen, sailors and bathers; nearby, the huge man-made *Lake Texoma* is also developing excellent opportunities for all water sports; the scenery surrounding the lake is beautiful. The ride from Madill to Durant via the mile-long Roosevelt Bridge offers interesting views.

NATIONAL PARK IN OKLAHOMA *Platt National Park,* see page 113.

NATIONAL FOREST IN OKLAHOMA *Ouachita Nat.F.,* U.S. 59, 270, 271 (Winding Stair and Kiamichi Mts.; Rich Mt. at Ark. border is of interest to naturalists because of the amazing number of species of trees and plants.)

STATE PARKS 9 state parks, 4 historic sites, numerous waysides. For details write to Division of Recreation and State Parks, Oklahoma Planning and Resources Board, State Capitol Building, Oklahoma City 5, Oklahoma.

OREGON

For information, write to Travel Information Department, Oregon State Highway Commission, Salem, Oregon.

THE COAST OF OREGON At the mouth of the Columbia River, *Astoria* is the oldest white settlement in the state, established as a fur trading post in 1811. An excellent spot to survey its setting is the observation platform of the 125-foot-high *Astor Column* on Coxcomb Hill; from there one enjoys a splendid panorama of ocean and river, city and docks, ferries and deep-sea trollers. The monument is decorated with a continuous pictorial strip wound around the column in a spiral, depicting the colorful story of the fur-trading fort now a fishing port. The city's waterfront is fascinating, with its salmon nets hundreds of feet long, and boats and teams of horses manipulating the nets. Besides salmon, Astoria handles millions of pounds of tuna, cod, clams, crabs and even sharks. The week before Labor Day, a great water-sports festival is held every year, climaxed by the Astoria Salmon Derby. *Oregon's Coastal Highway,* one of America's showplaces, is described on page 156, together with *Seaside,* the popular bathing resort, *Cannon Beach* and Haystack Rock, *Otter Crest State Park, Devil's Punch Bowl, Agate Beach,* the picturesque old fishing town of *Newport,* the *Sea Lion Caves, Coos Bay, Port Orford* and the highest point of the road at Carpenterville, near the California state line. On the southern coast of Oregon a rocky peninsula juts out into the ocean, where, in 1851, a group of prospectors fought their way out of an ambush of hostile Indians, an event commemorated by *Battle Rock State Park.*

NORTHERN OREGON *Portland* is one of America's "rose cities"; its International Rose Test Gardens are exciting, and the Rose Festival in June is a great event for Portlanders and visitors. The city is described on page 152. The spectacular *Columbia River Highway* with Crown Point, the Columbia River Gorge, the Multnomah Falls, Bonneville Dam and the Celilo Falls are described on page 152. Portland's great landmark, the snow-capped *Mt. Hood* with Timberline Lodge, is described on page 154. In the northeastern part of the state, the city of *Pendleton* is a farming and ranching supply center. Every September it is host to the Pendleton Round-Up, a three-day rodeo and Indian ceremonial which is one of the gayest and most colorful pageants of the Northwest. There are large camps of real tepees; covered wagons are pulled by teams of twelve longhorns plodding along under their wooden yokes and in the center of town, Happy Canyon invites the celebrants to saloons, gambling houses and dance halls.

CENTRAL OREGON The *Southern Cascades* with *Mt. Hood* and *Mt. Jefferson* are described on page 154. South of Mt. Jefferson, the following spot is of interest: *Cove Palisades State Park*, west of Culver, established around the "Cove," a 1,000-foot canyon where the Deschutes and the Crooked Rivers unite. Trout fishing is fine in both rivers and the scenery is magnificent. The *McKenzie Lava Fields,* one of the largest lava beds in Oregon, consisting of thousands of acres of cinder cones and volcanic dust, can be seen from *McKenzie Pass,* on highway 28. Approaching the pass, the *Three Sisters* are among the spectacular peaks of the Cascades. The town of *Bend* is the starting point of the 87-mile-long *Century Drive,* a loop of scenic roadway south and east of the Three Sisters. Elk Lake, Deschutes River and the Devil's Chair are popular points for sightseeing, fishing and hunting. The drive leads to crystal lakes, glacial meadows and mountain forests. In Bend proper, thousands of waterfowl may be watched in Drake City Park. *Pilot Butte State Park* is to the east of Bend; the attraction in this park is a 500-foot-high cinder cone whose summit, accessible by automobile, offers a splendid view of the snow-capped Cascades. Twelve miles south of Bend, *Lava River Caves State Park* preserves a geologically unique phenomenon: a natural tunnel 5,460 feet long and 35 feet high. *Crescent Lake* and *Odell Lake* as well as several smaller ones can be reached from highway 58; this is a popular recreational area, with emphasis on boating and horseback riding.

THE WILLAMETTE VALLEY OF NORTHWESTERN OREGON The fertile and beautiful valley of the Willamette River is one of Oregon's most densely populated areas. South of Portland, *Champoeg State Park* contains picnic sites and a museum of Oregoniana; on the site of the park the first provisional government of the territory was established by Americans in 1843, before it was legally determined whether the region would belong to Great Britain or the United States. In Oregon City, the *McLoughlin Mansion* of 1846 is now a museum of Oregon relics and a National Historic Site; its builder, Dr. John McLoughlin, was a director of the Hudson's Bay Company and for all practical purposes, the ruler of the northwest country. The state capitol at *Salem* is a beautiful modern building, with a huge symbolic figure of the Pioneer. To the east are Silver Falls State Park, the Detroit Dam and, on the western slopes of the Cascades, *Breitenbush Springs,* a resort with some fifty mineral hot springs. *Eugene* is the home of the *University of Oregon.*

EASTERN OREGON *Enterprise* is the gateway to the magnificent *Wallowa Mountains,* a mountain wilderness with, however, a few "civilized" spots. At *Wallowa Lake* and its lodge not only fishing and all water sports are available but also riding and golfing. At the southern end of the lake, bighorn sheep may be observed in a game refuge. Glacier Lake with Eagle Cap in the background is another beauty spot. On the Idaho state line, the *Grand Canyon of the Snake River* is truly wild country; the gorge is deeper than that of the Grand Canyon of Arizona. A good view of the roaring river may be had from the lookout tower of Hat Point, see also under Idaho, page 140. On the dry plateau near John Day, the *John Day Fossil Beds State Park* permits a glance into the early eras of the earth. Fossils have been unearthed there of huge mastodons and miniature horses, of giant sloths and saber-toothed tigers. In *Canyon City,* next to John Day, the four-room cabin built in 1864 by the poet Joaquin Miller is a museum now; the trees he planted still bear fruit. *Owyhee Dam,* one of America's major reclamation projects, and at 405 feet, the second highest dam on earth, creates a 52-mile-long lake and irrigates about 100,000 acres of land.

SOUTHERN OREGON *Crater Lake National Park,* one of the continent's truly unique sights, is described on page 154. To the southwest, *Oregon Caves National Monument* has been established at a chain of great limestone and marble caverns, extending underground for miles and having, in some places, sixty foot ceilings. The rock formations are of weird and varied beauty. Guided tours are available. South of Crater Lake, the region of *Upper Klamath Lake* attracts students of wildlife. The lake itself is the largest fresh-water body west of the Rockies and its shores are lined with the rookeries of waterfowl. Particularly interesting are the huge numbers of white pelicans which like to nest at Upper Klamath Lake, nearby Lake Ewauna and the Link River on which the city of Klamath Falls is located. Most of the nesting areas have been set aside as bird refuges by the Federal Government. Once upon a time there was also a Lower Klamath Lake, but it vanished when the Klamath Basin Irrigation Project was constructed. To the east, highway 395 passes through a most picturesque spot north of Valley Falls. On the western side there are the rippling waters of *Lake Abert;* on the eastern side, *Abert Rim* rises steeply for 2,000 feet, like a huge, 19-mile-long sector of the Chinese Wall. The foot of the rim proved a fertile hunting ground for archaeologists who found there pictographs and arrowheads, fossils and skeletons. Unfortunately, Abert Lake dries out in years of drought. Few tourists travel to the *Hart Mountain Antelope Refuge* east of Abert Lake, but occasionally a thrilling sight can be seen from the highway: Over the plain, set off by barren mountains in the distance, a herd of sixty or seventy antelopes runs by, a picture reminiscent of the African steppe. About 10,000 pronghorn antelopes, America's largest herd, live in this refuge.

NATIONAL PARK IN OREGON *Crater Lake National Park,* see page 155.

NATIONAL FORESTS IN OREGON *Deschutes Nat.F.,* U.S. 28, 97 (snow-clad peaks; ice caves; waterfalls; mountain lakes; includes Century Drive from Bend; several wilderness areas). *Fremont Nat.F.,* U.S. 395 (Abert Rim and Antelope Refuge; Oregon desert). *Malheur Nat.F.,* U.S. 28, 395 (Joaquin Miller Cabin at Canyon City; ponderosa pine forests; archers' hunting reserve; miles of fishing streams). *Mt. Hood Nat.F.,* U.S. 30, 99 (Mt. Hood; Mt. Jefferson; Timberline Lodge; Multnomah Falls; glaciers; lakes; alpine wildflower meadows). *Ochoco Nat.F.,* near Prineville, U.S. 28, 97 (natural parks; ponderosa pine forests; beaver colonies; frontier day army post, scene of bitter range wars). *Rogue River Nat.F.,* surrounding Oregon Caves, U.S. 99 (trout streams; water falls; lakes; forests of sugar pine and Douglas fir). *Siskiyou Nat.F.,* near southern Oregon coast, U.S. 99, 101, 199 (famous fishing grounds in lower Rogue River Gorge, home of Port Orford cedar and Oregon myrtle). *Siuslaw Nat.F.,* U.S. 20, 99, 101 (bordered by Pacific Ocean; sand dunes; stands of Sitka spruce, hemlock, rhododendron, azaleas). *Umatilla Nat.F.,* near Pendleton, U.S. 30, 395 (on the old Oregon Trail; Blue Mountains; hot sulphur springs). *Umpqua Nat.F.,* north of Crater Lake Nat. Park, U.S. 99 (spectacular North Umpqua Cataracts; Diamond Lake). *Wallowa Nat.F.,* near Enterprise, U.S. 30 (snow-capped peaks; glaciers; Snake River and Imnaha Canyons from Grizzly Ridge Road). *Whitman Nat.F.,* near Baker, U.S. 28, 395, 30 (Blue and Wallowa Mountains). *Willamette Nat.F.,* U.S. 20, 28, 54 (McKenzie Pass Highway; Mt. Jefferson and Three Sisters Wilderness Areas; snow-capped peaks; hot springs; most heavily timbered national forest in the U.S.).

STATE PARKS 180 state parks and areas, 11 historic sites. For details, write to State Parks Department, 402 Livesley Building, Salem, Oregon.

PENNSYLVANIA

For information write to Vacation and Recreation Bureau, Department of Commerce, Harrisburg, Pa.

EASTERN PENNSYLVANIA *Philadelphia* is an historical, industrial and cultural center, the seat of the University of Pennsylvania; it is described on page 44. The American Sanctuary of *Valley Forge* is described on page 44. From the neighborhood of Valley Forge the famous *Pennsylvania Turnpike* runs across the state, for 327 miles, to the Ohio border. The first one of America's cross-country toll roads, it is still considered the most spectacular one, with seven long tunnels leading through seven mountain ranges and now connects with the New Jersey and Ohio Turnpikes. East of Philadelphia, on a peninsula in the Delaware River near Tullytown, William Penn's summer home *Pennsbury Manor* has been reconstructed. The establishment consists of the residence and the stables, a brew house and a smoke house. The scenic road along the Delaware leads from Washington's Crossing to the picturesque artist's colony of *New Hope;* the town's setting of a quiet canal, great shade trees, bridges and solid fieldstone houses has often been called an Old World landscape, yet its character is "Old Pennsylvania" in its own right. The same pleasant atmosphere prevails in *Doylestown,* west of New Hope, where the museum of the Bucks County Historical Society exhibits the early settlers' tools in fully equipped colonial shops; a collection of Pennsylvania-Dutch iron stove plates is unique and decorative. Near Kennett Square, not far from the Delaware border, *Longwood Gardens* is the fabulous estate of Wilmington's Du Pont family, a spectacular park with a 3-acre conservatory and lovely fountains; it is open to the public (see also under Delaware). The *Pennsylvania-Dutch Country* and *Lancaster* with its famous farmer's market are described on page 46. Lancaster is also the site of Wheatland, President Buchanan's home; the mansion is open to visitors. The *Landis Valley Museum* near Lancaster illustrates interestingly the civilization of the Pennsylvania-Dutch since 1710, in furniture and clocks, tools and guns, paintings and books, glassware and pottery. Northeast of Lancaster, the *Cloister at Ephrata* has been restored and welcomes visitors; the buildings, erected in 1732, were occupied by a group of monastic Seven-Day-Baptists who wrote and composed their own sacred hymns and made an interesting contribution to American church music. Near Baumstown, not far from Reading, the *Daniel Boone Homestead* has been restored, on the site of the explorer's birthplace; it is a stone house with pioneer furnishings. At Schnecksville near Allentown, the *Trexler-Lehigh Game Preserve* maintains herds of bison, elk and other game animals. *Bethlehem* is famous on two counts: It is the seat of a great steel industry, and the home of the excellent Bach Choir and its annual Bach Festival; also Lehigh University is located there. Originally a Moravian settlement, Bethlehem still preserves several ancient Moravian buildings like Bell House, Sisters' House, Gemein Haus and Old Chapel. At the *Delaware Water Gap* the river cuts through the Kittatinny Range, creating a deep, three-mile gorge; this is a gateway to the *Pocono Mountains* and Stroudsburg, a popular vacation area described on page 46. The Pocono Wild Animal Farm, near Stroudsburg, exhibits mountain goats and llamas, kangaroos and deer. In the Berwick-Wilkes-Barre-Scranton anthracite district, some companies offer guided tours into the coal mines. To the east, near the New York state border, the making of fine, hand-cut crystal glassware may be observed at *White Mills,* at the Dorflinger Glass Works.

CENTRAL PENNSYLVANIA Throughout central Pennsylvania, numerous *Limestone Caverns* are open to the public. Near the New York state line, the Tioga Point Museum at *Athens* displays Indian and frontier relics. To the south, *Eagles Mere* is a popular summer resort on Eagles Mere Lake. At *Sunbury,* on the Susquehanna River, the site of Fort Augusta is marked by a museum and a model of the fort. *Hershey,* east of Harrisburg, is one of America's chocolate centers, with a luxury hotel, rose gardens, golf courses, an amusement park, and a museum; the chocolate-manufacturing plant is open for inspection. *Harrisburg,* the state capital, is described on page 46. Near the Maryland state line, on highway 194 between Hanover and Littlestown, the stables of the *Hanover Shoe Farms* may be visited; famous trotters are raised there. The most outstanding event in the development of the *Gettysburg National Military Park* was Lincoln's Gettysburg Address when he dedicated a part of the battlefield as a military cemetery. Today, 26 miles of roads wind their way past markers and monuments, breastworks and artillery; the Eternal Light Peace Memorial and the High-Water Mark Monument, at the spot of the farthest Confederate advance, are outstanding; observation towers overlook the battlefield and a cyclorama painting illustrates the details of the most important battle of the Civil War. Guided tours are available. The park has a lovely hill and woodland setting, and the old college town of Gettysburg does not seem to have changed much since the fateful July of 1863. Northwest of Gettysburg, near the town of Trough Creek, the huge *Balanced Rock* hangs in a precarious equilibrium over the gorge of Trough Creek, in Trough Creek State Forest. One of the landmarks in American railroading is the *Horseshoe Curve* at *Altoona;* the railroad tracks form a big U on their way through the Alleghenies. To the northeast, *State College* is the seat of *Pennsylvania State University.* Nearby in *Bellefonte,* trout fishing in Spring Creek is said to be so excellent that the area is called a "fishermen's paradise." Tourists interested in airplane construction may visit the Piper Aircraft factory near *Lock Haven,* northeast of Bellefonte. In a picturesque setting in the central north of the state, the *Pine Creek Gorge* is a thousand feet deep and about 50 miles long; it is called the Grand Canyon of Pennsylvania. Surrounding the chasm are Colton Point State Park and Leonard Harrison State Park with lookout points high above the canyon, and with recreational facilities.

WESTERN PENNSYLVANIA *Kane* is known for its Lobo Wolf Pack; the large and fierce beasts, supplemented by a number of Arctic wolves, may be seen in a fenced-in preserve in which they roam freely. At *Johnstown,* an Incline Plane Railway carries visitors and cars to a 500-foot summit which offers a splendid panorama of the city. Near the West Virginia state line, 11 miles southeast of Uniontown, Fort Necessity has been reproduced at the site of the first battle in which young George Washington took part. Nearby is the burial place of General Braddock. To the south, at New Geneva, *Friendship Hill* is a museum containing many historical documents. It was formerly the home of Albert Gallatin, one of our first secretaries of the treasury. *Pittsburgh* is one of the world's great steel and manufacturing centers; visitors should know, however, that the city's smoke control system works effectively. No longer is Pittsburgh enveloped in "smog"; it's a bright community today, as cheerful and healthy as any city its size. Historically it developed from Fort Duquesne, later Fort Pitt, at the confluence of the Monongahela and Allegheny rivers which form the Ohio. The peninsula is the "Golden Triangle," Pittsburgh's business district. The rest of the city has spread to the surrounding hills and a unique communication system negotiates rivers and ridges: There are 18 bridges, several tunnels, and a number of "inclines," cable cars that lift people and autos to the top of the hills. Mt. Washington Incline, across the Monongahela from the Golden Triangle, rises to a height of 400 feet and offers a fine panorama. In the Oakland District, the *University of Pittsburgh* has an unusual campus; its 42-story Cathedral of Learning is an impressive skyscraper. Nearby are the *Stephen Collins Foster Memorial* which honors the Pittsburgh-born composer of America's favorite folk tunes, the Carnegie Institute of Technology, and the Mellon Institute, an important industrial research center. Other outstanding organizations are the Buhl Planetarium, the Institute of Popular Science, the Allegheny Observatory in Riverview Park and the Syria Mosque of the Pittsburgh Symphony Orchestra. Schenley Park, the city's largest, contains an excellent botanical conservatory. To the northwest at *Ambridge,* the once flourishing Christian-communal settlement of the Harmonists, *Old Economy,* may be visited; it consists of the Great House of 35 rooms, the granary, music hall, and other structures filled with early-19th-century relics. *Pymatuning Lake* in the northwestern corner of the state is a large, man-made body of water with 78 miles of shoreline. The surrounding state park is a popular area for fishing and water sports in summer, and for skating and iceboating in winter. In the northwest of the state, particularly in *Cook Forest State Park* on the Clarion River, large stands of virgin timber and an abundant wildlife still remain. At *Titusville,* the Drake Well Memorial Park has been established around the world's first well that was drilled for oil, produced oil, and initiated a new industrial era. In a museum, Colonel Drake's primitive apparatus and some of his papers and personal belongings may be seen. On Presque Isle, in Lake Erie, opposite the city of *Erie,* the obelisk of the Perry Monument commemorates Perry's victory in the Battle of Lake Erie; the commodore's reconstructed flagship "Niagara" may be inspected at the foot of State Street.

NATIONAL FOREST IN PENNSYLVANIA *Allegheny Nat.F.,* near Warren, U.S. 6, 62, State 59 (Allegheny Mountains, Watermill Race ski trail, virgin timber stands, 300 miles of trout streams).

STATE PARKS 54 state parks and monuments, 57 picnic areas. For details write to Bureau of Parks, Dept. of Forests and Waters, Harrisburg, Pa.

RHODE ISLAND

For information, write to Recreation Bureau, Rhode Island Development Council, State House, Providence 2, R.I.

NORTHERN RHODE ISLAND *Providence,* the state capital, is particularly attractive around College Hill, where *Brown University* has a beautiful campus; fine old residences reflect the wealth of this seaport turned industrial center. The First Baptist Meeting-House with its slender spire is one of the city's loveliest buildings; the Brown commencement has been held there since 1775. Roger Williams Park has splendid rose gardens, flower displays and a colonial-furniture museum. The old Slater Mill at *Pawtucket,* erected beside the Blackstone River in 1793 by Samuel Slater, is the birthplace of the cotton textile industry in America; pieces of primitive 18th century machines are displayed in the ancient two-and-a-half-story frame building.

SOUTHERN RHODE ISLAND At *Bristol,* on the eastern shore of Narragansett Bay, Colt Drive is a scenic waterfront road along the bay, on the large Colt Estate. *Newport,* one of "the last resorts," had its heyday around the turn of the century. The expression "the 400" as a symbol of social prominence originated there because Mrs. William Astor's ballroom held exactly 400 guests. Today the pompous "cottages" (some costing two or three million dollars when they were built seventy or eighty years ago) can best be seen on an eleven-mile loop drive (also called the "Ten-Mile Drive") which takes the sightseer past the most spectacular estates like the Breakers, the Marble Palace,

the Stone Villa. Hikers will find the Cliff Walk beautiful; it follows the shore for three miles, between velvety lawns and masses of rocks and boulders sprayed with salty foam. The historic old port city is, in many ways, more interesting than the millionaires' palaces. Around Washington Square with the Commodore Perry Statue, such interesting buildings as the Old City Hall of 1761, the Old Colony House, the first Sabbaterian meeting house in America, the first synagogue in America and the Redwood Library, one of the country's earliest, reflect the city's historical and cultural importance. At the northern edge of Trouro Park, the so-called Old Stone Mill is an impressive circular fieldstone structure of medieval appearance. Its origin is unknown; some believe that it was built by Vikings in the 11th century. It fired the imaginations of Longfellow and James Fenimore Cooper, who mention it in their novels. Newport's Coaster's Harbor Island is the birthplace of the nation's naval training; at the Naval Training Station the old frigate "Constellation," the country's first man-of-war, is an interesting relic. On the western shore of Narragansett Bay, *Wickford* is the seat of the State Lobster Hatchery. In nearby *Exeter,* the South County Museum exhibits colonial crafts and Americana. *Saunderstown,* to the south, maintains the Gilbert Stuart birthplace as a memorial to the famous colonial portrait painter. South of Narragansett *Scarborough Beach* and *Sand Hill Cove* are recreational areas. *Block Island* may be reached by ferry from Providence, Newport, Point Judith or New London. It is a summer resort and deep-sea-fishing center, especially for swordfish and tuna.

STATE PARKS 20 state parks, forests and reservations, 4 parkways, numerous wayside picnic areas. For details, write to Division of Forests and Parks, Dept. of Agriculture and Conservation, State House, Providence 2, R.I.

SOUTH CAROLINA

For information, write to Research, Planning and Development Board, Columbia, South Carolina.

THE COAST OF SOUTH CAROLINA *Charleston,* one of America's "character towns," and the famous *Cypress, Magnolia,* and *Middleton Gardens* with their acres of blossoming azaleas and camellias are described on page 62. *Edisto Beach State Park* with its beach of white sands and waving palm trees is a popular recreation spot, 50 miles southwest of Charleston. *Beaufort County* is an exceedingly picturesque area, consisting largely of sixty-five islands. Among its attractions are several historic ruins of churches and fortifications (for instance, of Fort Frederick of 1731) which are remnants of "tabby" structures—tabby being a building material of shells, lime and sand. The city of Beaufort has some fine colonial buildings like St. Helena's Church and many stately ante-bellum residences. The neighboring island of St. Helena has a large population of Gullah Negroes, said to be the purest African race in America. Parris Island is a U.S. Marine Corps Training Station. On the coastal highway north of Charleston, near the town of McClellanville, *Hampton Plantation* with its pillared mansion is the home of Archibald Rutledge, the poet; it was begun by his family in the 1730's. Between McClellanville and the ocean, the Cape Romain National Wildlife Refuge has been established. South of Georgetown the *Belle Isle Gardens* are famous for their huge live oaks spreading their branches above beds of bright flowers. North of Georgetown, the state-owned *Brookgreen Gardens* are interesting; four old rice plantations were merged to make this park containing an impressive avenue of gigantic moss-hung live oaks, formal boxwood gardens, a noted outdoor collection of sculptures and a game preserve. To the north of the state,

235

Myrtle Beach is one of the state's outstanding seaside resorts.

CENTRAL SOUTH CAROLINA   In *Columbia*, the state capitol is an historical landmark. When General Sherman shelled the building in 1865, his artillery left in the walls holes and scars now covered by bronze stars; the Confederate Relic Room contains historical collections. Columbia is also the site of the University of South Carolina and Woodrow Wilson's boyhood home. Between the low coastal country and the uplands of the Piedmont Plateau, the Sand Hills in the Long-Leaf-Pine Belt are a region where all equestrian sports are cultivated. *Camden* is one of the oldest of the mid-southern winter resorts; horse shows and polo matches are important events, and the Springdale Course is noted for steeplechase racing. Near *Sumter*, the Swan Lake Gardens and the Dunndell Gardens with their large displays of Japanese iris are tourist attractions. To the south, at Summerton, the *Fort Watson Memorial* honors the storming of the British fort by General Francis Marion, "the Swamp Fox." At Orangeburg, the *Edisto Gardens* include large stands of wisteria, azaleas and a rose test garden; there are facilities for swimming and picnicking. *Aiken* calls itself the polo capital of the South, because like Camden, it is a resort frequented by horse-lovers. Polo ponies, hunters and jumpers are trained there, and the surrounding parks and forests offer quiet roads for horseback riding and horse-and-buggy driving. North of Aiken, in Edgefield, General Gary's *Oakley Park* is an ante-bellum residence filled with family heirlooms; it is open to visitors. Near McCormick, close to the Georgia state line, the *John de la Howe State School* is a unique institution; founded in 1797, this manual-training school, which teaches various trades, cooking and dairying, welcomes visitors.

NORTHERN SOUTH CAROLINA   *Lancaster* is the reputed site of *Andrew Jackson's Birthplace. Kings Mountain National Military Park* near Gaffney commemorates a Revolutionary victory, when regular British troops surrendered to American frontiersmen, in 1780. The park offers a ridge drive past markers and monuments, and the museum contains a diorama of the battle. North of Greenville, *Caesar's Head* is a rock rising 1,200 feet above the Saluda River, with a lookout platform and a recreational area. Nearby to the southwest, *Table Rock State Park* is another popular goal. At Clemson, near the Georgia border, *Fort Hill* was the home of John C. Calhoun. The stately plantation mansion still contains many of its original furnishings; visitors are welcome.

NATIONAL FORESTS IN SOUTH CAROLINA   *Francis Marion Nat.F.*, near McClellanville on the coast, U.S. 17, 52 (picturesque moss-hung oaks, flowering yucca, dogwood, holly; many "meteor bays"; ruins of early colonial plantations and settlements). *Sumter Nat.F.*, partly near the Georgia state line, U.S. 25, 76, 176 (Piedmont and Blue Ridge Mountains; huge stands of rhododendron; Walhalla trout hatchery).

STATE PARKS   18 state parks, 6 wayside picnic areas. For details, write to Division of State Parks, South Carolina State Commission of Forestry, 506 Calhoun State Office Building, Columbia, S.C.

SOUTH DAKOTA

For information, write to Publicity Office, State Highway Commission, Pierre, South Dakota.

EASTERN SOUTH DAKOTA   *Sioux Falls* is a meat packing center. Its Pettigrew Museum displays fine Indian handicrafts, especially of the Sioux.

CENTRAL SOUTH DAKOTA   *Pierre* is the state capital, and the seat of an Indian school. The State Museum in Soldiers' and Sailors' Memorial Hall contains interesting Indian relics, among them rare "bull boats" of buffalo hide. To the northwest of, Pierre, the *Cheyenne River Indian Reservation* is quite picturesque, since most of its 4,000 Sioux live in tents.

WESTERN SOUTH DAKOTA   That unique area comprising the *Badlands National Monument, Rapid City,* the *Black Hills with Mt. Rushmore National Memorial, Wind Cave National Park, Lead* with the Homestake Mine and *Deadwood* is described on page 106. Deadwood, by the way, celebrates the era of Wild Bill Hickock and Calamity Jane each year in August, in the "Days of '76." *Belle Fourche* is the northern gateway to the Black Hills, an old cattle center where an annual "Black Hills Roundup" attracts cowboys and tourists early in July. *Jewel Cave National Monument,* near Wind Cave National Park, is a cavern studded with sparkling calcite crystals justifying the name "Jewel" Cave. South Dakota is still a great Indian country and in *Rosebud and Pine Ridge Indian Reservations,* in the southern center of the state, some 19,000 Indians live, partly at least, in the ways of their forebears. They are excellent horsemen and as the reservations include good grazing lands, quite a few are self-supporting cattle ranchers. About half of the Indians are full-blooded.

NATIONAL PARK IN SOUTH DAKOTA   *Wind Cave National Park,* see page 106.

NATIONAL FOREST IN SOUTH DAKOTA   *Black Hills Nat.F.*, U.S. 14, 16, 85 (spectacular canyons and waterfalls, crystal caves; historic gold rush era; Homestake Mine; logging and lumbering operations; Harney Peak, highest point east of the Rockies; Mt. Rushmore Memorial; gold, silver and feldspar mining).

STATE PARKS   42 state parks and recreational areas. For details, write to Division of Forestry and Parks, Pierre, South Dakota.

TENNESSEE

For information, write to Division of State Information, 115 State Office Building, Nashville 3, Tennessee.

EASTERN TENNESSEE   *The Great Smoky Mountains National Park* which lies partly in North Carolina, partly in Tennessee is described on page 60. The popular resort of *Gatlinburg* is the northern gateway to the *Great Smoky Mountains.* A favorite goal of mountain climbers is Le Conte, with a height of 6,593 feet one of the highest peaks east of the Rockies. *Knoxville* is the supply depot for the eastern Tennessee Mountains and the nerve center of the TVA system, where visiting engineers from India and New Zealand, Argentina, Australia and every other corner of the world study the huge Tennessee Valley rehabilitation project, with a view of applying similar methods to their public works at home. Knoxville is also the seat of the University of Tennessee. North of the city, *Norris Dam* was the first TVA dam to be completed, in 1936. The lake formed by the dam is a vacation area, with Norris Park and Big Ridge Park offering all water-sports facilities. Norris Freeway leads to a lookout peak affording a fine view of the dam and the lake. In nearby *Oak Ridge,* the Museum of Atomic Energy has exhibits explaining the work and research of the famous Oak Ridge plant. For a broad panorama of *Chattanooga,* on the Georgia state line, a ride to the summit of 2,225-foot-high *Lookout Mountain* is recommended, either by car on a scenic highway or by incline railway. On top of the mountain, Point Park, the Rock City gardens and the Lookout Mountain Caverns with Ruby Falls are sightseeing attractions. Bloody battles were fought there during the Civil War and monuments mark the battlefields. From what is now *Chickamauga and Chattanooga National Military Park,* General Sherman started his notorious march to the sea. On the other side of the Tennessee River canyon, *Signal Mountain* is a popular lookout point high above the picturesque countryside; the mountain is so-called because of the Indian smoke signals which had emanated from there. Nearby *Chickamauga Lake,* one of the TVA reservoirs, offers all water sports.

WESTERN TENNESSEE   In *Nashville,* the state capitol on Cedar Knob affords a good view of the city. In Centennial Park an authentic reproduction of the Parthenon in Athens has been erected; it contains an art gallery. Fort Nashborough, the frontier post from which Nashville developed, has been reconstructed. Vanderbilt University and Fisk University, the latter one of America's largest Negro colleges and the home of the famous Jubilee Singers, are located in Nashville. 12 miles northeast of Nashville, Andrew Jackson's home, *The Hermitage,* is not only an historic shrine but also one of America's loveliest mansions. The original furnishings are still there and the garden is preserved as it existed in "Old Hickory's" days. Both the general and his wife Rachel are buried there. In the northwestern corner of the state, *Reelfoot Lake* is a region of wild and eerie beauty; during the New Madrid earthquake of 1811, a cypress forest was half-submerged, creating a fantastic lake 14 miles long. Huge beds of lotus flowers and water lilies add colorful touches. Fishing for all mid-continent species is said to be wonderful there, and duck hunting is popular. *Memphis,* the world's largest cotton market, is considered by many the most typically southern city. Two of its institutions have become famous: the Memphis Cotton Carnival, held every May, and Beale Street, home of the songs called "blues." In *Shiloh National Military Park,* near the meeting point of Tennessee, Mississippi and Alabama, markers and a museum commemorate the bloody 1862 Battle of Shiloh.

NATIONAL PARK IN TENNESSEE   The northwestern part of *Great Smoky Mountains National Park,* see page 60.

NATIONAL FOREST IN TENNESSEE   *Cherokee Nat.F.,* in the eastern mountains of the state, U.S. 421, 19E, 19W, 25, 64, State 68, 67 (rugged mountain country, deep river gorges; the Ducktown Copper Basin is a striking example of deforestation and erosion).

STATE PARKS   15 state parks, 7 state forests, 1 state memorial park. For details, write to Division of State Parks, Dept. of Conservation, Nashville 3, Tennessee.

TEXAS

For information, write to Texas Highway Department, Austin 14, Texas.

THE COAST OF TEXAS   The countryside around *Port Arthur* is that of the Deep South, Louisiana style, with Spanish moss and cypress swamps, and the city itself has a sub-tropical charm, with palm-lined streets and magnolia-shaded gardens. But the life blood of the region is oil, and visitors (and photographers) will find the tall, star-topped memorial column flanked by two oil derricks an intriguing sight. Neighboring *Beaumont* is also an important harbor and oil town; the famous Spindletop Field is only three miles away. North of Beaumont, *The Big Thicket* is an impenetrable jungle of two million acres traversed by streams said to teem with fish. The colorful Gulf port of *Galveston,* the "millionaires' city" of *Houston* and the *San Jacinto Battlefield* where Texas won her independence are described on page 116. *Corpus Christi* is both an industrial

ocean port and a lively Gulf Coast playground; opportunities for swimming, sailing and fishing abound. Spearing flounders on the bottom of a shallow bay at night is an exciting Gulf Coast sport. A gay and carefree spirit permeates the Buccaneer Days carnival held every June, the annual Tarpon Rodeo celebrated shortly afterwards and the sailing handicap regatta from Corpus Christi to Galveston.

EASTERN TEXAS   In *Texarkana* the state line runs through the heart of the city; the eastern half belongs to "wet" Arkansas, the western half to "dry" Texas. South of Texarkana, *Caddo State Park* is a huge, fantastic and eerily beautiful maze of bayous, cypress swamps, half-sunken banks, moss-draped live oaks, including large Caddo Lake on the Louisiana border. Fishes and wildlife abound, and the native Caddo Negroes are noted guides. To the west, the town of *Tyler* is "the Rose Garden of the World." This is an outstanding rose-growing district and the Municipal Rose Garden displays all the varieties of the region. South of Tyler, *Huntsville* proudly calls itself "the Mount Vernon of Texas." For there the first President of the Republic of Texas, Sam Houston, had his last home, and there he died. Houston's law office, his residence, the Steamboat House where he passed on and the Sam Houston Memorial Museum welcome visitors.

CENTRAL TEXAS   *Waco,* a great cotton market, is the seat of Baylor University, which owns the most complete collection of Browning manuscripts, first editions and other Browningiana. Southeast of Waco, *Marlin* is an outstanding health resort; mineral water gushes from hot springs 3,350 feet deep. In *Longhorn State Park,* southwest of Waco, the Longhorn Cavern is a large, partly explored limestone cave with lovely crystal formations; guided tours are available. *Austin* is the state capital and the home of the *University of Texas;* the French Legation of the Republic of Texas points to a proud era in the history of the state. 85 miles from Austin, the 1,850-foot-high *Bear Mountain* offers a magnificent panorama; on the summit, Balanced Rock is a huge boulder resting precariously on two granite points. West of Austin, *Fredericksburg* is a German settlement; its houses with their thick walls, steep roofs and outside stairs have the look of the old homes along the Neckar and the Rhine. A well-known German tradition is the annual singing contest, the Saengerfest, in May. *San Antonio* with the *Alamo* and the lovely old *Spanish Missions* is described on page 118. 25 miles to the east, *Medina Lake* is a recreational area with 96 miles of shoreline; fishing for bass, crappie and catfish is popular. Also near San Antonio is *Palmetto State Park,* a miniature Yellowstone with mud geysers and hot and cold sulphur springs. 90 miles southeast of San Antonio, *Goliad's* La Bahia Mission is a Texas historical shrine, the scene of the Fannin massacre of 1836. "Remember Goliad!" became one of the Texas' slogans, on their road to victory; the ruins of the presidio and the mission are open to visitors. The *Paint Rock Pictographs* on a slope by the Concho River, about 70 miles south of Abilene, are interesting. In lively colors Indian artists have painted hundreds of subjects; the latest ones must have been added at the time of the missions, since they depict devils in the Christian tradition.

NORTHERN TEXAS   "Persian lamb" fur coats are made of the pelts of newly-born Karakul sheep. One of the largest American flocks is maintained on the *Karakul Sheep Ranch,* 25 miles southwest of Wichita Falls; the original sheep were imported from southern Russia. East of Wichita Falls, *Gainesville* has become famous for its non-profit community circus; an all-amateur troupe of Gainesville citizens, it offers excellent entertainment. *Dallas* is a streamlined modern metropolis, rich from oil and cotton, literate and sophisticated, the style center of the Southwest. Its Neiman-Marcus store is one of the country's most elegant and most expensive shops. Dallas has a fine symphony orchestra, and is the seat of Southern Methodist University. Its Fair Park is modern and impressive, the scene of the Texas State Fair, a tremendous show; its Texas Hall of State is a pioneer museum. Among the city's parks White Rock Lake Park is outstanding; it contains 2,300 acres of woods, trails, picnic sites and a lake. *Fort Worth,* the friendly rival of Dallas, is equally rich and equally modern but retains a more typically Western atmosphere of friendliness. It is the home of Texas Christian University. Among the city's attractions are the Botanic Gardens in Trinity Park, the Texas Frontier Centennial Park, with its Texas Pioneer Memorial Tower, and the Will Rogers Memorial Coliseum which seats 10,000 people. The annual Fort Worth Fat Stock Show is an outstanding event. North of Forth Worth, two man-made lakes offer fishing and water-sports facilities. *Eagle Mountain Lake,* at a distance of 14 miles, and *Lake Bridgeport,* 50 miles away. West of Fort Worth, *Mineral Wells* is a noted health resort with several mineral springs.

TEXAS PANHANDLE Once a desolate and forbidding ranch country, the Texas Panhandle is now, in large part, a prosperous agricultural region growing grain, cotton and vegetables, with oil bringing in additional wealth. *Amarillo,* the center of the Panhandle, grew from "a huddle of buffalohide shacks" to a modern, progressive city. South of Amarillo, in Canyon, the *Panhandle-Plains Museum* exhibits a fascinating collection of relics from the days of the longhorns; around its entrance is displayed the brands of all the major Panhandle ranches, including the famous XIT brand of the region's first big ranch. Nearby, the *Palo Duro Canyon State Park* is located around a deep river gorge with steep walls.

WESTERN TEXAS *El Paso,* the ancient crossroads between Mexico and the north, *Pecos, Balmorhea State Park* with its huge spring, Fort Davis and the *Davis Mountains* with McDonald Observatory, and the "oasis" of *Alpine* are described on page 114. *Big Bend National Park,* a fascinating mountain wilderness facing Old Mexico across the Rio Grande, is described on page 120.

SOUTHERN TEXAS *Laredo,* locale of a famous cowboy song, is the starting point of the Pan American Highway to Mexico City. Across the Rio Grande, Nuevo Laredo is popular with tourists because of its bullfights and night life. Between the Rio Grande and the Gulf, south of Corpus Christi, the *King Ranch* is one of the largest cattle ranches on earth; it's the size of Rhode Island. Managed along scientific lines, the creation of the famous Santa Gertrudis breed of cattle is its major achievement. The lower Rio Grande Valley was once largely a desert; modern irrigation has turned it into a rich farming region producing citrus fruit, cotton and early vegetables. *Brownsville,* the center of the region, enjoys a strongly Mexican atmosphere, and the annual Charro Days Festival, during the week before Lent, is a gay fiesta with Latin American overtones.

NATIONAL PARK IN TEXAS *Big Bend National Park,* see page 120.

NATIONAL FORESTS IN TEXAS *Angelina Nat.F.,* in central Texas near Lufkin, U.S. 59, 69 (stands of longleaf pine on hills and of hardwoods along river bottom; Angelina River; Boykin Lake). *Davy Crockett Nat.F.,* near Crockett, U.S. 287, State 94, 103 (shortleaf-loblolly pine woods; hardwoods in bottoms). *Sabine Nat.F.,* near the Louisiana state line, U.S. 96, State 21 (Sabine River and overflow lakes; Boles Field Fox Hunt Area).

Sam Houston Nat.F., near Huntsville, U.S. 75, 190 (part of the "Big Thicket" area).

STATE PARKS 47 state parks, 5 state forests, hundreds of wayside picnic areas. For details, write to Texas State Parks Board, 106 East 13th Street, Austin, Texas.

UTAH

For information write to Tourist Information, State Road Commission of Utah, 210 State Capitol Building, Salt Lake City, Utah.

NORTHERN UTAH *Bear Lake* is a popular water sports area both for Idaho and Utah; white sandy beaches line this 25-mile long fresh-water lake. On highway 39, the traveler from Ogden to Woodruff rides along the Ogden River on the bottom of 1,000-foot-high *Ogden Canyon.* This picturesque gorge sometimes gives the impression of a dead-end street; the canyon walls seem to close in on the road. At other spots the canyon widens into delightful, wooded camping sites. The road touches the Ogden Snow Basin, a winter-sports center. *Salt Lake City,* world capital of Mormonism and seat of the University of Utah, and the *Great Salt Lake* are described on page 168. Approaching Salt Lake City from the Nevada state line, the highway crosses the *Great Salt Lake Desert,* a grassless desert in the most austere sense of the word. Its *Bonneville Salt Flats* are a hundred square miles of hard, level, white salt, with barren mountains at the horizon. This is an eerie region indeed, especially if you see mountain peaks standing upside down, or hills and lakes floating in the sky; such visions are, of course, mirages, quite a frequent occurrence. Practically speaking, the flats are used as an ideal automobile racing course, and several speed records have been established there; also salt mining operations are carried on. *Sandy Open Pit Copper Mine* is located in Bingham Canyon, twenty miles southwest of Salt Lake City. Observation platforms for visitors make it possible to get an interesting view of America's largest open pit copper mine and its various operations and activities. South of Salt Lake City, near the Sandy mine, *Timpanogos Cave National Monument* offers guided tours through a large limestone cave; curious are its helictites, a strangely twisted form of stalactites. *Provo* is a steel center and the home of *Brigham Young University;* the city has picturesque surroundings of mountains, canyons and waterfalls. Near the Colorado border, *Dinosaur National Monument* is an area of rich fossil beds and rugged canyons, weirdly shaped cliffs and Indian pictographs on the walls of caves. Bas reliefs of dinosaur bones are clearly imprinted into the walls of the excavation quarry. In the museum, skeletons of flying reptiles are especially interesting.

SOUTHERN UTAH The fascinating sights that can be seen when traveling south on highways 160 and 47, are described on page 170: *Arches National Monument, Dead Horse Point, Moab, Natural Bridges National Monument,* the *Great Goose Necks, Monument Valley,* and *Rainbow Bridge National Monument. Hovenweep National Monument* lies half in Utah, half in Colorado. It consists of prehistoric cliff dwellings and pueblos; the most stately ruin is called Hovenweep Castle. At Fruita in central southern Utah, *Capitol Reef National Monument* is a spectacular red sandstone "reef" topped with white sandstone domes; the monument covers 37,000 acres and includes strange rock formations like the Great Organ, canyons, natural bridges, and Indian pictographs. Three fabulous sightseeing attractions of southwestern Utah are described on page 172: *Zion National Park, Bryce Canyon National Park* and *Cedar Breaks National Monument. Kanab,* on the Arizona border, is a "location town" like Moab. Because of its spectacular surroundings, Western motion pictures are often filmed there.

NATIONAL PARKS IN UTAH *Zion National Park* and *Bryce Canyon National Park*, see page 172.

NATIONAL FORESTS IN UTAH *Ashley Nat.F.*, partly in Wyoming, U.S. 30, 40, State 44 (includes eastern half of the Uinta Mountain Range, highest American range extending east and west with 13,498-foot-high Kings Peak; High Uintas Wilderness Area mostly above 10,000 feet). *Cache Nat.F.*, partly in Idaho, U.S. 30S, 89, 91, State 39 (Bear River and Wasatch Ranges, Minnetonka Cave, Logan and Ogden Canyons). *Dixie Nat.F.*, near Cedar City in southwest of state, U.S. 91, 89 (includes Table Cliff Point from where peaks in four states—Colorado, Arizona, Nevada, Utah—can be observed on a clear day; spectacular colored cliffs). *Fishlake Nat.F.*, near Richfield, U.S. 89, 91 (Thousand Lake Mountain Scenic Area, Petrified Wood Scenic Area). *Manti-La Sal Nat.F.*, near Ephraim and Monticello, U.S. 89, 50, State 10, 29, 31 (its skyline drive crosses high alpine meadows, sylvan glades, and colorful canyons; east part of forest stands on top of huge coal deposits; Indian writings and battlefields). *Sawtooth Nat.F.*, U.S. 30S, State 70 (see under Idaho). *Uinta Nat.F.*, U.S. 40, 50, 91, 189 (near Provo deep canyons and waterfalls, mixed oak-maple-aspen-spruce forest, beautiful in fall colors). *Wasatch Nat.F.*, near Salt Lake City, U.S. 91, 40, 189, 30S, 50, State 152, 210, 65, 36, 80 (Alpine Scenic Highway, Timpanogos Cave, Mirror and Grandaddy Lakes, Alta and Brighton Skiing Areas with lodges and chair lifts).

STATE PARKS 5 state parks and monuments. For details write to Tourist Information, State Road Commission of Utah, 210 State Capitol Buildings, Salt Lake City, Utah.

VERMONT
For information write to Publicity Director, Vermont Development Commission, Montpelier, Vt.

NORTHERN VERMONT The pleasant Vermont town of *St. Albans* was the scene of one of the most daring raids of the Civil War. A troop of Confederates "invaded" Vermont from Canada, took the town, looted the banks of $200,000, and vanished back into Canada. St. Albans Bay is noted for excellent bass and perch fishing. *Burlington*, with the *University of Vermont*, is described on page 28. The city's Fleming Museum displays Indian relics of the Vermont area and owns also a fine collection of Oriental art. A steamboat ride on Lake Champlain is recommended, and sportsmen will find the lake a good fishing ground for pike, perch and bass. Along the wooded and hilly lakeshore there are numerous popular vacation spots. To the east, *Stowe* is Vermont's great ski resort (see also p. 28). It lies in the shadows of Mt. Mansfield, the highest peak in the state; the summit may be reached either by toll road or chair lift. To the north, the highway runs through a spectacular gap at the base of Mt. Mansfield called Smugglers' Notch. Elm-shaded *St. Johnsbury* lies in the center of the maple sugar country, and the Cary Maple Sugar Co. is a tourist attraction; the town's Natural Science Museum has a good display of the state's fauna and flora. North of St. Johnsbury, an area of dozens of lakes invites sportsmen and vacationists. Lake Memphremagog, which lies partly in Canada, is the largest.

CENTRAL VERMONT *The Long Trail of the Green Mountains* runs the whole length of the state for 260 miles, from Blackinton, Massachusetts, to Canada. It is popular with hikers who find overnight shelters at intervals. *Monpelier's* state capitol is built of Vermont granite; the town possesses several interesting his-

toric relics, among them the first printing press brought to the colonies. *Barre* is the world's leading producer of monument granite; the operation of the quarries on Millstone Hill is a fascinating spectacle (see also p. 29). West of Barre, at Fayston, *General Stark Mountain* offers a splendid view; a chair lift takes visitors to the top. *Middlebury* is a beautiful old college town, the seat of Middlebury College whose foreign-language schools are nationally known. The town's Sheldon Museum displays an old Vermont blacksmith shop, country store and post office. *Rutland* and nearby *Proctor* are famous for their marble quarries and marble finishing plants; some of their quarries are among the deepest on earth; in Proctor the exhibit of the Vermont Marble Company is most interesting (see also p. 29). Rutland is a popular resort and seat of the Green Mountain Club (maintaining trails in the mountains) and the Green Mountain Horse Association (opening and maintaining marked bridle paths). East of Rutland, the tiny village of *Plymouth* lies quietly among the wooded hills; its general-store-and-post-office building is the birthplace of Calvin Coolidge who also took his presidential oath of office there; he is buried near his birthplace.

SOUTHERN VERMONT In *Weston*, the Vermont Country Store has been restored as an emporium of the 1890's; it sells Vermont specialties and attracts large numbers of tourists. To the southwest, near the lovely resort of *Manchester*, the *Mount Equinox Skyline Drive* is a scenic toll road to the summit of 3,816-foot-high Mount Equinox from where a beautiful Vermont view may be enjoyed. Near the modern city of *Bennington*, "Old Bennington" is an historical outdoor memento of Ethan Allen, his Green Mountain Boys, the Catamount Tavern, and the Battle of Bennington. Old Bennington's museum owns an historical collection and an art gallery (see also p. 29). *Brattleboro* is picturesquely located on the Connecticut River; the town is noted as a producer of organs.

NATIONAL FOREST IN VERMONT *Green Mountain Nat.F.*, U.S. 4, 7 (Green Mountain Range, "Long Trail," Champlain Valley).

STATE PARKS 13 state parks, 7 state forests. For details write to Vermont Forest Service, Montpelier, Vt.

VIRGINIA
The best time to visit Virginia is spring, when the whole state sparkles brightly with beautiful spring flowers. *Garden Week in Virginia*, held every year during the last week of April, presents the "Old Dominion" at its best; many interesting ante-bellum homes with colorful gardens are open to visitors. Circulars with all details may be obtained from the Garden Club of Virginia, Jefferson Hotel, Richmond 19, Va. For general information about Virginia write to Division of Publicity and Advertising, Department of Conservation and Development, Richmond 19, Virginia.

TIDEWATER VIRGINIA *Alexandria*, a few miles south of Washington on the western bank of the Potomac, preserves a dignified colonial atmosphere. Mementoes of George Washington abound: The general attended Christ Church, planned the French-Indian campaign with Braddock at Carlyle House, and ate and drank at Gadsby's Tavern; to him the George Washington Masonic National Memorial Temple is dedicated. *Mount Vernon*, the plantation homestead and burial site of George and Martha Washington, is described on page 52. To the south, *Fredericksburg* is a shrine of American history. George Washington went to school there, and the home of his mother Mary is furnished as it might have been in her day; visitors are welcome. His sister, Betty Washington Lewis, lived at *Kenmore*, a stately colonial mansion, now a museum. Also the law offices of James Monroe are in Fredericksburg; they contain various Monroe relics, including the desk on which the fifth President of the U.S. wrote the Monroe Doctrine. Nearby, the *Fredericksburg and Spotsylvania National Military Park* commemorates four major battles of the Civil War which were fought there between 1862 and 1864. Gun pits, trenches, markers, the house in which General Stonewall Jackson died and a museum with relief maps, dioramas, and gun collections may be inspected. To the east, near Colonial Beach, the *George Washington Birthplace National Monument* has been established; the Memorial Mansion is open to visitors. Nearby, to the southeast, *Stratford Hall* is the birthplace of three famous Lees, Robert E. Lee the general, and Richard Henry and Francis Lightfoot Lee, both signers of the Declaration of Independence. The restored mansion reflects baronial country living. In the southern corner of the peninsula formed by the Potomac and the Rappahannock, *"King" Carter's Church near Kilmarnock* is practically unchanged since 1732 when it was built by a wealthy planter called "King" Carter. Across Chesapeake Bay, on the open Atlantic coast, *Chincoteague Island* is a hunting and fishing resort. An interesting wilderness touch is provided by a herd of wild ponies which roam the salt-marshes; every year in July, a "pony penning day" is held. Recrossing Chesapeake Bay to Mathews and Gloucester Counties, the numerous daffodil farms with their acres of blossoms are a sight to behold in springtime. To the east, *Richmond*, the capital of Virginia, originally built on seven hills by the James River, has now spread over a large area along the river. It is both a modern industrial city and a great historic center. The state capitol, designed by Thomas Jefferson, was the scene of the treason trial of Aaron Burr, and later became the home of the Confederate Congress; there General Robert E. Lee took over the command of the Confederate armies. The old White House of the Confederacy is now the Confederate Museum. Back in colonial days, in 1775, in Richmond's St. John's Church Patrick Henry coined the challenging words "Give me liberty or give me death." Other attractions are the home of John Marshall, the great jurist; the Virginia Museum of Fine Arts; the Edgar Allan Poe Shrine in the city's oldest house; the Carillon Tower in Byrd Park and the bright gardens of Maymont Park. Tourists interested in Virginia tobacco and the manufacture of cigarettes may take a guided tour through the plants of the Liggett & Myers Tobacco Co. *Westover*, 25 miles from Richmond, is considered one of America's most beautiful plantation homes; it was built about 1735. Around Richmond, a number of military parks commemorate various battles that were fought there; most important among the parks is the *Petersburg National Military Park* where the Confederate forces made their last stand in 1864. Southeast of Richmond, restored *Williamsburg* and the Colonial National Historical Park comprising *Jamestown* and *Yorktown* are described on page 52. At the mouth of the James River, *Newport News* is a busy shipbuilding town; the nearby *Mariners Museum* is an outstanding collection of ships' models, maritime prints, and nautical documents; the city's favorite bathing resort is Buckroe Beach. Across Hampton Roads, the sailor's town of *Norfolk* is the gateway to the famous hunting regions of the Back Bay (waterfowl) and the Dismal Swamp (small game animals); it is also the starting point for 25 miles of fine beaches; *Virginia Beach*, with its white sands, its 6 miles of beaches, excellent hotels and elegant clubs, is one of the best-known resorts on America's Atlantic Coast.

CENTRAL VIRGINIA   The *Great Falls of the Potomac*, north of Washington, D.C., are described under Maryland. The remnants of an iron forge established by George Washington are still visible. To the southwest, *Manassas National Battlefield Park*

commemorates, with markers and a museum, two important battles of the Civil War. In *Winchester,* the office of young Washington may be inspected; it was used by him when he worked as a surveyor for Lord Fairfax. The *Skyline Drive* and *Shenandoah National Park* are described on page 50. In the Shenandoah Valley, near the Skyline Drive, a number of limestone caverns may be visited on guided tours; the more important caves are Crystal, Skyline (near Front Royal), Shenandoah, Endless (near New Market), Grand (near Waynesboro), Massanutten, and Luray; the *Luray Caverns* are especially well-known. At the entrance to the caverns, the Luray Singing Tower is equipped with a 47-bell carillon. In the Shenandoah Valley at Mt. Solon, the *Natural Chimneys* are seven huge rock towers rising above the plain. In *Staunton*, the Birthplace of Woodrow Wilson is open to visitors. Also a historical doll museum may be inspected. East of the Skyline Drive, *Charlottesville* with the *University of Virginia*, Thomas Jefferson's *Monticello*, Monroe's *Ash Lawn*, and the old Michie Tavern are described on page 50. South of Charlottesville, the *Appomattox Court House National Historical Monument* has been established at the site of General Lee's surrender to General Grant; among the historical monuments is the restored McLean House where the truce terms were drafted. To the south, at the North Carolina state line, the city of *Danville* is noted for its old-established tobacco auctions which are held from mid-September to the winter months; visitors are welcome at the auctions.

WESTERN VIRGINIA   Near the West Virginia border, *Hot Springs* is a fashionable resort with the elegant Homestead Hotel. Southeast of Hot Springs, the city of *Lexington* in the Shenandoah Valley is the burial place of two southern heroes, Robert E. Lee and Stonewall Jackson; this "shrine of the South" is also the home of Washington and Lee University, and of Virginia Military Institute. South of Lexington, the *Natural Bridge* is a huge stone arch, 215 feet above Cedar Creek; it has been a famous sightseeing spot since the days of George Washington. Today a highway leads over the arch, and a musical pageant with the illuminated natural bridge as a background is performed nightly during the summer. The *Blue Ridge Parkway* connects the Skyline Drive with the Great Smoky Mountains in North Carolina; it is described on page 58. At *Roanoke*, modern commercial center of western Virginia, the scenic drive to *Mill Mountain* is outstanding. From the summit a splendid panorama of the city, the Blue Ridge and the Allegheny Mountains may be enjoyed. A 100-foot neon star on the mountainside above the city is visible for 50 miles. To the south on milepost 176 of the Blue Ridge Parkway, the restored *Mabry Mill* illustrates the small mountain industries of the pioneer South. Nearby to the east is *Fairy Stone State Park*. At *Pocahontas*, on the West Virginia state line, the *Exhibition Mine* may be visited; all mining operations are explained. To the southwest, near *Tazewell*, reconstructed Fort Witten of 1767 is open all year. *Abingdon*, near the Tennessee border, is a center for arts and skills of the southern mountains, for pottery making, weaving and wood carving; its Barter Theater is nationally known. Every mid-August an Arts and Crafts Festival and a Barter Theater Festival are held. To the west, the *Natural Tunnel* at *Clinchport* provides space for a small river and a railroad track; the tunnel may be visited on a trail. Nearby at *Big Stone Gap*, the *Southwest Virginia Museum* depicts the story of the region in historic relics.

NATIONAL PARK IN VIRGINIA   *Shenandoah National Park*, see page 50.

NATIONAL FORESTS IN VIRGINIA   *George Washington NatF.*, partly in West Virginia, U.S. 11, 33, State 42, 260 (orginally surveyed by George Washington, includes Blue Ridge and 3 other ranges, Crabtree Falls, Shenandoah and Warm Springs Valleys) . *Jefferson Nat.F.*, U.S. 11, 220, 21, 52, 23, 58 (includes Blue Ridge Parkway and Appalachian Trail; Mt. Rogers, with 5,719 feet the highest peak in Virginia; transitional zone between Northern and Southern floras) .

STATE PARKS 9 state parks, 3 recreational areas, numerous wayside picnic areas. For details write to Division of Parks, Virginia Conservation Commission, Life Insurance Co. of Virginia Building, Richmond 19, Va.

WASHINGTON

For information write to Washington State Advertising Commission, Transportation Building, Olympia, Washington.

WESTERN WASHINGTON *Puget Sound,* "one of the world's great seascapes," is described on page 148. Near the Canadian border, the town of *Lynden* is a bit of Holland in Washington. Dutch customs and the Dutch language are still cultivated there, and in springtime the town is surrounded by brightly blooming fields of daffodils and tulips. *Bellingham* is a pleasant city on Puget Sound, opposite the San Juan Islands. Nearby Mount Baker National Forest, an all-year recreational area, can be reached by a scenic highway. The picturesque seaport city of *Seattle,* gateway to Alaska, is described on page 148. Two state parks near Seattle are popular: Saltwater State Park and Twanoh State Park across the bay at Bremerton. *Olympic National Park* and the Olympic Loop Highway are described on page 146. The white peak of Mt. Rainier forms a splendid background to the industrial and commercial city of *Tacoma.* West of Tacoma, *Shelton* is a logging town where the daily speech is spiced with lumberjack expressions. In *Olympia,* the State Capitol, the Temple of Justice, and the War Memorial form an impressive architectural group near the bay. South of Olympia, in the prairie country, the Tenino Mounds are grass covered symmetrical cones with flat tops. Their origin and purpose is a puzzle to anthropologists since the cones are not burial mounds; possibly they were Indian buffalo decoys. Twelve miles south of Chehalis, *Lewis and Clark State Park* is a popular recreation area. Along the coast, just below Aberdeen, *Twin Harbor State Park* has a very large attendance of visitors; it is Washington's only state park on the Pacific Ocean proper. *Long Beach,* at the mouth of the Columbia River, has a wonderful, truly "long" beach; it is 300 feet wide and 28 miles long; auto races are often held on the hard sand.

CENTRAL WASHINGTON The *Northern Cascades* with *Mount Baker, Lake Chelan* and *Mount Rainier National Park* are described on page 150. Where Lake Chelan touches highway 97, a popular resort area has sprung up; a boat ride to the northern end of the lake takes visitors into a wilderness of jagged mountains where such peaks as Old Goat, Baldy and Stormy are mirrored in the water. Where highway 10 crosses the Cascades, *Snoqualmie Pass* is a spectacular stretch of road drilled through rock tunnels and hewn into canyon walls; it is a spot of record snowfalls—up to 400 inches in a year. To the northwest, near the town of Snoqualmie, the 270-foot-high cataract of the *Snoqualmie Falls* is a splendid spectacle, enhanced by a number of miniature falls on its rocky sides. *Mount St. Helens* as seen from Spirit Lake is one of America's famous sights. An automobile road leads to the beautiful lake, and even the timberline can be reached by car. But the ascent to the peak, over cliffs, glaciers and crevasses is difficult. East of Mt. St. Helens, snow-capped *Mount Adams* rises to a height of 12,307 feet; the area abounds with trout streams. Ice Cave, to the south, may be visited by descending a ladder into a cavern with columns of crystal and a floor of ice. On the northern shore

of the Columbia River, west of the Bonneville Dam, *Beacon Rock* is a 900-foot-high monolith, the world's second largest; a zigzag trail leads to its top. Also on the northern bank of the Columbia River, south of Goldendale, a replica of the prehistoric Stone-henge structure of England stands on a cliff above the river—quite an incongrous sight. It was erected by Samuel Hill, the railroad tycoon who also established, nearby, the *Maryhill Museum of Fine Arts;* the latter displays, among other relics, a collection of personal belongings of European royalty. In the *Yakima Indian Reservation,* Old Fort Simco has been restored as it looked in 1856. In the village of White Swan the "long houses" where tribal meetings are held, welcome visitors in July. The Yakima ritual of the "root-digging-and-salmon-run thanksgiving" is a famous ceremony. To the north, 25 miles east of Ellensburg, the *Gingko Petrified State Forest* is a 3,000-acre preserve of gingko trees which millions of years ago were buried under volcanic ash and turned into opal; numerous fossilized trees still stand upright, as they had grown originally. To the north, *Wenatchee* is the world's apple capital; it lies in the center of four valleys covered with irrigated orchards; its two-day apple festival is a gay event. Eleven miles southwest of Wenatchee, visitors may watch the spillways and fish ladders of *Rock Island Dam* from observation platforms.

EASTERN WASHINGTON *Grand Coulee Dam,* the biggest concrete structure ever raised on earth, and *Roosevelt Lake* are described on page 142. Near Coulee City, *Dry Falls State Park* preserves an ancient gorge, now dry, where at one time the Columbia River plunged over a cataract with a volume 40 times that of Niagara Falls. *Spokane,* capital of the "inland empire," is a great trading center; nearby are 76 lakes, all within easy reach. Northeast of the city, a scenic drive leads to the top of 5,000-foot-high *Mount Spokane;* Mt. Spokane State Park is a favorite area for summer camping and winter sports. At the bend of the Columbia River near Pasco, the *Hanford Atomic Energy Plant* is one of the largest nuclear fission projects. West of Walla Walla, the *Whitman National Monument* honors Marcus Whitman and his wife Narcissa who established an Indian mission and school on the site; they were killed by the Indians in 1847.

NATIONAL PARKS IN WASHINGTON *Mount Rainier National Park,* see page 150. *Olympic National Park,* see page 146.

NATIONAL FORESTS IN WASHINGTON *Chelan Nat.F.,* U.S. 97 (includes 55-mile-long Lake Chelan) . *Colville Nat.F.,* U.S. 395 (Roosevelt Lake, impounded by Grand Coulee Dam, with a scenic drive along the lake) . *Gifford Pinchot Nat.F.,* U.S. 99, 830 (Mt. Adams with scenic Evergreen Highway; Spirit Lake; several wild areas). *Mt. Baker Nat.F.,* U.S. 99 (superlative mountain scenery; snow-capped peaks, glaciers, alpine lakes; North Cascades Wilderness Area) . *Olympic Nat.F.,* U.S. 99, 410, 101 (dense forests of big trees, spectacular snowy peaks, lakes, streams) . *Snoqualmie Nat.F.,* U.S. 10, 410 (Snoqualmie Falls; largest known Douglas fir tree; Mather Memorial Parkway) . *Wenatchee Nat.F.,* U.S. 2, 10, 97 (snow-capped peaks, lakes, alpine meadows, rare wildflowers, fishing streams; Wenatchee Lake) .

STATE PARKS 50 state parks, 6 recreational areas, 3 scientific sites, 9 wayside historic sites. For details write to State Parks and Recreation Commission, 100 Dexter Ave., Seattle 9, Washington.

WASHINGTON, D.C.

For information write to Greater National Capital Committee, Convention and Tourist Bureau, Washington Board of Trade, Star Building, Washington, D.C.

WASHINGTON, D.C.   Our national capital is described on page 48. As an educational center, Washington is the seat of *George Washington University* and American University. In residential Georgetown, *Georgetown University* is a leading Catholic institution.

WEST VIRGINIA

For information, write to West Virginia Industrial and Publicity Commission, State Capitol, Charleston 5, W.Va.

NORTHERN WEST VIRGINIA   *Morgantown* is the home of the University of West Virginia. In the narrow Northern Panhandle between Pennsylvania and the Ohio River, *Moundsville* is the site of one of the country's largest Indian burial mounds; the structure measures 900 feet in circumference and is 79 feet high. The interior has been excavated and may be inspected by visitors. The industrial city of *Wheeling*, also in the Panhandle, possesses the widely known Oglebay Park in the hilly, wooded countryside; the park offers all sports facilities, an historical and regional museum and summer performances of plays, operettas and concerts.

EASTERN WEST VIRGINIA   *Harpers Ferry*, at the junction of the Shenandoah and Potomac Rivers, in the Eastern Panhandle, was the scene of John Brown's anti-slavery raid, in 1859. The engine house, which served Brown and his men as a fort until his capture there, is now a museum on the campus of Storer College. Nearby *Charles Town,* founded by George Washington's brother Charles, is a lovely city of fine old homes and big shade trees. Seven of its elegant homes were built by Washington's relatives; a few of the mansions have been restored. To the northwest, *Berkeley Springs* has been a health resort with mineral-medicinal springs since the days of the Revolution. To the south, *Cacapon State Park* is a popular recreational area. From Prospect Rock four states may be seen on a clear day. To the west, the recently restored *Fort Ashby* was built at the command of George Washington. To the south, *Lost River State Park* can be reached by a scenic skyline drive. *Monongahela National Forest* (see below) is a huge wooded area along the eastern border of the state. In the mountains near the Virginia state line the *Smoke Hole Cavern, Seneca Caverns* and *Seneca Rock* are tourist attractions. In the limestone caves guided tours are available. Seneca Rock consists of glistening white sandstone and rises spectacularly as 1,000-foot-high towers. To the south, *Spruce Knob* (4,860 ft.) is the highest mountain in the state.

SOUTHEASTERN WEST VIRGINIA   *White Sulphur Springs* is one of America's most famous resorts, and its Greenbrier Hotel a fabulous hostelry. The spa was the outstanding fashion center of the planter's society of the South, before the Civil War, and the summer seat of several 19th-century presidents. It still is a fashionable vacation spot. Neighboring *Lewisburg* is a leisurely county seat. Its shady lanes, colonial homes, Old Stone Church of 1796 (built of limestone blocks) and General Lewis Hotel, with its unique collection of pioneer guns, pokers and warming pans, combine to create an atmosphere of the Old South. The West Virginia State Fair is an important event.

WESTERN WEST VIRGINIA   In *Parkersburg* on the Ohio River the City Park is noted for its pioneer museum and its lily pond. Farther south, also on the Ohio, *Point Pleasant* commemorates its battle of 1774 with a tall stone shaft and a log house museum displaying pioneer relics. In *Charleston,* the state capitol is crowned with a 300-foot-high guilded dome. To the southeast, *New River Gorge* and *Hawks Nest State Park* make a picturesque tourist spot. To the south, at the Virginia state line, near Blue-field, *Pinnacle Rock State Park* is a popular recreational area in the mountains.

NATIONAL FOREST IN WEST VIRGINIA   *Monongahela Nat.F.*, U.S. 33, 219 (includes Spruce Knob, highest point in West Virginia; Blackwater Canyon and 60-foot falls; Seneca rock on historic Seneca Indian Trail; the botanically curious Cranberry Glades, called a "misplaced Arctic tundra"; unexplored limestone caves; beaver colonies) .

STATE PARKS   15 state parks, 7 state forests, 74 roadside parks, 8 wayside picnic areas. For details, write to Division of State Parks, Conservation Commission, Charleston, W.Va.

WISCONSIN

For information, write to Recreational Publicity Division, Conservation Department, Madison, Wisconsin.

NORTHERN WISCONSIN   When approaching the harbor of the city of Superior, boats travel past the group of *Apostle Islands*, with their spectacular red cliffs. The islands are an old French fishermen's settlement called the "Twelve Apostles." *Superior*, the iron-ore port, is a "twin" of Duluth. Ten miles to the south, *Pattison State Park* is located on highway 35; this scenic spot contains the 165-foot-high Big Manitou waterfall, the highest in Wisconsin. To the south, *Interstate Park* has been established at the Dalles of the St. Croix River—a spectacular wilderness. The forest-and-lake country of northern Wisconsin is one huge vacationland where water sports and winter sports flourish, with *Rhinelander* a center of the resort area. South of Rhinelander, *Rib Mountain State Park* near Wausau includes Wisconsin's highest summit, at an altitude of 1,940 feet. This is principally a winter playground, with toboggan runs, ice-hockey fields, ski tows and ski trails. At the tip of the peninsula between Green Bay and Lake Michigan, *Peninsula State Park* is a large forest with trails, bridle paths and other recreational facilities. Brown County with the city of *Green Bay* is an important cheese area; numerous small cheese factories sell their delicious products in their own stores along the roads. In Green Bay, the Neville Museum preserves relics of early fur-trading and lumbering days. The Roi-Porlier-Tank cottage of 1776, Wisconsin's oldest building, is located there.

SOUTHERN WISCONSIN   The *Wisconsin Dells, Devils Lake State Park* and Wisconsin's capital, *Madison,* with such famous institutions as the *University of Wisconsin* and the U.S. Forest Products Laboratory, are described on page 94. Just west of Madison, at *Mt. Horeb* in the "Valley of the Elves," *Little Norway* is a fascinating outdoor museum of a dozen log buildings, all replicas of such Norse structures as an early settler's house and a cobbler's shop. *Milwaukee* supposedly has been made famous by beer, and those interested in the brewing process will find guided tours available in most of the famous breweries. Milwaukee is not only an industrial center; with its magnificent lake shore, its city-wide system of parks, its conservatory, sunken gardens and zoo, it is also one of the country's most beautiful cities. A symphony orchestra and two art galleries are cultural centers. In the city's surroundings, dozens of inland lakes are within easy reach. In *Racine* lovers of modern architecture will be interested in the functional buildings of the Johnson Wax Company, designed by Frank Lloyd Wright, Wisconsin-born dean of American architects and international leader in modernistic design. *Lake Geneva* with Yerkes Observatory is described on page 95. To the west, *Mineral Point* is known for the row of Cornish-style houses built by Cornish miners after 1832, when mineral deposits were discovered in the neighborhood. Near Prairie du Chien, northwest of Mineral Point, *Wyalusing State*

Park is a pleasant recreational area of forests and caves, high bluffs and green valleys at the junction of the Wisconsin and Mississippi Rivers.

NATIONAL FORESTS IN WISCONSIN *Chequamegon Nat.F.,* U.S. 2, 63; State 13, 64, 70, 77 (hundreds of northern lakes; pine spruce and balsam forests) . *Nicolet Nat.F.,* U.S. 8,141; State 17, 32, 55, 64, 70, 139 (northern Wisconsin lake region; trout streams and scenic rivers; hardwood and evergreen forests) .

STATE PARKS 29 state parks, 7 state forests, numerous wayside picnic areas. For details, write to Forests and Parks Division, Wisconsin Conservation Department, State Office Building, Madison 2, Wisconsin.

WYOMING

For information, write to Commerce and Industry Commission, 213 Capitol Building, Cheyenne, Wyoming.

NORTHERN WYOMING In the northeastern corner of the state, *Devils Tower National Monument* is a unique kind of mountain: It has the shape of a gigantic tree stump, rising 600 feet above the ridge from which it seems to grow; even the outside of the rock is grilled like bark. Pleasant woodlands surround the tower, and a museum tells its story. *Sheridan,* to the west, is noted for its beautiful parks; the Sheridan Rodeo in July is one of the state's most popular festivals. West of Sheridan, where state highway 14 crosses the Bighorn Mountains, *Bald Mountain* is an attraction on two counts: One is the broad panorama of the Bighorn Basin, the other the Indian Medicine Wheel, a stone wheel measuring 245 feet in circumference, a ceremonial structure laid out by an unknown Indian race. A town which retains a real frontier flavor is *Tensleep,* on U.S. highway 16 west of the Bighorn Range. It is surrounded by sheep and cattle ranches, and scenic Tensleep Canyon is nearby. The name is based on the Indians' method of measuring distances; it means ten days or ten "sleeps" of travel, in this case from Fort Laramie. *Cody* was founded by Colonel William F. Cody, known throughout the world as Buffalo Bill. He lived there for twenty years and was a driving power behind the Shoshone Irrigation Project and Buffalo Bill Dam. He is honored in the *Buffalo Bill Statue* and the *Cody Museum* (a reproduction of his log ranch house) and in the city's annual stampede, held during the first week in July. Just outside of Cody, highway 14–20 leads through the spectacular five-mile gorge of Shoshone Canyon.

NORTHWESTERN WYOMING *Yellowstone National Park,* "the world's greatest outdoor volcanic museum," is described on page 136. The beautiful *Grand Teton National Park* is described on page 138.

CENTRAL WYOMING There are several points of interest around the trading center of *Casper.* To the north the *Teapot Dome,* a U.S. Naval Petroleum Reserve, made political history on the scandalous side in the 1920's. To the west, *Hell's Half Acre* is an area of twisted caverns, stone figures and spires; one section,

called Devil's Kitchen, has been opened as a park. To the south, *Independence Rock* is a stone tower almost 200 feet high and measuring about 1,500 feet in circumference; the early traders who blazed the Oregon Trail carved their names into the rock, turning it into a monument to the pioneer spirit. Nearby, 218-foot-high *Pathfinder Dam* creates the large Pathfinder reservoir. To the northwest, *Hot Springs State Park* near Thermopolis is a recreational area.

SOUTHERN WYOMING The history of *Cheyenne,* the state capital, is particularly colorful; in the days of Indian attacks, of badmen and vigilantes this was the rip-roaring Wild West. With such traditions, Cheyenne's Frontier Days Celebration is one of the country's best shows of its kind; it is held in the last week of July. In the Supreme Court Building a good collection of Indian relics may be seen. Frontier Park is a preserve for a herd of buffaloes. To the north, *Fort Laramie National Monument* comprises the remnants of an important trading post and garrison of 1834; the ruins of sixteen buildings are being restored. In the days of the Oregon Trail covered wagons stopped there by the dozens, forty-niners on their way to the gold fields sought protection in the fort against the Indians and the Pony Express maintained a horse-changing station there. The *Red Desert* in southern Wyoming is a little-known, colorful wilderness which preserves a remnant of the romantic Old West: Herds of wild horses still roam its lonely canyons and mesas. All of the mustangs are hardy, and some are magnificent specimens. Systematic roundups in which the herds are spotted from airplanes will sooner or later abolish these picturesque survivors from the days of the *conquistadores.* In the southwestern corner of the state, *old Fort Bridger* is the center of a state park including some of the early buildings of the fort and the old Pony Express station. The fort was founded by Jim Bridger, the famous scout, discoverer of the Great Salt Lake and the Paul Bunyan of the Rockies.

NATIONAL PARKS IN WYOMING *Yellowstone National Park,* see page 136. *Grand Teton National Park,* see page 138.

NATIONAL FORESTS IN WYOMING *Bighorn Nat.F.,* U.S. 14, 16, 87 (Bighorn Mountains, snow-capped peaks, glaciers, over 300 lakes, Indian Medicine Wheel) . *Bridger Nat. F.,* in western Wyoming, U.S. 89, 189, 187 (includes Wind River Mountain Range and Bridger Wilderness Area) . *Medicine Bow Nat.F.,* near Laramie, U.S. 30 (Medicine Bow and three other ranges; many lakes and fishing streams with beaver colonies) . *Shoshone Nat.F.,* near Cody, U.S. 14, 20, 287 (rugged Absaroka Mountains and Beartooth Plateau with perpetual snow; Gannett Peak, with an altitude of 13,785 feet the highest mountain in Wyoming; the largest glaciers in the Rocky Mountains; hundreds of lakes; five wilderness areas) . *Teton Nat.F.,* near Jackson, U.S. 89, 187, 287, State 22 (unspoiled scenic back country famous for big game herds; 4 mountain ranges; Continental Divide; famous Jackson Hole country) .

STATE PARKS 3 state parks For details, write to Commerce and Industry Commission, Capitol Building, Cheyenne, Wyoming.

SIGHTSEEING GAZETTEER OF CANADA

ALBERTA

For information write to Alberta Travel Bureau, Legislative Building, Edmonton, Alberta.

NORTHERN ALBERTA *Wood Buffalo National Park,* between

Athabasca and Great Slave Lakes, is a preserve of America's largest herd of wood buffaloes, a species bigger than plains buffaloes; not easily accessible to the public. *The Yellowknife Wilderness Area* is accessible only by air; it is an outstanding region for fishing, hunting, and "roughing it."

EASTERN ALBERTA Near the golf course of *Medicine Hat,* a cairn marks the site of Police Point, headquarters of the Northwest Mounted Police from 1883 to 1891. 43 miles to the south, *Elkwater Lake Provincial Park* is a popular playground.

CENTRAL ALBERTA *Edmonton* is the capital of Alberta, with impressive Legislative Buildings, museum and dome. It is the seat of the University of Alberta. In the lake country around Edmonton, *Elk Island National Park* is a fenced preserve for large herds of buffalo, deer, elk and moose; the 75 square miles of the park contain all recreational facilities. 88 miles northeast of Calgary, on highway 9, the *Badlands of the Red Deer River Valley* are a wilderness of geological interest; a section of the Badlands, Dinosaur Park, has been set aside as a tourist attraction, a fantastic region of ravines, flats, coulees and red shale hills. Petrified forests, prehistoric oyster beds and Horseshoe Canyon are decorated with strange formations known as dolomites and ammonites. This was a stamping ground of prehistoric monsters and fossils are found frequently. Scenically, the valley abounds in thrilling vistas which occasionally take on a grand-canyon splendor.

WESTERN ALBERTA *Waterton Lakes National Park* is the Canadian section of the Waterton-Glacier International Peace Park, a famous mountain playground of snowy peaks and lovely lakes. See also page 134. To the northeast, in the Galt Gardens near *Lethbridge,* a cairn commemorates the opening of the first coal mine in Alberta in 1872. Southeast of Lethbridge, on the Milk River, *Writing-on-Stone Park* preserves ancient Indian picture writings on rocks of grotesque shapes; picnic grounds are available. *Calgary* is the modern trading center of a rich farming and ranching area. The *Calgary Stampede,* held the second week in July, is Canada's most famous rodeo; the contests include an exciting chuck-wagon race. On the city's St. George Island, the wild animals of a modern zoo are supplemented by the concrete-and-plaster forms of huge dinosaurs, brontosaurs and sabre-toothed tigers which roamed the prehistoric jungles of Alberta; traces of their existence are found in the Badlands. *Banff National Park* with Banff city, *Lake Louise* and Chateau Lake Louise are described on page 130. *Jasper National Park* with the *Columbia Ice Field* is described on page 132.

CANADIAN NATIONAL PARKS IN ALBERTA *Wood Buffalo National Park,* not easily accessible to the public. *Elk Island National Park,* near Edmonton, see above. *Waterton Lakes National Park,* see above, and page 134. *Banff National Park,* see page 130. *Jasper National Park,* see page 132.

PROVINCIAL PARKS 23 provincial parks. For details write to The Alberta Travel Bureau, Legislative Building, Edmonton, Alberta.

BRITISH COLUMBIA

For information write to British Columbia Government Travel Bureau, Dept. of Trade and Industry, Victoria, B.C.

THE COAST OF BRITISH COLUMBIA *Victoria,* the beautiful capital of British Columbia on the southern tip of Vancouver Island, is famous for its colorful flower gardens and its British atmosphere; it is described on page 148. *Nanaimo,* to the north on the island, is an old trading post of the Hudson's Bay Company, with the original log house still on the site; it enjoys excellent boat service from downtown Vancouver. Nanaimo is the gateway to Canada's Evergreen Playground, to the Forbidden Plateau, Strathcona Provincial Park and the Campbell River country which is famous for fishing. To the west, *Port Alberni* at the head of the picturesque Alberni Canal can be reached by

driving through giant forests. *Vancouver,* dramatically located between the mountains and the sea, is described on page 144; the city is the home of the University of British Columbia. The *Inside Passage* to Alaska, with Ocean Falls, Prince Rupert, and Ketchikan, Alaska's southernmost port, is described on page 144. In Prince Rupert as in Ketchikan, fish canneries and totem poles are the tourist attractions.

INTERIOR BRITISH COLUMBIA In the eastern part of the province, a number of national parks preserve the most beautiful and spectacular sections of the Canadian Rockies. Together with Banff and Jasper National Parks in Alberta and several provincial parks they form the greatest mountain-park system in America. *Mount Revelstoke National Park* includes 7,983-foot-high Mt. Revelstoke; its principal attraction is an alpine region of dozens of lovely, clear, little lakes, of open stands of the slender spires of alpine firs and a carpet of wildflowers; the park contains championship ski runs and a ski jump. Nearby *Glacier National Park* protects the superb Selkirk Mountains, with towering summits, jagged ridges and glistening glaciers; since it is a true wilderness without automobile roads, only hardy hikers and climbers will cherish it; they can reach the park by the Canadian Pacific Railway, leaving the train at Glacier Station. On the west slope of the Rockies, *Yoho National Park* encompasses lofty peaks like Mt. Balfour (10,741 feet), magnificent cataracts like the Seven Sister Falls, two ice fields on the Continental Divide and clear, lovely lakes like Emerald and O'Hara. The word Yoho, by the way, is an Indian expression meaning, "it is wonderful." *Kootenay National Park* is a strip of mountain scenery on both sides of the Banff-Windermere Highway; the road leads through Sinclair Canyon with bright red walls, past the resort of Radium Hot Springs, the Iron Gates, and Marble Canyon with a natural bridge and a 70-foot waterfall. Lovers of the untouched wilderness will appreciate *Wells Gray Provincial Park,* to the northwest; it is an undeveloped lake-and-mountain area of unusual scenic beauty. In the southwest corner of the province, on the U.S. borderline, *E. C. Manning Provincial Park* lies on highway 3 between Hope and Princeton. Its features are mountain trails, alpine meadows, huge beds of wildflowers, and a varied wildlife. All recreational facilities are available, including skiing.

CANADIAN NATIONAL PARKS IN BRITISH COLUMBIA *Mount Revelstoke, Glacier, Yoho* and *Kootenay National Parks,* see above.

PROVINCIAL PARKS 61 provincial parks. For details write to Parks and Recreation Division, Dept. of Lands and Forests, Victoria, B.C.

MANITOBA

For information write to Bureau of Travel and Publicity, Dept. of Industry and Commerce, Winnipeg, Manitoba.

EASTERN MANITOBA *Whiteshell Forest Reserve* is a wilderness area of woods and lakes on the Ontario border, accessible by highway; it is noted for good fishing. *Lake Winnipeg* is a huge body of water, with several summer resorts at its southern end; steamboats serve the small shore communities like Norway House, on the lake's northern inlet; Norway House was founded as a trading post of the Hudson's Bay Company, in 1825; there the Cree syllabic system was invented.

CENTRAL MANITOBA *Winnipeg,* the capital of Manitoba, is a pleasant modern city whose Assiniboine Park contains beautiful flower beds, a conservatory, a zoo, and various sports fields. The Manitoba Pipers Association Picnic is held in that park late in July, and the old Scottish traditions of Manitoba are revived in lively competitions for pipers, drummers, and Highland dancers. The annual Music Festival has made a name for itself throughout Canada. Twenty miles north of Winnipeg, on the west bank of the Red River, *Lower Fort Garry* is an historic stone fort built by the Hudson's Bay Co. in the 1830's. West of Winnipeg, the city of *Portage la Prairie* is the site of Fort La Reine, built by La Vérendrye in 1738. North of the town, *Lake Manitoba* is a huge fishing ground.

WESTERN MANITOBA On the U.S. border, the *International Peace Garden* has been established by Manitoba and North Dakota to commemorate the traditional peace and friendship between Canada and the United States. A cairn consisting of rocks from both countries stands on the international boundary. *Riding Mountain National Park* has been established on the vast plateau of Riding Mountain which rises to a height of 2,200 feet. On the eastern and northeastern edge it towers 1,100 feet above the prairies, in a steep escarpment, and offers a splendid panorama of the fertile plains below. The park's main attractions are its magnificent forests of spruce, pine, and maple, and its numerous lakes. The largest is 9-mile-long Clear Lake whose name is well chosen; its waters are so crystal-clear that one can see, on its bottom, the bubbles of the springs that feed it. 85 miles of motor roads wind through the park, and all sports facilities are available. Highway 10 which crosses the park, penetrates far into the north country. It passes through The Pas where a cairn honors the memory of Henry Kelsey, fur trader and daring explorer of the Hudson's Bay Company, and ends at *Flin Flon*, on the Saskatchewan border. Sportsmen who look for the thrill of fishing in a real, far-away wilderness will enjoy this spot. Highlight of the season is the Flin Flon Trout Festival at the end of June. Both The Pas and Flin Flon are served by the Canadian National Railway.

NORTHERN MANITOBA In the high north, on Hudson's Bay *Churchill* was discovered in 1619, by the ill-fated Danish explorer Jens Munck. The Hudson's Bay Co. established its first fort there in 1688. The ruins of *Fort Prince of Wales*, on the shore of the Bay, date back to 1733; they are today a National Historic Park.

CANADIAN NATIONAL PARKS IN MANITOBA *Riding Mountain, Lower Fort Garry,* and *Fort Prince of Wales National Parks,* see above.

NEW BRUNSWICK

For information write to Government Bureau of Information and Tourist Travel, Fredericton, New Brunswick.

SOUTHERN NEW BRUNSWICK The southwestern coast of New Brunswick is so picturesque that it attracts many painters. There are beautiful resorts like St. Andrews, a golfer's paradise; islands like *Campobello* and *Grand Manan* are popular vacation areas; the latter's tower-like cliffs rise from the ocean for hundreds of feet, a metropolis of thousands of sea gulls and strayed tropical birds. The sturdy boats, the cod and lobster fisheries, the young sailors, the women gathering dulse (an edible seaweed)—all these sights create a fascinating local atmosphere. *Saint John* was called for the name which Champlain gave the river when he landed there in 1604 on the feast day of St. John the Baptist, but the city proper was founded in 1783 by expatriated royalists from New England. The outstanding feature of the harbor is the constant movement of the water, the difference between high and low tide which may be as much as 30 feet; at low tide the fishing schooners at the Market Slip pier lie in the mud. A phenomenon caused by the huge tides is that of the Reversing Falls, with the waters of the Saint John River gushing

in a torrent one way or the other, according to the outgoing or incoming tide. King Square Park and the historic New Brunswick Museum are other attractions. To the northeast, *Fundy National Park* rises from the bay in terraces, with a sculptured shoreline of sheltered coves and promontories battered by waves. While the shore of the park is of rugged grandeur, the interior is sylvan and hilly, an idyl of mixed forests and small lakes. There are facilities for all sports. Farther northeast near Sackville, *Fort Beauséjour National Historic Park* commemorates the French-English struggle for the possession of Canada; the old French fort was built from 1751 to '55. To the north, *Shediac* is a popular seaside resort offering excellent sailing conditions in Northumberland Strait and fine swimming; normally the ocean water is pleasantly warm in the strait. *Fredericton* is the small but dignified capital of the province, with impressive legislative buildings, a cathedral, and the University of New Brunswick. Located on the Saint John River, Fredericton is the gateway to the great fishing and hunting regions of the province; just above the town, a salmon pool is famous among sportsmen.

NORTHERN NEW BRUNSWICK In the huge, roadless forest-and-hill country of the province, the *Plaster Rock-Renous Game Refuge* is one of America's great preserves of the black bear, the moose, the white-tailed deer, and of such smaller fur bearers as mink, muskrat, red fox, raccoon, beaver, otter, wildcat, lynx, and weasel. In the northwestern corner of the province, *Edmundston* is the supply center for the *Saint John River Valley* which stretches throughout the eastern part of New Brunswick. The broad river, the hilly banks with wide views, the prosperous villages with their large apple orchards (their McIntosh apples are famous), the lush meadows and stands of trees create a lovely landscape of peace and plenty. At *Hartland,* the river may be crossed on the world's longest wooden covered bridge.

CANADIAN NATIONAL PARKS IN NEW BRUNSWICK *Fundy* and *Fort Beauséjour National Parks,* see above.

NEWFOUNDLAND

For geographic and climatic reasons, sportsmen rather than sightseers visit this rocky island, the tenth largest in the world. Its 200 rivers, particularly the Humber, Portland Creek and the Serpentine, offer excellent salmon fishing. Also brown trout and land-locked salmon are caught in a number of lakes. This island's rocky shores are studded with picturesque fishing villages where millions of cod dry on rickety scaffolds. *St. John's,* the capital, is an interesting city with whale, seal and cod fisheries. The airport of *Gander* is well known to transatlantic airplane passengers.

For further information, write the Newfoundland Tourist Development Board, St. John's, Newfoundland.

NOVA SCOTIA

For information write to Nova Scotia Bureau of Information, Provincial Building, Halifax, Nova Scotia.

SOUTHERN NOVA SCOTIA *Halifax,* founded in 1749, the capital of the province, is of great interest both historically and scenically. In Canada's history it played a leading part, for it has the country's oldest Protestant church (St. Paul, built 1750), and was the site of the first Canadian printing press (1751), which printed Canada's first newspaper in 1752; it had Canada's first public school, first public gardens, first dockyard and its first post office. It was a garrison and fortress from the beginning, and still is the principal base of Canada's fleet. For a magnificent view of Halifax Harbour, visitors ride to the highest hill in the city, which is crowned by the Citadel, a squat, gray old fort that has never been attacked. At the southern end of the city's peninsula, Point Pleasant Park is a resort area with several old forts and historic structures like the Martello Tower, which was built in 1796 by Queen Victoria's father, the Duke of Kent. North West Arm, a three mile inlet, is an ideal harbor for yachts, canoes and other pleasure craft; the blue surface of its water is set off by green hills ashore; from the National Memorial Tower in Fleming Park, a superb view of the city may be enjoyed. Downtown, Province House is an impressive structure. Halifax is also the home of Dalhousie University. To the southwest, *Lunenburg* is a picturesque fishing port whose fishing fleet is one of the world's largest; one of its schooners, the "Bluenose," won international fame as the North Atlantic champion. Deep-sea fishing flourishes all along the coast, and the annual International Tuna Cup Match held at *Wedgeport,* on the southern coast, is indeed an international contest attracting thousands of sportsmen. On the Bay of Fundy, *Port Royal National Historic Park* honors a unique event in Canada's history, in the reconstructed "Habitation," a fortified trading post erected by Champlain and de Monts in 1605. It was the first permanent white settlement in North America, north of the Spanish empire. At this spot the first conversions to Christianity in Canada were made, the first road was built and the first play was written and performed. Nearby, at Annapolis Royal, *Fort Anne National Historic Park* contains the restored fort, a museum and an historical library. On the Minas Basin, *Grand Pré Memorial Park* is a popular recreational area. Nearby to the southeast, the Haliburton Memorial Museum at *Windsor* is the estate of a Nova Scotia judge and author who erected the villa, on a hill above the Avon River, in 1836; it can be inspected in its original state. Between Windsor and Halifax, *Uniacke House* at Mount Uniacke was built in 1813–15 by Richard John Uniacke, Attorney-General of Nova Scotia from 1797 to 1830. It is a large mansion with a white-pillared portico, and still filled with the original furniture. It is open to the public.

NORTHERN NOVA SCOTIA   *Cape Breton Island* is the northern part of the province. In its center, a cluster of beautiful lakes impressed the first French settler deeply, particularly at sunset, so that the Frenchman called the lakes "Bras d'Or," "Arms of Gold." *Sydney,* Nova Scotia's second largest city, is closest to Great Britain of all American ports. It is both an industrial city (coal and steel) and a popular summer resort. 23 miles to the south, *Fortress of Louisbourg National Historic Park* preserves the ruins of one of the most impressive military establishments on the American continent: the walled city of Louisbourg erected by the French early in the 18th century. The present park contains interesting excavations and an historical museum. In the north, *Cape Breton Highlands National Park* is a landscape of solitary grandeur; it is touched, on three sides, by the scenic Cabot Trail. On the eastern shore the coves and valleys, the hills and vales are reminiscent of the Highlands of Scotland; the western shore is rugged, and the rocks rise from the ocean to heights of 1,500 feet. Both freshwater and saltwater fishing is good in the park, and the east coast offers a special treat to deep-sea fishermen: It is one of America's best fishing grounds for swordfish. Ingonish and Neil Harbour are the centers of the swordfishing industry.

CANADIAN NATIONAL PARKS IN NOVA SCOTIA   *Port Royal, Fort Anne, Fortress of Louisbourg* and *Cape Breton Highlands National Parks,* see above.

ONTARIO
For information write to Department of Travel and Publicity of the Province of Ontario, Toronto, Ontario.

EASTERN ONTARIO   The "greatest ship highway in the world" is the *Soo Canal* between *Sault Ste. Marie* in Ontario and the city of the same name in Michigan. Watching the traffic in the canal is a great sightseeing attraction; of the huge locks, one is located in Canada. The whole area is described on page 92. On the northern shore of Lake Huron, *Manitoulin Island* is the largest freshwater island on earth. *Georgian Bay* is an immense arm of Lake Huron, with a shoreline broken by hundreds of sheltered bays, and an archipelago of about 30,000 islands along its eastern coast. Rocky capes, sandy bays, wooded islands, picturesquely winding channels, and myriads of fish in the sparkling waters make this region a wonderful summer playground. Along the eastern shore, *Georgian Bay Islands National Park* consists of 30 islands of which Beausoleil is the largest. Also Flowerpot Island belongs to the park; it is located about 100 miles northwest of Beausoleil. The island's feature is a couple of eroded stone pillars which stand on the shore like two huge flower pots. Small trees and shrubs which grow in the fissures on top heighten the illusion. This region was "Huronia," the ancient home of the Great Huron Indian Federation which was almost annihilated by the Iroquois. Near *Midland,* on the south shore of Georgian Bay, the Indian Village and Jesuit Mission of St. Ignace was burned and destroyed in the massacre of 1649, an event which is commemorated today in the *Martyr's Shrine* of Midland. To the south at Stratford, the *Stratford Shakespearean Festival* is famous for its annual midsummer season of excellent dramatic performances of plays by Shakespeare and, occasionally, other classical dramatists. Art exhibitions are held in conjunction with the festival which draws thousands of visitors from Canada and the U.S. At the southern tip of Ontario, *Windsor* is located on the left bank of the Detroit River, opposite America's automobile capital; for obvious reasons, Windsor has become Canada's automobile capital. South of Windsor, near Amherstburg, *Fort Malden National Historic Park* commemorates, through an historic museum, an old British fort which used to stand on the site. Built about 1797 the fort played an important part in the War of 1812. *Point Pelée National Park* is the most southerly point of Canada. If you fly westward on the park's latitude, you will land in California—a surprise to those who think of Canada in terms of the far north. Point Pelée's broad, sandy beaches and shady groves of maple trees, oaks and red cedars have indeed a Southern charm. The park is also a fascinating bird sanctuary, on one of the continent's principal bird migration routes. Thousands of Detroiters and Windsorites enjoy the park during the summer. To the east, the *Niagara Falls* are described on page 40. The Canadian sector of the falls is larger in volume and more beautiful than the American sector, and the shore park of the Canadian city of Niagara Falls offers the best view of the great natural spectacle as a whole. To the north, *Toronto* is built on a slope below a plateau which gradually rises from Lake Ontario to a height of 300 feet. It is the capital of Ontario and Canada's second largest city, essentially a British-Canadian community. In its center, in Queen's Park, the old Parliament buildings are of red sandstone, and the new additions of blue dolomite stone. There are 69 other parks, among them Exhibition Park which houses the *Canadian National Exhibition,* the biggest annual exhibition on earth. The city's seat of higher learning is the University of Toronto. *St. Lawrence Islands National Park* is in the Canadian section of that most picturesque region usually called *The Thousand Islands,* described on page 38. The Canadian park consists of a mainland area and 13 islands whose granite and limestone cliffs rise from the blue channels; everywhere there are pleasant groves of birch, pine, oak and maple. Some of the islands, for instance Aubrey, Beau Rivage and Gordon, are equipped with wharves, bathing beaches and camping facilities. To the north, overlooking the St. Lawrence River at Prescott, *Fort Wellington National Historic Park* preserves an impressive fortress which was erected during the War of 1812. The pentagonal earthworks enclose a massive stone building with walls three feet thick. It serves as a museum now. To the north, *Ottawa* is located on the right bank of the Ottawa River, on a chain of hills which rises from the river bank to an altitude of 155 feet. The scenery is beautiful, and from Parliament Hill one can clearly see the Chaudière Falls with their cloud of spray. Also the curtain-like Rideau Falls are near. The Rideau Canal separates the city into an Upper Town (largely English), and a Lower Town (largely French). As the capital of the country, Ottawa possesses imposing government buildings, most of them erected on Parliament Hill, in Victorian Gothic, in 1860. Besides the legislative buildings, the Royal Mint, the National Museum, the National Art Gallery, the War Memorial and the Dominion Observatory are tourist attractions. Rideau Hall at Rockcliffe Park, the governor general's mansion, and the campus of the University of Ottawa are also of interest. Nearby Lake Deschénes is a popular summer resort, and skiing in the Laurentian Hills to the north is the favorite winter sport. West of Ottawa, *Algonquin Provincial Park* comprises 2,700 square miles of unspoiled natural beauty. It is a sanctuary for deer, moose, and beaver, with numerous lakes and streams. Camp sites and accommodations are available.

WESTERN ONTARIO *Lake of the Woods*, on the Manitoba border, is a great resort area with Kenora, "Queen of the North." This playground offers 2,000 square miles of water and woods, 14,000 islands, and too many delightful bays and inlets to be counted. From small boats and big cruisers visitors fish for muskies and lake trout, walleyes and small-mouth bass. To the east, the *Rainy Lake-Fort Frances Region* is a vast tract of evergreen forests with the earmarks of a true wilderness: There are hundreds of lakes which have no names; in fact, their number is not known either. The district has been described as "the greatest canoe country in North America." *Quetico Provincial Park*, together with the Superior National Forest on the U.S. side of the border, forms a huge water-and-woods wilderness ideal for canoeing; parts of it are a "forest primeval" of white pines. It is a rugged and beautiful country for experienced "voyageurs." The railroad touches the park in the north. On the shore of Lake Superior, the neighboring cities of *Fort William* and *Port Arthur* are popular starting points for the great hunting and fishing wilderness. But at the same time they are also the trading centers of the busy Thunder Bay region which produces gold, silver, iron, and grain. The cities' waterfront with miles of bustling docks, wharves, and the continent's biggest grain silos is interesting to watch.

CANADIAN NATIONAL PARKS IN ONTARIO *Fort Malden, Point Pelée, Georgian Bay Islands, St. Lawrence Islands,* and *Fort Wellington National Parks,* see above.

PROVINCIAL PARKS 6 provincial parks. For details write to Department of Lands and Forests, Parliament Buildings, Toronto, Ontario.

PRINCE EDWARD ISLAND
For information write to Prince Edward Island Travel Bureau, Charlottetown, P.E.I.

PRINCE EDWARD ISLAND Of all Canadian provinces, "P.E.I." is the smallest, and one of the loveliest. The whole island is a beautiful park, with a lacy shoreline of tidal streams, lagoons, and inlets, with gently rolling hills, prosperous farms and lush forests, and picturesque red sandstone cliffs in the south. In 1534 Jacques Cartier described the island as "the fairest that may possibly be seen, and full of beautiful trees and meadows." After more than four centuries, the explorer's "endorsement" is still true. There is only one city on the island, *Charlottetown*, which is also the capital of the province. It is picturesquely located at a spot where three rivers merge into a fine harbor. Victoria Park, facing the port, the Exhibition Grounds, and the Harris Memorial Art Gallery are tourist attractions. St. Dunstan's University is nearby. North of Charlottetown, *Prince Edward Island National Park* is a 25-mile coastal strip on the Gulf of St. Lawrence, a fine, smooth sandy beach of reddish color, set off by sand dunes and red sandstone cliffs; some sections are well forested, and stands of white birches and dark spruces have a northern beauty of their own. All sports are available, but swimming, sailing and fishing in the many sheltered bays are most popular. There are numerous picturesque and idyllic fishing villages on the island, for instance *Mount Carmel* in the southwestern corner. It is an Acadian settlement which seems to have been transplanted from Brittany not hundreds of years ago, but yesterday. Traditional handicrafts flourish, particularly the making of hand-hooked rugs with gay patterns. An interesting specialty of the island is the raising of silver foxes.

CANADIAN NATIONAL PARK ON PRINCE EDWARD ISLAND *Prince Edward Island National Park,* see above.

QUEBEC
For information write to Provincial Publicity Bureau, Québec, Que.

SOUTHERN QUEBEC Entering the Province of Quebec from New England, visitors will find, in the so-called *Eastern Townships*, very much the same landscape as south of the border, with pleasant forests, hills and lakes. One of the largest lakes of the region, Memphremagog, is partly in Vermont, partly in Quebec. *Sherbrooke*, the "Queen of the Eastern Townships," has a spectacular location on the scenic slopes of two rivers, the Saint-François and the Magog. To the west, *Fort Chambly National Historic Park*, 20 miles from Montreal, contains the reconstruction of a stone fort of 1711; some of its massive walls are the originals, and also the ancient dungeon has been restored. Not far away, 12 miles south of St. Johns, *Fort Lennox National Historic Park* preserves the remains of one of Canada's largest old fortresses, built in 1759 by the French to stop the advance of the English from the south. Since it was used as a military post until 1870, the fortified buildings, the ramparts and the 60-foot-wide moat are still intact.

THE ST. LAWRENCE VALLEY OF THE PROVINCE OF QUEBEC *Montreal*, Canada's largest metropolis, second largest French-speaking city on earth and the biggest inland seaport in the world, is described on page 21. Among the city's famous churches are Notre Dame, St. James Cathedral and St. Joseph's Oratory (Brother André's shrine). Montreal is also the seat of *Mc Gill University* and of the University of Montreal. To the northeast on the St. Lawrence River, *Les Trois-Rivières* has very old traditions. The city started as a trading post in 1615, and many of its streets are today as winding and narrow as they were when laid out hundreds of years ago by pioneers from Normandy and Brittany. The Ursuline Convent dates back to 1696, the Récollet Monastery to 1698 and the Boucher de Niverville manor house is a relic of the feudal system. But next to the mementoes of a proud French past there are the modern mills: Trois-Rivières is one of the world's greatest pulp and paper manufacturing centers. *Québec*, the capital of the province, is described on p. 20. It is the only walled city on our continent, with a famous citadel and a much-photographed city gate. Among the historic buildings are the Convent of the Ursulines, the Church of Notre Dames des Victoires and the Basilique de Notre-Dame of 1647. L'Université Laval is the premier French university in North America. Québec is also a haven for gourmets; the town's French restaurants are excellent. A few miles north of Québec, *Ste. Anne de Beaupré* is a widely known shrine whose basilica is dedicated to Ste. Anne, the mother of the Virgin Mary. As many miraculous cures have been reported there, it is sometimes called the Lourdes of America. Farther north on the left bank of the St. Lawrence, the fashionable summer resort of *Murray Bay* with the Manoir Richelieu is described on p. 20. On the same page a description of the *Gaspé Peninsula* is found. The Gaspé's brightest spot, the village of Percé, with its rock in the sea and its historic mountains, is an unforgettable sight.

QUEBEC'S NORTH COUNTRY   The huge mountainous area of the *Laurentian Hills* is described on p. 20. This region has recently developed into a great ski center, with all winter sports facilities and such cross-country ski trails as the Maple Leaf Trail. The picturesque small French-Canadian towns add an intriguing foreign accent to a skiing vacation in the Laurentians. The famous *Saguenay River Region* is usually enjoyed from a steamboat. At the mouth of the river, shielded by a rocky promontory, *Tadoussac* has a unique history; it was not only one of the first French trading posts in America, but also played a leading part in the history of the Indians. Long before the 16th century, Indians gathered here for a great barter fair and festival, coming from as far north as Hudson's Bay and from as far south as Florida. Proceeding up-river to Bagotville, today's boats move between canyon walls 900 feet high. Cape Trinité and Cape Éternité are huge rocks rising precipitously from the water. River cruises may be taken from Montreal or Québec, or steamboat trips from Tadoussac. The area is also accessible by highway. At the western end of the Saguenay region the *Lake St. John Area* was lonely backwoods country not so long ago; today it is Quebec's newest industrial empire, sparked by one of the greatest hydro-electric developments in America. Huge plants have been established there, smelting ores, manufacturing aluminum and making pulp and paper. But the lake is large, and there are still plenty of opportunities for fishermen; the sportsmen's specialty is "ouananiche," landlocked salmon, said to be the finest fighter in North American fresh water.

NATIONAL PARKS IN QUEBEC—*Fort Chambly* and *Fort Lennox Nat'l Historic Parks,* see above.

PROVINCIAL PARKS   Some of Quebec's huge provincial parks are traversed by one or two automobile roads, like *Laurentides Park* and *La Vérendrye Park.* Others are great game reserves in the North Country, like *Mont Tremblant Park,* the *Kipawa Reserve,* and high up north the *Chibougamau Reserve. Gaspesian Park* is in the interior of the Gaspé Peninsula.

SASKATCHEWAN

For information write to Bureau of Publications, Regina, Saskatchewan.

SOUTHERN SASKATCHEWAN   *Regina,* the capital of the province, is a pleasant city surrounded by rich agricultural lands; it has a beautiful Legislative Building in an attractive park-and-water landscape on Lake Wascana. Regina is also the training headquarters for the Royal Canadian Mounted Police. To the west, *Moose Jaw* is an important railroad point; its grain elevators rise from the prairie like huge towers. To the north, *Saskatoon* is a lovely college town, the seat of the University of Saskatchewan which includes a well equipped medical school.

NORTHERN SASKATCHEWAN   *Prince Albert,* about 100 miles north of Saskatoon, has a flavor all its own. On one hand it is a quiet farming community, but the discovery of uranium and other minerals in the north country give it occasional touches of a boom town. 36 miles north of the city, *Prince Albert National Park* is a vast region of rocks, woods, and water, still filled with the memories of trappers and fur-traders, explorers and Indians. The park's special feature is its wonderful canoeing, for the park contains hundreds of lakes, and many of them are connected by little rivers and streams. From the dock at Waskesiu, canoe journeys of various durations may be undertaken. Several lakes in the park are of special interest; on Montreal Lake, for instance, a tribe of the Cree Indians has its reservation, and on the same lake the Hudson's Bay Company maintains a trading post. Halkett Lake, adjacent to the park highway, has an exceptionally fine sandy beach. Lake Lavallée is a famous wildlife sanctuary: Its islands are covered with the rookeries of a bird which we usually associate with the Deep South, the white pelican. The quaint "relics of a twilight, antediluvian age" have their extensive nesting grounds in this clear, cool northern lake. There are also large colonies of double-crested cormorants. A golf course, tennis courts and bowling greens are available along with all other sports facilities. Superb fishing for fighting freshwater species like northern pike, a special far-north variety of pickerel, and lake trout is found at *Lake La Ronge;* although the lake is located in the wilderness of the far north, the village of La Ronge, at the end of highway 2, offers modern accommodations.

CANADIAN NATIONAL PARKS IN SASKATCHEWAN   *Prince Albert National Park,* see above. *Fort Battleford Historic National Park,* northwest of Saskatoon, preserves a Mounted Police Post of 1876.

PROVINCIAL PARKS   9 provincial parks. For details write to Tourist Branch, Bureau of Publications, Regina, Saskatchewan.

ALPHABETIC LISTINGS OF ACCOMMODATIONS

IN THE

NATIONAL PARKS AND NATIONAL MONUMENTS

IN THE UNITED STATES

AND THE NATIONAL PARKS IN CANADA

(1) *Accommodations in the National Parks in the United States*

Acadia N.P., Maine: Campgrounds in park; various accommodations available in the resorts and villages of Mt. Desert Island.—*Big Bend N.P.,* Texas: Campgrounds in park; National Park Concessions, Inc., of Big Bend Nat. Park, Texas, operates cabins, restaurant, photo store, grocery store and service station at the Basin, in the park; saddle horses are for rent; hotels, motels, and restaurants in the towns of Marathon and Alpine, Texas.—*Bryce Canyon N.P.,* Utah: Campgrounds in park; the Utah Parks Co. of Cedar City, Utah, operates lodge, cabins, cafeteria and grocery store; saddle horses and motor bus tours are available.—*Carlsbad Caverns N.P.,* New Mexico: Overnight accommodations along the highway leading to the park; a store, a day-nursery and an underground lunchroom are operated in the park.—*Crater Lake N.P.,* in Oregon: 4 public campgrounds in park; the Crater Lake National Park Co. (summer address: Crater Lake, Oregon; winter address: 603 Wilcox Building, Portland, Oregon) operates lodge, cabins, dining room, cafeteria, motor bus tours.—*Everglades N.P.,* in Florida: Motels and hotels in Homestead, Florida City, and Everglades; limited campgrounds in the park; lunchroom, service station, charter boats at Coot Bay during winter.—*Glacier N.P.,* Montana: Campgrounds in park; the Glacier Park Co. (summer address: East Glacier Park, Montana; winter address: 1310 Great Northern Building, St. Paul 1, Minnesota) operates hotels, cabins and chalets in the park, and general stores at Many Glacier, Rising Sun, and Lake McDonald; saddle horses, boats and motor bus trips to Waterton Lakes N.P. in Canada are available.—*Grand Canyon N.P.,* Arizona: On South Rim, public campgrounds are available all year 'round; the Fred Harvey Co. of Grand Canyon, Arizona, operates a hotel, lodge, cafeteria, cabins, and motor bus service; saddle horses and saddle mules (for trips into canyon) may be rented; open all year. On North Rim, public campgrounds are available during summer; the Utah Parks Co. of Cedar City, Utah, operates lodge, cafeteria, bus service, and saddle horse service during the summer.—*Grand Teton N.P.,* Wyoming: Public campgrounds are available, also overnight camps for hikers and pack trains. Guide service for mountain climbers. Lodges, motor courts and dude ranches in the city of Jackson and in Jackson Hole.—*Great Smoky Mountains N.P.,* North Carolina and Tennessee: Public campgrounds in park; lodges, hotels and motels in Elkmont, Gatlinburg, Bryson City, Cherokee, and Fontana Village; lodges on top of Mount Le Conte, Snowbird Mountain, and on other picturesque spots.—*Hot Springs N.P.,* Arkansas: A public campground is maintained in the Gorge, at the foot of Hot Springs Mountain; hotels, motels, cottages, and apartments in the city of Hot Springs.—*Isle Royale N.P.,* Michigan: Public campgrounds are maintained on island; National Park Concessions, Inc. (summer address: Rock Harbor Lodge, Isle Royale National Park, Rock Harbor, Mich., all-year address: Mammoth Cave Hotel, Mammoth Cave National Park, Mammoth Cave, Ky.) operates lodges with limited accommodations; camp and photo supplies at lodges.—*Kings Canyon N.P.,* California: See Sequoia and Kings Canyon National Parks.—*Lassen Volcanic N.P.,* California: The Lassen National Park Co. (summer address: Manzanita Lake, Cal., winter address: P.O. Box 188, Mineral, Cal.) operates a lodge, bungalows, cabins, tents, a restaurant, a general store, a service station and a rowboat service at Manzanita Lake. At Summit Lake, pack and saddle horses may be rented. Skiing facilities are available during winter months at the Sulphur Works Skiing Area. Outside of park, all-year accommodations are available in and around Mineral.—*Mammoth Cave N.P.,* Kentucky: Public campground and picnic area in park. National Park Concessions, Mammoth Cave, Ky., operates a hotel, cabins, and cottages, and the Snowball Dining Room underground.—*Mesa Verde N.P.,* Colorado: Public campgrounds in park. The Mesa Verde Co., Mesa Verde Nat. Park, Colorado, operates the Spruce Tree Lodge, cabins and tents; pack and saddle horses may be rented.—*Mount Rainier N.P.,* Washington: The Rainier Nat. Park Co., Box 1136, Tacoma 1, Wash., operates the Paradise Inn and lodge, with cafeteria and fountain service; the Sunrise Lodge, with cafeteria and store; the Longmire Inn with cafeteria, fountain, and store. There is also the Lodge at Ohanapecosh, with store and housekeeping cabins and facilities for hot mineral baths.—*Olympic N.P.,* Washington: Public campgrounds in park. Inn, lodge, cabins, cottages; saddle horses, boats, and guides. There are many hotels and resorts on the Olympic Peninsula; for information write to Olympic Peninsula Resort and Hotel Association, Colman Ferry Terminal, Seattle, Wash.—*Platt N.P.,* Oklahoma: Public campgrounds and picnic areas in park. Accommodations of various types are available in the city of Sulphur and other neighboring towns.—*Rocky Mountain N.P.,* Colorado: There are numerous hotels, inns, and lodges near and in the park. For information write to Estes Park Chamber of Commerce, and Grand Lake Chamber of Commerce. Bear Lake Lodge, Brinwood Hotel, Camp Woods, Forest Inn, Grand Lake Lodge, Spragues Lodge are well-known establishments.—*Sequoia and Kings Canyon N. Parks,* California: Public campgrounds in park; the campground at Lodgepole has a natural swimming pool. The Sequoia and Kings Canyon Nat. Parks Co., Sequoia National Park, Cal., operates lodges, camps, stores, restaurants, service stations, and saddle horse services at Giant Forest in Sequoia N.P. (all-year 'round), and at General Grant Grove in Kings Canyon N.P. (closed during winter except for the lunch counter); the company also maintains tent accommodations, a store, a lunchroom and a service station at Cedar Grove, South Fork of the Kings River (closed during winter). During July and August, the company operates a High Country Base Camp at Bearpaw Meadow in Sequoia N.P., with tent and dining accommodations.—*Shenandoah N.P.,* Virginia: Public campgrounds and picnic areas in park. The Virginia Sky-Line Co., Inc., Luray, Va., operates a hotel, lodges, cabins, and stores at several locations.—*Wind Cave N.P.,* South Dakota: Public campgrounds in park, also lunchroom and fountain service during summer. Near the park are numerous hotels and motels, in Hot Springs and elsewhere.—*Yellowstone N.P.,* Wyoming, Montana and Idaho: Public campgrounds in park; the Yellowstone Park Co. (summer address: Yellowstone Park, Wyoming; winter address: P.O. Box 1699, Helena, Montana), operates hotels, lodges, cottages, tourist cabins, cafeterias, transportation service, groceries-and-photo stores and service stations at various points; boats, fishing tackle and saddle horses may be rented.—*Yosemite N.P.,* California: Large public campgrounds in park; the Yosemite Park & Curry Co., Yosemite National Park, California, operates hotels, lodges, cabins, tents, transportation service, grocery stores, photo stores, garages, service stations and swimming pools, at various points. Pack and saddle horses and bicycles may be rented.—*Zion N.P.,* Utah: Public campgrounds in park, open all year. The Utah Parks Co., Cedar City, Utah, operates Zion Lodge with cabins, cafeteria, store, and transportation service; saddle horses, guides and all-expense motor tours to neighboring sightseeing attractions are available.

(2) *Accommodations at the National Monuments in the United States*

Note: Not mentioned here are the National Monuments without tourist accommodations at the monument or nearby, the historic shrines in densely populated areas and the monuments of minor importance.—*Arches Nat.M.,* Utah: Accommodations in Moab, 5 miles distant; saddle and pack horses for hire.—*Badlands Nat.M.*, South Dakota: Cedar Pass Lodge with cabins, restaurant, souvenir store, service station at Interior, S.D.—*Black Canyon of the Gunnison Nat.M.*, Colorado: Public campgrounds and picnic areas on both rims; hotels and motels in nearby towns.—*Capulin Mountain Nat.M.*, New Mexico: Picnic area at western base of Capulin Mountain; supplies and accommodations in the towns of Capulin and Folsom.—*Cedar Breaks Nat.M.*, Utah: A public campground is maintained; the Utah Parks Co., Cedar City, Utah, operates a lodge with cabins, during summer months.—*Chiricahua Nat.M.*, Arizona: Public campgrounds in Bonita Canyon, near headquarters; accommodations, meals, and saddle horses at Silver Spur Ranch.—*Colorado Nat.M.*, Colorado: Public campground and picnic area at monument headquarters; supplies and accommodations in nearby towns.—*Craters of the Moon Nat.M.*, Idaho: Public campgrounds at monument headquarters; the Crater Inn (postal address: Arco, Idaho) offers cabins and meal service during summer months.—*Death Valley Nat.M.*, California and Nevada: One public campground. On government land the Wildrose Service Station (P.O. Box 4, Trona, Cal.) operates also tourist cabins. On private lands, various accommodations are available; well-known are the Furnace Creek Inn and Ranch, the Stovepipe Wells Hotel, and Scotty's Castle at Goldfield, Nev.—*Devils Tower Nat.M.*, Wyoming: Public campgrounds and picnic areas near monument headquarters; motor courts are available nearby.—*Dinosaur Nat.M.*, Utah and Colorado: One public campground; accommodations at Vernal, Utah, 21 miles away.—*Great Sand Dunes Nat.M.*, Colorado: Public campground near dunes; accommodations at nearby Alamosa.—*Jewel Cave Nat.M.*, South Dakota: Public campground near monument headquarters; accommodations in nearby towns.—*Joshua Tree Nat.M.*, California: Public campgrounds with fireplaces available, but campers must bring fuel and water; accommodations in Twentynine Palms and Joshua Tree.—*Lava Beds Nat.M.*, California: Public campground and picnic area available; accommodations and supplies in nearby towns.—*Lehman Caves Nat.M.*, Nevada: Public campground, picnic facilities, cabins and lunchroom available.—*Muir Woods Nat.M.*, California: Meal service and souvenir store.—*Oregon Caves Nat.M.*, Oregon: Public campground at Greyback, on approach road, 8 miles from monument; Oregon Caves Resort, Inc., Grants Pass, Oregon, operates lodge, cabins, restaurant, souvenir store.—*Organ Pipe Cactus Nat.M.*, Arizona: Campground near monument headquarters; service station at international boundary; accommodations at Ajo and Tuscon.—*Petrified Forest Nat.M.*, Arizona: Public campground available; food, gasoline and souvenirs at Painted Desert Inn and Rainbow Forest Lodge; accommodations at Holbrook, Ariz., 20 miles to the west.—*Rainbow Bridge Nat.M.*, Utah: Limited accommodations and saddle horses for excursion to Rainbow Bridge at Rainbow Lodge.—*Saguaro Nat.M.*, Arizona: Picnic area at monument headquarters; accommodations in Tuscon.—*Timpanogos Cave Nat.M.*, Utah: Picnic facilities, lunchroom and store with supplies near monument headquarters; accommodations in nearby towns.—*White Sands Nat.M.*, New Mexico: Picnic facilities, soda fountain and souvenirs at monument headquarters; accommodations in Alamogordo and also Las Cruces.

(3) Accommodations in the National Forests in the United States

Send 25 cents to Superintendent of Documents, U.S. Government Printing Office, Washington D.C., and ask for the booklet *National Forest Vacations*, issued by the Forest Service of the U.S. Department of Agriculture; the booklet lists recreation and campground facilities for each national forest in the U.S.

(4) Accommodations in National Wildlife Refuges in the United States

In a few outstanding refuges overnight accommodations are operated by concessionaires in the *Okefenokee National Wildlife Refuge* in Georgia, the *Imperial and Havasu National Wildlife Refuges* in Arizona and California and the *Mattamuskeet National Wildlife Refuge* in North Carolina.

(5) Accommodations in the State Parks in the U.S.

Write to the state agencies indicated at the end of each state chapter in the Sightseeing Gazetteer, page 209.

(6) Accommodations in the National Parks in Canada

Banff N.P., Alberta: Hotels, lodges, motels, apartments and bungalows in and near Banff, at Lake Louise and along the Banff-Jasper Highway; the Banff Springs Hotel in Banff and the Chateau Lake Louise at Lake Louise are world famous.—*Cape Breton Highlands N.P.*, Nova Scotia: Keltic Lodge and Cape Breton Highlands Bungalows are within the park; lodges and cabins are available just outside the park at Ingonish, Neils Harbour, Cheticamp, Pleasant Bay and Cape North.—*Elk Island N.P.*, Alberta: Cabins in the park; hotel accommodations at Lamont (4 miles distant) and Edmonton (30 miles distant).—*Fundy N.P.*, New Brunswick: Fundy Park Chalets are located in the park; other accommodations are available at the nearby town of Alma.—*Georgian Bay Islands N.P.*, Ontario: There are no accommodations in the park, but they are available at Tobermory, Midland, Honey Harbour, Penetang, Owen Sound, and other neighboring communities.—*Glacier N.P.*, British Columbia: No accommodations in the park.—*Jasper N.P.*, Alberta: Hotels, lodges and cabins in and around Jasper, at Miette Hot Springs, Athabasca Falls, Amethyst and Maligne Lakes, Sunapta Falls, Columbia Icefield. The modern Jasper Park Lodge is outstanding.—*Kootenay N.P.*, British Columbia: Hotels, lodges and bungalows at Radium Hot Springs, Kootenay Flats, Kootenay Crossing, Vermilion Crossing, Marble Canyon.—*Mt. Revelstoke N.P.*, British Columbia: Heather Lodge in the park; hotel and bungalow accommodations in the town of Revelstoke adjacent to the park.—*Point Pelee N.P.*, Ontario: Aviation Inn and Point Pelee Lodge in the park; additional accommodations close to the park.—*Prince Albert N.P.*, Saskatchewan: Hotels, apartments, and cabins at Waskesiu Townsite and Waskesiu Narrows.—*Prince Edward Island N.P.*, Prince Edward Island: Hotels, lodges and cabins at Dalvay, Stanhope, Brackley Beach, and Cavendish.—*Riding Mountain N.P.*, Manitoba: Hotels, lodges, motels and bungalows at Wasagaming Townsite.—*St. Lawrence Islands N.P.*, Ontario: No accommodations in the park; they are available at towns and cities along the St Lawrence River from Kingston to Cornwall.—*Waterton Lakes N.P.*, Alberta: Hotels, lodges and cabins at Waterton Lakes Townsite, Cameron Lake, and Waterton River Bridge.—*Yoho N.P.*, British Columbia: Hotels, lodges and bungalows at Field, Emerald Lake, Wapta Lake, Lake O'Hara and Yoho Valley.

(7) Accommodations in the Provincial Parks in Canada

Write to the provincial agencies indicated in the Sightseeing Gazetteer, page 243.

INDEX
of Places to Go